T5-AFY-991

™

References for the Rest of Us! ®

BESTSELLING BOOK SERIES

Are you intimidated and confused by computers? Do you find that traditional manuals are overloaded with technical details you'll never use? Do your friends and family always call you to fix simple problems on their PCs? Then the *...For Dummies®* computer book series from IDG Books Worldwide is for you.

...For Dummies books are written for those frustrated computer users who know they aren't really dumb but find that PC hardware, software, and indeed the unique vocabulary of computing make them feel helpless. *...For Dummies* books use a lighthearted approach, a down-to-earth style, and even cartoons and humorous icons to dispel computer novices' fears and build their confidence. Lighthearted but not lightweight, these books are a perfect survival guide for anyone forced to use a computer.

Already, millions of satisfied readers agree. They have made *...For Dummies* books the #1 introductory level computer book series and have written asking for more. So, if you're looking for the most fun and easy way to learn about computers, look to *...For Dummies* books to give you a helping hand.

IDG BOOKS WORLDWIDE

1/99

Windows® 2000 Registry

FOR DUMMIES®

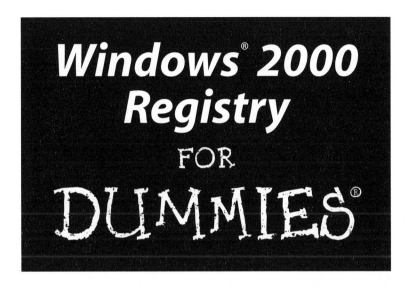

Windows® 2000 Registry

FOR

DUMMIES®

by Glenn Weadock, MCSE

Illustrated by Emily Sherrill Weadock

IDG
BOOKS
WORLDWIDE

IDG Books Worldwide, Inc.
An International Data Group Company

Foster City, CA ◆ Chicago, IL ◆ Indianapolis, IN ◆ New York, NY

Windows® 2000 Registry For Dummies®

Published by
IDG Books Worldwide, Inc.
An International Data Group Company
919 E. Hillsdale Blvd.
Suite 400
Foster City, CA 94404
www.idgbooks.com (IDG Books Worldwide Web site)
www.dummies.com (Dummies Press Web site)

Library of Congress Catalog Card No.: 99-66498

ISBN: 0-7645-0489-4

Printed in the United States of America

10 9 8 7 6 5 4 3 2

1B/SQ/RS/ZZ/IN

Distributed in the United States by IDG Books Worldwide, Inc.

Distributed by CDG Books Canada Inc. for Canada; by Transworld Publishers Limited in the United Kingdom; by IDG Norge Books for Norway; by IDG Sweden Books for Sweden; by IDG Books Australia Publishing Corporation Pty. Ltd. for Australia and New Zealand; by TransQuest Publishers Pte Ltd. for Singapore, Malaysia, Thailand, Indonesia, and Hong Kong; by Gotop Information Inc. for Taiwan; by ICG Muse, Inc. for Japan; by Intersoft for South Africa; by Eyrolles for France; by International Thomson Publishing for Germany, Austria and Switzerland; by Distribuidora Cuspide for Argentina; by LR International for Brazil; by Galileo Libros for Chile; by Ediciones ZETA S.C.R. Ltda. for Peru; by WS Computer Publishing Corporation, Inc., for the Philippines; by Contemporanea de Ediciones for Venezuela; by Express Computer Distributors for the Caribbean and West Indies; by Micronesia Media Distributor, Inc. for Micronesia; by Chips Computadoras S.A. de C.V. for Mexico; by Editorial Norma de Panama S.A. for Panama; by American Bookshops for Finland.

For general information on IDG Books Worldwide's books in the U.S., please call our Consumer Customer Service department at 800-762-2974. For reseller information, including discounts and premium sales, please call our Reseller Customer Service department at 800-434-3422.

For information on where to purchase IDG Books Worldwide's books outside the U.S., please contact our International Sales department at 317-596-5530 or fax 317-596-5692.

For consumer information on foreign language translations, please contact our Customer Service department at 1-800-434-3422, fax 317-596-5692, or e-mail rights@idgbooks.com.

For information on licensing foreign or domestic rights, please phone +1-650-655-3109.

For sales inquiries and special prices for bulk quantities, please contact our Sales department at 650-655-3200 or write to the address above.

For information on using IDG Books Worldwide's books in the classroom or for ordering examination copies, please contact our Educational Sales department at 800-434-2086 or fax 317-596-5499.

For press review copies, author interviews, or other publicity information, please contact our Public Relations department at 650-655-3000 or fax 650-655-3299.

For authorization to photocopy items for corporate, personal, or educational use, please contact Copyright Clearance Center, 222 Rosewood Drive, Danvers, MA 01923, or fax 978-750-4470.

is a registered trademark under exclusive
license to IDG Books Worldwide, Inc.
from International Data Group, Inc.

About the Author

Glenn Weadock, MCSE is president of Independent Software, Inc., a consulting and training firm he founded in 1982 after graduating from Stanford University's engineering school. Glenn has taught technical computer topics to thousands of students in the United States, United Kingdom, and Canada in more than 200 seminars since 1988. A recognized authority on Windows, he served as one of twelve expert witnesses in the Microsoft antitrust case, and millions of viewers saw him on CNN during the one and one-half seconds he was on camera.

This is Glenn's seventh book about Windows and thirteenth book overall. He wrote *MCSE Windows 98 For Dummies* and *Small Business Networking For Dummies,* and co-authored *Windows 98 Registry For Dummies, Windows 95 Registry For Dummies,* and *Creating Cool PowerPoint 97 Presentations,* all from IDG Books, Worldwide, Inc. He also wrote *Bulletproofing Windows 98, Bulletproofing Windows 95, Bulletproofing NetWare,* and *Bulletproof Your PC Network,* all from McGraw-Hill. Glenn has been in the Windows 2000 beta program since Beta 1, which he survived through a combination of therapy and medication. He is a Microsoft Certified Systems Engineer and a member of the Association for Computing Machinery and American Society for Training and Development.

About the Illustrator

Emily Sherrill Weadock is the director of Independent Software's Digital Art Studio. An award-winning computer graphic artist whose work has been featured in magazines and competitions from San Francisco to Frankfurt, Emily's talent ranges from technical illustration to broadcast-quality 3-D animation and multimedia development. She has illustrated 13 books to date, including *Small Business Networking For Dummies* and *The Portable Businessaurus,* and is the co-author of *Creating Cool PowerPoint 97 Presentations,* the most popular advanced guide to PowerPoint. Before trading brushes for mice, Emily enjoyed success as a mixed-media construction artist and studied art at SMU and Baylor Universities.

ABOUT IDG BOOKS WORLDWIDE

Welcome to the world of IDG Books Worldwide.

IDG Books Worldwide, Inc., is a subsidiary of International Data Group, the world's largest publisher of computer-related information and the leading global provider of information services on information technology. IDG was founded more than 30 years ago by Patrick J. McGovern and now employs more than 9,000 people worldwide. IDG publishes more than 290 computer publications in over 75 countries. More than 90 million people read one or more IDG publications each month.

Launched in 1990, IDG Books Worldwide is today the #1 publisher of best-selling computer books in the United States. We are proud to have received eight awards from the Computer Press Association in recognition of editorial excellence and three from Computer Currents' First Annual Readers' Choice Awards. Our best-selling *...For Dummies®* series has more than 50 million copies in print with translations in 31 languages. IDG Books Worldwide, through a joint venture with IDG's Hi-Tech Beijing, became the first U.S. publisher to publish a computer book in the People's Republic of China. In record time, IDG Books Worldwide has become the first choice for millions of readers around the world who want to learn how to better manage their businesses.

Our mission is simple: Every one of our books is designed to bring extra value and skill-building instructions to the reader. Our books are written by experts who understand and care about our readers. The knowledge base of our editorial staff comes from years of experience in publishing, education, and journalism — experience we use to produce books to carry us into the new millennium. In short, we care about books, so we attract the best people. We devote special attention to details such as audience, interior design, use of icons, and illustrations. And because we use an efficient process of authoring, editing, and desktop publishing our books electronically, we can spend more time ensuring superior content and less time on the technicalities of making books.

You can count on our commitment to deliver high-quality books at competitive prices on topics you want to read about. At IDG Books Worldwide, we continue in the IDG tradition of delivering quality for more than 30 years. You'll find no better book on a subject than one from IDG Books Worldwide.

John Kilcullen
Chairman and CEO
IDG Books Worldwide, Inc.

Steven Berkowitz
President and Publisher
IDG Books Worldwide, Inc.

WINNER
Eighth Annual
Computer Press
Awards ≥1992

WINNER
Ninth Annual
Computer Press
Awards ≥1993

WINNER
Tenth Annual
Computer Press
Awards ≥1994

WINNER
Eleventh Annual
Computer Press
Awards ≥1995

IDG is the world's leading IT media, research and exposition company. Founded in 1964, IDG had 1997 revenues of $2.05 billion and has more than 9,000 employees worldwide. IDG offers the widest range of media options that reach IT buyers in 75 countries representing 95% of worldwide IT spending. IDG's diverse product and services portfolio spans six key areas including print publishing, online publishing, expositions and conferences, market research, education and training, and global marketing services. More than 90 million people read one or more of IDG's 290 magazines and newspapers, including IDG's leading global brands — Computerworld, PC World, Network World, Macworld and the Channel World family of publications. IDG Books Worldwide is one of the fastest-growing computer book publishers in the world, with more than 700 titles in 36 languages. The "...For Dummies®" series alone has more than 50 million copies in print. IDG offers online users the largest network of technology-specific Web sites around the world through IDG.net (http://www.idg.net), which comprises more than 225 targeted Web sites in 55 countries worldwide. International Data Corporation (IDC) is the world's largest provider of information technology data, analysis and consulting, with research centers in over 41 countries and more than 400 research analysts worldwide. IDG World Expo is a leading producer of more than 168 globally branded conferences and expositions in 35 countries including E3 (Electronic Entertainment Expo), Macworld Expo, ComNet, Windows World Expo, ICE (Internet Commerce Expo), Agenda, DEMO, and Spotlight. IDG's training subsidiary, ExecuTrain, is the world's largest computer training company, with more than 230 locations worldwide and 785 training courses. IDG Marketing Services helps industry-leading IT companies build international brand recognition by developing global integrated marketing programs via IDG's print, online and exposition products worldwide. Further information about the company can be found at www.idg.com.
1/24/99

Dedication

To Jeff Kremer, for being a constant friend for many years and so that he can impress girls by showing them this dedication, at least until they realize that there must be a couple hundred "Jeff Kremers" in the world.

Author's Acknowledgments

I thank my wife Emily, not only for her fine illustrations, but also for her support and encouragement while I ate, drank, and breathed the Windows 2000 Registry. (Especially for waking me from that chilling nightmare about excessive access control restrictions on the HKLM key.) Thanks go as always to my agent, Mike Snell; my friend and colleague, Mark Wilkins, for the technical edit; my level-headed project editor, Kyle Looper; my bright (in both senses) acquisitions editor, Joyce Pepple; and all the other people at IDG Books who worked to ensure a high level of quality and clarity at every stage. I thank Darin Linnman at Waggener-Edstrom, who kindly arranged to get me answers from extremely busy Microsoft engineers on some pretty obscure questions. I thank all the beta program newsgroup participants, from Microsoft and everywhere else, who gave of their time and energy not only to improve Windows 2000 during the development stages, but also to help each other understand its inner workings.

Finally, special thanks go out in advance to readers who take the time to let us know about 1) any errors of fact or omission, which we've tried really hard to avoid but which sometimes sneak in anyway, and 2) any cool new Windows 2000 Registry tips, which we'll try to include in future editions.

Publisher's Acknowledgments

We're proud of this book; please register your comments through our IDG Books Worldwide Online Registration Form located at http://my2cents.dummies.com.

Some of the people who helped bring this book to market include the following:

Acquisitions, Editorial, and Media Development

Senior Project Editor: Kyle Looper

Acquisitions Editor: Joyce Pepple

Copy Editor: James Russell

Technical Editor: Mark Wilkins

Media Development Editor: Marita Ellixson

Associate Permissions Editor: Carmen Krikorian

Media Development Coordinator: Megan Decraene

Editorial Manager: Leah P. Cameron

Media Development Manager: Heather Heath Dismore

Editorial Assistant: Beth Parlon

Production

Project Coordinator: Maridee V. Ennis

Layout and Graphics: Karl Brandt, Joseph Bucki, Barry Offringa, Jill Piscitelli, Maggie Ubertini, Dan Whetstine, Erin Zeltner

Proofreaders: Laura Albert, John Greenough, Paula Lowell, Marianne Santy

Indexer: Liz Cunningham

Illustrator: Emily Sherril Weadock

Special Help: Amanda Foxworth

General and Administrative

IDG Books Worldwide, Inc.: John Kilcullen, CEO; Steven Berkowitz, President and Publisher

IDG Books Technology Publishing Group: Richard Swadley, Senior Vice President and Publisher; Walter Bruce III, Vice President and Associate Publisher; Joseph Wikert, Associate Publisher; Mary Bednarek, Branded Product Development Director; Mary Corder, Editorial Director; Barry Pruett, Publishing Manager; Michelle Baxter, Publishing Manager

IDG Books Consumer Publishing Group: Roland Elgey, Senior Vice President and Publisher; Kathleen A. Welton, Vice President and Publisher; Kevin Thornton, Acquisitions Manager; Kristin A. Cocks, Editorial Director

IDG Books Internet Publishing Group: Brenda McLaughlin, Senior Vice President and Publisher; Diane Graves Steele, Vice President and Associate Publisher; Sofia Marchant, Online Marketing Manager

IDG Books Production for Dummies Press: Debbie Stailey, Associate Director of Production; Cindy L. Phipps, Manager of Project Coordination, Production Proofreading, and Indexing; Tony Augsburger, Manager of Prepress, Reprints, and Systems; Laura Carpenter, Production Control Manager; Shelley Lea, Supervisor of Graphics and Design; Debbie J. Gates, Production Systems Specialist; Robert Springer, Supervisor of Proofreading; Kathie Schutte, Production Supervisor

Dummies Packaging and Book Design: Patty Page, Manager, Promotions Marketing

◆

The publisher would like to give special thanks to Patrick J. McGovern, without whom this book would not have been possible.

◆

Contents at a Glance

Introduction *1*

Part I: Start Your Engines: Introducing the Registry *11*

Chapter 1: Why Does the Registry Matter? 13
Chapter 2: Registry Backup 101 33
Chapter 3: Editing the Registry without a Registry Editor 61
Chapter 4: Registry Editors, from Headlights to Taillights 91

Part II: Rally Map: The Registry's Structure *127*

Chapter 5: Where the Files Are 129
Chapter 6: The Registry's Logical Structure 151

Part III: Mag Wheels and Pinstripes: Customizing the Registry *177*

Chapter 7: Customizing Security with the Registry 179
Chapter 8: Customizing User Profiles 199
Chapter 9: Customizing the Desktop 219

Part IV: Flat Repair: Troubleshooting the Registry *237*

Chapter 10: A Dozen Registry Problems (And Solutions!) 239
Chapter 11: Restoring the Registry 253

Part V: For Rally Masters Only: The Networked Registry *265*

Chapter 12: Network Management and the Registry 267
Chapter 13: Network Services and the Registry 279

Part VI: The Part of Tens *289*

Chapter 14: Ten (Or So) Registry Tricks 291
Chapter 15: Ten (Or So) More Registry Tricks 311
Appendix: About the CD 329

Index *335*

IDG Books Worldwide End-User License Agreement.....359

Installation Instructions...............................361

Book Registration Information.......................Back of Book

Cartoons at a Glance

By Rich Tennant

"Well, let's look in the Registry and see what your life preferences have been."

page 127

"Jeez—I thought the Registry just defined the wallpaper on the screen."

page 177

page 11

Fax: 978-546-7747
E-mail: richtennant@the5thwave.com
World Wide Web: www.the5thwave.com

page 265

page 237

page 289

Table of Contents

Introduction *1*

About This Book 2
Conventions Used in This Book 4
What You're Not to Read 5
Foolish Assumptions 5
How This Book Is Organized 6
    Part I: Start Your Engines: Introducing the Registry 7
    Part II: Rally Map: The Registry Structure 7
    Part III: Mag Wheels and Pinstripes: Customizing the Registry 7
    Part IV: Flat Repair: Troubleshooting the Registry 8
    Part V: For Rally Masters Only: The Networked Registry 8
    Part VI: The Part of Tens 9
Icons Used in This Book 9
Where to Go from Here 10

Part I: Start Your Engines: Introducing the Registry 11

Chapter 1: Why Does the Registry Matter? 13

What Does the Registry Do? 13
    Defining the Registry 14
    What was wrong with INI files? 17
    The Registry's role 19
What's New with the Windows 2000 Registry? 23
    Plug and Play info 24
    More security 24
    Active Desktop and IE 24
    Active Directory 25
    Different save and restore procedures 26
Rule #1: Saving the Registry 26
    How to save 26
    When to save 28
    Fix Windows 2000 bugs 28
    Recover from crashes 29
    Make the desktop easier to use 30
    Speed up Windows 2000 31
    Increased security 31
    Control servers 32
Leveraging Your Registry Knowledge 32

Chapter 2: Registry Backup 101 ....**33**

Why Backups Matter 34
When to Back Up the Registry 35
   Landmark backups 35
   Scheduled backups 36
Where to Back Up 37
What to Back Up 38
   LOG files 39
   SAV and Repair files 39
   Dogs without tails 40
   ALT files 40
   $$$ files 41
   User-specific files 41
How to Back Up 42
   Why backing up is hard to do 42
   Making startup diskettes (even if they do ignore the Registry) 43
   Method #1: Microsoft Windows Backup 44
   Method #2: The Emergency Recovery Diskette 52
   Method #3: REG from the Resource Kit tools 53
   Method #4: Bootin' and batchin' 54
   Method #5: Export and import 56
The Bottom Line 58

Chapter 3: Editing the Registry without a Registry Editor **61**

What's So Risky about Registry Editors? 62
What's So Safe about Alternatives? 64
   Extending a helpful hand 64
   Simplifying complex changes 65
   Taking care of non-Registry files 66
Control Panels 67
   Primary control panels 69
   Secondary control panels 77
   Showing your control panel who's driving 77
The Setup Program 81
My Computer and Explorer 82
Opening a Program with Another Application 84
System Policy Editor 86
Application Software 88

Chapter 4: Registry Editors, from Headlights to Taillights **91**

Cautions and Alerts 92
   Registry Rule #1 92
   Registry Rule #2 92
Why Two Registry Editors? 93
REGEDIT: The Jaguar E-Type 94
   REGEDIT part 1: Getting graphic 97
   REGEDIT part 2: At your command 109

REGEDT32, the GMC Hummer 111
    Adding REGEDT32 to your desktop 111
    Anatomy of the REGEDT32 window(s) 112
    Customizing REGEDT32 behavior 115
    Changing stuff 116
    Adding and deleting 118
    Finding 119
    Printing 119
    Exporting and importing 119
    Setting security 120
Taking the Editors Out for a Spin 122
    Where's the setting? 123
    How can I change it? 124
    A tarnished victory 125
    An unqualified success 125

Part II: Rally Map: The Registry's Structure 127

Chapter 5: Where the Files Are 129

Getting Physical 130
    Viewing and printing Registry files 132
    How Windows wakes up: SYSTEM 136
    What Windows does once awake: SOFTWARE 137
    Who can do what: SECURITY and SAM 138
    The "P" in "PC": Files containing user settings 139
    DEFAULT 142
    USERDIFF 142
    Transaction logs: *.LOG 142
    SYSTEM.ALT 143
    The original Registries: *.SAV and REPAIR 144
    Backup files 144
Registry-Related Files Not Part of the Registry 145
    Bringing order to chaos, sort of: *.POL 145
    NTUSER.INI 146
    GPEDIT.MSC 147
    POLEDIT.EXE 147
    *.REG 147
    *.INF 147
    *.MSI 148
    SECEVENT.EVT 148
    REGEDIT.EXE 148
    REGEDT32.EXE 148
    Profile files and folders 149

Chapter 6: The Registry's Logical Structure **151**

   The Basic Components 152
      Branching out 153
      All keyed up 154
      Adding value 155
   Gross Registry Anatomy 160
      HKEY_LOCAL_MACHINE (HKLM) 161
      HKEY_CURRENT_CONFIG (HKCC) 168
      HKEY_CLASSES_ROOT (HKCR) 169
      HKEY_USERS (HKU) 174
      HKEY_CURRENT_USER (HKCU) 175

Part III: Mag Wheels and Pinstripes:
Customizing the Registry *177*

Chapter 7: Customizing Security with the Registry **179**

   Windows 2000 Security in Six Pages or Less 180
      Computer accounts: Pre-logon security 181
      Logon security: Getting in the door 181
      User and group rights 182
      Permissions 182
      Security for stored data 183
      Security for transmitted data 184
      System and group policies 184
      Auditing 185
   Securing the Registry 185
      Registry key permissions 186
      Auditing Registry events 189
   Securing Computers and Users with Policies 192
      Accessing the Group Policy snap-in 193
      Computer and user policies 194
      Templates 195
      Policies on the network 196

Chapter 8: Customizing User Profiles **199**

   What's a User Profile? 200
   When to Use Profiles 201
      Many drivers, one car 202
      Nomad's LAN 202
   Setting Up User Profiles 203
      Local profiles 203
      Roaming profiles 206

What Profiles Do to the Registry 209
    Now where's that file? 209
    A spare set of keys 213
Mandatory User Profiles 214
Managing User Profiles 215
Profile Downsides 215
    Luxury tax 1: Performance 216
    Luxury tax 2: Convenience 216
    Luxury tax 3: Size 217

Chapter 9: Customizing the Desktop ....**.219**
Customizing for Speed 220
    Depersonalizing menus 220
    Slippin' and slidin' around the road 221
    Taking fast laps around your menus 223
    Turbocharging your keyboard 223
    Disabling folder memory 224
Streamlining Common Activities 224
    Expanding the Start menu 224
    Pruning the search tree 225
    More convenient encryption 226
    Making desktop icons for control panels 226
    Opening My Computer in Explorer view 227
    Adjusting file type associations 228
Window Dressing 231
    Changing application-related icons 231
    Adding info to your tips 232
    Sorting the Start menu 233
Filling Security Holes 234

Part IV: Flat Repair: Troubleshooting the Registry *237*

Chapter 10: A Dozen Registry Problems (And Solutions!) ....**.239**
Registry Editors Display Error Messages 240
I Get Errors When Backing Up the Registry 241
System Policies Aren't Working 242
I Can't Reverse Restrictive Policies 243
The Registry Editor Policy Doesn't Restrict Other Editors 244
Group Policies Aren't Working 244
User Profiles Load Slowly Over a Modem 245
Importing a REG File Doesn't Work 246
    Missing keys 246
    Unwanted duplicates 247
    REG and INF files aren't working on other PCs 247

I Can't Find Stuff in the Registry that I Know Is There 248
REGEDT32 doesn't find value names or data 248
Context menu search strings 248
Find command follies 249
The short and long of it 249
I'm Low on Registry Quota . . . Whatever That Is 249
"Another Installation Is in Progress" 250
Office 2000 Programs Quit after Launch 251

Chapter 11: Restoring the Registry **253**
Partial Restores 254
Last Known Good = Smart First Step 254
Restoring a key, or two, or three 255
Restoring a whole hive 257
Full Restores 259
Restoring the Registry with Microsoft Windows Backup 260
Restoring the Registry with REGEDIT — Not! 262
Restoring the Registry with the
Emergency Recovery Diskette 263
Restoring the Registry with the Recovery Console 263
Restoring the Registry with a batch file 264

**Part V: For Rally Masters Only:
The Networked Registry** **265**

Chapter 12: Network Management and the Registry **267**
The Registry and the Rollout 268
LAN-based installation methods 268
Tales from the script 269
Implementing the scripted setup 275
Editing Remote Registries 275
Getting set up for remote Registry editing 276
Running REGEDIT remotely 277
Running REGEDT32 remotely 277
Limiting remote Registry access 278

Chapter 13: Network Services and the Registry **279**
TCP/IP 279
Automatic IP addressing 280
IP security 280
TCP/IP tuning 280
Removing and reinstalling TCP/IP 281

TCP/IP Applications and Services 281
  DHCP 281
  DNS 282
  Telnet 283
  WINS 283
Internet Information Server 284
Improving Server Performance 285
  Just browsing 285
  Give me all your cache 286
  A Terminal Server tweak 287

Part VI: The Part of Tens 289

Chapter 14: Ten (Or So) Registry Tricks 291
Peek Inside a Windows Installer Package 292
Remove Programs from the Install/Uninstall List 295
Let Windows "Run" Amok 296
Recover a Lost Internet Explorer Password 299
Hiding Selected Control Panels 300
Set the DUN Logon Option 301
Set NumLock for the Logon Screen 302
Set Background for the Logon Screen 303
Change the Default Setup Location 305
Annotate the Registry 306
Photo Finishes 307
  Snapshotting 307
  REGMON 308
Rules and REGs 308

Chapter 15: Ten (Or So) More Registry Tricks 311
Enable AutoComplete in Command Windows 312
What's New on the Menu? 314
  Removing a file type 315
  Adding a file type 315
Customize System File Protection 316
Move Those Event Logs 318
Log Some New Stuff 320
Create Application-Specific Sound Schemes 321
Lock Out File Type Changes 322
Telling DUN When to Be Done 323
Less Power to You 324
Change the Registered Organization and Owner Names 325
Run a Program Automatically 326
Run Registry Editor as Administrator without Restarting 327

Appendix: About the CD 329
    System Requirements 329
    Using the CD 330
    What You'll Find 331
        Registry Editors and managers 331
        Registry monitors 331
        Handy utilities 332
    If You Have Problems (Of the CD Kind) 333

Index...................................*335*

IDG Books Worldwide End-User License Agreement......*359*

Installation Instructions...................................*361*

Book Registration Information ....*Back of Book*

Introduction

● ●

*T*he Registry is a crazy-quilt collection of settings and details about the hardware and software in a Windows 2000 PC. The Registry isn't the brain of Windows 2000, but it's a lot like its spine: that is, where most of the nerve endings come together. And, like your spine, the Registry is vitally important.

Windows 2000 can't even get up in the morning without the clues that Microsoft has tucked away inside the Registry. After startup, Windows 2000, and the programs you run with it, use the Registry many thousands (yep, *thousands*) of times in a typical computing session — to find necessary files, recall user preferences, enforce security restrictions, and perform hundreds of other actions.

If something goes wrong with your Registry, you may not be able to use your computer until you fix it. If something goes wrong with a program you're running, or with Windows 2000 itself, you may need to use the Registry to repair it. If a hacker knows more about the Registry than you do, you could be at risk for some of the more insidious viruses around.

On a lighter note, the Registry can be fun (and not just in the intellectual sense that "calculus can be fun"). You can customize Windows 2000 in some slick ways that you can't do otherwise. You can also customize lots of Windows 2000 PCs very quickly, if you administer a network for example, by leveraging the power of the Registry and its related tools. You can get a great look at how Windows works by spying on the Registry when you make system changes. And you can share your Registry hacks with others.

As important and cool as it is, though, getting information about the Registry has never been easy. Mindful of the dangers of tinkering with this pseudo-database, Microsoft only dribbles out Registry structure details on a "need to know" basis. So (drum roll, please) here's *Windows 2000 Registry For Dummies,* which provides the information you need to use the Registry safely, protect the Registry from problems that can range from inconvenient to disastrous, and customize Windows 2000 to your liking. I include specifics on how to make Windows 2000 do what you want (as opposed to what Microsoft thinks you want) by tweaking the Registry. I explain cool Registry features that many Windows 2000 users may not even know about, such as user profiles, hardware profiles, and group policies. I even go into some of the networking issues connected with Windows 2000 Server, TCP/IP services, and Active Directory — but don't worry, these subjects stand apart so you don't have to read them if you don't care about them.

My hope is that *Windows 2000 Registry For Dummies* is the only book you need to read or own on the subject, unless you're a professional programmer, in which case you may need to buy five or six books (but read this one first!). My goal is to include everything that the vast majority of my readers would need to know about the Registry.

About This Book

This book presents the essentials of the Windows 2000 Registry concisely, conversationally, and (I hope!) clearly. I quickly bring you up to speed on the absolute minimum you must know about the Registry in order to use Windows 2000 safely. I then take you further and show how you can use the Registry to do cool and useful things with your computer.

You probably know already that Windows 2000 isn't really one product, it's two: *Windows 2000 Professional* (what we used to call "Windows NT Workstation"), and *Windows 2000 Server*.

If you're using the Server product, does that mean you're not a professional? And why, after calling the workstation product "Workstation" for several years, does Microsoft suddenly change it to "Professional" and confuse everybody? For that matter, why change from "NT 5.0" to "Windows 2000?" Does Microsoft really want us to change operating systems every year? Send your cards and letters to Microsoft Corporation, Annoying Product Names Division, Redmond, WA, USA. But first read the next paragraph.

To be a little more precise, "Windows 2000" is actually *more* than two products. The Server version is available in three flavors: regular "Windows 2000 Server," "Windows 2000 Advanced Server" (formerly "Windows NT Server, Enterprise Edition," which apparently was not a good enough name) and "Windows 2000 Datacenter Server" (a product with no immediate ancestor).

The bottom line in all this is that most of the stuff in this book applies to both the "Professional" and "Server" products. When some material applies solely to one and not the other, I'll let you know. Most of the network-related material, which deals more with the server product, is in Part V. Also, because we wanted to get this book out before the year 2010, I didn't test everything in this book with the Advanced Server or Datacenter Server products. I wrote this book on a local area network running Windows 2000 Professional on the clients and Windows 2000 Server (the "regular" version) on the server. Most of what I discuss about the "regular" server product should apply also to the Advanced Server and Datacenter Server products, but I offer no guarantee on that point.

Windows 2000 Registry For Dummies is not a tutorial. You don't have to do everything in Chapter 1 before going on to Chapter 2. You can jump here and there, finding out cool Registry tips and tricks along the way. The one caveat to this general theme is that before getting into the more heady aspects of the Registry Editors, you should read Chapter 2 on backing up your Registry and then actually make a good backup for safekeeping. Then you can relax and explore.

Windows 2000 Registry For Dummies is a reference. You don't have to commit all the various facts about the Registry, Plug and Play, and user profiles to memory (lucky for you!). Use the Table of Contents to find the topic you're interested in. Or, use the index to zero in on the specific term you're looking for. Find the information you need, put it into action, and then set this book back on the shelf (preferably where you can get to it easily!).

If you bought this book but you're actually running Windows NT 4.0 rather than Windows 2000, some of the material will apply and some won't. I don't guarantee that any specific tip here works in NT 4. I also don't guarantee that any specific tip works in some future revision of Windows 2000; this book is based on the initial commercial version. (Having said that, chances are good that 98 percent of what's here will still work with future versions of Windows 2000.)

You may also want to know that IDG Books offers two other Registry books: _Windows 95 Registry For Dummies_ and _Windows 98 Registry For Dummies_, both by my colleague, Mark Wilkins, and me.

You should know right up front that this book deals with a potentially risky subject. Viewing the Registry and modifying it through the various Windows 2000 control panels isn't especially dangerous, but modifying the Registry directly, using a Registry Editor or other similar utility, can be. _You can accidentally render a Windows 2000 PC unbootable, trash software settings, and lose data files as a result of using the Registry Editor._ You should _always_ create a fallback position for yourself in case something goes wrong. For example, back up your hard disk regularly and back up the Registry files before you make any changes to them. Chapter 2 goes into detail on how to perform these backup tasks. I'll remind you of this caution periodically throughout the book where appropriate. If you don't heed my advice and you get yourself into trouble, Chapter 13 may help you avert total disaster, but I can't guarantee it.

Finally, this book is as scrupulously accurate as I could make it. Everything you read here is something I've tested personally, usually on more than one computer. Also, every word has been scrutinized and authorized by my technical editor (and author in his own right), Mark Wilkins. Nevertheless, if you find what looks like a mistake, please let the publisher know via the online registration site described in the back of this book so that we can research and correct it if necessary. We'll thank you in the acknowledgments section of this book's next edition.

Conventions Used in This Book

I've tried to standardize how I tell you to do things and how I refer to things, because I know that you don't want to guess at what to do. Check out the following conventions:

- ✔ I say "double-click" to mean activating a desktop icon, even though you can single-click icons to activate them in the Windows 2000 Active Desktop's so-called "Web view."

- ✔ When I show you a keyboard shortcut, I put a + sign between the two keys that you press simultaneously. For example: Ctrl+C.

- ✔ When I show you a series of commands that you use your mouse and menus to accomplish, I put an arrow between the commands. For example: File⇨Save As.

- ✔ When I show you a message that you get from the computer, I print that message in a monospace font, similar to what you would see on a manual typewriter. For example: It is now safe to turn off your computer.

- ✔ When I show you something that you type into Windows 2000 or another Windows 2000 application, the information to enter is presented in a bold font. For example: **REGEDT32.**

- ✔ When I show you stuff to enter at the command prompt or code to enter, it appears in monospaced font and capitalized. For example:

```
XCOPY C:\WINNT\SYSTEM32\CONFIG\SYSTEM E:\REG\ /Y
```

- ✔ When I name a directory path, that also appears in monospaced font, but not necessarily capitalized. For example: C:\Documents and Settings.

- ✔ When I refer to the Windows 98 and Windows 95 product line, I economize by using the term "Windows 9x." When I refer to the Windows 3-point-whatever series of products (Windows 3.0 and 3.1, Windows for Workgroups 3.1 and 3.11), I use the term "Windows 3.x."

- ✔ When I refer to a Registry key, I put that key in an italic font. (In cases where I must break a key because it's too long for a line, I do so after a slash.) For example: *HKLM\SOFTWARE\Classes.*

- ✔ When I refer to a Registry value, I put the value name in an italic font. For example: *AutoReboot.*

This is a hands-on book, so I give you lots of steps to follow to accomplish your Registry magic. The bolded portion of these steps are things for you to do; unbolded stuff is explanatory, as in the following example:

1. **Save any data files in open programs and close the programs.**

   This step isn't strictly necessary, but I like to walk on the safe side of the street.

2. **Give your PC the three-finger salute (Ctrl+Alt+Del) to display the Windows Security dialog box.**

3. **Click Explorer and End Task.**

What You're Not to Read

Here and there, you'll see information marked with the Technical Stuff icon or in sidebars. This is information that isn't necessary for you to get the job done. Don't feel bad about skipping right over this stuff. If you're interested, however, go ahead and read it. Nothing ventured, nothing gained.

Foolish Assumptions

I've written this book for the broad audience of people who work with Windows 2000, whether for business or pleasure. You may be a home PC user who wants to protect that machine from common problems and tune it up in useful ways. You may use Windows 2000 at work, where you can't afford the downtime that Registry problems can create. You may be a part-time or full-time network administrator who's responsible for managing multiple Windows 2000 PCs and wants to know how to set them up for minimum maintenance and maximum reliability. You may also be a consultant of one stripe or another who needs to advise others about using Windows 2000. You may even be a programmer who wants a quick and friendly introduction to the Registry.

The few assumptions I do make about you as a reader are as follows:

- **You use Windows 2000 and know enough about it to get around the desktop.** If I refer to the taskbar, the My Computer icon, or the Windows Explorer, you know what I'm talking about.

✓ **You don't necessarily want to become a computer expert, but you want to understand Windows 2000 more thoroughly so that you can take maximum advantage of its capabilities.** If this book alone doesn't slake your thirst for Registry knowledge, I include references to a variety of additional resources on the Registry throughout the text.

✓ **You're conscientious enough to actually make Registry backups before trying the various changes I suggest in this book.** (If you're not, and you prefer to live dangerously, please return this book for a refund, with which you can buy a ticket for a high-altitude bungee jump.)

✓ **You have a bona fide copy of Windows 2000 and all the files that it comes with, either on hard disk, CD-ROM, or network drive.** (Some of the utilities this book discusses aren't installed as part of a typical Windows 2000 installation, so you need to install them as a separate step — a procedure that requires access to the original Windows 2000 files.)

✓ **You don't expect to write Windows 2000 programs as a result of reading this book.** If you're a programmer, you can get a lot of great information from this book, and you certainly need to know about the Registry in order to write good Windows 2000 software. But writing programs isn't my main focus here.

✓ **You don't expect to configure a network as a result of reading this book.** Some of the topics in this book pertain to a network environment, but I don't tell you how to build a network here. For this sort of information, check out *Small Business Networking For Dummies* by me (IDG Books, Worldwide, Inc.) if you work in a company with under 100 employees, or *Networking For Dummies,* 3rd Edition, by Doug Lowe (IDG Books, Worldwide, Inc.) for a more general treatment.

✓ **You're no "dummy"; you just need the basics on the subject in a hurry.**

If this sounds like you, read on!

How This Book Is Organized

As with most ...*For Dummies* books, you can dip in and out of specific chapters according to what your interests are and what level of knowledge you already have about particular subjects. You can certainly read this book cover to cover, and I do my best to keep it interesting if you do. However, each chapter is designed to give you all the information you need on a specific topic and not leave you hanging if you haven't read the entire book up to that point.

The book uses a road rally metaphor to help explain the purpose of the book's six main parts. Think of this book as a race around the highways and byways of the Windows 2000 Registry. So put on your driving gloves and sunglasses, and take a look at the following map before you hop in the Z3.

Part I: Start Your Engines: Introducing the Registry

This part starts out by answering the question "Why do I need to know about the Registry, anyway?" I tell you what the Registry is, what it does, and what's new in the Registry since Windows NT 4.0. The first chapter also gives you a taste of the sorts of things you can do with the Registry once you gain some familiarity with it. Chapter 2, hands-down the single-most important chapter in the book, lays out the detailed procedures for backing up the Registry. Follow these guidelines and you can experiment with the Registry in the secure knowledge that if you damage something, you can always get back to where you were before you started experimenting.

Chapter 3 presents the various ways you can change Registry settings without actually directly editing Registry contents, for example with Windows 2000 control panels. (Whenever you have a choice between using a Registry Editor and a control panel, use the control panel; it's safer.) Finally, Chapter 4 introduces the two Windows 2000 Registry Editors (yep, you get two) and helps you understand when to use which.

Part II: Rally Map: The Registry Structure

Part II takes a closer look at how the Registry is put together. Chapter 5 explains what actual files constitute the Registry (yes, there's more than one), where you can find them on your PC, how to see them (they're normally hidden from view, and for good reason), and what they contain. Understanding where these files are and what they do is essential to being able to back up the Registry so you don't get into trouble that you can't get out of easily. Chapter 6 takes a look at the Registry structure from a different angle, namely, the "logical" structure. The Registry may consist of several separate files, but it appears as a single, multilevel database when you view it with either Registry Editor, and you need to understand how Microsoft has organized that database in order to use the Registry Editors effectively.

Part III: Mag Wheels and Pinstripes: Customizing the Registry

In Part III, you discover how to use the Registry to customize Windows 2000 to your liking. Chapter 7 goes into detail on how you can customize the Registry to control what a user can do on any given Windows 2000 machine. The Group Policy utility and the System Policy Editor are the Registry-modifying tools that this chapter explores, and they're useful whether you're implementing a company network or just trying to figure out how to prevent little Johnny from inadvertently trashing your home Windows 2000 PC. This chapter also looks at how you can protect yourself from yourself, and certain viruses, by slapping some security on individual Registry keys. Chapter 8 investigates user profiles, a cool technique for making the Registry look and act differently depending on who logs on to the PC (also very handy for both company networks and home computers).

Chapter 9 explains ways you can tune the Registry to squeeze more speed out of Windows 2000, change how the operating system looks to the user, and do things you didn't know Windows 2000 could do — such as provide a multiple-choice list for choosing the program you want to use when right-clicking a data file.

Part IV: Flat Repair: Troubleshooting the Registry

Windows 2000 is not perfect. It can break in a thousand different ways, many of which relate in one way or another to the Registry. Part IV helps you deal with the occasional problems that may crop up. Chapter 10 presents a dozen common Registry-related Windows 2000 problems, plus suggestions for correcting them (or at least recovering from them). Chapter 11 gives you step-by-step instructions for recovering from Registry disasters when Chapter 10 doesn't help, and you must restore the Registry using an earlier version.

Part V: For Rally Masters Only: The Networked Registry

For those of you who work on a network (and maybe even help keep one running), Part V covers material of particular interest to you. I've segregated it out so that readers who aren't on a network don't have to wade through stuff that's irrelevant to them.

Chapter 12 explains how you can customize the Windows 2000 setup program so that after you install Windows 2000, the Registry looks the way you want it to look. This chapter also discusses remote Registry editing for those troubleshooting sessions you may encounter just after a Windows 2000 roll-out. Chapter 13 deals with Registry settings that help control various network services, including Active Directory and the TCP/IP "alphabet soup" programs (DNS, DHCP, and so on).

Part VI: The Part of Tens

The "Part of Tens" is a standard feature of *...For Dummies* books. Chapter 14 presents ten or so Registry tricks that I think you'll enjoy discovering. Chapter 15 presents even more! Following The Part of Tens is the book's appendix, which describes the software goodies enclosed on the CD-ROM.

Icons Used in This Book

Several graphical icons highlight certain kinds of material throughout this book:

This icon guides you to other sections of the book where you can find more information relative to the topic at hand.

You get a CD-ROM with this book, and this icon alerts you that the accompanying text refers to software on that disc.

This icon means I've succumbed to the temptation to editorialize a little. Other knowledgeable people may disagree with these opinionated comments, but they *are* based on experience.

This icon points out a bit of knowledge or a comment that's worth committing to your long-term memory.

Here's material you can skip if you don't care about the nitty-gritty details, but may want to read if you like to know a bit more than the average bear.

Short suggestions, hints, and bits of useful information appear next to this icon.

Use this icon to avoid a *gotcha* — a common Registry pothole. Most of these little warnings come from my own experience fiddling around with the Registry. Benefit from my mistakes!

I hope that this book provides a bounty of useful information that makes your Windows 2000 experience more rewarding, fun, and trouble-free. If you can think of ways I could make it even better, please visit the Web site at the back of the book and let me know.

Where to Go from Here

If you don't know much about the Registry, you can find out the background stuff in Chapter 1; otherwise, proceed directly to Chapter 2 to find out how to safeguard your Registry. Network administrators may want to take special note of Chapters 12 and 13. After that, it's happy driving in whichever chapters interest you most.

Part I

Start Your Engines: Introducing the Registry

In the history of the personal computer, Mel and Frank's "Lube 'n Tune" represented the first true garage start-up.

Whoa Mel. Registry looks about full.

In this part . . .

Part I of this book is where you get ready for your road trip across the asphalt jungle of the Windows 2000 Registry, learning the background you need and the tools you'll use to fine-tune your Registry in the safest possible way. In these chapters, you find out why the Registry matters, and what you can do if you understand a little about its inner workings. Many people can drive a car, but they don't have a clue about how their engine works. That's fine if your car never breaks down, but if it ever does, a little automotive savvy can mean the difference between a slight inconvenience and a total nightmare. And so it is with the Registry.

This Part also discusses how to create all-important Registry backups, so that if you accidentally drive your Ford Expedition into a ditch, you can hop into the Miata that you keep stowed in the Ford's cargo bay, and be on your way. (If that sounds impractical, I'm guessing you've never seen the size of the Expedition, whose marketing slogan is "When a car's this big, you don't *have* to drive well.") You discover the safest ways to edit the Registry — many of which don't involve a Registry Editor, because even Mario Andretti doesn't want to drive his Ferrari to the grocery store. And you find out how to use the two Registry Editors that Microsoft provides, so you can switch gracefully between a manual transmission and an automatic as the situation demands. So read on, get familiar with the heart and soul of Windows 2000, and see how long I can keep up this automotive analogy. It should be fun.

Chapter 1

Why Does the Registry Matter?

In This Chapter

▶ Defining the Windows 2000 Registry

▶ Comparing the Registry to INI files

▶ Finding the new features

▶ Discovering examples of what you can do with the Registry

▶ Leveraging your Registry knowledge

*N*ever mind that the Microsoft-supplied product documentation all but ignores the Registry; every user needs to know about the heart of Windows 2000. In this chapter, I provide you with an aerial view of the Registry from which you can see what the Registry does and why it's fundamental to just about everything you can do in Windows 2000. More importantly, I give you some ideas of how you can use the Registry to improve and customize your Windows 2000 system.

For those of you who got your feet wet doing stuff with your *INI files* in Windows 3.*x* (by which I mean Windows 3.1, Windows for Workgroups 3.1, and Windows for Workgroups 3.11), I ground you in the differences between the old INI files you're used to and the new Registry paradigm. (For those of you new to Windows, INI files are text files that contain settings for Windows and Windows programs. The Registry replaces most INI files.)

So sit back in your driver's seat, open up the first envelope in this wild cross-country road rally, and get ready to read about the trip that's in store for you.

What Does the Registry Do?

This section looks at what the Registry is and what it actually does for a Windows 2000 PC.

Defining the Registry

If Windows 2000 were a sports car that you owned, then the Registry would be the car's electrical system. You may never give the wiring much thought until the day you buy a radar detector (essential for road rallies), plug it into a miswired cigarette lighter, and fry its circuitry so that when you whip by the hidden State Patrol car at 110 mph, you are shocked at the speed with which you get pulled over. Or, you may never think of your car's electrical system until the day you decide to improve or customize the sound system with a CD changer, amplifier, and five-speaker "home theater on wheels."

The Registry is much the same. You need to understand it in order to fix certain problems that can crop up and to customize Windows 2000 to your liking. Here's my attempt at a one-sentence definition of what the Registry is and all it does:

> *The Registry is the central store of information that Windows 2000 and Windows 2000 programs use to track all the software and hardware on the machine, including details about how that software and hardware are configured.*

The following sections expand on key aspects of this definition in more detail.

Central storage location

One of the key features of the Registry is that it brings information that was formerly scattered around the computer's hard drive into a single place. But understanding this explanation depends on understanding what I mean by the word *place.* The Registry contains more than one file (there are several, but the exact number depends on whether the Windows 2000 PC is set up for multiple users), but the Registry's actual files don't necessarily all exist in a single directory.

The Registry still *seems* like a single place, however, because you can view all the Registry information from a single window if you use one of the Registry Editor tools (REGEDIT.EXE and REGEDT32.EXE) that come with Windows 2000, as shown in Figure 1-1. The Registry Editors are covered in Chapter 4.

Nevertheless, with Windows 2000 Server, Microsoft is moving away from the concept of having the Registry contain every possible configuration setting. The company has set up a new database, *Active Directory,* which maintains lots of information about how the network is organized. Most of the low-level details about network nuts and bolts remain in the Registry, though. As you read this book, you'll discover that in some cases, features overlap between Active Directory and the Registry.

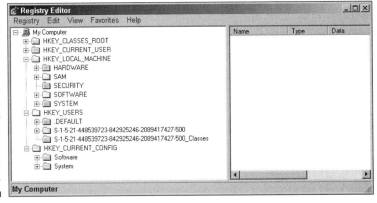

Figure 1-1:
REGEDIT
lets you
see the
complete
Registry
database
within a
single
window.

Software information

Windows 2000 is a highly configurable operating system, meaning that users and administrators can make zillions of settings after installing the base operating system. Similarly, most Windows 2000 programs offer a dizzying array of optional settings, so, if you prefer white text on a blue background in your word processor, you can set up the program that way.

One of the Registry's main functions is to keep track of your PC's software configuration (including Windows 2000 itself). The Registry handles this job well with so-called *32-bit programs* — which are written expressly for Windows 2000, 9*x*, or NT — but not so well with *16-bit programs*, such as those written for Windows 3.*x*.

If every program in the world were completely compatible with Windows 2000, then the Registry would know all the setup and configuration details for every program on your PC. However, Computerdom is an imperfect kingdom. The Registry's ability to track your software is subject to the following limitations:

- ✔ **Windows 2000 and 9*x* programs.** Even 32-bit programs don't always store every setting in the Registry. Instead, they may use *private INI files* that the Registry doesn't understand. For example, some settings for Adobe Acrobat Reader, a 32-bit application, are stored in ACROREAD.INI. Furthermore, if you're on a network with Active Directory, network administrators can *publish* applications so that their settings reside in Active Directory instead of the client's Registry.

- ✔ **Windows 3.*x* programs.** Because Windows 3.*x* has a Registry of sorts (only one section), Windows 3.*x* programs do update the Windows 2000 Registry with some information at install time — such as the *file association* information that tells the program to run whenever you double-click a file with a specific suffix. Windows 3.*x* programs don't make all the entries that Windows 2000 and Windows 9*x* programs typically make, however, such as the information that programs use to "sign in" with

Windows and effectively say, "This computer has program ABC installed on it, and here's how to uninstall it later." The Windows 2000 Registry also can't always capture information that Windows 3.x programs typically put into the WIN.INI file or a private INI file. (Note that Windows 2000 doesn't support Windows 3.x programs that try to talk directly to PC hardware or that use *virtual device drivers,* or VxDs.)

✔ **DOS programs.** DOS programs don't make any entries into the Registry, because DOS programs neither know about Windows nor care about it. If you want to know how a DOS program is set up, you must look at the program's own configuration files, and possibly also the DOS startup files, which in Windows 2000 are CONFIG.NT and AUTOEXEC.NT in the `C:\WINNT\SYSTEM32` folder.

The Windows 2000 Registry stores *most* of the details about Windows 2000 and 32-bit Windows 2000 and 9x programs; *some* of the details about Windows 3.x programs; and *none* of the details about DOS programs.

Hardware information

In Windows 2000, the Registry tracks all the hardware on your PC.

✔ First, the Registry contains information about *32-bit device drivers* — programs designed especially to enable the Windows 2000 operating system and the hardware device to communicate with each other. (Windows 2000 comes with hundreds of different 32-bit device drivers, and the Windows 2000 setup program installs most of the necessary ones automatically.)

✔ Second, the Registry contains information about which computer resources each bit of hardware is using — stuff like interrupts, ports, memory addresses, and the like.

✔ The hardware devices in a Windows 2000 PC may have a variety of configurable settings: for example, whether your network interface card uses the coax cable connector or the twisted-pair cable connector, or whether your monitor uses a resolution of 1024 x 768 or 800 x 600. The Registry tracks all these optional settings so that users don't need to recreate them every time they boot their PCs.

✔ Fourth, packrat that it is, the Registry even keeps details about hardware that you *used* to use with the PC but later removed — presumably on the off chance that you may reinstall it later on.

These facts go a long way toward explaining why you can't just move all the Registry files from one PC to another and expect things to work!

Windows 2000, like Windows NT 4.0 before it, does not support older, 16-bit device drivers (also known as *real-mode* device drivers) that may work with Windows 9x or 3.x. That explains why, if you have a CONFIG.SYS file in the root directory of your boot drive, Windows 2000 ignores it.

What was wrong with INI files?

And now, a few words about INI files — a concise history, a summary of their shortcomings, and their role in Windows 2000.

A bit o' history

Windows 3.*x* saved software and hardware settings in various places and forms, but it stored most of these settings in text files having the extension .INI, such as WIN.INI, SYSTEM.INI, CONTROL.INI, and PROGMAN.INI. The INI stands for *initialization,* because Windows looks at these files when it starts up. (Windows and Windows programs also look at some of the INI files after startup, too.)

In addition to these *system* INI files, *private* INI files contain information that allows individual programs to run, and can appear in various places on the hard drive, including the application's own directory. EXCEL.INI is an example of a private INI file. Private INI files exist because WIN.INI has a 64K limitation and can't hold every setting for every program without bursting its belt.

All INI files follow the same simple formatting rules: Section headings are in square brackets, items underneath section headings can appear in any order, items under the wrong heading don't work, a leading semicolon *comments out* a line so that Windows doesn't process it, and so on. You can (with rare exceptions) edit any INI file with a simple text editor, such as Windows Notepad. Figure 1-2 shows an excerpt from an INI file essential to Windows 2000, BOOT.INI.

Figure 1-2: INI files aren't dead; in fact, Windows 2000 uses this one to find the operating system!

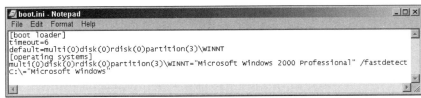

INI faults

What's the problem with INI files? Why replace the INI file structure with the new Registry system? Well, the INI file system has never been ideal. Here's a short list of its shortcomings:

✔ **Flat structure.** You can't have a subsection underneath a main section; one level of structure is all that's available, limiting the ability of Microsoft and application developers to organize INI file settings more finely.

✔ **Size limit.** Each INI file can be no larger than 64K. (Although this limitation no longer applies in Windows 2000, it was a big problem for Windows 3.*x* users. Individual applications had to install private INI files to keep WIN.INI under 64K.)

✔ **Scattered locations.** Although you can say with certainty where the core Windows INI files are (they all have to be together), you never know where programs may put their private INI files.

✔ **Poor separability.** Some INI files contain both machine-specific settings and user-specific settings. As a result, it's difficult to have all the user settings — wallpaper, program groups, and so on — follow a roaming user who may work on different networked PCs at different times, or multiple users of the same home PC.

✔ **Poor programmability.** With no capability to provide different data types, such as numeric, binary, and so on, programmers have less flexibility in creating and reading INI file data.

✔ **No remote administration.** Without third-party add-ons, such as remote-control software, no convenient way exists for a network administrator to connect to a PC and access its INI files.

Enter the Registry

The first attempt to address some of the INI files' shortcomings was the Windows 3.*x* Registry, although Microsoft actually called it the *Registration Database* (see Figure 1-3). Much narrower in scope than the Windows 2000 Registry, the Registration Database limited itself to file type associations (which data files go with which programs), compound document creation (embedding or linking a chunk of spreadsheet data into a word processing program), and drag-and-drop behavior.

The Registration Database represented a good first step toward consolidating at least certain categories of Windows information, and it did a good enough job to encourage Microsoft to extend the concept dramatically in Windows 95, 98, NT, and now 2000.

So are the INI files now obsolete in Windows 2000, given that the new Registry is much more comprehensive than the Windows 3.*x* Registration Database? It's a nice thought but unfortunately not yet reality. Try running Windows 2000 without BOOT.INI, and you won't get very far. However, you can be thankful for small mercies: Unlike Windows 98, you *can* run Windows 2000 without WIN.INI and SYSTEM.INI. Just be aware that WIN.INI and SYSTEM.INI are important to ensure compatibility with the 16-bit Windows 3.*x* applications that use them. For example, if WIN.INI isn't present, the setup program for some Windows 3.*x* applications fail.

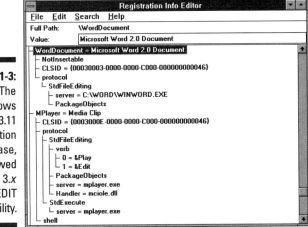

Figure 1-3:
The
Windows
3.11
Registration
Database,
as viewed
by the 3.*x*
REGEDIT
utility.

If you install Windows 2000 over a previous version of Windows and use the same directory (usually C:\WINDOWS) for the new operating system, Windows 2000 automatically migrates various settings from CONTROL.INI, PROGMAN.INI, SYSTEM.INI, and WIN.INI into the Registry (along with previous Registry settings, too!). Microsoft calls this feature *INI file mapping.* You can see the details of which INI file settings map to which Registry settings by exploring *HKLM\SOFTWARE\Microsoft\Windows NT\CurrentVersion\ IniFileMapping.* Also, when you install a new Windows 3.*x* program, Windows 2000 uses these mappings to redirect INI file settings into the Registry.

Putting aside system INI files for a moment, many private INI files still exist on any given Windows 2000 machine. You can quickly check the INI files on a given machine by choosing Start➪Search➪For Files or Folders and typing ***.INI** in the Search for Files or Folders Named field (I count three-dozen separate INI files on a Windows 2000 PC with only three common applications installed!). Although I could understand why 16-bit Windows 3.*x* programs used private INI files, Microsoft breaks its own rules by using private INI files for some of its own Windows 2000 applications, such as Office 97, TechNet, and even Internet Information Server (IIS). Clearly, private INI files are going to be with us for some time.

The Registry's role

After you understand what the Registry is, you may wonder what its role is in a Windows 2000 machine. What does it actually *do?* Go ahead and refill the coffee cup now, because the list is a long one!

Recording installation choices

The Registry fires up and gets working during the Windows 2000 installation program. When a user — either an *end user* (the person who purchases a computer) or a *PC vendor* (a computer retailer) — first installs Windows 2000, that user can specify what pieces of Windows 2000 to install: networking components, optional services, and so on. The setup program records those choices in the Registry.

Setting up hardware

Your Windows 2000 PC is likely different from mine, because Windows 2000 supports a great many hardware devices, such as graphics accelerator cards, CD-ROM drives, modems, hard disks, and so on. When Windows 2000 starts, it must set up all those devices by assigning them the *resources* that they need to function. These resources include *interrupts* that devices use to request the PC's attention, *memory* areas that they use to communicate with the PC, software *drivers* that form the link between the devices and Windows 2000, and so on.

Windows 2000 permits you to define different *hardware configurations,* or hardware *profiles.* For example, you may work with a notebook computer on the road, but you attach that notebook to a docking station with a different display, keyboard, and network connection when you're in the office. The Registry stores these hardware profiles so that Windows 2000 can configure itself properly depending on the hardware configuration that you need at the time. Chapter 6 discusses hardware profiles in more detail.

Setting up Windows 2000

You can change many of the Windows 2000 operating system settings, so Windows 2000 needs to know how to set itself up for operation when it starts. Here are a few examples of startup information contained in the Registry:

- ✓ What time zone to use
- ✓ Where to find the Windows 2000 system files
- ✓ What device drivers to load into memory so that Windows 2000 can interact with the PC's hardware
- ✓ What to do in case Windows 2000 crashes

And here are some examples of Registry settings that apply to a Windows 2000 PC in a network environment:

- ✓ The computer's network name
- ✓ The server that Windows 2000 should look for when the user logs on to the network

    ✔ (Windows 2000 Server) How to divide processor time between fore-
    ground applications and background server tasks

    ✔ The order in which to load different network components, if the PC con-
    nects to more than one kind of network

Running startup programs

The Registry maintains a list of programs to run when Windows 2000 starts,
independent of the list that you can create by manually modifying the Start
menu. The Registry's run list typically includes programs that absolutely,
positively must run every time that Windows 2000 starts, such as network
communication programs and antivirus utilities.

The Registry can also run certain programs one time only. This option typically comes into play when an application needs to restart the computer in
the middle of an installation routine and then pick up where it left off. The
Run Once Registry feature may also be used the first time you turn on a new
PC, launching welcome screens and other first-time configuration routines
that you never see again.

Defining how Windows 2000 appears

The Registry tells Windows 2000 how to get dressed in the morning. It specifies all the display options the user can set, such as what screen resolution to
use, how many colors to display, what wallpaper to use, what fonts and sizes
to use for icon titles, and so on. It also tells Windows 2000 what icons and
folders to put onto the desktop and what icons to place in the *system tray*
(the little box at the opposite end of the taskbar from the Start button).

The Registry keeps track of each person's preferences so that when someone
logs on, Windows 2000 displays the desktop designed by that person. If users
roam from machine to machine in a PC network, the Registry maintains desktop preferences on a network server so that when the user logs on to the network, Windows 2000 fetches the user's preferences from the server. Chapter 8
discusses these features, which go by the name of *user profiles*.

Determining component behavior

Windows 2000 is the most advanced expression to date of Microsoft's
Component Object Model, or COM, which is a sort of philosophy of modular
software design. For every different *object* — for now, just think of objects as
different sorts of data files, like spreadsheet files and word processing documents — you can perform a different set of actions. For example, you can
play a sound file, and you can also play a digital video file. But you can't *play*
a spreadsheet; instead, you can open it, print it, and so on. COM is a way of
keeping track of what sorts of actions are appropriate for different types of
documents, and what precise commands Windows runs when you choose
one of those actions. DCOM, or *Distributed COM,* extends the concept to
objects that live on different machines.

The Registry has a central role in the component model because the Registry stores all the information about what different kinds of objects can do. This section lists three examples.

Specifying what double-clicking or single-clicking does

You can run a program in Windows 2000 by double-clicking (or single-clicking if the Active Desktop is actually active) a data file that's associated with that program. Double-click a file with the TXT suffix, and you typically run Notepad. The Registry tells Windows 2000 which program to run when a particular type of data file is double-clicked. (Yes, you can change this behavior!)

Specifying what dragging and dropping does

Windows 2000 and its programs enable you to do a variety of things by dragging and dropping icons from point A to point B: You can print a file, graft a chunk of data into a different document, compress or decompress a file, and much more. The Registry controls all the drag-and-drop behavior for the various types of data files that it knows about.

Defining right-click behavior

The right mouse button, which in Windows NT 3.5 was about as useful as a radar detector on a tricycle, is a very busy little rodent appendage in Windows 2000. When you right-click a file of any kind in Windows 2000, a *context menu* appears, listing the choices available for that file: open, print, delete, and so on. The context menu can change depending on what type of file you right-click on. The Registry specifies the appearance and function of the context menu for every data type defined on the system.

Most Windows 2000 programs store *user-definable* settings in the Registry. For example, if you're processing words, you can choose to turn the automatic spell-checking feature off (especially if you're writing about computers and your article has lots of weird abbreviations). Windows 2000 programs also store *user-specific* (as opposed to user-definable) settings in the Registry, such as a list of most recently used files. These sorts of application settings should be kept in the Registry, although in reality, many programs (including some written by Microsoft) use other ways to track user settings, too — such as the time-honored INI files (see the "What was wrong with INI files?" section, earlier in this chapter).

Reporting configuration data to administrators

On a network of PCs, administrators and troubleshooters often need to know the details of a computer's configuration, but they can't always physically go to the user's computer. The Registry can report a user's PC configuration to a remote administrator, as long as both the user and administrator are connected to the same network. That network must be a *client/server* type (such as Novell NetWare or Windows NT Server) that uses a centralized database of users and passwords.

Conspiracy theories

Why doesn't Microsoft tell you about the Registry if it's so important and you can do so much with it? Here are my theories:

✔ Microsoft thinks that telling users how to modify the Registry is like giving the Porsche keys to a 15-year-old boy. (My view is that with proper instruction, a 15-year-old boy can drive a Porsche responsibly, as long as a 15-year-old girl isn't in the car, too.)

✔ Microsoft intended the Registry to be a behind-the-scenes database with which users should never need to directly interact. (In a perfect world, that might be true, but ours isn't.)

✔ Microsoft knows that its bare-bones Registry editing tools, REGEDIT and REGEDT32, are hastily assembled, inelegantly designed, and break almost every rule of user-friendly software design, so they don't want to call attention to them. (I wouldn't either.)

✔ They couldn't figure out how to explain the Registry. (Okay, it takes me about 400 pages just to lay out the basics, so I can sympathize.)

Pick your favorite theory; the truth is probably a combination of all of these. Just remember that Microsoft's scant documentation of the Registry is no indicator of its importance. When you buy a house, you don't get a manual describing it, either, but it's probably the most valuable thing you'll ever buy.

The bottom line is that the Registry handles just about every chore on a Windows 2000 PC and influences the chores that it doesn't handle. Now you can begin to understand why the Registry is so important, why every Windows 2000 user needs to take steps to protect it, and why you can do so many things to improve the functioning of Windows 2000 after you understand it.

What's New with the Windows 2000 Registry?

Okay, so why a new book about the Windows 2000 Registry? Many books cover the Windows NT 4.0 Registry, and isn't Windows 2000 nothing more than a renamed NT 5.0? Be cautious, *mi amigo.* The Windows 2000 Registry shares lots of similarities with NT 4.0, which incidentally is why the upgrade path from NT 4.0 is a whole lot smoother than from any other Windows version; but the new Registry presents some significant differences, also.

Plug and Play info

Windows NT 4.0 was, quite frankly, a pain in the driver's seat when it came to hardware compatibility. The operating system wouldn't work with lots of hardware, and even the devices that would work with NT 4.0 required lots of manual fiddling and finagling. Microsoft published some Plug and Play add-on software for NT 4.0, but between you and me and the rest of the world, it never worked very well.

The Plug and Play standard, which has been around since Windows 95, finally makes it as an integral part of the NT platform in Windows 2000. Plug and Play ain't perfect in Windows 2000, but it does help make installing new hardware easier. It also makes it easier to rip out old hardware you no longer want.

Plug and Play maintains a database of hardware settings that helps automate the process of assigning and unassigning computer resources to specific devices. Guess what? That database is in the Registry!

Another Windows NT 4.0 bugbear was power management. Windows 2000 takes a few steps forward here with support for newer standards, although its dropping of support for some APM (Advanced Power Management) computers may mean some inconvenience for some of you in readerland. In any event, the Registry is, once again, in the thick of things. It contains details on how to put devices to *sleep* (that is, into power-saving mode) and how to wake them up.

More security

The Registry adds settings to increase the number of access restrictions that Windows 2000 can impose. It also adds a nifty mechanism for setting up multiple Windows 2000 PCs to all use the same set of restrictions: the policy file — which is an optional Registry file that you can create with the new Group Policy tool (on an all–Windows 2000 network) or the System Policy Editor utility (on a network with Windows NT clients). Chapter 7 tells you all about policy files.

Active Desktop and IE

Windows NT typically adopts the user interface settings of the previous version of Windows 9x. For example, Windows NT 4.0 adopts the Windows 95 look and feel. In similar fashion, Windows NT 5.0 (whoops, I mean Windows 2000) adopts the Windows 98 user interface, complete with the Active Desktop's Web view and various integration features with Internet Explorer. As with Windows 98, if you use Windows 2000, you're going to use

Internet Explorer — whether you like it or not. (You can find ways to mitigate the influence of Internet Explorer on your desktop, however, many of which involve tweaking the Registry; Chapter 9 has examples.)

Active Directory

One of the most important new features of Windows 2000, at least for network users, is Active Directory (AD). (Everything is *active* at Microsoft these days.) AD is supposed to act like a master Rolodex for your whole network: It contains details on all network resources, from users and groups to printers and programs. Actually, AD is a bit more like a security guard holding a master Rolodex, because AD also handles access control.

The Active Directory database appears only on the various server versions of Windows 2000. If you're not interested in Windows 2000 Server, you're probably not interested in Active Directory.

So how does AD relate to the Registry? The Registry contains a number of AD-related settings, even though AD maintains its own information in a separate database (the file NTDS.DIT, which, unlike the Registry, is a bona-fide, industrial-strength, extensible database). Plus, AD can associate Registry settings with directory objects, as it does, for example, when you use the Group Policy tool to enforce restrictive Registry settings for users, groups, or domains across the network.

Many new Registry entries exist for the new programs, features, and hardware support files that come with Windows 2000. In fact, the Windows 2000 Professional Registry starts life at about 9MB before you even install any applications — that's about four times the typical initial size of the Windows 98 Registry.

Some of the areas that have added to the Windows 2000 Registry's size include the following:

- New digital video, animation, and other multimedia settings
- Internet browser capabilities that appear in Windows NT 4.0 only if Internet Explorer is installed (and Internet Explorer 5, which comes with Windows 2000, takes about 2.5MB more Registry space than IE4!)
- Settings for the *Active Desktop,* the update to the Windows NT 4.0 user interface
- Security-related settings for e-mail and Java
- New power-management features that Windows didn't control in earlier versions
- More support for voice modems and computer telephony

✔ Device support for the Universal Serial Bus (USB), Digital Versatile Disc (DVD), and other new hardware types

✔ New desktop-management capabilities for networked PCs

Different save and restore procedures

For those of you who have worked with Windows NT and have come to know and love the RDISK program for backing up Registry information, be advised: RDISK is gone as of Windows 2000. The Emergency Repair Disk has somewhat less capability than it did in Windows NT, and not only does it not contain any part of the Registry anymore, it doesn't hold any Active Directory settings, either. (Thankfully, other ways exist to back up the Windows 2000 Registry, as Chapter 2 explores.) In fact, while I'm on the subject of backups, I have a few comments on how to save the Windows 2000 Registry before you make any changes to it.

Rule #1: Saving the Registry

If you've been reading this chapter from the start, you've probably begun to realize that Windows 2000 depends upon the Registry to much the same extent that your rally car depends on its tires. If anything happens to the Registry, Windows 2000 becomes a zero-mph Ferrari. The First Rule of the Registry, therefore, is as follows:

> *Periodically save a "known good" copy of the Registry where it's out of harm's way.*

Chapter 2 gives you details on various ways to save the Registry, but here's what you absolutely must know in a nutshell.

How to save

You have several choices as to how you save the Registry. Here, I just mention one: the Emergency Repair Disk (ERD for short).

Actually, although you may reasonably assume that the Emergency Repair Disk contains the Registry, it doesn't. The Windows 2000 Registry is far too large to fit onto a single diskette. What happens (and this is going to sound a little weird) is that when you make the ERD, you get the opportunity to make a backup copy of the Registry files to a special folder on your hard drive.

(Assuming you've installed Windows 2000 into the usual folder C:\WINNT, this special Registry backup folder is C:\WINNT\repair\RegBack.) Windows 2000 can then use that backup copy to restore the Registry in certain circumstances.

The ERD method may not be a perfect Registry backup solution — what if Windows 2000 can't get to your hard drive, for example? Or what if your hard drive fails? The ERD wizard doesn't give you a graphical dialog box where you can select an alternative destination location (grrr). So, you may want to explore the other backup options in Chapter 2 when deciding on a bullet-proof Registry backup strategy. For now, though, the ERD method is a whole lot better than nothing, and it has the virtue of being mighty easy.

Activate the ERD wizard by choosing Start⇔Programs⇔Accessories⇔System Tools⇔Backup and then select the Emergency Repair Disk button, as shown in Figure 1-4. (Chapter 2 gives you the step-by-step procedure for putting Backup in a more convenient desktop location.)

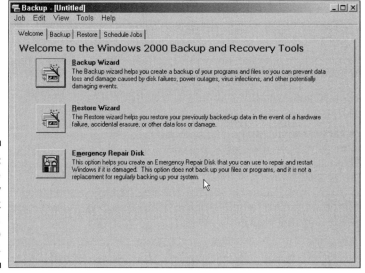

Figure 1-4: Get to the Emergency Repair Disk wizard via the Backup utility.

You'll see a prompt to put a diskette into your A drive, and a check box labeled Also back up the registry to the repair directory. This backup can be used to help recover your system if the registry is damaged. Click in the check box and then click the OK button. When the backup operation is complete, click OK again to close the dialog box. You can now use Windows Explorer to check out the date stamps on the files in C:\ WINNT\repair\RegBack. At this point, you have at least some measure of protection against Registry damage.

When to save

Always save a copy of the Registry at the following times:

- ✔ As soon as you finish a Windows 2000 installation and everything seems to work. (I became *very* familiar with this approach when testing Windows 2000 in the beta stages!)
- ✔ As soon as you fire up a new PC that came with Windows 2000 and (again) everything seems to be working fine.
- ✔ Before you install or remove any program, except perhaps the minor *applets* (such as Calculator and Notepad) that come with Windows 2000.
- ✔ After you install or remove any program and everything looks like it's working right.
- ✔ Before you make any significant changes with the control panel or Microsoft Management Console (for example, installing network software is significant, but changing the time and date is not).
- ✔ Before you make changes with the System Policy Editor, which is a Registry-editing wolf in sheep's clothing, or with the new Group Policy tool.
- ✔ Whenever you make any security changes such as modifying passwords or adding new users and groups.
- ✔ Before you even think about running REGEDIT, REGEDT32, or any similar utility.
- ✔ Every three months or 3,000 miles.

So what can you *do* with the Registry, besides make backup copies of it to ensure against future problems? Quite a lot. Chapters 7 through 9 provide many examples of how you can use the Registry to customize a Windows 2000 PC. For now, here's a sampling of five useful things you can do after you understand the Registry's ins and outs.

Fix Windows 2000 bugs

Windows 2000 comes with bugs that range from the cosmetic to the serious. An example of a serious bug is one that prevents many parallel-port Zip drives from working with the new operating system. When you try to tell Windows 2000 to use one of these popular removable-cartridge drives, by running the Add/Remove Hardware wizard, Windows 2000 stubbornly refuses to detect the drive.

The fix is to tell Windows 2000 to allow devices that use older parallel port specifications. How do you tell Windows 2000 to do this if you're upgrading a hundred PCs to Windows 2000 over a network? You modify the Registry! (See Figure 1-5 for the grisly details, and Chapter 12 for how to make Registry changes over a network. If you need to fix this bug on a single PC, you can edit the Registry with REGEDIT or REGEDT32, but it's safer to double-click the parallel port in the System control panel's Device Manager and check the box labeled `Enable Legacy Plug and Play Detection`.)

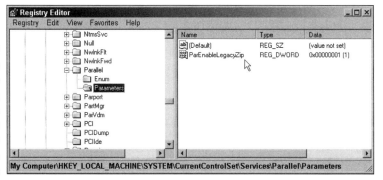

Figure 1-5:
A Registry fix lets you use a drive that you otherwise couldn't.

Recover from crashes

Not only can Windows 2000 crash, but it can also damage the Registry when it crashes. The situation gets worse when you consider that many (all?) application software vendors don't write perfectly reliable programs — those programs can crash Windows 2000, too, and they can also damage the Registry.

You can recover gracefully from a Windows 2000 system with a damaged Registry if you heed the earlier section ("Rule #1: Saving the Registry") on backing up the Registry. For example, if you use the Backup utility to create an Emergency Repair Disk (ERD), you can re-run the Windows 2000 setup program in *Recovery Console mode* to get the Registry back to where it was the last time you ran the ERD wizard. ERD isn't the only way to get out of trouble, though. Chapter 11 goes into some depth on various step-by-step procedures for restoring a damaged Registry and when to use them.

Make the desktop easier to use

You can customize the Registry to make the Windows 2000 desktop more user-friendly. For example, when you right-click a data file, a *context menu* pops up and gives you the option to *Open* the file. The file type association stored in the Registry determines which program runs: For example, opening a file having a BMP file type (the three-letter filename suffix) runs the Microsoft Paint program. In many situations, however, users may use more than one program to work with a given type of file. Microsoft Paint may be fine for casual editing of a BMP graphic — changing a couple of pixels here and there — but a user may need to use a more powerful tool, such as Adobe Photoshop, for more serious editing, such as applying color corrections to a scanned photograph. By using the Registry, you can change the context menu so that it offers a convenient list of all the programs the user may need (see Figure 1-6 and Chapter 9).

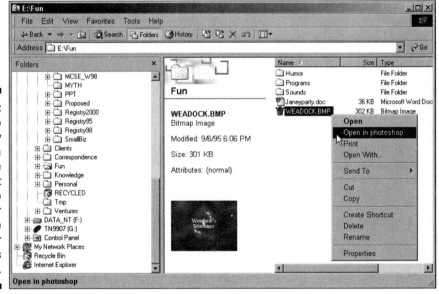

Figure 1-6: Changes to the Registry enable a more convenient menu to appear when the user right-clicks a data file.

Speed up Windows 2000

Various user interface settings in Windows 2000 tend to slow down how fast the operating system feels in daily use. For example, when the user points at a Start-menu entry that leads to a subsidiary menu, the hesitation that Windows 2000 makes is a "feature" that makes the desktop feel more sluggish than it needs to. You can't modify this hesitation with a control panel, but you can use your knowledge of the Registry to reduce the lag time for a snappier response. Chapter 9 tells you how to perform this customization as well as several others.

Increased security

Windows NT 4.0 offered many tools for limiting user access to the operating system. Windows 2000 lets you control the desktop even more thoroughly, and all the security features happen via the Registry. Security is very important in a business environment, but it also can be convenient on a home PC (you don't want your 6-year-old making direct Registry edits!).

A great security feature is the ability to run the Local Group Policy utility, which can disable the REGEDIT and REGEDT32 programs. When you disable the Registry editors, any user (including a 6-year-old child) who tries to run it sees the screen shown in Figure 1-7. Chapter 3 gives you the procedure, and Chapter 7 deals with the Local Group Policy and Active Directory Group Policy utilities in detail. The gist, though, is that the Registry makes security-related programs like these possible, and those programs, in turn, can help protect the Registry.

Figure 1-7:
One Registry security feature prevents users from editing the Registry with REGEDIT or REGEDT32.

Control servers

For those of you who plan on running Windows 2000 as a network server operating system, the Registry is how you control some of the network settings that pertain to server functions. From the fine details of the network *language* (TCP/IP, NWLink, and so on) to the inner workings of Active Directory, much of what you must do to administer and fine-tune a Windows 2000 server involves tweaking Ye Olde Registry. Chapters 12 and 13 provide some Registry-related suggestions for those of you running Windows 2000 Server.

Leveraging Your Registry Knowledge

Microsoft seems highly committed to the Registry concept, which has evolved substantially over the last few years. Windows 3.*x* employed the concept to a limited extent, and with each successive Windows release, the operating system has relied more heavily on the Registry. I believe we are at a fork in the road in the Registry's development on the server side — the Active Directory database is likely to assume some of the network-related tasks that the Registry has managed in the past — but I have no doubt that the Registry will continue to evolve in future versions of Windows.

The good news is that after you read this book, the knowledge you gain will continue to be useful and applicable for years to come — not always the case with computer books. If you still have to work with NT 4.0, Windows 95, or Windows 98, there's enough similarity between the Registries of all these different products to make you feel at home — even if you do have to bone up on the aspects of the Registry that are unique to each operating system.

Chapter 2

Registry Backup 101

• •

In This Chapter

▶ Discovering why you need to make Registry backups

▶ Understanding how to use Microsoft Windows Backup and REG

▶ Dealing with the backup "Ws" — when, where, and what

▶ Creating your own custom Registry backup batch file

▶ Using export files as a backup technique

• •

> *Fastening ourselves into a Formula I car is a big business, because our six point seat belts are so complicated that they cannot be buckled up by a driver by himself . . . If we stop somewhere along the track to check something or repair a minor fault — which means we have to unbuckle ourselves — then we have to drive slowly back to the pits afterwards to be buckled in again. To fail to do this would be the worst possible disregard for elementary safety precautions.*
>
> — From *The Art and Science of Grand Prix Driving*, by Niki Lauda, Motorbooks International, 1977

*N*obody in his or her right mind would go on a race track, or even a cross-country road rally, without seat belts— even if the seat belts require two people to buckle, as Niki Lauda describes. Backing up the Registry before you do anything to change its contents is a safety precaution that is just as elementary, and just as important, as buckling up in a race car. Making a Registry backup can be a little complicated, too, like fastening those six-point Formula I belts. However, making a backup isn't all that difficult after you set up your computer to make the process fast and convenient.

In Chapter 1, I introduce the First Rule of the Registry, restated here:

> *Periodically save a "known good" copy of the Registry where it's out of harm's way.*

The most important action that you can perform as a result of reading this book is to back up the Registry. If I can help you get into the habit of backing up your Registry successfully, then this book has paid for itself in one chapter. (Think of the other 14 chapters as a bonus!)

You may have heard something about how Windows 2000 makes Registry backups for you automatically, and that's sort of true. However, in this chapter I show you that those automatic backups are limited in some important ways. Rely on them blindly, and you may find your backup against a wall. (Please remember to tip your wait staff.)

My job here, then, is to present the why, when, where, what, and how of Registry backups and describe enough alternatives so that you can choose a method — or, more likely, a combination of methods — that works best for you. After you set up a Registry backup plan and adhere to it, you can relax a little whenever you need to modify the Registry. Even if you do make a mistake (and at some point mistakes are inevitable), you can always get back to where you were before. If only life in general could work that way!

This chapter focuses on *creating* backups, and Chapter 11 looks more closely at *restoring* from your backups. The later chapter discusses some of the same programs that I discuss here, in the context of disaster recovery.

Why Backups Matter

Here's why you really do need to back up the Registry, and why I devote a whole chapter to the subject:

- The Registry is at the center of everything that Windows 2000 does, as Chapter 1 explains. Problems with your Registry can affect every program on your PC and even prevent Windows 2000 from starting properly.

- In severe cases, a damaged Registry may require you to completely reinstall Windows 2000 and perhaps even all Windows 2000 applications, if you don't have a good Registry backup.

- The Registry is vulnerable to damage from disk media failure (hard drives, like spark plugs, eventually go bad) and from buggy software install and uninstall programs.

- Windows 2000 does a crummy job of making its own Registry backups, as the sidebar "Driving by the seat of your pants" explains.

- Windows 2000 keeps the Registry files open, even in the new so-called "safe mode," which means that you can't just back 'em up with a simple command like COPY or XCOPY.

- Damaging the Registry during a session with a Registry Editor is easier than running a STOP sign in the middle of the Nevada desert.

- The Registry files aren't text files. Unlike an INI file, if something goes wrong with the Registry, you can't fix it by loading it in a simple program like Notepad.

Driving by the seat of your pants

You would think that, given the Registry's importance, Windows 2000 would make automatic periodic backups of every significant Registry file, for example, at each reboot. Apparently, the Microsoft engineers who designed the Windows 2000 Registry backup features didn't agree. Windows 2000 doesn't automatically back up the Registry to *.DA0 files like Windows 95 does, and Windows 2000 doesn't automatically back up the Registry to RB*.CAB files like Windows 98 does.

Does Windows 2000 do *anything* by way of automatic Registry backups? Well, two things come to mind.

First, Windows 2000 does maintain a mirror image of the SYSTEM file (its name is SYSTEM.ALT). However, SYSTEM.ALT lives on the same hard drive and, in fact, in the same folder as the original SYSTEM file, so this isn't perfectly safe by any means. And no such mirror image exists for the other Registry files: SAM, SOFTWARE, and so on.

Second, you can tap the F8 key at the Windows 2000 text boot prompt and choose a boot option called "Last Known Good Configuration." This boot option tells Windows 2000 to use the device driver configuration at the previous successful boot. The "Last Known Good Configuration" option can be useful if you've added, changed, or deleted a device driver and thereby somehow bollixed up the Windows 2000 normal operations. However, this option only affects one part of the Registry. (If you're curious, that part is *HKLM\System\CurrentControlSet*. If that's Greek to you, don't worry; Chapter 4 explains the terminology.)

Bottom line? Windows 2000 protects certain parts of the Registry to a limited extent, but it sure doesn't perform a full backup on a regular basis.

When to Back Up the Registry

A solid Registry backup plan includes both *landmark* and *scheduled* backups.

Landmark backups

A *landmark backup* is a backup that you perform at an unscheduled time, when backing up seems prudent. In this book, I usually display the *Warning* icon to point out when a landmark backup makes sense, but here's a general list of situations that call for a Registry backup:

- ✔ As soon as you finish a Windows 2000 installation and everything seems to work. (I got *very* familiar with this approach when testing Windows 2000 in the beta stages!)

- ✔ As soon as you fire up a new PC that came with Windows 2000, and (again) everything seems to be working fine.

✔ Before you install or remove any program, except perhaps the minor *applets* (such as Calculator and Notepad) that come with Windows 2000.

✔ After you install or remove any program and everything looks like it's working right.

✔ Before you make any significant changes with the control panel or Microsoft Management Console (for example, installing network software is significant, but changing the time and date is not).

✔ Before you make changes with the System Policy Editor, which is a Registry-editing wolf in sheep's clothing, or with the new Group Policy tool.

✔ Whenever you make any security changes such as modifying passwords or adding new users and groups.

✔ Before you even think about running REGEDIT, REGEDT32, or any similar utility.

✔ Whenever the moon is full.

If you're reading this book start to finish, the preceding list may seem familiar (that's because I present it in Chapter 1, too). Sorry, but certain points bear repeating, and you may be the kind of reader who always skips a book's first chapter. (I usually do!) Anyway, *For Dummies* books are made so that you can jump around, so linear readers, please forgive any occasional reprises.

Scheduled backups

A *scheduled backup* (also known as a *recurring backup*) is a backup that occurs on a regular basis. For example, many computer users back up everything on their hard drives to a tape drive once a month; that's called a full backup.

You have to remember to perform one kind of scheduled backup, while the computer remembers the other kind for you. Having the computer remember to perform the backup is usually better, but it takes a bit more planning. You need a scheduling program, such as the Scheduled Tasks utility that comes with Windows 2000. If you're a dyed-in-the-wool NT 4.0 user, you may prefer the AT.EXE command-line program that comes with Windows 2000, or the graphical version (WINAT.EXE) that comes with the separately available *Windows 2000 Resource Kit*.

If you want to use the Microsoft Windows Backup program that comes with Windows 2000, you can schedule your backups from within the Backup program (for details, see "Method #1: Microsoft Windows Backup" later in this chapter). When you do so, a new icon appears in your Scheduled Tasks folder.

Microsoft Backup, Scheduled Tasks, AT.EXE, and WINAT.EXE all rely on the *Task Scheduler* service, which normally starts automatically at boot time. You can check the status of this service with the Services control panel.

The online help for the Scheduled Tasks program lays out the details for specifying the file you want to run (it doesn't have to be Microsoft Windows Backup) and how often you want to run it (every Friday night at 2:00 a.m., for example). Access the Scheduled Tasks utility by choosing Start➪Programs➪ Accessories➪System Tools➪Scheduled Tasks, or Start➪Settings➪Control Panel➪Scheduled Tasks.

The online help for Microsoft Windows Backup implies that you can't back up the Registry of a remote machine, but that's just not true. If you're on a network, you can use the backup program that comes with Windows 2000 to set up periodic, unattended Registry backups over the network. The "Method #1: Microsoft Windows Backup" section later in this chapter provides details. This type of backup is a very slick solution! You can also use other server-based backup programs to achieve the same results.

Scheduled backups that include Registry files can be risky if they overwrite older scheduled backups. Sometimes you don't notice a Registry-related problem right away, and if a scheduled backup wipes out an earlier scheduled backup, it may create a backup with the same problems that your current active Registry files have. If you use scheduled Registry backups, which is a great idea, save the files in a location different from the location that you use for your landmark backups.

Where to Back Up

Here are the places that you can back up your Registry files to, in approximate order of desirability (details of your particular situation may change the order I present here):

- ✔ **A network drive.** You're likely to have plenty of space on a network drive, and you're protected if your hard drive fails totally. Most network managers periodically move server backups off-site, too, which is good in the event of fire, flood, locust plague, and so on.

- ✔ **A removable optical drive.** Optical drives such as CD-R, CD-R/W, and writable DVD have many virtues, including speed, media life, and resistance to magnetic fields.

- ✔ **A removable cartridge drive.** The popular Iomega Zip and Jaz drives are examples. The media isn't as reliable or long-lived as optical discs, but a hard drive crash doesn't trash your backup, and you can store backup media off-site.

✔ **A tape drive.** This method is usually slower than a removable cartridge drive or optical disc, depending on the specific hardware. You still protect yourself against a hard drive failure this way, and you can store backup media off-site.

✔ **A diskette drive.** This method is *much* slower than network, cartridge, or tape backups, and you should use it only with backup software that can create a multiple-diskette set containing your entire Registry. (If you use the Microsoft Windows Backup program for backing up just the Registry to diskette, don't back up the entire "system state," which is much larger than the Registry. See the "Method #1: Microsoft Windows Backup" section later in this chapter for more info.)

✔ **A second local hard drive.** If you're fortunate enough to have two hard drives in your PC, backing up Registry files to the second drive is faster and safer than backing up to a different directory on your first hard drive. You couldn't do this with the Windows NT 4.0 backup program, but you can with Windows 2000.

✔ **A different directory on your local hard drive.** Very fast, but hard drive failure wipes out your backup.

What to Back Up

First, a terminology note: For the rest of this chapter, I'm going to assume that your Windows 2000 system resides in C:\WINNT, which is the usual name for the main operating system folder. Other books and magazine articles, allowing for the possibility that you've installed Windows 2000 into a differently named folder, use the technical-looking term *%systemroot%* to refer to "the folder where Windows 2000 lives." I'm allergic to potentially confusing notation, so if you're in the one-tenth of one percent of people who has installed Windows 2000 into C:\WINDOWS2000PRO or F:\WINNT or some other name, please mentally substitute that location wherever you see "C:\WINNT" in this book.

Now, take a look in C:\WINNT\SYSTEM32\CONFIG, headquarters of the Registry (see Figure 2-1). You see a couple dozen or so files. (If you *don't* see these files, then in Windows Explorer, choose Tools⇨Folder Options⇨View, select the Show Hidden Files and Folders radio button, and deselect the Hide Protected Operating System Files (Recommended) check box. You can also use the new Folder Options control panel, if that's more convenient, although I usually have an Explorer window open at all times.) Do you need to back 'em all up? The short answer is no, although you may choose to do so for the sake of thoroughness. This section will help you decide which files you need to back up.

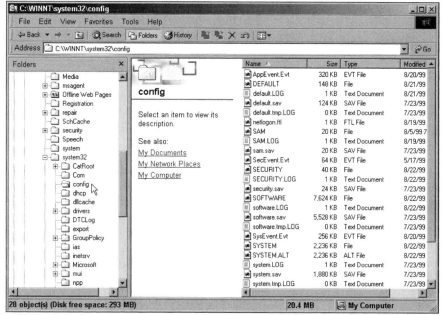

Figure 2-1:
A typical
listing of
Registry
files.

The following sections break these files down by their suffixes. For more details on each file and what it does, please refer to Chapters 5 and 6. I limit the discussion here to the bare minimum you need to know in order to set up a sound backup routine.

LOG files

The .LOG files (DEFAULT.LOG, SAM.LOG, SECURITY.LOG, SOFTWARE.LOG, SYSTEM.LOG, and in a separate location, NTUSER.DAT.LOG) only become useful if your PC suddenly and unexpectedly shuts down in the middle of a Registry update of some kind. So these aren't critical to back up in the normal course of business, but it doesn't hurt to include them. I suppose that in an unusual circumstance you may be glad you did. They're normally not very large, either.

SAV and Repair files

Some folks are confused about the exact purpose of the SAV files, and at least one popular book on the NT 4.0 Registry has inaccurate information on the subject. Here's the deal: The .SAV files (DEFAULT.SAV, SAM.SAV, SECURITY.SAV, SOFTWARE.SAV, and SYSTEM.SAV) are versions of the Registry in its infant state, the day Windows 2000 was installed onto the PC. They're not backup copies of Registry transactions. They're snapshots of the baby Registry before Windows spanks it. (Sort of like the SYSTEM.1ST file in Windows 95 and 98, if you know those products.)

If you want to get really precise about this (and precision is always a good thing when it comes to the Registry), the *.SAV files are snapshots of the baby Registry after the completion of the setup program's *text mode*, but before completion of the setup program's *graphics mode*. The *.SAV files are basically there in case the graphical part of the setup program blows up, in which case setup can restart without having to build everything from scratch.

For you Registry backyard mechanics out there, snapshots of the baby Registry *after* completion of setup's graphics mode may be found in C:\WINNT\REPAIR. If you look, you'll probably see that these files (which do *not* have the SAV extension) have time stamps around a half an hour to an hour later than the SAV files. This set of files is more useful than the SAV files, as it represents a slightly more recent Registry snapshot.

It's probably wise to save one copy of these *.SAV and C:\WINNT\REPAIR files somewhere, although if you need to go back in time this far in order to resurrect a dead PC, most likely you're better off just reinstalling Windows 2000. In any case, I don't recommend backing up the SAV and repair files on a recurring basis, as they don't ever change unless you reinstall the operating system.

Dogs without tails

The most important Registry files in the C:\WINNT\SYSTEM32\CONFIG folder are the ones with no extension on the filename: DEFAULT, SAM, SECURITY, SOFTWARE, SYSTEM. Any self-respecting Registry backup scheme should include these rascals.

ALT files

Well, you only have one of these, and that's SYSTEM.ALT. Unless your PC shut down abnormally at the precise moment that a Registry modification was taking place, SYSTEM.ALT is a mirror image of the SYSTEM file, one of the principal Registry files.

I feel the same about SYSTEM.ALT as I do about the LOG files — go ahead and back up this file if it doesn't present any inconvenience (in terms of backup size or speed), but otherwise don't worry too much about it. At least 999 times out of a thousand, if you back up SYSTEM, you don't need to back up SYSTEM.ALT as well.

$$$ files

If you see files with names like SOF$$$$$.$$$, then your Windows 2000 installation didn't finish normally, because these are leftover files that the setup program should have cleaned up at the end of the operating system installation. As long as everything's working okay for you, you can delete these files. You've no reason on earth to back them up. But I would be a tad nervous about whether Windows 2000 installed properly onto your PC if you see loose ends like this that didn't get tied up.

User-specific files

Not all the Registry files live in C:\WINNT\SYSTEM32\CONFIG. The user-related settings (which live in files named NTUSER.DAT) can reside in various places, depending on whether you installed Windows 2000 over an earlier version of Windows or as a fresh install. Chapter 5 goes into all the gory details, but suffice it to say here that these files will either live under the C:\Documents and Settings\<username> folder, or under the C:\WINNT\PROFILES\<username> folder. You'll find a separate NTUSER.DAT file for every user who's got an account on that Windows 2000 PC.

Wanna see how many copies of NTUSER.DAT you have on your Windows 2000 PC? Use the Windows 2000 search facility (formerly called "Find"). Click Start➪Search➪For Files or Folders and type **NTUSER.DAT** in the Search for Files or Folders Named field. Then press Enter. (I normally select the Local Harddrives option from the Look In drop-down box.) You'll see some NTUSER.DAT.LOG files, too; their function is described in the earlier "LOG files" section.

The ability to have multiple copies of NTUSER.DAT means that different users can log on to the same PC and see their own settings. On a network, users can log on to any network PC and see their own settings. These settings live in NTUSER.DAT and in user-specific folders like Favorites, My Documents, the Start Menu, and so on. I discuss this "roaming" capability, which Microsoft now likes to call *IntelliMirror*, in greater depth in Chapter 8.

Most Registry backup solutions ignore multiple NTUSER.DAT files because you can't predict exactly where they'll be, but you need to back these guys up — they're part of the Registry. You may also need the other various user-specific folders in your backup strategy, too. Remember these issues when you read the following section.

How to Back Up

You don't have to buy any software in order to make Registry backups. You just have to know about the tools and techniques that are available to you already and the advantages and disadvantages of each.

Why backing up is hard to do

One of my favorite scenes in a road-rally movie is the moment in which the driver rips the rear-view mirror off the inside of his windshield, tosses it out the window, and proclaims to his perplexed partner, "First rule of Italian driving: What's behind you doesn't matter!" I knew from my own experience with Italian sports cars that the rear window is usually so small that you can't see anything even *with* the rear-view mirror, which made the joke even funnier to me.

It turns out, unfortunately, that backing up the Registry is no easier than backing up a Lamborghini that's had a mirror-ectomy. The big problem in backing up the Registry is that as long as Windows 2000 is running, the main Registry files are "in use." That is, a program or the operating system itself could potentially write to a Registry file at any moment.

Imagine what would happen if you were copying the SYSTEM file to a Zip drive, and at the same time, a program was writing some information to the Registry. (Programs, and Windows 2000 itself, write data to the Registry pretty often, so this isn't just some theoretical scenario.) Your copy of the file might contain some of that information, but not all of it, in which case your Registry would now be internally inconsistent. In theory, Windows 2000 could "lock out" the Registry from any write operations as long as the COPY operation is going on. However, in that case, any number of programs and operating system services could crash, because they all think that they can write to the Registry whenever they need to.

If none of that makes any sense to you, then think of this analogy: You can't be writing on a piece of paper at the same time you're photocopying it. You have to put the paper down. Trouble is, Windows 2000 never "puts the Registry down," although I know a few people who do.

The bottom line is that if you try to copy active Registry files in the normal way, such as with a drag-and-drop movement in Windows Explorer, you get an error such as that in Figure 2-2. You could copy Registry files in Windows 9*x* without this error, but the NT platform (remember, Windows 2000 equals Windows NT 5.0) is a lot less inclined to let you bend the rules of proper computing behavior.

Backup à la mode?

Now, some of you may have heard about the Windows 2000 *safe mode.* Others may have some experience with safe mode in Windows 95 or 98. In those operating systems, you can boot into safe mode and the operating system does not activate the Registry. So, you can do things like back up and restore Registry files in the Windows 9x safe mode that you wouldn't (or shouldn't) attempt in the normal mode.

The question naturally arises: Can't I boot Windows 2000 into safe mode and copy the Registry files that way? Unfortunately, no. It turns out that when you boot Windows 2000 into safe mode (you can do so by tapping the F8 key at the text-mode boot prompt and selecting "Safe mode" or "Safe mode command prompt"), Windows 2000 *still* activates the Registry. And, doggone it, that means you *still* can't copy the files. In this respect, the Windows 2000 safe mode is a lot different than the Windows 9x safe mode.

Figure 2-2:
Windows 2000 doesn't let you copy files that are in use.

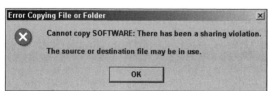

Making startup diskettes (even if they do ignore the Registry)

Before I get into the ways that you can back up the Registry, let me just clear up a little potential confusion by discussing one action that you may reasonably think would create a Registry backup, but doesn't. Namely, creating Windows 2000 startup diskettes.

You can create a set of Windows 2000 startup diskettes by using either the MAKEBOOT.EXE or MAKEBT32.EXE program from the BOOTDISK folder on your Windows 2000 CD. (Use MAKEBOOT.EXE from a DOS or Windows 3.x machine, and use the slightly quicker MAKEBT32.EXE from a Windows 9x, NT, or 2000 PC.) These startup diskettes come in mighty handy on a PC that doesn't support booting from the CD-ROM drive when the system becomes so mangled that it can't boot from the hard drive. Here's the procedure:

1. **Pop your Windows 2000 CD into your CD-ROM drive and have four freshly formatted diskettes at the ready.**

   I assume that D is the designated letter for the CD-ROM drive. Your mileage, as they say very quickly on car commercials, may vary.

2. **Click Start⇨Run.**

3. **In the Open dialog box, type** D:\BOOTDISK\MAKEBOOT A: **if you're running DOS or Windows 3.x, or type** D:\BOOTDISK\MAKEBT32 A: **if you're running Windows 9x, NT, or 2000.**

4. **Pop in diskettes as requested, labeling them as you go.**

Although you can boot Windows 2000 with these diskettes, *they don't contain your Registry files!* (Try this method and see whether you can find any of the aforementioned Registry files on these diskettes.) Go ahead and make startup diskettes by all means; you may need them to restore the Registry using some of the methods this chapter discusses later. Just don't expect to back up your Registry onto these diskettes; that's not what they're for.

Microsoft warns that you can't use startup diskettes from a Windows 2000 Professional machine to boot up a Windows 2000 Server machine, and vice versa.

Method #1: Microsoft Windows Backup

The general-purpose backup program that comes with Windows 2000, NTBACKUP.EXE or *Microsoft Windows Backup,* can back up your entire disk drive, including the Registry. It can compress files on the fly, and if you have to use a diskette drive as your target device, Backup has no trouble creating a multiple-diskette backup to deal with files (like SYSTEM) that are typically too large to fit on one diskette. It can also back up to a good variety of target devices, including Zip, Jaz, and writeable optical drives, as well as the more traditional tape drives and network directories. It logs its activities, too (typically in C:\Documents and Settings\<username>\Local Settings\ Application Data\Microsoft\Windows NT\NTBackup\data). Furthermore, you don't have to reboot your PC to use NTBACKUP.

Perhaps best of all, NTBACKUP is able to make a backup of your Registry even though the files are open and "in use." That is, NTBACKUP can copy Registry files even when COPY and XCOPY and drag-and-drop can't. For years now, full-fledged backup programs have provided the ability to back up open, active files, and that's just one reason such programs are good to have around. How does NTBACKUP accomplish this magic? The answer is far too complex to discuss in this book. *[This is Glenn's way of telling you that he doesn't know. — Ed.]* The important thing is that it does.

About the only major drawback of using NTBACKUP to clone your Registry is that the program requires Windows 2000 to be running in order to restore the files. The implications are:

- ✔ If you experience total hard disk meltdown and you have to replace the drive, you first have to reinstall Windows 2000 onto the drive before you can run NTBACKUP in order to restore the files you backed up earlier. True, you can specify a minimum install and save some time, but doing so is still a pain and adds an hour or so to your recovery time.

- ✔ If your Registry is so trashed that you can't boot Windows 2000 at all, even in "Safe mode," then you can't run NTBACKUP to restore your Registry. (Can you say, "Catch 22"?) Here again, you may be faced with a reinstall (and, in extreme cases, a reformat before the reinstall) before you can restore your backup.

Another drawback of NTBACKUP is that you can't save all your backup settings and options to a disk file so that you can run NTBACKUP with a single click. All you can save is the list of files you want to back up. This limitation is all the more annoying in that the command-line version of the program (which, by the way, runs at the Windows 2000 command line, which isn't the same as a DOS prompt!) doesn't offer every option that the graphical version does. Network managers need to write scripts that use the command line, so I have to disagree when Microsoft states that the new NTBACKUP may be all you need for an enterprise-wide backup solution. One of these days, Microsoft will ship a backup program that's truly ready for prime time.

Meanwhile, however, NTBACKUP is an adequate day-to-day tool for Registry backups. However, before you decide to use it as your sole method, read the rest of this chapter and consider other methods that don't require Windows 2000 to be up and running in order to restore the backed-up Registry. Meanwhile, the next couple of sections explain how to use NTBACKUP to back up the Registry. The procedure isn't difficult, but it isn't obvious, either, and it involves some terms that you probably haven't heard before.

Creating a backup

To make a backup with Microsoft Windows Backup, start by running the program (Start➪Programs➪Accessories➪System Tools➪Backup). At the initial screen that says Welcome to the Windows 2000 Backup and Recovery Tools, you can select the Backup Wizard radio button to use the built-in wizard, which works pretty well; or, you can click the Backup tab and design your backup job in the utility's main window as shown in Figure 2-3. The latter method is a little more flexible so that's what I discuss here.

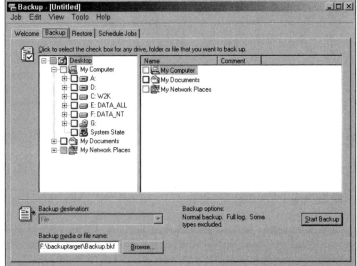

Figure 2-3:
Create your
backup job
at the
program's
main
screen.

The general procedure is as follows (I give you specific details later in this chapter): You choose which directories or files you want to back up in the two Explorer-like windows that occupy most of the main screen. (You can choose Job➪Save Selections As, which lets you create a disk file such as REGISTRY.BKS containing your file selections. You can later load those file selections in one fell swoop by choosing Job➪Load Selections.) Then, choose Tools➪Options to set your preferences for this backup job. Pick a target device in the lower-left corner of the window, click the Start Backup button in the lower-right corner, set a few final options, and you're off to the races.

Why didn't Microsoft just put all the backup options on the Tools➪Options menu instead of putting some on the menu and others on the dialog box that pops up when you click the Start Backup button? The answer is beyond me. Just be aware that you need to check both places to set all the possible backup choices. You also can't save all those choices along with your file list, as you can, for example, with a Windows 98 Backup *job file.* In NTBACKUP, you have to choose your backup options each time you back up (although you can, at least, save a file list with the Job➪Save Selections command). *Yeccchh.*

Tricks and traps for backing up the Registry

So, now that you know the basics of running Microsoft Windows Backup, how do you create a backup job that backs up Ye Olde Registry? In order to accomplish this, you need to understand the term *system state.*

In Computer Science 101, programming students learn that the "state" of a computer system includes every detail necessary to describe that system: everything from the contents of random-access memory to the files on the hard drive. (An analogy may help: The "state" of a rally car, for example, would include how much oil is in the engine, how old the tires are, what direction the car is pointing, how many expired registration certificates are in the glove box, and so on.)

Microsoft uses the phrase *system state* to mean something similar in Windows 2000. The company defines the system state to include the following specific elements:

- ✔ **The Registry.** (Ta-daa!) However, you'll see that when you back up the system state, you don't quite get *all* the Registry, even if you do get most of it.

- ✔ **The boot files.** Specifically, NTLDR and NTDETECT.COM, if you're interested. These are the minimum files that you need to boot Windows 2000.

- ✔ **The COM+ Class Registration Database.** This will probably be empty on a Windows 2000 Professional machine; it has to do with software components that may be accessed over a network.

- ✔ **All the system files in the** C:\WINNT **folder.** These files (most of which have the suffix DLL) amount to at least 200 megabytes. Thankfully, you can exclude them when backing up the system state, at least from NTBACKUP's graphical interface. (You *don't* have the option to exclude them using NTBACKUP's command-line interface.)

And, for those of you running Windows 2000 Server, the system state includes the following additional (and potentially large!) elements:

- ✔ **The Active Directory database**, if the PC is a domain controller. (Active Directory is a network-wide naming system, about which I'll have more to say in Chapters 8, 12, and 13. A domain controller is responsible for authenticating users who log on to the network.)

- ✔ **The SYSVOL folder**, again, if the PC is a domain controller.

- ✔ **The Certificate Services database**, if the PC is running that service.

The *only* way you can back up the local Registry in Microsoft Windows Backup is to select the System State check box in the directory tree on the main backup window. (Checking the folder C:\WINNT\SYSTEM32\CONFIG, or checking the individual files therein, works when you back up a remote Registry but doesn't work when you back up your own Registry. NTBACKUP lets you check 'em, but it won't back 'em up. Remember, these are not ordinary files, so ordinary procedures don't apply.)

When you do choose to back up the system state, NTBACKUP gives you the opportunity to exclude the system files in the C:\WINNT folder, because they're so voluminous. When I make Registry backups, I generally omit these system files, because I catch them in my monthly or weekly full backups, anyway.

Even the system state backup bypasses the multiple possible copies of NTUSER.DAT and USRCLASS.DAT that make up the user-specific Registry files. So, if you want to create a backup job that includes all of these (which I strongly recommend), go check them as well. Remember, these files will either live under the C:\Documents and Settings\<username> folder, or under the C:\WINNT\PROFILES\<username> folder, depending on whether Windows 2000 is an upgrade of an earlier Windows system or not.

Going by the numbers

Okay, in this section I take you through a fairly typical sequence of steps in order to back up the Registry on a Windows 2000 Professional machine. Here we go.

1. **Run NTBACKUP by choosing Start⇨Programs⇨Accessories⇨ System Tools⇨Backup.**

   FYI, you can also choose Start⇨Run and enter **NTBACKUP** to activate the utility.

2. **Click the Backup tab.**

3. **Select the System State check box in the left windowpane.**

4. **Click the + sign next to the C: drive, and select the check box beside the Documents and Settings folder.**

   This folder contains all the user-specific versions of the Registry files NTUSER.DAT and USRCLASS.DAT for anyone who can log on to this computer. (If any user has a ton of data in his Documents and Settings\ <username> folder, as may happen when people store all their data files in My Documents, you can select the various NTUSER.DAT and USR-CLASS.DAT files individually if you only want Registry files in your backup.) When you've done this, the screen should look something like Figure 2-4.

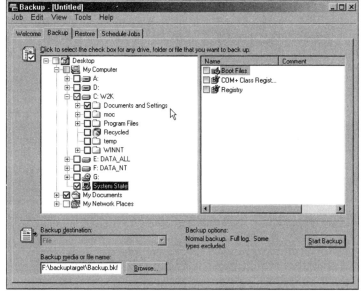

Figure 2-4:
This screen
shows the
entire
Registry
selected for
backup.

5. Choose Tools⇨Options to display the Options dialog box (see Figure 2-5).

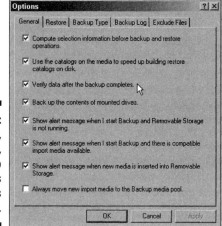

Figure 2-5:
Set most,
but not all,
backup
options
in this
dialog box.

6. **On the General tab, make sure that the Verify Data after the Backup Completes check box is selected.**

   It's smart to make the program perform a comparison check. This comparison makes the backup job take longer, but it ensures that your backup matches the original files exactly.

7. **On the Backup Type tab, select the Normal option.**

   You could choose a different type of backup, such as incremental or differential, if you're backing up an entire hard drive. The Normal setting is appropriate for a quickie Registry backup.

8. **On the Backup Log tab, select the Detailed option.**

   This option lets you confirm exactly which files NTBACKUP was successfully able to copy.

9. **Click OK to close the Options dialog box.**

10. **Click the Browse button in the lower left to select your target device.**

    This is where the backup file will go. It could be a diskette drive, tape drive, Zip drive, or pretty much any storage device that Windows 2000 understands.

11. **Click the Start Backup button.**

    You see the Backup Job Information dialog box (see Figure 2-6).

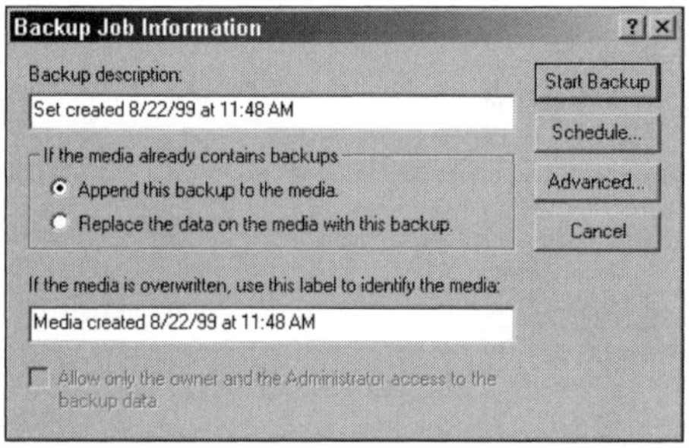

Figure 2-6:
This dialog box appears the first time (!) that you click the Start Backup button.

12. **Click the Advanced button (this is very important!).**

13. **Deselect the check box labeled** Automatically backup System Protected Files with the System State **(see Figure 2-7).**

    Leaving this check box selected causes pretty much the entire contents of C:\WINNT to be backed up the along with the Registry, adding some 200 megabytes or more to the backup set.

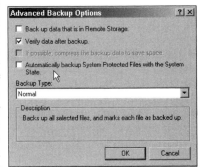

Figure 2-7:
Exclude the
system files
from your
backup if
you're
mainly
wanting to
back up the
Registry.

14. **Click OK to close the Advanced Backup Options dialog box.**

15. **Click Start Backup in the Backup Job Information dialog box.**

    Yes, you did this in Step 11, but this one actually starts the backup.
    (Hey, I don't write these programs, I just write about them.)

    You're off to the races!

Backing up a distant Registry

You wouldn't know it to read the NTBACKUP help file, but you can back up a
remote Registry. (I found this out from a helpful Microsoft engineer.) The
secret is to make sure that the remote computer has its *administrative shares*
activated. The administrative shares are hidden shared folders that end with a
dollar sign, like C$ and ADMIN$. You can see whether they're active by typing
NET SHARE at a command prompt. To activate these on a Windows 2000
Professional machine, make sure that the DWORD value *AutoShareWks* is set
to 1 in the *HKLM\System\CurrentControlSet\Services\lanmanserver\parameters*
key. On a Server machine, the *AutoShareServer* value is in the same key. After
you change these values, you must restart the PC for them to take effect.

Then, as long as you log on with an account that has either Administrator
rights or Backup Operator rights on the remote PC, you can run NTBACKUP,
click the Backup tab, navigate to the remote machine's C:\WINNT\
SYSTEM32\CONFIG folder, and select it. You can then choose a backup target,
which can be on your machine, the remote machine, or anywhere else that
has a network path you can access. The rest of the process works as
described in the previous section.

Method #2: The Emergency Recovery Diskette

As you may have figured out, the Registry is too large to fit onto a single diskette. *Way* too large. So how can a procedure that creates a single Windows 2000 emergency startup diskette be a Registry backup method?

When you make the Emergency Repair Diskette, or *ERD*, you get the opportunity to make a backup copy of the Registry files to a special folder on your hard drive — namely, C:\WINNT\REPAIR\REGBACK.) Windows 2000 can then use that backup copy to restore the Registry in certain circumstances.

This isn't a perfect Registry backup solution — if Windows 2000 can't get to your hard drive, or if your hard drive fails, you're sunk. That said, the ERD method is easy and definitely better than nothing.

Activate the ERD wizard by choosing Start⇨Programs⇨Accessories⇨ System Tools⇨Backup and then click the Emergency Repair Disk button on the Welcome tab as shown in Figure 2-8. You'll see a prompt to put a diskette into your A drive, and a check box labeled Also backup the registry to the repair directory. This backup can be used to help recover your system if the registry is damaged. Select the check box, ignoring the incorrect usage of the word "backup" in the first sentence (these are programmers, not writers), and click the OK button.

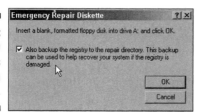

Figure 2-8:
ERD
(rhymes
with
"nerd").

When the operation is complete, click OK again to close the dialog box. You can now use Windows Explorer to check out the date stamps on the files in C:\WINNT\REPAIR\REGBACK. At this point, you have at least some measure of protection against Registry damage. When you repair a Windows 2000 system, you have the option of restoring the Registry that you created when you made the ERD. However, confusingly, you have to use the Recovery Console to do so. If you use the Emergency Repair procedure, Windows 2000 ignores your backups and restores the infant version of the Registry that was created when Windows 2000 was installed! Chapter 11 provides the somewhat bizarre details.

Method #3: REG from the Resource Kit tools

Windows NT 4.0 included as part of the separately available *Microsoft Windows NT 4.0 Resource Kit* a twin set of command-line programs named REGBACK and REGREST. Although REGBACK, the backup part of the set, was more useful back when NTBACKUP didn't support diskette drives and removable disk drives, its successor, REG.EXE, is still a handy tool if you like backing up to a disk device such as a Zip drive or network drive, you don't have to back up every single key (REG omits *HKLM\SECURITY*, for example), and you don't mind a command-line interface. You can install REG.EXE, along with several other Resource Kit tools, by running SETUP.EXE in the \SUPPORT\ TOOLS folder of your Windows 2000 CD.

REG is easy to use. Just open a command prompt session (Start⇨ Programs and enter **CMD**) and type

```
REG SAVE keyname filename
```

where *keyname* is the name of the key you want to save (which may optionally include a network machine name, as in *ralph**HKLM**SOFTWARE*\ *Microsoft*) and *filename* is the name of the file you want to create (which is a compressed binary file, not a text file as with a REGEDIT export). Type **REG SAVE /?** at a command prompt for complete syntax details. You can restore a backup file created by REG SAVE with the (you guessed it) REG RESTORE command. Type **REG /?** at a command prompt to see all the variations of the REG command.

A few points to note:

- ✔ REG only backs up currently active Registry files, so any alternative user files (NTUSER.DAT, USRCLASS.DAT) don't get backed up. You could write a batch file (see the next section) that would run REG to copy the active Registry files and XCOPY to copy any inactive files, such as those other NTUSER.DAT and USRCLASS.DAT files.

- ✔ REG works with network drives, but Microsoft recommends you use NTBACKUP instead of REG if you want to back up to a tape drive. Also, only *HKLM* and *HKU* are available for saving on remote machines.

- ✔ REG can't create a multiple diskette set; it has to see enough free space on the target device to create the specified Registry backup, or it fails with an error message.

- ✔ REG won't overwrite existing files with the same name on the target device (it fails with an error message), so if you use REG repeatedly, you have to clean out the target location first.

As with Microsoft Windows Backup, in order to use REG, you must be logged on to Windows 2000 as a user with the Back Up Files and Folders right. The built-in Administrator account has this right, as does any member of the Backup Operators group.

Method #4: Bootin' and batchin'

A good free solution for making Registry backups is to write a *batch file* that handles the job for you. (A batch file is simply a text file containing a sequence of commands that run one after another.) Creating a batch file has the following advantages:

- ✔ You can write your batch file so that it includes every Registry file, not just some of them.

- ✔ You can set it up to run everything automatically — no having to remember exactly what options you need to set, as in Microsoft Windows Backup, for example.

- ✔ If something goes wrong, you almost always get an error message.

- ✔ Unlike Microsoft Windows Backup, you can use this method even if you can't boot Windows 2000.

The bootin'-and-batchin' solution isn't right for everyone, however. Here are its disadvantages:

- ✔ You have to reboot your machine into a different operating system in order to use it. (Remember, you can't just copy those files while Windows 2000 is running.) Rebooting may be unacceptable on a server that's supposed to run continuously!

- ✔ If you use NTFS on the hard disk as your file system, you have to use third-party software to get your boot diskette to work with NTFS. If you use FAT32 on the hard disk as your file system, you can't use this method at all.

- ✔ You have to provide a DOS device driver for your target device; for example, you have to set up your boot diskette with the GUEST program if you want to back up to a Zip drive.

Writing a batch file involves a little bit of the "P" word — programming — but the programming is easy, and I give you a substantial head start.

If you're not comfortable with writing batch files, consider hiring (or bribing) someone who is and getting him or her to help you set up a batch file that works for you, based on my examples. Generally, programmers can be had for the price of a deep-dish pizza. (If you are a programmer, be sure to request extra cheese.)

Making a DOS boot diskette

Your first step is to make a boot diskette that won't boot you into Windows 2000 (you don't want to activate that Registry!), but will rather boot you into another operating system — good old DOS is a fine choice. If you have an old DOS boot diskette lying around, grab it. If you don't, you can kinda sorta make one from a Windows 95 or 98 system by creating a "startup diskette" using the Add/Remove Programs wizard in the control panel.

Your next chore is to set up your boot diskette with any drivers required for DOS to "see" your backup target device. For example, if you're backing up to a network, you'll need some commands in CONFIG.SYS and AUTOEXEC.BAT to load the requisite network software. Or if you're backing up to a Zip drive, Jaz drive, or something similar, you'll need the DOS drivers for that drive, which the drive manual should explain how to install. Of course, if you want to back the Registry up to diskette, you don't need any such drivers; all DOS boot diskettes understand how to communicate with drive A.

"Now, wait a minute, Glenn," you say. "I see where you're going with this, and it should work fine with a regular old FAT disk. (FAT, or File Allocation Table, is the most compatible kind of disk partition — it works with DOS, Windows 9*x*, NT, and 2000.) But here's the deal: I've formatted my hard drive using the NTFS file system that Microsoft recommends for Windows 2000. (NTFS stands for NT File System.) And when I boot to DOS, I can't see any NTFS disks, because NTFS isn't compatible with DOS. So what about them apples, Mr. Registry?"

I say, mash up them apples and let's have some cider, because the clever lads over at System Internals have written a dandy program called NTFSDOS.EXE. (It's on the CD-ROM that comes with this book.) Run this little guy after you boot to your DOS diskette, and you can magically see those NTFS disks plain as day. Not only can you see them, you can use regular DOS commands like XCOPY to copy them.

Write the backup batch file

So now you can use good old Notepad to make a REGBAK.BAT file (or whatever name you like as long as it has the .BAT suffix) that looks something like this, assuming that network drive F: is already set up via the CONFIG.SYS and AUTOEXEC.BAT files:

```
@ECHO OFF
ECHO About to back up Registry to F:\REG.
ECHO Press Ctrl+C to cancel this backup.
PAUSE
:The /L:D tells NTFSDOS to mount the drive as D.
NTFSDOS /L:D
:
: Copy the main files (the /Y means that XCOPY
```

(continued)

(continued)

```
: doesn't ask if it's overwriting an old file)
:
XCOPY D:\WINNT\SYSTEM32\CONFIG\DEFAULT F:\REG\ /Y
XCOPY D:\WINNT\SYSTEM32\CONFIG\SAM F:\REG\ /Y
XCOPY D:\WINNT\SYSTEM32\CONFIG\SECURITY F:\REG\ /Y
XCOPY D:\WINNT\SYSTEM32\CONFIG\SOFTWARE F:\REG\ /Y
XCOPY D:\WINNT\SYSTEM32\CONFIG\SYSTEM F:\REG\ /Y
:
: Now copy up all possible copies of NTUSER.DAT
: (DOCUME~1 is the DOS name for the
: "Documents and Settings" folder)
:
XCOPY D:\DOCUME~1 F:\REG\ /S
```

Ain't that cool? Incidentally, the /S at the end tells XCOPY to include all non-empty subdirectories underneath D:\DOCUME~1, ensuring that all user-specific versions of NTUSER.DAT and USRCLASS.DAT get backed up. You don't even have to know the usernames; XCOPY copies every user directory under the DOCUME~1 directory. Granted, this method may back up lots of other files that you may not want, such as each user's My Documents folder, Outlook Express files, and so on. If you know every user's name, and you only want Registry files in your backup, then you can substitute the last line above with a series of similar commands that back up only the NTUSER.DAT and USR-CLASS.DAT files (find them all fast with the Start menu's Search command).

Should you ever have to restore these files, you may run into the limitation that NTFSDOS.EXE only permits reading from NTFS partitions, not writing to them. However, you could work around this problem by buying NTFSCopy from the System Internals folks (hey, they've got to make a living). It's part of the NTFS Tools package, which is a bargain at twice the price. And no, they don't pay me to say that. (I wish they did. I need new skis.)

Method #5: Export and import

One of the simpler and more frequently recommended ways to back up your Registry is to run REGEDIT (one of the two Registry Editors that come with Windows 2000) to export the entire Registry to a text file. The procedure is as follows:

1. **Run the Registry Editor by choosing Start⇨Run, typing REGEDIT, and then clicking OK.**

2. **Choose Registry⇨Export Registry File to display the dialog box shown in Figure 2-9.**

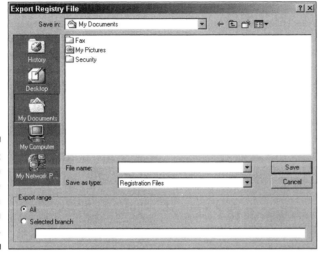

Figure 2-9:
Backing up
the entire
Registry to a
text file with
REGEDIT.

3. **Specify the target directory in the Save In field and name the file in the File Name field.**

   REGEDIT automatically gives the file the .REG suffix.

4. **Select the All radio button in the Export Range panel and then click Save.**

Although very easy, this procedure has a couple of problems.

✔ You can't restore a full Registry backup when Windows 2000 is running in its graphical mode and be completely certain that the resulting Registry is identical to the one you backed up. The reason for the uncertainty is that a REG file import can't delete existing Registry entries, it can only modify them or add new entries.

✔ The export procedure doesn't back up user settings for the non–logged-on users of a PC that's set up to handle multiple user profiles. However, the export procedure does back up the settings for the currently logged-on user and the default user.

You might expect REGEDIT to omit exporting value types that its user interface doesn't support, such as REG_EXPAND_SZ and REG_MULTI_SZ (see Chapter 4). It turns out, however, that the export procedure saves these values using a special numeric coding that enables REGEDIT to re-import them later — making REGEDIT smarter than it looks, much like racer Richard Petty. (Or Tom Petty, for that matter.)

Because of these problems, the REG file export is more appropriate for quickle, partial Registry backups — for example, when you're about to modify a particular Registry key and want to save the original — than for full backups.

You can create a REG file export using REGEDIT even if Windows 2000 won't start normally. Hit the F8 key at the text mode boot menu and choose "Safe Mode, Command Prompt" from the list. At the `C:\WINNT>` prompt, you can create a full export of the current Registry by using the following command, where *filename* is the filename that you specify:

```
REGEDIT /E filename.REG
```

The Bottom Line

Here's a summary of the key points in this important chapter, with my editorial comments in italics:

- ✔ Windows 2000 makes automatic backups of certain Registry components, but they live on the same hard drive as the original files and they don't include the whole Registry. *Don't rely solely on the automatic behind-the-scenes backups.*

- ✔ The Windows 2000 startup diskette set is okay for starting your PC in some situations, but it doesn't contain your Registry files. *Make a startup diskette set by all means, but don't think that doing so backs up your Registry.*

- ✔ Microsoft Windows Backup can back up your Registry, works with a variety of backup devices (including diskettes), can compress data on the fly, and can perform a post-backup comparison test. *Use this method to save Registry files to a device other than your main hard drive, but make sure you add the various NTUSER.DAT and USRCLASS.DAT files to the file list.*

- ✔ The REG utility is handy for partial backups, if you don't mind the lack of a graphical interface. It doesn't work with tape drives and it's impractical with diskettes, but it works with removable disk drives and network drives. *Use REG for partial backups on disk media, but not for full backups.*

- ✔ Creating your own boot disks and batch files works well. You can automate the process so you don't have to remember anything, and you can restore your backups even when Windows 2000 can't start. Also, using batch files enables you to back up your complete Registry even if you set up your PC to work with multiple users. However, creating batch files requires a little up-front work, maybe some third-party software, and perhaps even some expert help. *Use this method if you're familiar with batch file programming or you know someone who is, and you don't mind rebooting to back up or restore your Registry.*

✔ The REGEDIT Registry Editor's export feature is useful for backing up parts of the Registry, and you can restore your backups even if Windows 2000 can't start. However, you have no guarantee of being able to restore your Registry exactly as it was before when you use export files. *Use this method for partial Registry backups (selected keys only) but not as your only method for full Registry backups.*

This chapter has been a little complicated, and I apologize for that. Unfortunately, no single Registry backup solution is the best for every situation. If you go through this chapter carefully and choose the options that seem to work best for you, you'll be glad that I went into as much detail as I have. Choose a method or a combination of methods that's as easy and convenient as possible, so you'll actually make your Registry backups as often as you should. That, in turn, will let you sleep easier — which is important, considering the journey you're about to make through the narrow, twisted roads of Registry country.

Chapter 3

Editing the Registry without a Registry Editor

- -

In This Chapter

▶ Discovering why the Registry Editors are risky utilities

▶ Finding out why other alternatives to editing the Registry are safer

▶ Getting familiar with the Windows 2000 control panel applets

▶ Making the acquaintance of the new Microsoft Management Console

▶ Using My Computer and Open With to manage file type associations

▶ Uncovering the secret use of the System Policy Editor

- -

*M*any Windows 2000 features allow you to edit the Registry without using either of the two Registry Editor utilities, REGEDIT and REGEDT32. In this chapter, I introduce you to these Registry editing features and explain why they're preferable to either Registry Editor.

I give REGEDIT and REGEDIT32 their due in Chapter 4, where I also explain why you get two different Registry Editors with Windows 2000. (Psst. Each is good at different things and Microsoft hasn't bothered to combine their best features into a single tool.) I use both tools a lot in the chapters that follow as well as to perform a couple of cool tricks in this chapter.

REGEDIT and REGEDIT32 are the *only* tools that come with Windows 2000 for making many of the changes you may want to make to the Registry. However, if the First Rule of the Registry is to save it frequently, then the Second Rule is as follows:

> *Never use a Registry Editor unless no safer alternative is available.*

Or, put another way:

> *If you want to remove bugs from your windshield, a squeegee is better than a chisel.*

Whereas every other tool that Windows 2000 provides for modifying the Registry has some safeguards (even if they're minimal), the Registry Editors have few safeguards at all. I'm all for the chisel when nothing better is available, but fortunately Windows 2000 provides tools that are a bit less blunt to put a shine on your Registry.

You have to know what the "safer alternatives" are and what they do in order to follow this Second Rule of the Registry. For example, if you're aware that a Windows 2000 control panel can make a certain setting for you, then you can use the control panel instead of REGEDIT or REGEDT32 — and run much less risk of making a mistake that could ruin your whole day. Or even 'cause you to lose your job, start drinking, get divorced, and flee shamefully to Bulgaria, where you end up writing computer viruses for the Dark Avenger and live out your days in bitter obscurity, sobbing to yourself nightly in your lumpy, chilly bed, *Why didn't I use a control panel? Why?*

What's So Risky about Registry Editors?

Why is a control panel, for example, safer than a Registry Editor? Well, if you take as your starting point that almost nothing is more dangerous than a Registry Editor, just about *any* alternative is safer by default. Here's why:

- **Registry Editor changes occur immediately.** Most programs let you make whatever changes you want without committing them to disk until you choose File⇨Save. But take a look at the REGEDIT and REGEDT32 menus. No File menu! Changes that you make in these programs head straight for the Registry as soon as you make them (even though some don't actually take visible effect until Windows 2000 restarts). As a result, if you're just horsing around with a Registry Editor when the system crashes or experiences a power cut, you may be stuck with a damaged Registry.

- **Registry Editors offer no Undo feature.** Want to reverse yourself and nullify your last change? You'd better have a great memory, because neither REGEDIT nor REGEDT32 helps you retrace your steps. This lack of an Undo feature is a major pain. For example, imagine that you accidentally delete the value {25336920-03F9-11cf-8FD0-00AA00686F13}. This is a real Registry value identifying the file MSHTML.DLL, which can display Web graphics within Internet Explorer and in the Windows 2000 HTML Help system. Think you can remember it well enough to correct your mistake? I know *I* can't. There go all those Web page graphics, Windows Help screens, and HTML-view folders.

✔ **Registry Editors offer no warnings.** If you're about to do something that could really damage the Registry, such as delete a whole bunch of essential values, REGEDIT presents the same brief warning message that it presents when you delete a single, trivial value (see Figure 3-1). REGEDT32 presents a somewhat more informative message that indicates whether you're about to nuke a single value or a bunch of values (see Figure 3-2). However, neither program has built-in warnings to help the user distinguish between critical and noncritical changes.

✔ **Registry Editors' help needs some.** The online help for the Registry Editors continues to be a major embarrassment. For Microsoft to provide such important utilities with practically no information in the Help file was surprising in earlier versions of Windows, but inexcusable now that the company has had several years to address the deficiency. Want to know the purpose of the Registry's six primary branches? The REGEDIT help file doesn't even mention them! (The REGEDT32 help file, to its credit, does.) In fact, as Figure 3-3 shows, the REGEDIT help file consists of a total of fifteen little windows' worth of information — about the same amount of text as two pages of this book. REGEDT32 doubles that amount with 32 little windows, lifting its help system up from "woefully inadequate" to "sadly inadequate."

Figure 3-1:
The
standard
REGEDIT
deletion
warning.

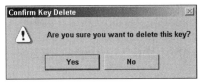

Figure 3-2:
A slightly
more
informative
REGEDT32
deletion
warning.

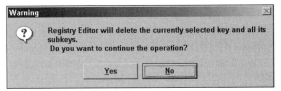

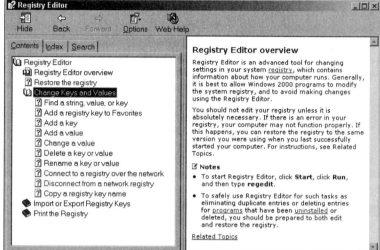

Figure 3-3:
The Registry
Editor's
helpless
help feature.

What's So Safe about Alternatives?

Most of the Windows 2000 alternatives to REGEDIT and REGEDT32 — and I'm talking here about things like control panels, dialog boxes, and property sheets — give the user more guidance to warn of certain potentially harmful actions, as well as make complex tasks much easier.

Extending a helpful hand

As an example, consider the issue of giving a Windows 2000 computer a *network name*. The network name identifies the computer to other computers on a local or wide-area network.

In the new Windows 2000 network naming scheme, which is based on the same set of standards used by the public Internet, a computer name (BarneyFifes-PC, DeputyDesk, and so on) can only contain letters, numbers, and hyphens. If you open the Network Identification dialog box, which you reach by right-clicking My Computer and choosing Properties⇨ Network Identification⇨Properties, you can receive this advice. Click the **?** icon on the dialog box's upper-right corner, click in the Computer Name field, and open the suggested Help window, as shown in Figure 3-4.

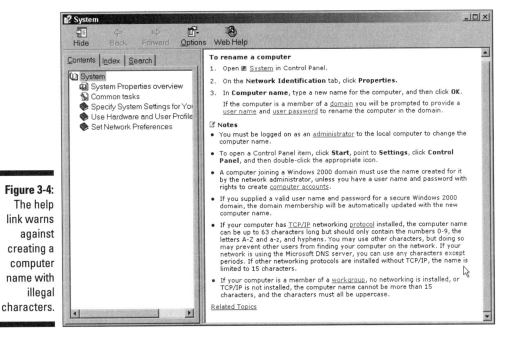

Figure 3-4:
The help
link warns
against
creating a
computer
name with
illegal
characters.

If you use a Registry Editor to change a computer name, however, you have no way of finding out that you shouldn't use characters such as the underscore ("_"). You wouldn't even know there's a problem until someone tries to access the misnamed computer over the network. The dialog box method not only warns you if you use the built-in help feature, it warns you if you put an "illegal" character in the Computer Name field. If you're cautious enough to use the dialog box, in other words, you have both a spare tire and a can of fix-a-flat spray on a road full of potholes.

Simplifying complex changes

Some of the chores you need to perform with Windows 2000 are mind-numbingly complex if you attempt to perform them by directly editing the Registry. For example, changing the display's color scheme — which takes just a few clicks in the Display control panel's Appearance tab — can involve dozens of changes to the Registry.

Take a look at Figure 3-5, which shows a couple dozen or so Registry entries that Windows 2000 modifies in *HKCU\Control Panel\Colors*. (The *WindowMetrics* key, pointed to in the figure by the arrow cursor, contains a dozen or so more changes.)

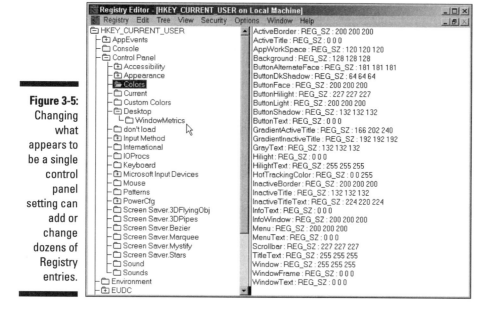

Admittedly, I'm giving you an extreme case: Certain control panel settings only change one or two Registry entries. Even in those cases, however, you can make the change using the control panel more easily than you can figure out precisely which Registry entries correspond to the change and precisely what to type into REGEDIT or REGEDT32 to accomplish it.

Taking care of non-Registry files

Sometimes, Windows 2000 settings don't reside in the Registry at all, but rather in one of the INI initialization files. For example, check out Figure 3-6, which you get to via Start⇨Settings⇨Control Panel⇨System⇨Advanced⇨ Startup and Recovery. Some of the settings you can make on this property sheet do live in the Registry, but the Display List of Operating Systems for *x* Seconds setting lives in the BOOT.INI text file. (The reason for this is that the Registry hasn't yet loaded when you see the text mode boot menu.) The property sheet "knows" where these respective settings belong, so you don't have to.

A few other INI files exist in Windows 2000, also, and letting the system's various property sheets and control panels worry about them is certainly more convenient.

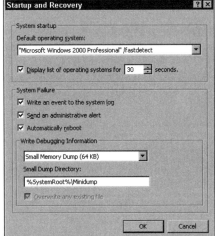

Figure 3-6:
This
property
sheet has
some
settings that
live in the
Registry and
some that
live in
BOOT.INI.

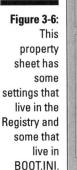

Control Panels

In general, this book saves the nitty-gritty details of Registry settings for situations where you can't change or view a setting more safely or conveniently any other way. For example, I don't tell you exactly which Registry settings get modified when you change the desktop wallpaper, because it's easier and safer to change it in the Display control panel. My guess is that you don't want to know the difficult and risky way to do things unless no better option is available.

Having said that, there may be times when you legitimately need to see what effect a control panel (or any other action, for that matter) has on the Registry, or when you're just curious and want to understand more about what the control panels actually do. Chapter 14 presents some tools and techniques for tracking Registry changes (wherever they may come from), and the list of control panels in this section gives you clues as to which control panels affect which Registry branches.

The Windows 2000 control panels are the most common and useful alternatives to the Registry Editor for making changes to the Windows 2000 configuration. Most of the control panels modify the Registry; but some also modify various INI files on the disk, too, as well as the new Active Directory database in a networked environment.

Microsoft Management Console: Control panel, part deux

Windows 2000 uses a new kind of control panel in addition to the older *.CPL files. This new variation is called *Microsoft Management Console*, or *MMC* for short. Microsoft used MMCs in a few products (such as its Internet server software) prior to Windows 2000, and it seems to be the way the company is moving. I predict the *.CPL files will be history in Windows 2010. So this new approach is worth a few words now.

MMC is a bit like a standard car chassis within which software developers can put whatever engine they want. That is, the framework has some consistent elements, but the contents of any given MMC window may vary greatly. The left window is a hierarchical, Explorer-like "console tree" showing the individual *snap-ins* that actually do useful work; examples of snap-ins are Device Manager and Event Viewer. The right window is the Details pane showing the contents of the active snap-in highlighted in the console tree. The menu bar contains the Action and View menus, but the choices beneath these menus can and do vary widely.

The level of standardization that MMC provides is pretty minimal, and MMC windows are no more user-friendly than tabbed property sheets — in fact, the MMC windows are a little less "discoverable." However, one cool benefit is that you can put together your own MMC "control panels" with any combination of snap-ins. That's something you can't do with the traditional control panel files, and it's sure to come in handy for those who have to spend a lot of time configuring or managing Windows 2000 systems.

The preconfigured MMC consoles that appear when you choose Start⇨Settings⇨Control Panel⇨Administrative Tools are easily distinguishable from traditional control panel files by the presence of a shortcut arrow on the icon. These shortcuts point to *.MSC files on disk, which run the MMC host program MMC.EXE. If you want to experiment with making your own "mission control" MMC consoles, choose Start⇨Run, enter **MMC**, and when the Microsoft Management Console is up and running, choose Console⇨Add/Remove Snap-In, click Add, and select the snap-ins you want. An example of a custom MMC console appears below.

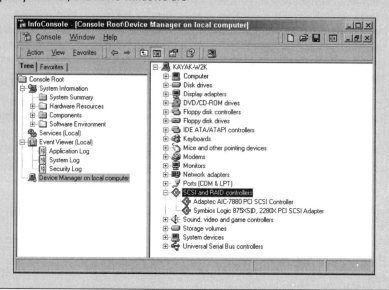

Which control panel icons appear when you click Start⇨Settings⇨ Control Panel depends on which control panel files (they have the suffix .CPL) are present in the C:\WINNT\SYSTEM32 directory. In fact, one way to hide a particular control panel is to remove or rename the associated .CPL file, but take care: Some CPL files, such as MMSYS.CPL, handle more than one control panel icon. A better way to control access to control panels is to use the System Policy Editor or Group Policy utility, as described in the following tip.

If you want to hide certain control panels from other users, you can do that with the Group Policy tool. For example, you can run the Local Group Policy utility by choosing Start⇨Run, and entering **GPEDIT.MSC**. Select User Configuration\Administrative Templates\Control Panel and modify the Hide Specific Control Panel Applets setting. Chapter 7 offers more information on Group Policies.

In the Administrative Tools area of the control panel are a number of different-looking quasi-control panels called *MMC consoles* (see the sidebar titled "Microsoft Management Console: Control panel, part deux"). In the rest of this chapter, I refer to these guys as control panels, too, even though strictly speaking they're not CPL files. The fact is that they act like control panels and they can modify the Registry like control panels. If it looks like a duck, swims like a duck, and quacks like a duck, then we may as well call it a duck.

Having said that, these two ducks are different subspecies, because the MMC ducks have a somewhat different user interface than the CPL ducks. So the control panel has become a fairly messy pond. Don't worry, you'll get used to it!

Primary control panels

The primary control panels are those that appear on just about every Windows 2000 PC. You can fire up the control panel main screen by choosing Start⇨Settings⇨Control Panel (see Figure 3-7). The view here is pretty much the same from Windows 2000 Professional or Windows 2000 Server, the main difference being that the Professional version has the Users and Passwords control panel. (Windows 2000 Server manages users and passwords via Active Directory control panels in the Administrative Tools folder.)

When you open the Administrative Tools folder, however, the view is likely to be quite different. Figure 3-8 shows a typical snapshot of the folder on a Windows 2000 Professional machine, and Figure 3-9 shows the folder on a Windows 2000 Server machine (demonstrating that network administrators are busy folk!).

Slick tip: You can add most of the Server's administrative tools to a Windows 2000 Professional machine by popping a Windows 2000 Server CD into the machine and double-clicking ADMINPAK.MSI on the CD's \I386 folder. Doing so lets you do lots of network management stuff remotely, without being on the server PC itself.

The last column of Table 3-1 tells you the more important part or parts of the Registry that the particular control panel modifies. I explain the structure of the Registry in Chapters 4 and 6, so check out those chapters to figure out what a *Registry key* is and where it lives in the Registry.

Figure 3-8:
The
Windows
2000
Profes-
sional's
Administra-
tive Tools
are few.

Figure 3-9:
Windows
2000
Server's
Administra-
tive Tools
are many
and scary.

Table 3-1		Control Panel Effects on the System and Registry	
Control Panel	*Filename*	*Description*	*Main Registry Keys Affected*
Add/Remove Hardware	HDWWIZ.CPL	Activates the Add New Hardware wizard, a series of question-and-answer dialog boxes that guide you through the process of installing a new device (such as a sound card). The wizard modifies the hardware-related Registry settings by reading INF files supplied by the device manufacturer.	*HKLM\Enum, HKLM\hardware, HKLM\System\ CurrentControlSet\ Services\Class*
Add/Remove Programs	APPWIZ.CPL	Enables you to conveniently install and uninstall compon-ents of Windows 2000 as well as 32-bit Windows 2000 app-lications that supply their own installation and de-installation programs.	*HKLM\SOFTWARE* for settings affect-ing all users, *HKCU\Software* for settings affect-ing individual users, *HKLM\ SOFTWARE\ Microsoft\Windows\ CurrentVersion\ Uninstall* for the deinstallation info
Administra-tive Tools	N/A	A virtual folder leading to a variety of Microsoft Manage-ment Console snap-ins, such as Computer Management, Event Viewer, Performance, and Services. Some of these appear in this table individually.	N/A
Date/Time	TIMEDATE.CPL	Enables you to set the clock and time zone. Access it quickly by double-clicking the clock on the taskbar.	*HKLM\System\ CurrentControlSet\ Control\Time ZoneInformation*

Control Panel	Filename	Description	Main Registry Keys Affected
Display	DESK.CPL	Enables you to change screen size, color options, wallpaper, screen saver settings, monitor power-saving settings, visual effects, the desktop view (as Web page or not), display acceleration settings, and the desktop color scheme. Easily accessible by right-clicking any empty area of the desktop and choosing Properties.	*HKCC\Display\ Settings, HKCU\ Control Panel\ Desktop,* *HKCU\Control Panel\Colors,* *HKCU\Control Panel\Appearance,* HKU for each user, and several others
Folder Options	N/A	Not really a control panel, actually a shortcut to the dialog box that you can see from My Computer⇨Tools⇨ Folder Options.	*HKCR*
Fonts	N/A	Functions a little differently from most other control panels — actually is a shortcut to viewing the directory in Explorer. Opens a window showing all the OpenType, TrueType, and PostScript fonts installed on the system. You can add or delete fonts from this window.	*HKLM\SOFTWARE\ Microsoft\ Windows\ CurrentVersion\ Fonts*
Game Controllers	JOY.CPL	Changes joystick settings (usually for computer games).	*HKLM\System\ CurrentControl Set\control\Media Resources\joystick*
Internet Options	INETCPL.CPL	Sets Internet Explorer options (but not other browser options). A quick way to get to this control panel is to right-click the Internet Explorer icon on the desktop and choose Properties.	*HKCU\Software\ Microsoft\Internet Explorer, HKLM\ Software\ Microsoft\Internet Explorer*

(continued)

Table 3-1 *(continued)*

Control Panel	Filename	Description	Main Registry Keys Affected
Keyboard	MAIN.CPL	Handles key repeat delay and repeat speed, as well as the text insertion cursor blink rate (don't ask why that last one is a keyboard setting).	*HKCU\Control Panel\Keyboard*
Licensing	LICCPA.CPL	On Windows 2000 Server only; changes from "per server" to "per seat" licensing or vice versa, changes number of client licenses.	*HKLM\SYSTEM\ CurrentControlSet\ Services\ LicenseInfo*
Mouse	MAIN.CPL	Enables you to set not only mouse preferences but also cursors (or mouse pointers).	*HKCU\Control Panel\Cursors, HKCC\Display\ Settings,* and (typically) *HKCU\ Control Panel\ Mouse, HKU* for each user
Network and Dial-Up Connections	NCPA.CPL	Functions as the nerve center for all your network and dial-up settings, such as which network communications language you want the PC to use. Get here quickly by right-clicking the My Network Places desktop icon and choosing Properties.	*HKLM\Enum\ HKLM\Network, HKLM\System\ CurrentControlSet\ Services\Class\ . . .~\NetClient, . . .~\Network, Net* (and *NetService,* and *. . .~\NetTrans*)
Password	PASSWORD.CPL	Enables you to set up the PC for remote administration (for example with the Remote Registry Editor), set up user profiles so multiple people can use the same PC, and change the Windows logon password.	*HKLM\System\ CurrentControlSet\ PwdProvider, Control\ HKU* for each user
Phone and Modem Options	TELEPHON.CPL	Runs the Install New Modem wizard if no modem is set up, or the Modem's control panel otherwise. Set modem speeds, dialing properties, and communications options here.	*HKLM\System\ CurrentControlSet\ Services\Class\ Modem, HKLM\ Enum*

Control Panel	Filename	Description	Main Registry Keys Affected
Power Options	POWERCFG.CPL	This control panel sets the computer's power-saving features, such as turning off a hard drive after so many minutes of inactivity.	*HKCU\Control Panel\PowerCfg, HKU for each user*
Printers	N/A	Opens a special folder called the Printers folder, where you can adjust settings such as resolution, print darkness, and so on. (Functions similarly to the Fonts control panel.)	*HKLM\System\ CurrentControlSet\ Control\Print\ Printers, HKCC\ System\ CurrentControlSet\ Control\Print\ Printers*
Regional Options	INTL.CPL	Enables you to set location-specific preferences for how Windows 2000 displays numbers, currency, and time-and-date information.	*HKCU\Control Panel\ International*
Scanners and Cameras	STICPL.CPL	If you have one or more scanners or digital cameras installed, this control panel offers configuration options.	*HKLM\SYSTEM\ CurrentControlSet\ Services\StillCam, HKLM\SYSTEM\ CurrentControlSet\ Services\StiSvc, HKLM\SYSTEM\ CurrentControlSet\ Control*
Scheduled Tasks	N/A	Opens a special folder called Scheduled Tasks, where you can specify programs to run in the future on a recurring or one-time basis.	*HKLM\SECURITY\ RXACT, HKLM\ SECURITY\Policy*

(continued)

Table 3-1 *(continued)*

Control Panel	Filename	Description	Main Registry Keys Affected
Sounds and Multimedia	MMSYS.CPL	Enables you to associate sounds (for Windows 2000 and certain applications) with particular events, such as minimizing a window or closing a program. Also enables you to set audio, video, digitized music, and CD music preferences (for example, whether to play back video clips at original size or full screen).	*HKCU\AppEvents, HKCU\Software\ Microsoft\ Multimedia, HKCU\Software\ Microsoft\ Windows\Current Version\ Multimedia, HKLM\ System\ CurrentControlSet\ Control\Media Resources, HKLM\ System\Current ControlSet\ Services\Class\ CDROM, HKU for each user*
System	SYSDM.CPL	Enables you to tune Windows 2000 performance and set startup/shutdown options (Advanced tab), run downhardware problems and setup multiple hardware configurations (Hardware tab), copy or change user profiles (User Profiles tab), and change the computer's name (Network Identification tab).	*HKLM\System\ CurrentControlSet\ Control\ FileSystem, HKCC\ Config\ Display, HKLM\Enum,* and *HKLM\Config.* Can also modify SYSTEM.INI
Users	INETCPL.CPL	An alternative user interface for setting up multiple user profiles, duplicating features in the Passwords control panel.	*HKCU\Software\ Microsoft\Internet Explorer\Main, HKCU\Software\ Microsoft\ Windows\Current Version\ Internet Settings, HKCU\ Software\ Microsoft\ Windows\Current Version\Explorer, HKU for each user*

Secondary control panels

I define secondary control panels as those that may or may not appear on a given PC: control panels that pertain to specific applications you may install or that you obtain from other sources (such as the Microsoft Office programs). Here is a list of a few common secondary control panels, but many others exist:

- ✔ **32-Bit ODBC** (File: ODBCCP32.CPL): You may see this one if you use Microsoft Access or any other database program that speaks the Structured Query Language (SQL).

- ✔ **Personal Web Manager** (File: PWS.EXE): Here's an example of a control panel that isn't a CPL file. This one manages the version of Microsoft's IIS Web server that ships with Windows 2000 Professional. Install this utility via the Add/Remove Programs wizard.

- ✔ **Find Fast** (File: FINDFAST.CPL): This control panel comes with Microsoft Office 97 and 2000 and is supposed to make opening Office documents faster. It's famous for slowing down machines, though, so I usually turn it off.

- ✔ **QuickTime 32** (File: QT32.CPL): Here's where you can set preferences for playing digital movies (*.MOV) that use Apple's QuickTime format.

- ✔ **TweakUI** (File: TWEAKUI.CPL): This control panel is a freebie from Microsoft provided on the separately available *Microsoft Windows 2000 Resource Kit* CD-ROM.

Showing your control panel who's driving

If you're like me, you're always looking for ways to reduce the number of clicks, double-clicks, and keystrokes that common Windows procedures require. One way to save clicks when using the control panels is to put them onto the Start menu in such a way that you can pluck the particular control panel you need from a cascading menu (see Figure 3-10), instead of having to select the icon in the main control panel window and wait for Windows 2000 to display the window's graphics.

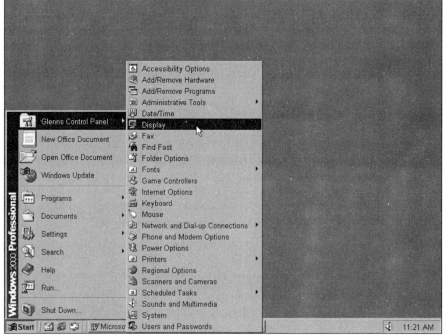

Figure 3-10:
Saving
mouse
clicks with a
cascading
control
panel menu.

Microsoft's answer

One approach is to use a new setting that Microsoft built into Windows 2000. If you choose Start⇨Settings⇨Taskbar & Start Menu, click Advanced, and check the Expand Control Panel check box (see Figure 3-11), then you get a cascade effect when you choose Start⇨Settings⇨Control Panel. This setting is a welcome addition and may be fine for many readers. However, it has the drawback of being "hardwired" into the operating system. That is, you can't change the location of the cascading control panel; it must remain off the Settings entry on the primary Start menu.

For the curious, the Expand Control Panel check box modifies the *HKCU\Software\Microsoft\Windows\CurrentVersion\Explorer\Advanced\ CascadeControlPanel* Registry value. Incidentally, you can also cascade the My Documents, Printers, and Network & Dial-Up Connections menu options — but, again, only from their preset locations.

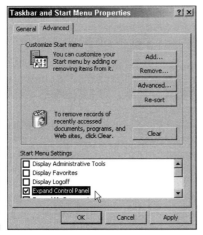

Figure 3-11:
Windows
2000 lets
you cas-
cade control
panels, but
only in a
fixed
location.

An even better answer

In order to create a cascading control panel menu that you can place wherever the heck you want, you have to create a Start menu item that points to
the Windows 2000 control panel *object*. All objects have a unique identifier,
called a *Class ID* (or CLSID, as it appears in the Registry). This identifier needs
a word or two of explanation, because it's an important Registry concept.

Every kind of object in a Windows 2000 system, including data file types
(such as a PowerPoint slide show) and program modules (such as the code
that displays and processes dialog box radio buttons), has a special Class ID
all to itself. Notice that I say "every *kind* of object" has its own unique identifier, not every *object*. That is, if you create three different PowerPoint slide
shows, they don't have three different Class IDs; all three are part of the same
"class" and share the same Class ID.

First, you have to figure out which Class ID runs the control panel. You won't
be modifying the Registry to do this, but it's still a good idea to make a
backup before you run REGEDIT (see Chapter 2 for details if you're not sure
how to back up the Registry). Once you've made a Registry backup, follow
these steps (note that many of them require right-clicking):

1. **Choose Start⇨Run, type REGEDIT in the Open field, and click OK.**

   The Registry Editor window appears. I recommend using REGEDIT here,
   rather than REGEDT32, because REGEDIT is better for searching the
   Registry.

2. **Press the left arrow repeatedly if necessary to get all the way back to
   My Computer; then press Ctrl+F to bring up the Find dialog box.**

Make sure all the check box options inside the Look At rectangle are selected. (You don't yet know exactly where you're going to find the control panel Class ID; checking all three boxes tells REGEDIT to look everywhere it can.)

3. **Type** control panel **in the Find What field and click the Find Next button. Press F3 if needed, until you find the Class ID.**

The Class ID for the control panel object appears as a long string of seemingly random letters and numbers next to an opened folder in the left windowpane (see Figure 3-12). You could jot this long Class ID down on a piece of paper (it's 21EC2020-3AEA-1069-A2DD-08002B30309D), but you might make a mistake, and there's an easier way: copy the Class ID to the invisible Windows Clipboard.

4. **Right-click the opened folder in the left windowpane.**

5. **Choose Copy Key Name.**

This action copies the key's name, including the Class ID, to the Windows Clipboard. We'll paste it into a folder name in a minute.

6. **Close the Registry Editor by clicking the close box in the upper-right corner (it looks like an X).**

Now it's time to create the control panel item on the Start menu in Steps 7 through 12.

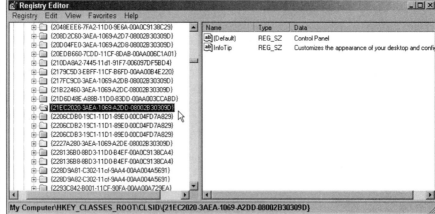

Figure 3-12:
Finding the control panel's class identifier using a Registry Editor.

7. **Right-click the Start button and choose Explore.**

You should see an Explorer window showing the structure of the Start menu, and the Start Menu folder should appear highlighted in the left windowpane.

8. **Choose File⇨New⇨Folder to create the new menu entry for the control panel.**

I'm creating the cascading control panel right off the main Start menu, but you can change the location in the left windowpane to put it wherever you wanted in your menu structure.

9. **In the highlighted area for the new folder's name, type** My Control Panel. **(including the final period).**

10. **With the folder name still highlighted, press Ctrl+V to paste the Class ID from the Windows Clipboard into the space right after the period.**

11. **Delete everything to the right of the period except the Class ID number and its enclosing curly braces, and press Enter.**

    Putting the Class ID right after the period in the folder name tells Windows 2000 to make this new folder work just like the control panel object. You can use this little trick with other Class IDs, as I show you in other parts of this book.

12. **Close the Explorer window by clicking the close box in the upper-right corner.**

Now, click the Start button to see your new menu, with the My Control Panel entry on it. Move the mouse up to highlight My Control Panel, hold it there for a second or so, and Windows 2000 displays a cascading menu showing each individual control panel. Best of all, you can now move your cascading Control Panel entry wherever you want, instead of having to accept Microsoft's hardwired location on the Start⇨Settings menu. You've just made your control panel easier to use, you've one-upped the Microsoft programmers (always a gratifying feeling), and you've discovered that every Windows 2000 object has a unique identifying number in the Registry. And if you think *that's* moderately cool, I can assure you that you ain't seen nothin' yet. We're just starting to hint at the power of the Registry.

The Setup Program

The Windows 2000 setup program, WINNT.EXE (if you're installing from DOS or Windows 3.*x*) or WINNT32.EXE (if you're installing from Windows 9*x* or a previous version of Windows NT), is responsible for copying Windows 2000 files onto a PC and for building the very first version of the Registry on that PC.

If you're reading this book because you already have a Windows 2000 PC and you want to make it work better, what actually happens during setup doesn't concern you a great deal. You probably never plan to run it again, and you shouldn't need to. However, if you're responsible for other Windows 2000 PCs, you may be interested to know how you can customize the setup program to build a Registry that's more nearly the way you want it from the very start. Chapter 12 provides all the details.

Deciding not to reinstall Windows 2000 to fix your Registry

For nigh on a decade, reinstalling Windows has been a favorite suggestion of technical support staff who can't figure out any other way to fix a given problem. At some point in your experience with Windows 2000, you may encounter a technician or Help Desk analyst who tells you to reinstall the operating system. Be very cautious before accepting such advice!

When you reinstall Windows 2000, depending on the method that you use, the installation program may create a brand-new Registry for you from scratch. It's possible that doing so will fix the particular problem you've run into, but the cure may be worse than the disease. If you reformat the hard drive before reinstalling Windows 2000, or if you install Windows 2000 into a different directory than the one you installed to originally, you zap all the customizations you've made to the Windows 2000 desktop. All the Registry entries for application software you've installed also get zapped. You end up having to reinstall all your software and reenter all your software-specific configuration settings.

True, you can just reinstall Windows 2000 over your existing installation and retain most, if not all, of your application settings. An in-place upgrade reinstalls all system files, so re-running

setup is one way to fix file corruption. But because this method leaves some settings in place, it may not resolve the problem you're facing. For example, if you reinstall Windows 2000 because your modem stops working, you could end up with two modems defined in the control panel, neither of which will work!

Reinstalling Windows 2000 is rarely necessary to fix a problem. (I am *not* talking about the beta program here, during which I reinstalled Windows 2000 about 2000 times — that's just life in the prerelease lane.) If a software vendor tech support person (including Microsoft) tells you to reinstall Windows, politely ask to speak to a senior tech support analyst who may be able to give you more specific and less drastic advice. For example, the Last Known Good boot option may be able to conveniently restore your Registry to the last version that worked. You can also try using the Emergency Repair Diskette and the Recovery Console (Chapters 10 and 11 contain details). Also, the new-for-NT System File Checker utility looks for system files and device drivers that show evidence of recent tampering or damage. (Select Start➪Run, enter **CMD**, and type **SFC /?** for details on this command-line utility.)

My Computer and Explorer

My Computer, which displays a single-paned window into the computer, is supposedly for "typical" Windows 2000 users, while Explorer, which displays a double-paned window, is for "advanced" users. Most Windows 2000 users get frustrated with the limitations of My Computer and end up using Explorer. Whichever navigational tool you prefer, you can use it to edit the Registry!

Most people don't think of either My Computer or Explorer as making changes to the Registry, but they can, and they're very convenient tools for certain kinds of changes. Open either program and choose Tools⇨ Folder Options, and then click the File Types tab. (Warning to NT 4.0 users: This stuff used to be on the View menu.) Or, you can double-click the new Folder Options control panel, if that's more convenient. However you get there, you should see the screen in Figure 3-13.

Figure 3-13 shows a window into the branch of the Registry that handles file-type associations. (See the little line of text that says `Registered file types`, just above the scrolling list? The word *Registered* clues you in to the fact that you're looking into the Registry.)

Typically, when you install a new application, that program registers one or more new filetypes, and they appear on the list in Figure 3-13 after installation. For example, in Figure 3-13, you can see that the BMP file type associates with the MSPAINT program. When you double-click (or single-click, in the Web view desktop) a file with the suffix .BMP, Windows 2000 runs Microsoft Paint — the little graphics editor that comes with Windows 2000 as an accessory program.

Two Explorers not named Lewis and Clark

As long as we're discussing Explorer, I should mention a terminology "gotcha" that confuses many Windows 2000 uses. The term *Explorer* actually means two entirely different things in Windows 2000: the file management program (Start⇨Programs⇨Accessories⇨Windows Explorer), and the Windows 2000 desktop shell itself.

Try this experiment: press Ctrl+Alt+Delete with no programs running, click Task Manager, and click the Processes tab. See the entry for EXPLORER.EXE? It's not referring to the file management program, because you're not running it. The Explorer entry refers to the Windows 2000 *shell*, or graphical user interface.

Now, if you're working on a test machine or a PC that you've backed up recently (because this next command could crash your system), click the entry for Explorer and then click the End Task button. The desktop elements, icons, taskbar, and so on, all vanish — exactly what you'd expect when you shut down the Windows 2000 user interface. (Mysteriously, your wallpaper may remain visible.) Restart with Ctrl+Alt+Delete.

When you press Ctrl+Alt+Delete with the Windows Explorer file management program running, it typically shows up as the name of the folder in the Task Manager's Application tab.

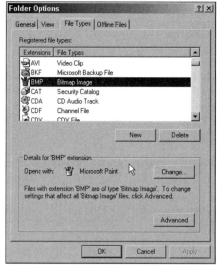

Don't make any changes to the Registered filetypes list just yet. Chapter 9 explores (pardon the pun) how you can use this property sheet as a user-friendly Registry Editor in order to make the Windows 2000 desktop more convenient. For now, I'll just mention that you may want to make a different program run when you double-click a particular kind of file — or even change the menu that appears when you right-click that file type. It's much nicer to make such changes here than in REGEDIT or REGEDT32, although in certain situations, such as dealing with data types that work with two or more different programs, you may have no choice but to use one of those tools.

Opening a Program with Another Application

At some point with an earlier version of Windows, you may have bumped into the tip that if you hold down the Shift key when right-clicking any highlighted data file in My Computer or Explorer, a new option, Open With, appears on the context menu that pops up. In Windows 2000, the Open With option shows up for most kinds of files, even when you *don't* hold down the Shift key. (I was never really clear as to why the "Open With" feature should require a "secret handshake" anyway, so it's good to see it out in the open.)

If you select Open With for the first time with a particular data file type, you see a dialog box that looks like Figure 3-14. You can then scroll through the list of registered program types and choose which one you want to use to open the selected data file. Or, you can click the Other button and navigate to any program you like.

Notice the little check box at the bottom of the scrolling list, with the label `Always use this program to open these files`. If you check the box, then from that moment on, any time you double-click a data file with the same suffix as the one you originally right-clicked, the program you've chosen will run the data file. (You can change this default association later by right-clicking the data file, choosing P̲roperties, and clicking Change.)

Figure 3-14:
The Open With dialog box lets you open a data file with any program.

In an attempt to make the Open With feature work even better, Windows 2000 now remembers programs you select with that feature and puts them on a cascading menu such as that in Figure 3-15. (The Choose Program option works just like the Other button in Figure 3-14, despite having a different name.) Unfortunately, Microsoft didn't think this feature through very carefully. If you try opening a data file with a program that *doesn't* work, that program shows up on the cascading menu anyway. (Take another look at Figure 3-15. I discovered this bug when, just for grins, I tried to use Internet Explorer to open an INI file.) Guess what's the only way you can remove such an incorrect entry? Hint: The answer starts with R.

The main point here is that the Open With dialog box lets you modify the list of file type associations that we looked at in the preceding section. Open With is a miniature Registry Editor, too! And although it works fine if you never make a mistake, it messes things up royally if you do. Verdict: The Open With feature is still safer than a Registry Editor, but only marginally so.

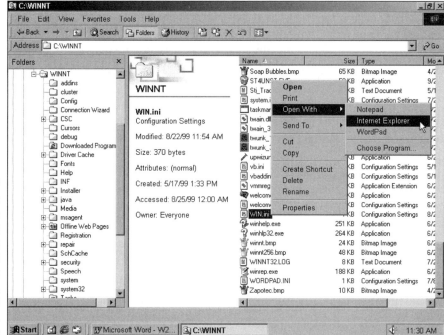

Figure 3-15:
The
cascading
menu
shows all
previous
attempts,
successful
or not.

System Policy Editor

And now, a bit of information on PC administration, for you network managers and parents with home PCs. The System Policy Editor, POLEDIT.EXE, has two roles in life. Its main job, which presumes a network environment, is to create *policy files* that modify the Registry and restrict what users can do on Windows NT 4.0, Windows 98, or Windows 95 client PCs. (Creating policies for Windows 2000 Professional clients is the job of the new Group Policy tool.) However, the System Policy Editor can also work as a Registry Editor for Windows 2000 — and a much more user-friendly one than REGEDIT or REGEDT32, at that.

The bad news is that if you have Windows 2000 Professional, you don't have the System Policy Editor. If you have a Windows 2000 Server CD, however, you can install the System Policy Editor (and a bunch of other stuff you may or may not want) by popping the CD into the drive of either a Windows 2000 Professional or Windows 2000 Server PC, navigating to the \I386 folder, and double-clicking ADMINPAK.MSI. Unfortunately, you can't specify exactly which administration tools you want from the ADMINPAK package; it's an all-or-nothing proposition.

Chapter 7 discusses the installation and use of the Policy Editor and Group Policy utility in more detail.

Just to give you a taste for how you can use the System Policy Editor to modify the Registry, here's how you would turn off a user's ability to run REGEDIT and REGEDT32 on a given Windows 2000 PC:

1. **Run the System Policy Editor by choosing Start⇨Run and entering** POLEDIT.

   Windows Installer puts the System Policy Editor in `C:\WINNT`, so you don't need to specify the full path to the file.

2. **Choose File⇨Open Registry.**

   Two icons appear in the System Policy Editor window, corresponding to the two active Registry files NTUSER.DAT and SYSTEM.

3. **Double-click the icon labeled Local User.**

   The Local User Properties window appears.

4. **Click the + sign to the left of the book icon labeled** System.

   The System book opens, and a new book labeled Restrictions appears underneath it.

5. **Click the + sign to the left of the book icon labeled** Restrictions.

   The screen should now look like Figure 3-16.

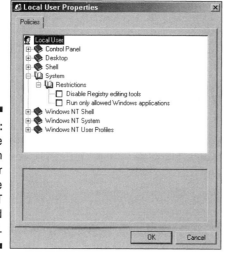

Figure 3-16:
Using the System Policy Editor to disable REGEDIT and REGEDT32.

6. **Select the Disable Registry Editing Tools check box.**

7. **Click OK.**

8. **Close the System Policy Editor by clicking the close box in the menu bar's upper-right corner.**

9. **Click Yes in the dialog box that asks you whether you want to save changes to the Registry.**

Now, try to run the Registry Editor by choosing Start⇨Run and entering **REGEDIT** in the Open field. Try it again with **REGEDT32**. Access to both Registry Editors is now *verboten* for the current user. (Don't forget to change it back if you're experimenting on your own PC and with your own logon name!) Incidentally, if you installed the TweakUI control panel from the separately available *Microsoft Windows 2000 Resource Kit*, TweakUI will be disabled now as well. (Good thing, as it changes many Registry settings.)

For those of you who are interested, you just changed the Registry entry *HKCU\Software\Microsoft\Windows\CurrentVersion\Policies\System\ DisableRegistryTools*. I explain the structure of the Registry in Chapter 6, if this looks a bit hairy to you right now.

Fortunately, access to the System Policy Editor is not forbidden by the change you just made, so you can run POLEDIT again and change the setting back to its original value. I should also mention in passing that disabling REGEDIT and REGEDT32 doesn't disable the Norton Registry Editor, if it's present, nor does it prevent users from importing Registry settings indirectly by selecting a REG file. Not exactly ironclad security, but good enough for many situations. In Chapter 7, I show you how to tighten up policy restrictions so that they're very difficult to sidestep.

Application Software

Last but not least, application software programs modify the Registry, both when installed and when users modify program settings to suit their own preferences. Here are the typical ways users can modify application program settings:

✔ **Choosing Tools⇨Options, or View⇨Options from the program's menu bar.**

Microsoft is inconsistent in where it places the Options choice, and other software vendors sometimes choose other locations. You might say the location of the Options command is optional.

✔ **Running a wizard.**

Wizards are little automated programs that lead you step-by-step through a procedure such as setting up an application program's user preferences. Microsoft's Internet Connection Wizard is an example: It runs the first time the user selects the Internet desktop icon.

✔ **Modifying an application's private INI file with Notepad.**

Private INI files are now considered clumsy and passé, but many programs still use them, including Microsoft TechNet, Microsoft Office, and so on.

✔ **Right-clicking the program icon and choosing Properties.**

This method often produces the same results as selecting Options from within a program menu, as in Microsoft Internet Explorer 5 (where the command has moved to Tools⇨Internet Options from its location on the View menu in IE4).

An application doesn't always let you change every setting that you may want to change. For example, Internet Explorer 5 always opens a particular page if a user tries to access an unknown Web site without establishing an actual Internet communications link. (The actual page that appears is OFF-CANCL.HTM, which you can see in Figure 3-17, but you won't find it in any file listing — Microsoft hid the file away inside the container file SHDOCLC.DLL.)

You may prefer a different file to run in this situation — say, a file on a network server that displays helpful information on how the user can create or use an Internet link. (Or maybe a file that, unlike OFFCANCL.HTM, you can modify without being a C++ programmer!) Changing this setting requires delving into the Registry with REGEDIT or REGEDT32.

The precise setting to modify is the *OfflineInformation* value in the key *HKLM\Software\Microsoft\Internet Explorer\AboutURLs*, but if that doesn't mean anything to you, don't worry — Chapters 4 and 6 explain it all.

The main point to remember is that if you can make an application setting via a menu option, wizard, INI file, or property sheet, do so. Save your Registry editing for cases that require it, and save your chisel for removing the iron boot that the authorities clamp onto the wheel of your parked car for having so many speeding tickets.

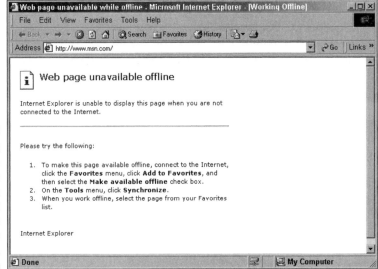

Figure 3-17:
A standard
IE5 page
that you
can't
change
without the
Registry.

Chapter 4

Registry Editors, from Headlights to Taillights

. . . .

In This Chapter

▶ Getting to know REGEDIT and REGEDT32

▶ Understanding when to use which Registry Editor

▶ Discovering how to add, change, and delete Registry entries

. . . .

> *The 4Runner may call itself a sport/utility vehicle, but back in the old coun-*
> *try its folks were plain trucks...The transfer case shift knob and other con-*
> *trols were placed truckishly, without a hint of ergonomics, and the ride was*
> *as hard as an income tax form.*
>
> —From *Age and Guile Beat Youth, Innocence, and a Bad Haircut,*
> P.J. O'Rourke, Atlantic Monthly Press, 1995

*K*nowing your tools makes working with the Registry safer, easier, faster, and more fun. This chapter lays out the fundamental features of Microsoft REGEDIT and REGEDT32.

The Windows 2000 Registry isn't a simple text file, so you can't use a program like Notepad to view or edit it. Also, the Registry consists of more than one file, so you need a program to bring these files together into a single view. The most common tools for viewing and modifying the Registry are the Registry Editor programs that come with Windows 2000: REGEDIT and REGEDT32. Getting familiar with the ins and outs of these programs is worth your while before doing any serious Registry tinkering.

These tools aren't as difficult as they look — the complicated underlying structure of the Registry just makes them *feel* difficult. Think of the Registry Editors as magnifying glasses that you use to examine an intricate fingerprint. Understanding the fingerprint's details may take some time, but the magnifying glass itself isn't hard to use.

If you've already learned your way around any modern word processor or spreadsheet program, you'll find, as I did, that the Registry Editors are much less complicated and much easier to master than those applications. If you spend an hour with the two Registry Editors and this chapter, you'll have the programs down cold. (Try saying *that* about most computer programs!)

Sometimes you want summer tires on your rally car, sometimes snow tires. Similarly, no one Registry editing tool is perfect, and I include several of the better shareware, trialware, and freeware utilities on the CD-ROM that comes with this book, so you can take them for a test drive.

Cautions and Alerts

Before getting going with the Registry Editors, I should restate the First and Second Rules of the Registry, which appear in Chapters 1 and 3.

Registry Rule #1

Periodically save a "known good" copy of the Registry where it's out of harm's way.

Before you even think about possibly coming close to running REGEDIT or REGEDT32, save your current Registry contents to a cool, dry place. Read Chapter 2, reread it, pick your favorite backup method, and then practice it a couple of times.

I'm not trying to harp at you like some back-seat grandpa that "35 miles an hour is too darn fast." I see you as more of an elite stunt driver, preparing to launch your vehicle through a wall of flames. As any seasoned stunt driver will tell you, your likelihood of success is proportional to your care and planning before you strap yourself into the driver's seat. Before you go up that ramp, you want to know what speed you need to attain, where on the ramp to align your car, and whether your clothing will protect you from the heat. Take it from someone who's been burned a few times: Don't screw up, back up.

Registry Rule #2

Never use a Registry Editor unless no safer alternative is available.

If you haven't read Chapter 3, now is a good time to skim over it at least. To recap briefly here: If you can make a desired system change using a control panel, Microsoft Management Console, Windows Explorer, Group Policy program, System Policy Editor, or a specific application program, do it there —

not in the Registry. Reserve the Registry Editors for those cases when no other method is available, because these are risky tools.

The Registry Editors make changes immediately, offer no undo feature, present little in the way of warnings or cautions, and feature built-in help that's mostly helpless. Much like a race-car cockpit, these tools have only the bare necessities to achieve their goals — no creature comforts here.

Why Two Registry Editors?

Windows 95 has a single Registry Editor. Windows 98 has a single Registry Editor. Heck, even good old Windows 3.1 has a single Registry Editor. So why does Windows 2000 need two of 'em?

Here's the scoop. REGEDT32 derives from early versions of Windows NT, while REGEDIT descends from the Windows 9*x* product line. (The immediately obvious difference in the "look and feel" of these two programs testifies to their different ancestries. For example, right-clicking keys and values does nothing in REGEDT32.) The two tools were designed by different teams at different times. They also perform different functions: For example, REGEDIT processes REG files, the mechanism that many programs use to install their own settings into the Registry.

The reason we still have two Registry Editors in Windows 2000 is simply that Microsoft doesn't see any profit in combining their features into a single unified tool. In Windows 2000, Microsoft has combined a lot of Windows 9*x* product line features with NT product line features. Rather than merge the useful features of both Registry Editors into a single utility, Microsoft just tosses both of the old programs onto the Windows 2000 CD so you can use one sometimes and the other sometimes. (The company pulled this stunt with Windows NT 4.0, too.)

Technical professionals griped about this problem in private beta-tester Internet newsgroups over a year before the commercial release of Windows 2000. They pointed out that Microsoft had had (at that time) four years to bring REGEDT32's user interface up to Windows 95 standards and to include proper search capabilities. Microsoft responded that Windows 2000 was too far along to make changes to the Registry Editors (nobody believed *that*), and the company assured us that changes would be considered for a future release of Windows.

My advice: Don't hold your breath for that bright day. Instead, master both tools, because they have different strengths. I'll do my best here to explain them in this chapter; as a start, Table 4-1 summarizes the key differences.

Table 4-1	A Tale of Two Registry Editors
REGEDIT	**REGEDT32**
Uses newer Windows 95/98 user interface	Uses older Windows 3.1 user interface
Can search: key names, value names, value contents	Can only search key names
Can search and edit remote Registries	Can search and edit remote Registries
Shows whole Registry in one window	Shows separate windows for each root key
Very similar to Windows 95/98 Registry Editor	Very similar to Windows NT 3.51/4.0 Registry Editor
Can export and import text files	Can export, but not import, text files
Cannot export or import binary files	Can export and import binary files
Offers no "read-only" mode	Does offer "read-only" mode, but not as default
Offers no security features	Supports full Windows 2000 access control and auditing
Lives in C:\WINNT folder	Lives in C:\WINNT\SYSTEM32 folder
Fully supports Windows 95/98 Registry data types only (string, binary, DWORD)	Supports full range of Windows 2000 Registry data types (string, binary, DWORD, multi-string, expandable-string, resource descriptor)

REGEDIT: The Jaguar E-Type

Jaguar cars (and I'm talking about the company before Ford bought it) are perfect examples of automobiles that look gorgeous, but lack certain important qualities under the skin. (We've all met a few people about whom something similar can be said!) Arguably the most beautiful Jaguar ever was the E-type, or XKE, which still turns heads today with its sleek, smooth lines.

The first of our two Registry Editors, REGEDIT, is a lot like the E-type: It looks modern and attractive and handles well on the road, but it's not capable enough to drive as your only car.

REGEDIT's sleek appearance follows in large measure from the fact that REGEDIT is the only one of the two Registry Editors that adheres, if only partially, to the user-interface design principles introduced by Windows 95.

- ✔ For example, in REGEDIT, you can right-click most anywhere and see a *context menu* of actions that you can take regarding whatever you just clicked.

- ✔ REGEDIT has just one window, with two panes: a pane in the neck, and a pane in the rear. (I'll be here all week.) But seriously folks, such a layout has its benefits: no losing track of where you are, no having to minimize one window to see another, no having to "cascade" multiple windows to be able to move from one part of the Registry to another.

- ✔ REGEDIT lets you see the Registry structure all at once, in its left window, using the tree-structured hierarchy popularized by Windows Explorer in Windows 95 (and now used in the Windows 2000 Explorer).

REGEDIT allows you to search almost every part of the Registry for a particular word or phrase. (The only part that REGEDIT can't search for is text strings that are part of a multi-string value and appear second or further down in the list; see Chapter 6 for more on the multi-string value type.) REGEDT32 still only lets you search key names. (Incidentally, *keys* are the containers that hold Registry data; think of them like the envelopes in a mailbox.) Plus, REGEDIT has the handy advantage of being able to save — and restore — Registry settings as human-readable text files.

So with all these advantages, why do I say that REGEDIT can't be the only car in the garage? Coming as it does from the Windows 95/98 world, REGEDIT lacks some key capabilities that are unique to the Windows NT and Windows 2000 architecture. The two "biggies" are as follows:

- ✔ **Security.** Windows 2000 lets you slap security on every object in the operating system, including the Registry. You can specify which groups of users can do what to specific parts of the Registry. Windows 98 and 95 don't have that kind of security, so REGEDIT doesn't know how to let you access or change security settings.

- ✔ **Special data types.** The Windows 2000 Registry includes some special data types that Windows 95 and 98 don't use, such as a data type called REG_MULTI_SZ that lets you put multiple text entries into a single Registry value. REGEDIT can't properly display or edit these special data types.

The rest of this section on REGEDIT discusses how to use the program in each of its two modes: graphical and command-line. You Windows NT veterans will also appreciate the sidebar, "For NT 4.0 users: What's new with REGEDIT?"

For NT 4.0 users: What's new with REGEDIT?

The versions of REGEDIT that ship with Windows 2000 and Windows NT 4.0 have a few differences. If you're familiar with NT 4.0, then you'll notice these differences with the newer version:

✔ You no longer see the root key *HKEY_DYN_DATA,* which is a good thing considering that Windows 2000 doesn't use it. (In Windows NT 4.0, you could see the key but nothing underneath it. In Windows 98 and 95, this key contains selected hardware and Plug-and-Play information.)

✔ A value's data type now appears in the value pane, sandwiched between the value name and value data.

✔ REGEDIT now has "memory." When you restart the program, it restores the window to show the key you were working on when you last shut it down. Some people like this feature; others hate it. You can turn it off, though, with a bit of trickery, as I explain in the "Taking the Editors Out for a Spin" section later in this chapter.

✔ The REGEDIT Help system (Help⇨Help Topics) uses the "HTML Help" engine introduced in Windows 98. HTML Help uses some of the same code to display Help topics that Internet Explorer uses to display Web pages. It's part of Microsoft's effort to make everything look like a Web browser.

✔ In Windows NT 4.0, double-clicking a REG file (which contains Registry changes) automatically merges the changes in the REG file with the current Registry. This behavior can create problems if users double-click a file to start it and thereby put stuff into their Registry that they don't really want, such as settings that pertain to an earlier version of a program that's since been updated. Happily, Microsoft fixed this problem in Windows 2000. Now, when you double-click a REG file, you see a warning message. It's not much, but it's enough to suggest that users are about to do more than open a data file and that they should cancel the operation if they're not sure about it.

✔ The new Favorites menu lets you create bookmarks to Registry keys you tend to visit a lot. This feature is similar to the list of favorite Web pages you can create in a Web browser.

Microsoft passed on making the truly major improvements, such as making REGEDIT aware of Windows 2000 security, giving it the ability to handle the full range of Registry data types, adding an "undo" feature, letting the user decide when to save changes instead of always saving them immediately and automatically, and fully supporting cut-and-paste operations. (These last three problems apply equally to REGEDT32.)

REGEDIT part 1: Getting graphic

You can run REGEDIT from the Windows 2000 graphical user interface *(GUI,* pronounced *gooey)* or from a DOS-like command prompt. You normally run REGEDIT graphically, but the command-prompt capability does come in handy from time to time — such as when you can't boot the GUI or when you're trying fancy batch-file tricks such as the ones I describe in the last section in this chapter.

Adding REGEDIT to your desktop

Windows 2000 doesn't put an icon for REGEDIT on your desktop or your Start menu after a typical installation, but it does copy the file REGEDIT.EXE to the C:\WINNT directory (or whatever you name your Windows 2000 directory). You can start the program by choosing Start⇨Run, typing **REGEDIT**, and clicking OK.

If you plan to spend a fair amount of time with REGEDIT, which I'm guessing is true or you wouldn't have dropped a few bucks on this book, you probably don't want to use the Start⇨Run method several zillion times. You can create a desktop icon for REGEDIT by right-clicking the desktop, choosing New⇨Shortcut, typing **REGEDIT** in the Type the Location for the Item field, clicking Next, and typing whatever label you like in the Type a Name for this Shortcut field. (Microsoft went a little wizard-happy with Windows 2000, as you can see here; the Create a Shortcut wizard would be simpler as a single two-field dialog box.)

If you're setting up Windows 2000 for someone else, remember that you probably don't want REGEDIT (or REGEDT32, for that matter) on the desktop or Start menu of novice users. You may want to use a system policy (on a standalone machine or NT 4.0 network) or a group policy (on a Windows 2000 network) to restrict the user's ability to run REGEDIT and REGEDT32; Chapter 7 provides details.

The race-car cockpit: Anatomy of the REGEDIT window

Figure 4-1 shows the REGEDIT window, which has many of the usual Windows program features: a *menu bar* at the top, a *status bar* at the bottom (which shows the full Registry path of the currently active selection), and *scroll bars* to help you navigate up, down, and side to side.

The REGEDIT window has two panes: The *key pane* to the left presents an Explorer-like hierarchical view of the Registry database, and the *value pane* to the right shows the contents of whatever key you highlight in the key pane. You can use the Tab key to jump quickly between the key pane and the value pane. (In some documents, Microsoft refers to the key pane as the *navigation pane* and to the value pane as the *topic pane*. Don't be confused.)

TIP

Storing REGEDIT out of harm's way

If you want to bury the REGEDIT command a little deeper than a desktop icon so that other people who may use your PC aren't tempted to run it, you can put the program on your Start menu along with other system tools. Here's the procedure:

1. **Right-click the Start menu button and choose Explore.**

   Most likely you'll see that the open folder is the Start Menu folder under the *<youruser-name>* folder which, in turn, is under the Documents and Settings folder. (If you see a different arrangement, don't worry, it just means you upgraded to Windows 2000 from an earlier version of Windows NT.)

2. **Click the + to the left of the Programs folder in the left windowpane under the open Start Menu folder to expand it.**

3. **Click the + to the left of the Accessories folder in the left windowpane to expand it.**

4. **Click the System Tools folder in the left windowpane.**

5. **Choose File⇨New⇨Shortcut to create the new menu entry for REGEDIT.**

6. **Type C:\WINNT\REGEDIT.EXE in the Type the Location of the Item field of the Create Shortcut dialog box.**

(If Windows 2000 resides in a directory other than WINNT, substitute the correct directory name.)

7. **Click the Next button and type Regedit in the Type a Name for this Shortcut field.**

   You can't just type "Registry Editor," because there are two of them, remember? You'll go through this same drill for REGEDT32.

8. **Click the Finish button and close the Explorer window by clicking the close box in the upper-right corner.**

   You can now run REGEDIT by choosing Start⇨Programs⇨Accessories⇨System Tools⇨Regedit.

You can modify the precise placement of the REGEDIT menu listing so that it appears wherever you want. Windows 2000 makes doing so easy: Just navigate through the menus to the REGEDIT item, and click-and-drag the item to whatever menu and position you desire. The ease of reconfiguring the Start menu in this way is one of the best improvements that Windows 2000 borrows from Windows 98.

Each folder icon in the key pane represents a Registry *key,* which is a location for storing data. (A key isn't the same as a folder in Explorer, although the icon is the same. An Explorer folder is almost always a file system directory, but a key is an internal Registry structure.) Many keys (the ones with + signs to their left) contain other keys, which may be called *subkeys* — much the same way directories on your hard disk may be called subdirectories if they reside inside another directory. (Again, just so you know, Microsoft sometimes calls subkeys *descendant keys,* I guess because it sounds more scientific, or because someone on staff is into genealogy.)

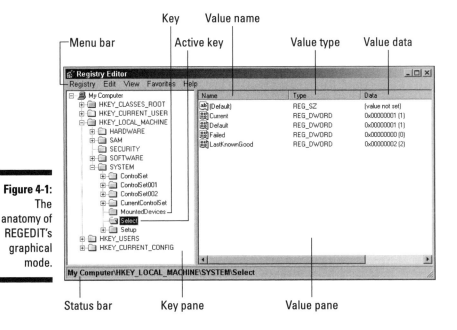

Key   Value name

Menu bar   Active key   Value type   Value data

Figure 4-1:
The
anatomy of
REGEDIT's
graphical
mode.

Status bar   Key pane   Value pane

You can expand the tree-like structure of the key pane by clicking the + sign
to the left of any key that has one or more subkeys, and you can collapse the
structure by clicking the – sign. Or, if you prefer, you can expand and collapse
the structure by double-clicking the folder icon itself (it's a bigger target!).
You can even right-click the folder icon and choose Expand or Contract from
the context menu. If you have good hand-to-mouse coordination, clicking the
+ and – symbols is your fastest method.

The active (selected) key in the key pane displays an open-folder icon, while
all the other keys display closed-folder icons. The key contents, called *values,*
appear in the value pane to the right. Every value has a

✔ **Name field,** such as *FileLocation,* that identifies the value.

✔ **Type field,** such as *REG_SZ,* that identifies the value's predefined type or
    format.

✔ **Data field,** such as *C:\WINNT,* that contains the value's setting.

Every key contains at least one value, named *Default,* which (if empty) shows
the message `value not set` in the data field; but a key can contain a whole
bunch of values, and many do.

These values have three types: *string, binary,* and *DWORD.* I explain these
value types more fully in Chapter 6, but for now just know that the string
type (indicated by a tiny icon in the value pane's Name column containing

the letters *ab*) is usually for text, and the binary and DWORD types (indicated by a tiny icon containing some 1s and 0s) are usually for numeric information. Demonically, string values can contain numbers, and often do.

REGEDIT doesn't properly handle some value types that you run across in Windows 2000, such as multi-string values. You can see these values, but not in their proper format, and you can only edit them as though they were binary data — not convenient at all and not a good idea to attempt!

Note: Key names aren't unique in the Registry, and the same key name may crop up in several different places. So, when I describe a particular key in this book, I usually give its complete location, such as *HKCR\Drive* or *HKLM\Software\Classes\Drive*. In these examples, I use abbreviations for the *branches*, also called *root* or *top-level* keys: for example, *HKCR* is short for *HKey_Classes_Root.* Chapter 6 discusses these primary keys in more detail.

The menu bar in REGEDIT has five menus, but only three of these menus are worth checking out:

- ✔ **The Registry menu** enables you to print, import, and export Registry data from and to text files, and connect to a remote user's Registry.

- ✔ **The Edit menu** lets you create, delete, rename, and hunt for keys (in the left windowpane) or values (in the right pane). You can also copy a key name to the Clipboard, which comes in handy from time to time — as when you're searching for complex or long key or value names.

Sometimes you don't want to copy an entire key name, with the full Registry path specification (that is, all the upper-level keys); you want to copy just the name of the currently selected key. Here's an alternative to the Copy Key Name command that lets you do just that. Right-click a key, choose Rename (which selects the key name), press Ctrl+C to copy the key name to the Clipboard, and finally press Esc (to avoid actually renaming the key). You can then press Ctrl+V to paste the name somewhere else. To copy a value's data field, double-click the value name and then press Ctrl+C to copy the data field.

- ✔ **The Favorites menu** lets you add the current key to a list of favorite keys (that is, keys you visit often), jump to an existing favorite key, or delete a key from the favorites list.

Two menus in REGEDIT are barely worth a glance:

- ✔ **The View menu** lets you turn the status bar on or off (why you'd ever want it off is a mystery to me), move the split bar separating the two panes (which you can do much more easily with the mouse), and refresh the display (which just updates the window to re-sort the contents alphabetically and display any changes that Windows 2000 or a Windows 2000 program may have made since you originally selected the key). You can refresh the display more easily by pressing F5. In other words, if you use a mouse, forget about the View menu.

✔ **The Help menu**, alas, provides very little. Go ahead and take five minutes to read the help screens at least once through; then you can forget
about this menu, too.

Sometimes, REGEDIT "grays out" a menu option if it isn't available for the
selected item. For example, you can't delete or rename any of the six main
Registry keys. (Good thing, too — you could crash the whole system.)

Changing stuff

Most of the changes you make to the Registry involve modifying a value that
already exists. REGEDIT makes this job pretty simple. The basic method is to
hunt around in the left windowpane (the key pane) until you find the key containing the value you need to change. (If you don't know exactly where that
key is, see "Finding" later in this section.) Make a particular key active by
clicking it. Then, change the value in the right windowpane (the value pane)
by using one of the following three methods:

✔ Double-click the value name. (Fastest method)

✔ Right-click the value name and choose Modify. (Slower method)

✔ Click the value name and choose Edit⇨Modify from the menu bar.
(Slowest method)

Which dialog box appears next depends on the type of value you selected.
The Edit String, Edit Binary Value, and Edit DWORD Value dialog boxes you
work with are shown in Figure 4-2. Chapter 6 describes the number format for
binary and DWORD values. Make whatever change is necessary in the Value
Data field and click OK. You may notice that in each case the Value Name field
is grayed out, meaning that you can't change the information in this field.
(Go ahead, try. I dare you.) The reason you can't change this info is that,
while you may have a legitimate reason to change a value's *data,* you're less
likely to need to change a value's *name,* and doing so runs the risk that
Windows 2000 or an application program can't find your renamed value. If
you're really certain that you need to rename a value, right-click the value
name in REGEDIT's value pane, and choose Rename. Legal characters are A
through Z, 0 through 9, space, and underscore.

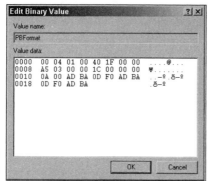

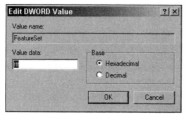

Figure 4-2:
Use the Edit
dialog boxes
to change a
string value,
a binary
value, or a
DWORD
value.

If you need to change a value's type, for example from binary to string, REGEDIT doesn't offer a command to do so. You have to delete the existing value and create a new one with the same name. This situation doesn't come up often, but I've occasionally created new values that use the incorrect type. For example, sometimes using a binary value when a DWORD value is required means that the Registry setting just won't work.

Sometimes a key appears in more than one place, as I describe in Chapter 6. If you've set up *user profiles,* that is, multiple user accounts on the same Windows 2000 PC, changing a setting for the current user doesn't change that setting for all other users. Chapter 8 explains user profiles in detail.

Adding keys and values

You can add two things to the Registry: a key or a value. Adding a key is simpler than adding a value. You can add a new key in a few different ways, but the way that makes the most sense to me is to follow these general steps:

1. **In the key pane (on the left), right-click the key that you want the new key to appear beneath, hierarchically.**

2. **Choose New⇨Key from the context menu and type in the key name over the** New Key #1 **text.**

3. **Press Enter.**

REGEDIT automatically adds the famous Default string value that every key must contain; the word Default appears in the value pane, to the right. (Note that the purpose of the Default value for any given Registry key varies depending on the context; sometimes it's not used at all, but the unwritten rules of the Registry state that it must be present.)

If you want an alternative method to add a new key, you can single-click the key under which you want the new key to appear, and use the menu bar to choose Edit⇨New⇨Key.

Adding a value to a key is almost as easy as adding a new key; you just have to know a little more information ahead of time. In addition to the value name, you need to be able to specify what type the value should be (string, binary, or DWORD) and what data it should contain. Follow these steps to add a value to a key:

1. **In the key pane, highlight the key in which you want to add the value.**

   For example, if you want to hide a particular file type so that it doesn't show up in My Computer's Tools⇨Folder Options⇨File Types list, you can do so by adding a Registry value. Hide the CHM file type (compiled HTML file, used in the Windows 2000 HTML Help system) by first high-lighting the key *HKCR\chm.file*.

2. **In the value pane, right-click anywhere within the pane except on an occupied entry in the Name column.**

3. **Choose New⇨String Value, New⇨Binary Value, or New⇨DWORD Value from the context menu.**

   Choose Binary Value for this example.

4. **Type in the value name over the** New Value #1 **text and press Enter.**

   For our example, type **Editflags**. This is a special value that controls what actions you can perform from the File Type list.

5. **Press Enter again.**

   The Edit String, Edit Binary Value, or Edit DWORD Value dialog box appears, depending on the value type you're editing. Edit Binary Value appears in this case.

6. **Type the value data in the Value Data field and then click OK.**

To complete our example, type the hexadecimal values **01 00 00 00**.
After you close REGEDIT, open the File Types list; Compiled HTML Help
file no longer shows up, which is handy if you don't want a user to be
able to change how CHM files behave.

You usually add a Registry value at the direction of a tech support
person, a tech note, a book like this one, or some other source, so you
can expect some guidance as to what value type and data to enter.

Adding keys and values to the Registry isn't as common as modifying keys
and values that already exist, but you will perform these tasks occasionally.
Sometimes you add keys and values for your own purposes, without affecting
Windows 2000 or application programs. Other times, as in the example in this
section, you may have to be careful that whatever keys and values you add
meet the formatting requirements that Windows 2000 or an application
expects. As always, back up the Registry before you add new entries to it.

Deleting keys and values

Destroying is usually easier than creating, and REGEDIT is no exception. To
delete pretty much anything — a key (as long as it's not one of the six main
ones), or a value of any type — just display it, right-click it, and choose
Delete. (Left-clicking the key or value and pressing the Delete key may be
faster, although some people prefer the mouse-only method.) You have to
answer Yes in the ensuing dialog box to complete the deletion, so you always
have an out if you choose Delete by accident or in haste.

Good thing you have an out, because after you delete something in REGEDIT,
you may have no easy way to get it back. (Chapter 11 gives you various methods that may work in some cases and that may not work in others.) The
Microsoft help files advise you to reboot and use the "Last Known Good" boot
option to restore the Registry, but I'm here to tell you that this procedure does
not restore the entire Registry, just one part of it (albeit an important part).

When you delete a key in the Registry, you also delete every value in that key
and every subkey underneath that key. Deleting a key is like sawing a big
branch off a tree: In doing so, you also remove every smaller branch that
grows from the big branch, and every leaf on all those smaller branches.

Before you delete a Registry key or value, save it by using REGEDIT's Export
Registry File command (see the section later in this chapter called "Exporting
and importing"). You may even want to designate a special directory on your
hard drive (C:\TEMPREG or something similar) for these exports. If everything works fine for a few days after you delete the key or value, you can then
delete the export file from your hard disk.

If you want to delete several values in a particular key, you can select a
bunch of adjacent keys by clicking the first one, holding down the Shift key,
and clicking the last. If you want to delete several nonadjacent values, hold

down the Ctrl key and click each value that you want to delete. Then right-click any highlighted value and choose Delete from the context menu that appears. (This tip only works with REGEDIT, not REGEDT32.)

Finding

Many times, especially when you're just getting familiar with the lay of the Registry land, you may know what a key is called or what a value name is, but you don't know precisely where something lives within the maze-like Registry structure. REGEDIT's Find command, although certainly imperfect, comes in mighty handy in such situations and is far and away superior to the find facility in REGEDT32.

Fire up the Find command by choosing Edit⇨Find from the menu or pressing Ctrl+F. However you get there, REGEDIT displays the Find dialog box shown in Figure 4-3.

Figure 4-3:
The Find
dialog box
in REGEDIT,
imprecise
labels
and all.

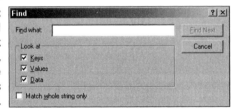

You can type in the value you're looking for in the Find What field and tell REGEDIT where to look by selecting the appropriate check boxes in the Look At area. Microsoft isn't precise with its wording here: The Keys check box is self-explanatory and correct, but the Values check box really means *value names* (the left column in the value pane), and the Data check box really means *value data* (the right column in the value pane).

If you know whether the data you're searching for resides in a key name, value name, or value data field, you can deselect the other two check boxes to speed your search a little, but I rarely recommend doing so — the speed difference isn't huge on today's hardware, and you could miss a relevant setting. If you want to find a string fragment but you're not sure you know the entire string, make sure that the Match Whole String Only check box is deselected.

Click the Find Next button to start your hunt. When REGEDIT locates a match, it highlights the appropriate entry in both the key and value panes. If you suspect that you'll have multiple matches, hit F3 (the "find next" key) to resume the search. When REGEDIT can't find any more matches, or if it didn't find any in the first place, it displays a dialog box saying: `Finished searching through the Registry`. (Yes, it *would* be nice if REGEDIT said "No matches found" if that's the case, but the program is an uncommunicative sonofagun.)

REGEDIT cannot find data in DWORD or binary values; it can only find data in key or string values. If you want to search for DWORD or binary values, export the key that you think contains the values (see "Exporting and importing" later in this section) and use your favorite word processor's Find command.

The Find command always starts with the currently selected key or value and works downward. So, if you've been bouncing about the Registry and you've selected something other than the My Computer icon that sits atop the six main Registry branches in the key pane, then you're not going to be searching the entire Registry when you press Ctrl+F. (The search operation never "wraps around" to the top of the document as the Find command in a decent word processing program does.) So, always click the My Computer icon before initiating a Registry search. It's a pain, but you get used to it. Or, use a better utility, such as Norton Registry Editor, which searches the entire Registry regardless of which key is highlighted.

Printing

Figuring that the best way to print all or part of the Registry is to choose REGEDIT's Registry⇨Print option (or press the shortcut, Ctrl+P) seems logical. The naked truth, however, is that this command is fine for a quick-and-dirty printing of little chunks of the Registry, but that's about it. Here's the procedure for this quick-and-dirty method:

1. **In the key pane, navigate to the key you want to print and then click it. The folder icon opens.**

2. **Choose Registry⇨Print to bring up the dialog box in Figure 4-4.**

Figure 4-4:
REGEDIT's
Print dialog
box, suitable
for short
printouts
only.

3. **Choose the printer you want in the Select Printer area, and click the Selected Branch radio button in the Print Range area.**

4. **Click OK, and fetch your hard copy.**

REGEDIT doesn't go in for niceties of appearance such as margin settings or other output formatting options, and neither does REGEDT32. If you want to print a serious chunk (a big key or, if you've lost your mind, the whole Registry, which can require several hundred pages), export the desired chunk to a text file, as described in the next section. You can then pull that text file into a bona fide word processing program, where you can play with the page margins, font style, font size, and so on, before you actually print. You can also delete chunks that you don't want to print, saving trees and speeding print time.

Exporting and importing

Exporting and importing is the last subject I touch on in this overview of REGEDIT's graphical *modus operandi*. Exporting and importing have very specific meanings in the context of the Registry, and you'll use these commands often if you read very much of this book.

Exporting a Registry key (or the whole Registry, for that matter) with REGEDIT creates a text file on disk with the suffix .REG. The text file contains the contents of the specified key, plus any subkeys under that key, plus all the associated values contained in those keys. (The original information stays in the Registry.)

REGEDT32 behaves differently than REGEDIT when you export a key! REGEDT32 normally exports Registry information to binary files, not text files. Knowing this can come in handy if you're exporting a large key to a diskette; the file will normally be smaller if exported from REGEDT32 than if exported from REGEDIT. But you can't view or edit the binary file.

You can view an exported REG file in any text editor (Notepad, for example) or word processor. You can also double-click a REG file to merge its contents into the current Registry, so exporting is a popular way of backing up a particular key before making changes to it. However, exporting the entire Registry can take a pretty long time, so this method isn't the most convenient way to back up your whole Registry database.

The procedure for exporting a Registry key is simple, although not quite as elegant as one might like:

1. **In the key pane, click the key you want to export to make it active, and choose Registry⇨Export Registry File.**

   It would be slicker if you could just right-click the key and export it from the context menu. The Export Registry File dialog box appears, as shown in Figure 4-5.

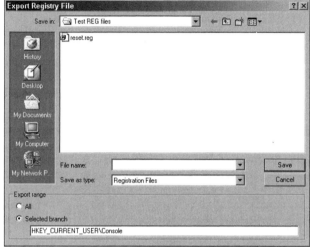

Figure 4-5:
You can
export a
key, or the
entire
Registry,
using
REGEDIT.

2. **Give your export file a destination in the Save In field.**

3. **Give your export file a name in the File Name field.**

   Incidentally, you can choose the Win9x/NT4 Registration File (REGEDIT4) option in the Save As Type box if you need to create a REG file that a Windows 9*x* or NT 4.0 operating system can import.

4. **Check that the Selected Branch radio button is selected in the Export Range area. (Select the All radio button only if you want to export the whole Registry.)**

5. **Click the Save button.**

Importing from a REG file is a similar process. Choose Registry➪Import Registry File from the menu bar and specify the REG file that you want to import in the Import Registry File dialog box. Alternatively, you can open Windows Explorer, find the REG file, and double-click it — or right-click the file and choose Merge from the context menu.

Importing a REG file can create new Registry entries and modify existing ones. REGEDIT doesn't warn you if the REG file you're importing is about to overwrite existing values. *Always* back up the Registry before importing a REG file.

Importing a REG file works flawlessly as long as you're adding values to the current Registry or changing existing values. The problem comes up when you want to import a REG file with *less* information: Importing a REG file doesn't delete existing keys or values. Assuming you're not stuck with a REG file that you or someone else made earlier, you can avoid this problem by exporting and importing with REGEDT32, which *does* wipe out the contents of a key that you're restoring. With REG files, though, the only way that you can be sure that the Import operation correctly restores the Registry is to delete the keys from the Registry *before* you import them from the REG file.

After you realize that REG files are the primary way that new programs add keys and values to the Registry, you can appreciate why Microsoft designed REGEDIT so that it doesn't delete existing data. You don't want new programs to be able to accidentally trash Registry entries created (and relied upon) by other programs.

Animation is for cartoons

Here's a tip for making REGEDIT more responsive to the touch. Microsoft has taken the "zooming windows" concept that it introduced in Windows 95 to an even-more-annoying level in Windows 2000. Not only do windows whoosh to and from the Taskbar when you minimize or maximize them, but menus slide into place from one corner to the other, and scrolling lists slink greasily up and down in animated motion. All this pointless movement slows you down when you work with REGEDIT, especially when you have to scroll through a large key such as *HKey_Classes_Root.*

Thankfully, you can turn Windows 2000's animation off. Open the Display control panel by right-clicking the desktop and choosing Properties. Click the Effects tab, and deselect the Use Transition Effects for Menus and Tooltips check box. REGEDIT feels much snappier without all that slipping and sliding, as will most other applications you use. (Unfortunately, no way exists to control the transition effects for certain programs and not others, so this is an all-or-nothing proposition.) Chapter 9 gives much more detail on dealing with Windows 2000 animations.

REGEDIT part 2: At your command

You may occasionally need to run REGEDIT in its so-called *command-line mode,* that is, from a command prompt (it's not really a "DOS prompt" anymore) rather than from the graphical Windows 2000 environment. For example, you may wish to include one or more REGEDIT commands in a batch file, as the last section in this chapter illustrates, or in a script, or from the NT command prompt. (However, you can't use REGEDIT in a real-mode computing session, as you could do in Windows 98 or 95; see the following sidebar for details.)

Running REGEDIT in command-line mode is riskier than running it in graphical protected mode because you can accidentally and easily type one wrong letter and damage the Registry. Only run REGEDIT in command-line mode after backing up the Registry.

The command line options are as follows, with optional entries in square brackets (you don't type the brackets). Note that *filename* should include the .REG suffix, and that *regpath* cannot use abbreviated key names like HKLM, but must use full names like *HKey_Local_Machine*.

```
REGEDIT /S filename1
REGEDIT /C filename2
REGEDIT /E filename3 [regpath]
```

- ✔ **The /S option** tells REGEDIT to perform an import operation "silently;" that is, without the usual confirmation dialog box stating that the information has been successfully added to the Registry. This option allows your batch file or script to run unattended.

- ✔ **The /C option** is the most dangerous one: It creates a brand-new Registry from scratch, importing the contents of filename2 — which must end in the suffix .REG and which should contain a full Registry export. REGEDIT doesn't look at filename2 to verify that it contains a full Registry, and if filename2 doesn't, you can end up worse off than before. *Back up your existing Registry if at all possible before using this option.*

- ✔ **The /E option** exports the Registry to filename3 (by the way, you should specify the .REG suffix as part of filename3). If you want to export only a portion of the Registry, you can specify the starting key as the *regpath*. (The *regpath* is just the key location.) For example, to export the contents of *HKEY_CURRENT_USER\Software* to the file SOFT.REG, type the following (and note that you can't use the *HKCU* abbreviation):

```
REGEDIT /E SOFT.REG HKEY_CURRENT_USER\Software
```

No real-mode Registry editing in Windows 2000

Some readers of this book may have experience with Windows 95 or 98. Those readers may know that if you find yourself in a situation where Windows 2000 doesn't boot properly, and you can't even get to the graphical environment, you can run REGEDIT from a DOS prompt, from a Safe Mode boot, or from the Windows 9x Single MS-DOS mode. In the Windows 9x family, such command-line operation uses the so-called "real mode" of the Intel processor, working pretty much like an old DOS machine: 640K of conventional memory, and so on.

Please put such thoughts out of your head in the Windows 2000 environment. Just for grins, I've tried running REGEDIT after booting a Windows 2000 system to a DOS prompt via a DOS boot diskette. I've also tried running REGEDIT (and REGEDT32, for that matter) in the new Recovery Console, which you get to via the Windows 2000 setup program. Neither option works. Knowing this might save some of you 9x jockeys some time if you ever have to troubleshoot your Windows 2000 system!

REGEDT32, the GMC Hummer

If REGEDIT is a Jaguar, then REGEDT32 is a Hummer: the go-anywhere, do-anything, defiantly non-aerodynamic military vehicle driven by soldiers, rich macho types like Arnold Schwarzenegger, and rich non-macho types having midlife crises. (And, I guess I should add, firefighters: My neighborhood fire department recently bought a specially equipped Hummer with downward-spraying water jets on the undercarriage, so in case of a brush fire, the volunteers can just drive over the fire and put it out. Try *that* with a weenie civilian sport-utility vehicle.)

The Hummer can do anything you need to do, but don't expect to be comfortable or to look good doing it. That's REGEDT32 in a nutshell. It can handle 2000-style security and 2000-style Registry data types. Its user interface, however, is a clunky holdover from Windows NT 3.51. You don't want to use REGEDT32 as your only Registry Editor, mainly because it can't search the Registry for value names or value data, only for key names. You also won't use it for day-to-day editing, as everything takes a click or two more in REGEDT32 than in REGEDIT. Having said that, if you need to deal with Registry security settings or multiple-string value types, you'll need to use REGEDT32.

If you've jumped straight to this section and skipped the previous section on REGEDIT, you may want to go back and read it now. In order to avoid a lot of duplication, I'm going to limit this section to the ways in which REGEDT32 works differently from REGEDIT.

Unlike REGEDIT, REGEDT32 has no command-line interface, so this section covers only the graphical interface.

Adding REGEDT32 to your desktop

The procedure for adding a link to REGEDT32 to your desktop or Start menu is the same as described for REGEDIT earlier in this chapter ("Adding REGEDIT to your desktop"), with two differences. In Step 6, you should specify C:\WINNT\SYSTEM32\REGEDT32.EXE as the item location, and in Step 7 you should specify Regedt32 as the item name.

For NT 4.0 users: What's new with REGEDT32?

As with REGEDIT, the Windows 2000 version of REGEDT32 has a couple of differences from the version that the company provided with Windows NT 4.0, in case you're familiar with that one. With the newer version:

✓ The REGEDT32 help system (Help⇨Help Topics) uses the "HTML Help" engine introduced in Windows 98. HTML Help presents help subjects in a window that uses some of the same code that Internet Explorer uses to display World Wide Web documents in a browser window.

✓ The Security menu has changed. Instead of containing three choices (Permissions, Auditing, and Owner), the new Security menu contains only one choice,

Permissions. To get to the auditing and owner settings, you click the Advanced button on the Permissions dialog box. Personally, I liked the older version better because it was more accurate (auditing really isn't a permissions issue) as well as better design (one-choice drop-down menus are inefficient).

REGEDT32 still has no "undo" feature, still saves changes immediately and automatically, and still can't search on value names or value data. But, to be fair, we all have to remember that changing that Security menu was *top* priority. Users could actually find the auditing and owner settings easily in the older version.

Anatomy of the REGEDT32 window (s)

The REGEDT32 user interface (see Figure 4-6) is an involuntary time machine, taking us back to the early 1990s and the look and feel of the Windows 3.*x* product line. Here are the key differences between REGEDT32's window and that of REGEDIT:

✓ Rather than a single unified window, you get a separate window for each of the five root keys. Each of these separate windows has its own key pane and value pane. Because of this design, REGEDT32 requires a Window menu that REGEDIT does not. From the Window menu, you can choose to cascade the five windows in an overlapping diagonal pattern, tile them in a mosaic fashion, or simply jump to one of the five windows that may be hidden behind another window.

✓ You can minimize, maximize, or resize any of the five independent windows, but you cannot close any of them individually. (You can close them all with the Registry⇨Close command, which you might do for example if you were about to connect to a remote Registry.)

✔ Sorry, no Favorites menu. That REGEDIT enhancement didn't make it over to REGEDT32. (Idle curiosity: If REGEDT32 is the only Registry Editor that Microsoft wants you to use, why is it enhancing REGEDIT but not REGEDT32?)

✔ You won't see a status bar in REGEDT32. That's a pity, because it's handy to know where you are. In this program, however, you have to use the scroll bars to discover your position within the Registry spaghetti bowl.

Instead of single-clicking as with REGEDIT, you expand the tree-like structure of the key pane by double-clicking the + sign that (another difference) appears *inside* the folder icon of any key that has one or more subkeys. You can collapse the structure by double-clicking the - sign. REGEDT32 doesn't support right-clicking anything.

As with REGEDIT, the active (selected) key in the key pane displays an open-folder icon, while all the other keys display closed-folder icons. The key contents, called *values,* appear in the value pane to the right. The value pane contains the same three fields that REGEDIT does — name, type, and data — but rather than line them up for you in three neat columns, REGEDT32 mashes them all together and puts colons (:) between them.

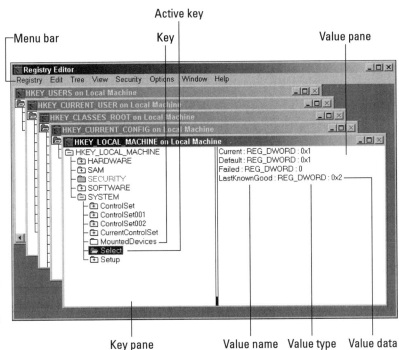

Figure 4-6: The anatomy of REGEDT32.

The values that appear in REGEDT32 can take on the three types discussed earlier in the REGEDIT section, as well as other types. REGEDT32 displays the value types with a rather cumbersome "nerdspeak" notation, as follows:

- REG_SZ means "string."
- REG_BINARY means "binary."
- REG_DWORD means "DWORD."
- REG_MULTI_SZ means "multi-string," a collection of strings.
- REG_EXPAND_SZ means "expandable string," a string that can contain an expandable variable.

Chapter 6 goes into more detail on these different value types, as well as a couple of other minor value types that you may encounter along the trip.

The menu bar in REGEDT32 has eight menus, as opposed to REGEDIT's five:

- **The Registry menu** enables you to print, import, and export Registry data to and from binary files and to text files, and connect to a remote user's Registry. (I look at that last capability in Chapter 12.)

- **The Edit menu** lets you create, delete, and rename keys (in the left windowpane) or values (in the right pane). You can't copy a key name to the Clipboard, as you can in REGEDIT's Edit menu, nor do you perform Registry searches from this menu, as you do in REGEDIT. You can also choose to modify a value by choosing the value's type from the four options at the bottom of this menu (Binary, String, DWORD, Multi-string).

- **The Tree menu** lets you expand and collapse Registry key hierarchies if you'd rather not use the double-click-the-folder-icon method.

- **The View menu** lets you move the split bar separating the two panes in any window (which you can do much more easily with the mouse) and refresh the display (assuming Auto Refresh on the Options menu is off) to show any changes that Windows 2000 or a Windows 2000 program may have made since you originally selected the key. The Refresh All option updates all open windows, while Refresh Active only updates the front window. You can refresh the active display more easily by pressing F6. (Yes, F6. I know, it's F5 in REGEDIT. User-interface consistency between applications has never been a top priority at Microsoft, apparently.) The Display Binary Data command is rarely used: It displays a highlighted value in binary format. Finally, the Find Key command is like REGEDIT's except it's on a different menu and only searches on key names.

- **The Security menu** has but one option, Permissions. I discuss this in more detail in the "Setting security" section later in this chapter, but here's your jumping-off point for controlling Registry key access and auditing.

✔ **The Options menu** controls various features of the program: the font used, whether Registry changes automatically display, read-only mode, whether a confirmation dialog box appears before permitting a deletion, and whether window positions get saved on exit.

✔ **The Window menu** lets you arrange the five windows in either a cascading overlap or a mosaic-like tile pattern and lets you jump right to a specific window.

✔ **The Help menu** provides a lot more information than the REGEDIT help menu, but that's not saying much.

Like REGEDIT, REGEDT32 "grays out" a menu option if it isn't available for the selected item. For example, if you haven't selected a value in the value pane, the bottom four options in the Edit menu appear grayed out.

Customizing REGEDT32 behavior

The Options menu is worth an extra minute here because some of it is really important. (I'll skip an analysis of the Font option on the grounds that you can experiment with it yourself if you don't like the default font.)

✔ **Auto Refresh.** If you select this option, REGEDT32 updates the display whenever the Registry changes, and the two refresh options on the View menu go dim (become unavailable). The default is for Auto Refresh to be selected (on), but whether you leave it that way depends largely on how fast your PC is. The performance impact can be annoying, causing REGEDT32 to take long pauses during an editing session. Even if you do use this feature, watch out: It doesn't work if you're editing a remote computer's Registry, even though REGEDT32 doesn't warn you that it's not working.

✔ **Read-Only mode.** This is a good feature that lets you muck about the Registry without fear of doing any damage. This feature should be in REGEDIT and should be the default setting in REGEDT32, but it isn't. You should turn this on (just select it and the check mark appears) right away; then, as long as the Save Settings on Exit check box is selected, REGEDT32 will stay in Read-Only mode until you change the setting back (such as when you really need to make a Registry change). The only drawback is a really annoying message that appears whenever you double-click a value (which you often have to do to see the value's entire contents), reminding you that you're in read-only mode. Microsoft should present the reminder only when the user attempts to change a value from its existing setting — or, better yet, "gray out" value data in read-only mode, so you can see it but it's obvious that you can't change it. I haven't found a way to turn off these messages. Send your postcards to Chairman Bill.

✔ **Confirm on Delete.** You should select this setting when you deselect the Read Only Mode check box; it instructs REGEDT32 to give you one final chance to change your mind before you delete a key or value. For those of you who disable the Windows Explorer confirm-on-delete feature for file system deletions, I gently remind you that REGEDT32 does not have a Recycle bin. (Note that this option is grayed out if you're in read-only mode, because you can't make any changes in that mode anyway.)

✔ **Save Settings on Exit.** If you want REGEDT32 to remember the other settings on the Options menu as well as the layout of the five root key windows, select this check box. Otherwise, REGEDT32 simply uses the default option settings and the same window layout every time you open the program.

Changing stuff

REGEDT32 works a little differently than REGEDIT when it comes to changing values.

✔ First off, you can't right-click a value and choose Modify, because REGEDT32 doesn't support right-clicking.

✔ Before you can change Registry values in REGEDT32, you have to be logged on as a user with the necessary permissions, which often means that you have to be an "administrator" or equivalent. (You also have to make sure that the Read-Only Mode check box is deselected; see previous section.)

✔ You can't just click a value and choose Edit⇨Modify, because that option doesn't exist on the Edit menu. Rather, you must choose a data type (binary, string, DWORD, or multi-string) from the Edit menu. This means that you can edit a value as though it had a different data type. I've been playing around with the Registry a long time, and I don't remember ever having to use this feature.

Double-clicking the value in the value pane brings up the appropriate value editor dialog box for that data type. This method is the fastest and safest for changing Registry data, and it's the one I recommend you use. (You can also click the value and then press the Enter key.)

The String Editor, Binary Editor, and DWORD Editor dialog boxes (see Figure 4-7) are similar to REGEDIT's, although the latter two give you the option to work in true binary mode (all 1s and 0s) if you choose (you never will!). It's worth mentioning that the String Editor dialog box works the same for regular strings (REG_SZ) and strings that contain variables (REG_EXPAND_SZ).

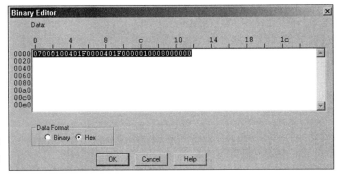

Figure 4-7:
The String,
Binary, and
DWORD
editors vary
little from
REGEDIT.

REGEDT32 has an editor that REGEDIT doesn't: the Multi-String Editor (see Figure 4-8). Some Registry values have multiple strings that the Registry treats as a single value. To modify a value with the REG_MULTI_SZ type, just double-click it and make your changes in the Multi-String Editor as you would in a text editor like Notepad. Each component string has its own line in this dialog box.

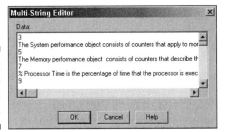

Figure 4-8:
REGEDT32's
Multi-String
Editor.

Incidentally, changing a value's name is even less convenient in REGEDT32 than in REGEDIT. REGEDT32 has no "rename" command, so you have to create a new key manually and then delete the old one. This shouldn't be too much of a problem, however, as you rarely need to rename keys.

Adding and deleting

Adding a key using REGEDT32 isn't quite as convenient as in REGEDIT, due to the lack of support for right-clicking. In REGEDT32, you have to click the key under which you want the new key to appear and choose Edit⇨Add Key. You see the dialog box in Figure 4-9, at which point you specify the key name and (optionally) a default data type for that key.

It won't come up often, but for the sake of completeness I should mention that REGEDT32 doesn't let you add a key immediately below the *HKU* or *HKLM* root keys. You have to use the Registry⇨Load Hive command to add keys at this high level, in which case you're probably doing so in order to inspect someone else's Registry.

Figure 4-9:
REGEDT32's
Add Key
dialog box.

Adding a value in REGEDT32 is a similar process. Select the key under which you want the new value to reside, then choose Edit⇨Add Value. Give the new value a name and a type in the dialog box shown in Figure 4-10, click OK, and enter the value data in the ensuing editor dialog box.

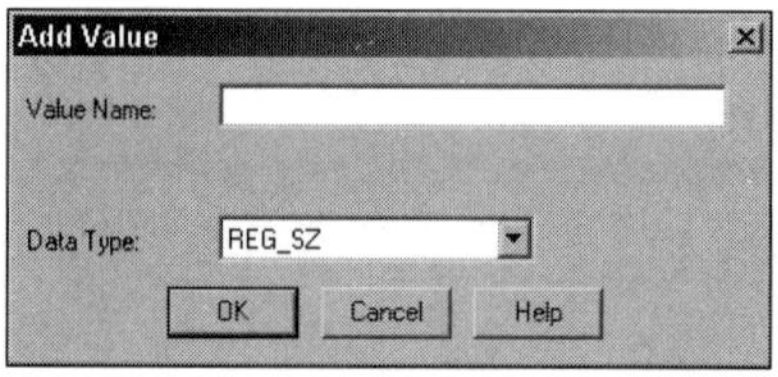

Figure 4-10:
REGEDT32's
Add Value
dialog box.

Deleting keys and values in REGEDT32 is a matter of clicking a key or value to select it and tapping the Delete key (or choosing Edit⇨Delete). Unfortunately, the Shift+click and Ctrl+click selection methods that I describe in the REGEDIT section don't work in the archaic REGEDT32 user interface. If you want to delete multiple items, you must do so one by one.

Here again, remember that deleting a key also deletes all the subkeys and values beneath that key, so it's prudent to back up a key you intend to delete, using the Registry⇨Save Key command.

Also, you have to have the appropriate security clearance to delete Registry keys. Again, that often means that you must be logged on as an administrator. And you have to make sure that the Read-Only Mode check box is deselected in the Options menu.

Finding

REGEDT32's search feature is far inferior to REGEDIT's, because it can't find text that you specify in value names or value data fields — only in key names. Here are a few other differences to note:

✔ The search feature ("Find Key") lives on the View menu, instead of the Edit menu where it lives in REGEDIT and most other Windows programs.

✔ REGEDT32 gives you an additional Match Case option (see Figure 4-11) that forces an exact uppercase or lowercase match and that you'll probably never use.

✔ You also get the option to search downward or upward from the currently highlighted key. (REGEDIT always searches downward.)

✔ The Ctrl+F and F3 Find shortcut keys don't work in REGEDT32.

REGEDT32's inability to find text in value names or value data fields is the main reason you'll use REGEDIT frequently, even though Microsoft says REGEDT32 is the better tool.

Figure 4-11:
Finding
keys in
REGEDT32.

Printing

REGEDT32 doesn't do much differently from REGEDIT when it comes to printing Registry output. The relevant commands are Registry⇨Printer Setup, where you can set a few printing options and Registry⇨Print Subtree, where you actually generate the printout.

Exporting and importing

When it comes to exporting and importing data, REGEDT32 has some significant differences from REGEDIT:

✔ Although you can save (export) a portion of the Registry as a text file by choosing the REGEDT32 Registry➪Save Subtree As command, the program cannot restore (import) Registry data from a text file. You probably won't use the Save Subtree As command often. (You should also know that this command does not create a REG file.)

✔ REGEDT32 can save and restore Registry data in *binary* format, which is a more compressed format than the text *.REG files that REGEDIT uses. The Registry➪Save Key and Registry➪Restore commands use a binary file format.

✔ When you restore a key in REGEDT32 with the Registry➪Restore command, the program doesn't perform a merge, as REGEDIT does, but rather completely replaces the key and its contents. So it's important to be sure that you're restoring in the right place. Highlight the key over which you want to restore a saved key by clicking it before you actually choose the Restore Key command.

Another difference has to do with the two commands Load Hive and Unload Hive. These commands, which REGEDIT does not offer, are mainly for repair work on someone else's Registry. (By the way, for now, just know that a *hive* is simply an odd name for a Registry file; I define the term more precisely in Chapter 5.) For example, you may want to load a hive from another computer if that computer can't boot properly (such as when it can only boot into safe mode), or if that computer can't connect to the network for you to able to edit its Registry remotely (in which case, for example, you could save the remote computer's hive to a Zip disk and then analyze it on your PC).

Think of loading a hive as a restore operation that, unlike the actual Restore Key command, does *not* overwrite existing data in the Registry. You can load a hive from a different computer, give the hive a temporary name, study and change keys and values that need changing, and then unload the hive. At that point, you can copy the hive back to the computer it came from.

When you load a hive, you must load it into either the *HKU* or the *HKLM* window. If you have a different window open, REGEDT32 "grays out" the Load Hive menu option.

Setting security

You have to use REGEDT32 whenever you want to change the security associated with a given Registry key. Choose Security➪Permissions to see the dialog box in Figure 4-12. If you click the Advanced button in the Permissions dialog box, you see a more thorough tabbed dialog box, as shown in Figure 4-13.

Key security involves three aspects: permissions, ownership, and auditing.

✔ **Key Permissions.** Every object in Windows 2000 has an associated Access Control List, or ACL, that defines who can do what with that object. Registry keys are objects, and in theory, you can assign a different set of access controls, or *permissions,* to every single key in the Registry!

Permissions can be powerful tools for keeping your Registry secure, but be very careful: Changing them incorrectly can crash your Windows 2000 system and make it unbootable!

✔ **Key Ownership.** The "owner" of a Registry key can perform some actions that others can't. For example, a key owner can assign permissions restricting who can do what with that key. If you're an administrator, then you're allowed to take ownership of any key. You may find it prudent to change the ownership of certain Registry keys, although you should not do so without expert guidance!

✔ **Auditing.** Windows 2000 can keep a record, or audit trail, of just about anything anyone could do with the Registry. You can click the Auditing tab of the Access Control Settings dialog box to add an auditing specification, consisting of who you want to audit and what Registry actions you want to audit. You can then view the audit logs through the Windows 2000 Event Viewer utility.

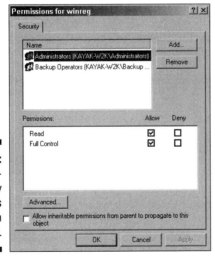

Figure 4-12:
The quick-and-dirty Permissions dialog box in REGEDT32.

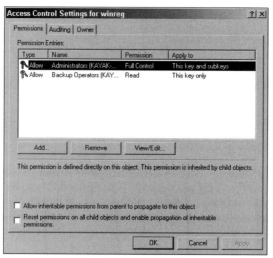

Figure 4-13:
The more
detailed
Access
Control
Settings
dialog box
lets you
control
auditing and
ownership.

Registry security is a pretty big topic, and Chapter 7 looks at these security settings in greater depth than I can in this already-lengthy chapter. So, for now, just be aware that these settings exist, and know how to get to them. The section that follows gives an example of how you can use security settings to modify the Registry's behavior, and how that technique can work both for you and against you.

Taking the Editors Out for a Spin

This chapter has included a lot of fairly abstract material, and it's about time to bring some of it to life. Here's a fairly cool real-world example of how to use REGEDIT and REGEDT32 in combination, along with a couple of other nifty Windows 2000 tricks, to accomplish a bit of magic and undo a potential annoyance that Microsoft added with the new version of REGEDIT.

You may not fully understand every step of this example, and that's perfectly okay. Chapter 14 goes into more detail on the nuances of REG files, for example, and Chapter 7 explores issues of Registry access control. The main point here is to demonstrate the power of the Registry and some of the relative virtues of REGEDIT and REGEDT32.

One of the changes that Microsoft made to REGEDIT between Windows NT 4.0 and Windows 2000 is that REGEDIT now remembers the last key you worked on and restores the viewing window to that key when you restart the program later on. Now, you may like that feature, but if you don't, Microsoft didn't provide the option to turn it off. Like one of Tom Sawyer's friends in the white-washing incident, being denied the option made me want it even more.

The process that I went through to create a "last-key-memory off switch" is illustrative enough of the kinds of things that you may want to do with the Registry that I take you through it step by step. If you want to follow along on your own system, great idea!

Where's the setting?

The first logical thing to do, I reckoned, is to figure out if this "last key memory" is somehow stored in the Registry. After all, REGEDIT has to put the last key information someplace, and the Registry seems a logical candidate. But where in the Registry?

When the question is "where," the answer is usually REGEDIT, because of its superior search capabilities. So I performed a small experiment. I fired up REGEDIT, navigated randomly to *HKEY_CURRENT_USER\Console*, and then closed REGEDIT. If the last key were in fact stored in the Registry, then I should be able to find the string *HKEY_CURRENT_USER\Console* somewhere in there, using REGEDIT's search facility.

So I ran REGEDIT again, clicked the My Computer icon at the top of the tree (to start the search at the beginning), typed Ctrl+F, selected all three check boxes to search everywhere possible, and entered *HKEY_CURRENT_USER\Console* as the text to find. As luck would have it, REGEDIT found the specified string, in the location *HKCU\Software\Microsoft\Windows\CurrentVersion\Applets\Regedit*, value name *LastKey*. (Okay, I could have guessed "LastKey" and searched on that. I wasn't that smart.) See Figure 4-14.

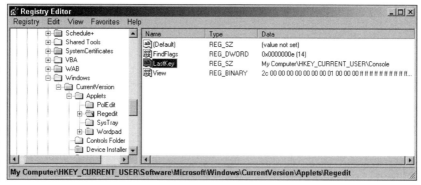

Figure 4-14:
The location of REGEDIT's LastKey memory.

How can I change it?

The smart thing to do at this point seemed to be simply to delete the *LastKey* value. Being a conscientious Registry hacker, I exported the *Regedit* key first, to the file REGEDIT.REG, just in case I needed to restore it later. Then I nuked the *LastKey* value. When I restarted REGEDIT, to my dismay, the program returned me to the last key location. Apparently REGEDIT simply restores the *LastKey* value on its own, when you exit the program.

Being too hardheaded to stop there, I did what any dogged Windows 2000 researcher would do. I went to the Internet newsgroups to see if someone cleverer than I had figured out an answer. And I found one solution that seemed pretty smart. One guy suggested using REGEDT32 to first set the value of *LastKey* to a null string ("") and then disable access permission to the *Regedit* key, effectively making the *LastKey* value read-only. If it couldn't be modified, it could never be changed from an empty string, and REGEDIT would always start at the top folder level. Very interesting!

You have to use REGEDT32 for this task, because it understands about access controls and REGEDIT doesn't. So I fired up REGEDT32, deleted the contents of *LastKey*, clicked the *Regedit* key, chose Security⇨Permissions, and cleared the Full Control check box for all the user accounts on the system. See Figure 4-15.

As I was doing this, I suddenly realized that the trick probably wouldn't work perfectly. Can you figure out why, at this point? (Hint: Take a closer look at Figure 4-14.) However, eager for any kind of a workable solution, I pressed on. I opened REGEDIT, went to a random key, closed and restarted REGEDIT, and voilà — no last key memory any more! Success!

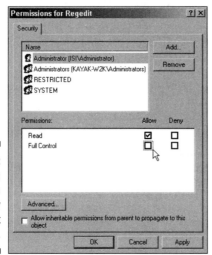

Figure 4-15:
Removing permission to modify the Regedit key.

A tarnished victory

Well, not really. At least, not total success. Here's the worry that I had when I was modifying the security of the *Regedit* key: When you restrict access to a key, you restrict access to *every value* in that key. (Permissions aren't granular enough to work at the value level.) Now, *LastKey* isn't the only value in *Regedit*. There are also the values *FindFlags* and *View*. I pretty much knew already what these values did, and another experiment bore me out. You know those three check boxes in REGEDIT's Find dialog box? REGEDIT remembers those settings from session to session, too, so you don't have to reset 'em every time. Sure enough, though, REGEDIT could no longer remember the check box settings now that I had restricted access to the *Regedit* key. I knew that the same would be true of the settings on REGEDIT's View menu.

So, I had a solution, but it wasn't a truly clean solution — it had undesired side effects. It also wasn't the kind of solution that required zero maintenance. What would happen if I ever logged on as a new user onto the Windows 2000 PC? I'd have to remember to run REGEDT32 and remove the Full Access permission to the *Regedit* key for that new user. I worried that if I took the easy road and stopped at this point, some of you wouldn't respect me in the morning. So I thought about the problem a little more.

An unqualified success

What I really wanted to do was to surgically reset the *LastKey* value to the null string every time I ran REGEDIT, without messing up any other settings and without imposing any ongoing maintenance responsibilities. Then I remembered that I could use a REG file to reset a single value in the Registry. So I created the file in Figure 4-16. (After you read Chapter 14, creating a file like this will be a piece of cake for you.) I called it RESET.REG.

Figure 4-16:
A REG file
that sets
LastKey to
the null
string.

Next thing was to test it. Remembering that I could run REGEDIT from the command prompt and that the /S qualifier made the program run "silently," I opened a command window (choose Start⇨Run and type **CMD**), changed to the folder where I was working, and typed the following command:

```
REGEDIT /S RESET.REG
```

Right afterwards, I typed

```
REGEDIT
```

which brought up the graphical REGEDIT window — with no last key memory. This was looking good. Now all I had to do was make it automatic. The easiest way to achieve that is to write a batch file, and that's what I did, using Notepad. The entire content of RESET.BAT is simply the two commands I'd just typed interactively:

```
REGEDIT /S RESET.REG
REGEDIT
```

Then I saved a shortcut to RESET.BAT on my desktop, set it to run minimized (so that the annoying command-prompt window wouldn't clutter things up on screen), and tested it. It worked like a charm — no noticeable delay in processing RESET.BAT, no unwanted side effects, and no need to modify Registry security if I ever logged on as a new user. At this point, my solution was clean enough to put into print, although I'm sure it's not the only way to accomplish the goal.

The morals of this story are as follows:

- ✔ Use REGEDIT when you need to find something in the Registry.
- ✔ Use REGEDT32 when you need to modify access to a Registry key.
- ✔ Changing the access controls on a Registry key changes access to all values inside that key; you can't control access to individual keys separately.
- ✔ Use REGEDIT with a REG file to change a Registry setting surgically, from the command line.
- ✔ Use a batch file to run REGEDIT conveniently and automatically.
- ✔ If you know your way around the Registry Editors, you change just about anything you want to change in Windows 2000 — even the way the Registry Editors work!

Now you know where the REGEDIT settings live in the Registry. If you're curious about where the settings are for REGEDT32, the answer is *HKCU\Software\Microsoft\Regedt32*.

Part II
Rally Map:
The Registry
Structure

The 5th Wave   By Rich Tennant

"Well, let's look in the Registry and
see what your life preferences have
been."

In this part . . .

Some car rallies are not strictly based on how fast you can get from Point A to Point B. After all, speed races reward contestants for breaking the law, and that's — well, that's just *wrong*, especially if you don't have a good radar detector.

Anyway, the *gimmick rally* doesn't focus on speed entirely. It requires you to end up at the right place at the right time, to be sure, so you can't just kick back and cruise. But this sort of rally also demands that you find the answer to certain questions along the way. These questions are contained in an envelope that you open at the start of the race. What's the name of the owner of the "Curl Up and Dye" hair salon on Route 44? How tall is the gas station sign at Main and Elm in the little town of Longneck? That sort of thing.

Winning a gimmick rally demands some knowledge of the area covered by the race. If you're visiting from out of town, you may eventually find the beauty shop, but Mabel will have gone home long before you do. Same with the Registry: Learn your way around, which is the goal of this part of the book, and you'll have both success and fun. Don't, and you not only won't win the race, you may find yourself lost in the bad part of town — late at night and out of gas.

Chapter 5

Where the Files Are

• •

In This Chapter

▶ Finding out where the heck the Registry really is

▶ Discovering why the Registry has multiple files

▶ Understanding transaction log files

▶ Uncovering the primordial Registry

▶ Locating policy files and other Registry-related files

• •

> *Never let a person drive your brand-new Porsche 911 Turbo who says, "Why does this car have two brake pedals?"*
>
> —From "Rituals of the Road," Jean Lindamood,
> *Automobile* magazine, 1995 special issue

*C*omedian Dana Carvey's parody of the colorful American politician Ross Perot included the line "I'm sorry, but I just can't understand something until I can see it, feel it, touch it, taste it, and pass it through my lower intestine." You may want to know, in a more sensory way, just what the Registry really is (although I don't recommend passing it through your lower intestine). What are the actual files on your hard disk (or on the network) that I am talking about when I say the "R" word? This chapter holds the answer, and it's a fairly important issue.

Why? Well, the fact is, you can't take proper care of your Registry unless you know what disk files it contains. Sure, you can run programs such as Microsoft Windows Backup without knowing exactly what files constitute the Registry. But if you don't at least know the what-and-where of the Registry files, you may miss some dangerous little quirks of these programs — such as the fact that Backup doesn't necessarily back up the complete set of Registry data! Windows 2000 also automatically backs up your Registry after a successful initial installation and whenever you create an Emergency Repair Diskette, and knowing where these backup files are located may just save your bacon one day.

If you set up Windows 2000 to take advantage of *user profiles,* which enable multiple users to log on to the same PC, or to log on to any network PC and see their own desktop setup (known as *roaming profiles*), then you need to know where these user-specific Registry files live. (Most Registry backup programs don't back up these user-specific files, so you may need to back them up separately if they're important to you.)

If you ever need to restore your Registry file backups during a troubleshooting session, you need to know where your files are — and which ones to restore. Here again, Registry backup programs don't always give you the flexibility to specify which files need to go where.

Finally, Windows 2000 contains a few files that aren't strictly part of the Registry but that relate to it in one way or another: REG, INF, MSI, and so on. If you don't know where these files are or what they do, you may inadvertently do some Registry damage that isn't easily undoable.

This chapter presents the skinny on the Registry files. After you're comfortable with their names, functions, and locations, you're like a rally driver who knows the layout of the road ahead: You're much better prepared to avoid the larger potholes, and much less likely to take a wrong turn at Albuquerque.

Getting Physical

You can look at the Registry in two ways: as a logical entity, in which you look at how the Registry's information is organized, or as a physical entity, in which you look at the actual locations of Registry files.

Chapter 6 explores the Registry's *logical structure*, which is the tree-like organization you see when you open REGEDIT. (Okay, it doesn't always seem all that logical, but that's the term nevertheless.) The logical structure is more abstract, but very useful when you're studying the Registry, modifying its contents, troubleshooting a PC, or writing a program.

The actual files on disk that make up the Registry constitute its *physical structure*. The physical structure is very useful when you're designing a backup strategy, restoring the Registry (or parts thereof) from an earlier backup, troubleshooting someone else's Registry, or trying to understand, create, or troubleshoot user profiles (a subject that I cover in depth in Chapter 8).

In this chapter, I look at this physical structure of the Registry. I discuss it first mainly because it's a little bit simpler than the logical structure. Figure 5-1 shows the physical structure of the Registry, and the rest of this chapter explains the various files and what they do.

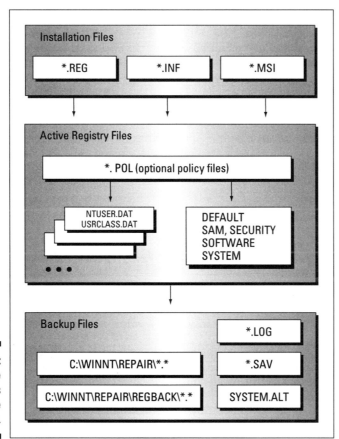

Terminology note: The main Registry files on disk are called *hives*, presumably because they're organizational structures with lots of little compartments. Or maybe because you break out in a rash after working with them for too long at a stretch. (The rash will go away if you just let it bee.)

Your Windows 2000 PC may not use all these files on a regular basis, or at all. If you have a simple, single-user, stand-alone PC, you don't have to worry about some of the files this chapter discusses. But even a non-networked PC uses most of these files.

Why have so many files in the Registry? Why not just have one big meaty file with everything in it? Although the "one monster file" design has a certain aesthetic appeal, a few very good reasons exist for separating the Registry into multiple files:

> ✔ Different users can create and see different user-specific settings (NTUSER.DAT, USRCLASS.DAT) based on their logon names, but all users on a machine can share the same machine-specific settings.

✔ On a network, the user-specific settings (NTUSER.DAT, USRCLASS.DAT) can live on a network server and "follow a user around" as he or she logs onto different machines.

✔ You can maintain a separate group of settings (DEFAULT) for the pre-logon desktop, while keeping every existing users' settings intact.

✔ The security-related parts of the Registry (SECURITY and SAM) can be restricted from view and protected against modification.

✔ If something goes haywire, you may be able to restore part of the Registry from an earlier backup instead of restoring all of it. The benefit of such a "surgical restore" is that you may lose less work.

Before looking at the Registry files in depth, however, you need to be able to view the Registry files, which the following section discusses.

Viewing and printing Registry files

Before you wander around your PC and look at the Registry's physical structure, you have to set up Windows 2000 so that you can see all the files on your disk with My Computer or Windows Explorer.

After a typical Windows 2000 installation, many files (including some Registry files) don't appear in these file management programs because Windows 2000 sets the files up with the *Hidden attribute,* the *System attribute*, or both attributes turned on. The first part of this section explains Windows 2000 attributes, and the second part tells you how to bend Windows 2000 to your will and display your hidden and system files.

File attributes in Windows 2000

PC files have had *attributes* since way back in the days of DOS. Attributes are special settings associated with a particular file. These attributes can be either informational, like the Archive attribute in the following list, or restrictive, like the other three attributes. The basic Windows 2000 file attributes include:

Attribute and Abbreviation	What It Means
Read-only (R)	You can't change or delete the file.
Hidden (H)	You can't see the file unless Windows Explorer is set up to show all files or unless you know the exact filename.
System (S)	The operating system uses the file, and you can't see the file unless Windows Explorer is set up to show all files, including "protected system files."
Archive (A)	The file has been added or changed since the last backup.

You can view these attributes — and change all but the System attribute — by right-clicking a file, choosing Properties, and viewing the General tab, as shown in Figure 5-2. If you look at the same General tab on a disk formatted with NTFS (NT File System), then you only see the status of the Read-only and Hidden attributes right away; if you click the Advanced button, as shown in Figure 5-3, you see the status of the Archive attribute, as well as three additional NTFS attributes (indexing, compression, and encryption) that FAT-formatted disks don't have.

In any case, whether you have an NTFS or FAT disk, if you need to modify a file's System attribute, you must use the ATTRIB command at the command prompt (get to the command prompt by choosing Start⇨Run and typing **CMD**). For some examples of using ATTRIB, read on.

Figure 5-2:
Viewing file
attributes
on a FAT-
formatted
disk.

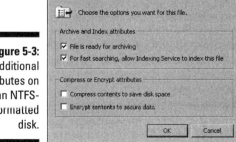

Figure 5-3:
Additional
attributes on
an NTFS-
formatted
disk.

Some files are so important that Microsoft won't let you see them even if you set up Windows Explorer to show files with the hidden attribute. These files have both the system and hidden attributes, and they're known as *superhidden* files. You can spot these guys because the General tab of their View dialog box shows the Hidden check box selected, but grayed out so you can't change it. The following section provides the trick to viewing superhidden files.

You can use a few grief-saving little tricks while working with the ATTRIB command, and you may need to use ATTRIB if you ever have to do Registry restoration surgery. So, here goes.

- ✔ If a file has both the Hidden and System attributes set, such as C:\NTLDR (which loads the operating system) does, you can't remove one attribute at a time — you have to remove both at once, using a command such as

```
ATTRIB -S -H NTLDR
```

- ✔ If a file has the Read-only attribute set and you want to remove that attribute so that you can write over the file, you have to either remove the System and Hidden attributes first, or remove all three attributes at once, as follows:

```
ATTRIB -S -H -R NTLDR
```

- ✔ You restore file attributes with the ATTRIB command by using a + instead of a - in the command.

- ✔ If you want to use the DIR command at a command prompt to see files with the System and Hidden attributes, you have to use **DIR /A** because otherwise the DIR command omits such files.

- ✔ Finally, you can use the ATTRIB command to display and print a file listing, like the DIR command does, but ATTRIB includes file attribute information. Open a command window and use the ATTRIB command with the /S qualifier, which means "include subdirectories." For example, to display all the files and directories under C:\WINDOWS, type **ATTRIB C:\WINNT*.* /S**, and if you want the output to go to a printer connected to your first parallel port, for example, type the **ATTRIB C:\WINNT*.* /S > LPT1:** command. The forward slashes are called *qualifiers* (or *switches*) because they qualify the command and "switch" different features of the command on or off.

Displaying hidden and superhidden files

Nothing is quite so confusing as reading a book that mentions a file you can't find. Often, the reason you can't find it is that the file is hidden or even *superhidden*. Here's how to display your hidden and operating system files so that you can find *all* the files on your PC:

1. **Open My Computer by double-clicking its desktop icon (or single-clicking it if you use the Web view desktop).**

2. **Click the My Computer icon in the left windowpane.**

   This ensures that the changes you're about to make will affect all folders and files on your PC.

3. **Choose Tools⇨Folder Options and then click the View tab in the Folder Options dialog box (see Figure 5-4).**

   If you prefer using the control panel, you can get to the Folder Options dialog box with the new Folder Options icon, too.

4. **Under the Hidden Files and Folders icon, select the Show Hidden Files and Folders radio button.**

   This choice forces Windows 2000 to display all files — even files that have the Hidden attribute, which appear in gray in Explorer.

5. **Clear the Hide File Extensions for Known File Types check box.**

   This choice forces Windows 2000 to display the full filenames, including suffixes, for all files.

6. **(Optional) Clear the Hide Protected Operating System Files (Recommended) check box, and click Yes to the ensuing dialog box (see Figure 5-5).**

   This restriction, which is new to Windows 2000 for you Windows NT 4.0 users, covers superhidden files; that is, files with both the System and Hidden attributes. As of this writing, Microsoft has made only one Registry-related file superhidden, and that's NTUSER.INI (see the "NTUSER.INI" section later in this chapter).

7. **Click OK and close the My Computer window.**

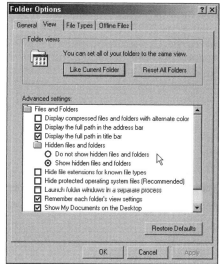

Figure 5-4:
Setting
up My
Computer
to show
hidden files
and file
extensions.

Figure 5-5:
Windows
2000 would
rather you
not look
under its
covers.

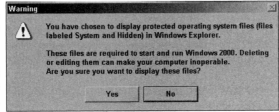

Warning ⚠ You have chosen to display protected operating system files (files labeled System and Hidden) in Windows Explorer.

These files are required to start and run Windows 2000. Deleting or editing them can make your computer inoperable. Are you sure you want to display these files?

[Yes] [No]

Printing file listings

At some time, you may want to print a list of files in a particular directory. Sorry! Windows 2000 Explorer still doesn't have a print command! See Chapter 9 for details on how to hack the Registry to add a directory print command. Also, check out the last bullet in the "File attributes in Windows 2000" section earlier in this chapter for a way to use the ATTRIB command to print a listing.

How Windows wakes up: SYSTEM

The SYSTEM file (which, like many Registry files, has no filename extension) typically lives in the C:\WINNT\SYSTEM32\CONFIG directory (see Figure 5-6, and replace "WINNT" with whatever you've named your main Windows 2000 folder if you've changed from the standard practice). If you're running a lobotomized PC with no local disk storage that boots from diskette or a remote-boot disk image, SYSTEM resides in the *machine directory* on the server, along with the other Registry files. I don't cover machine directories in this book, but if you need this kind of information, check out the *Microsoft Windows 2000 Resource Kit* from Microsoft Press.

The SYSTEM file contains information about the computer on which it resides: mainly hardware configuration data such as device driver information and device settings. SYSTEM also contains information about the various *services* that Windows 2000 can use, many of which are essential to a successful boot. Finally, SYSTEM contains some information to let the boot loader, NTLDR, know whether you're in the middle of installing Windows 2000 or not, so NTLDR can run the setup program again if the answer is yes.

If the SYSTEM file is damaged, Windows 2000 may not even be able to get out of bed in the morning. SYSTEM is the first of the Registry files that Windows 2000 accesses in the boot process, and it's therefore super-important.

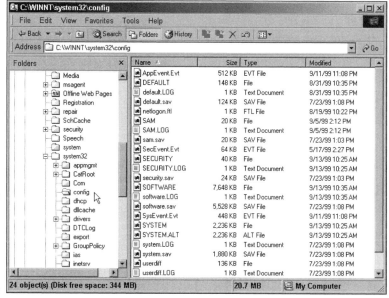

Figure 5-6:
A fairly
typical
CONFIG
folder.

None of the settings in SYSTEM change from user to user. SYSTEM is associated with a particular *computer*, not a particular *user*.

SYSTEM contains the information in the logical Registry branches *HKLM\SYSTEM* and *HKCC*. I explain these branches in Chapter 6.

What Windows does once awake: SOFTWARE

The SOFTWARE file makes its home in the same place as SYSTEM, in C:\WINNT\SYSTEM32\CONFIG. This very important file is where Windows 2000 itself and "well-behaved" Windows 2000 programs put non-user-specific details about their configuration — that is, any information that doesn't change from user to user.

When you make certain settings in the control panel, or when you install or remove a program, Windows 2000 modifies the SOFTWARE file. Many of the Registry hacks in this book modify the Windows 2000 settings in the SOFT-WARE file.

SOFTWARE contains the information in the logical Registry branches *HKLM\SOFTWARE* and *HKCR*. I explain these branches in Chapter 6.

Who can do what: SECURITY and SAM

The SECURITY and SAM files also reside in `C:\WINNT\SYSTEM32\CONFIG`. SAM stands for Security Accounts Manager, and its role has changed significantly between Windows NT 4.0 and Windows 2000.

The precise roles of the SECURITY and SAM files may not matter much if you're using Windows 2000 Professional as a stand-alone machine. So if you're in that category and you don't know what a "domain" or a "domain controller" is, you can skip the rest of this little section in good conscience.

- ✔ In Windows NT 4.0, the SAM file contains a list of all local or "workstation" users and groups as well as all domain users and groups (if the PC is on a domain-type network). I put "workstation" in quotes because I'm referring here to users and groups defined on the local computer, which is usually a Windows 2000 Professional machine but may also be a stand-alone Windows 2000 Server computer or a *member server* (a server that does not act as a domain controller). The SAM also contains information detailing the permissions that users have to access resources such as folders, files, and printers. (These permission details live in *Access Control Lists*, or *ACLs* — an acronym that you'll see often if you get very involved with Windows 2000 security.)

- ✔ In Windows 2000, the SAM file contains a list of all local or "workstation" users and groups just as it does in Windows NT 4.0, but it is no longer the primary storage area for domain users and groups — the Active Directory database takes over that function. The Active Directory also contains the ACLs for domain users and groups. However, in a *mixed-mode network* (that is, one that still has NT 4.0 domain controllers), the SAM file will act much as it did in Windows NT 4.0, for compatibility's sake. So, the Active Directory is the primary storage area for domain accounts, and the SAM is a secondary storage area for those accounts if the network has any NT 4.0 domain controllers.

One reason Microsoft is moving domain security information to the Active Directory database and out of the Registry has to do with size limits. The Registry-based SAM can only handle 40,000 entities (users, groups, computers, and so on) per domain. That number sounds like a lot, but for really big companies it can prove limiting. The Active Directory database can handle something like a million and a half entities, and it doesn't suffer as much performance degradation when it grows, either.

The SECURITY file contains some security-related stuff that SAM doesn't, such as the ability to use NT 4.0-style user and group policies. Networks with Windows 2000 Servers and no NT 4.0 servers use the Active Directory for user and group policy storage, so on such systems, the SECURITY file is likely to be pretty small.

You can't normally view the information in the SECURITY and SAM files with either Registry Editor, even if you log on as Administrator. If you're super curious, you can see some of this information by typing **AT *hh:mm* /INTER-ACTIVE REGEDT32** at the command prompt (which you can access by choosing Start⇨Run and then typing **CMD**), where *hh:mm* is a minute or two later than the PC's present time. At time *hh:mm*, the REGEDT32 Registry Editor appears, letting you peek inside *HKLM\SECURITY* and *HKLM\SAM*. (Chapter 4 covers the Registry Editors.) This trick works because the AT.EXE task scheduler, unlike the Scheduled Tasks utility, runs programs in the SYSTEM account's security context. Unfortunately, the information that you see is decidedly unimpressive. Most of the stuff in these files is encrypted. About the only aspect of SECURITY and SAM that you need to understand is how to back 'em up in good times and restore 'em in bad.

The SAM file contains the information in the logical Registry branch *HKLM\Security\SAM*, which is the same as *HKLM\SAM*. The SECURITY file contains the information in the branch *HKLM\Security*.

The "P" in "PC": Files containing user settings

I said earlier in this chapter that the Windows 2000 Registry splits out user-specific settings from machine-specific settings.

If you've installed Windows 2000 fresh or if you've installed it over a Windows 95 or 98 system, the user-specific settings live in two different folders:

- ✔ C:\Documents and Settings*<username>* is the home for NTUSER.DAT, which contains most of the user-specific settings for *username* (who already has an account on the system).

- ✔ C:\Documents and Settings*<username>*\Local Settings\ Application Data\Microsoft\Windows is the home for USRCLASS.DAT, a new file that contains per-user class registration information (more on this in a minute).

If you installed Windows 2000 over a previous version of Windows NT, then replace C:\Documents and Settings with C:\WINNT\PROFILES in the previous bulleted list and from this point forward in this chapter. I'm not sure why Microsoft decided to do things this way, but maybe the company is trying not to break certain existing applications that work with Windows NT 4.0. Whatever the reason, if you're a network administrator, you're going to have to keep track of whether any given PC has been upgraded from NT or is a fresh Windows 2000 install — for example, when you design a Registry backup strategy.

Let's look at these files in turn:

NTUSER.DAT

The NTUSER.DAT file contains information about the users who work with the PC, including: their desktop preferences, the control panel options they can set, the location of their list of Start menu programs, application-specific settings that apply to them (such as recently used file lists), and so on.

None of the settings in NTUSER.DAT are machine-specific. If you set up a Windows 2000 network so that users can log on from any machine with their own user ID and password, then their NTUSER.DAT files (among others) can follow them from machine to machine. NTUSER.DAT is associated with a particular *user,* not a particular *computer.*

NTUSER.DAT contains the information in the logical Registry branches *HKU* and *HKCU.* I explain these branches in Chapter 6.

NTUSER.DAT sports the *Hidden attribute,* unlike most of the other Registry files. If you consider that this file lives in a folder that users have full freedom to see and modify, the fact that NTUSER.DAT is hidden makes some sense. The theory is (I suppose) that because most users won't be mucking about in C:\WINNT\SYSTEM32\CONFIG anyway, the Registry files in that folder don't need to be hidden.

Windows 2000 creates a separate copy of NTUSER.DAT in subdirectories underneath the C:\Documents and Settings directory. The subdirectory names match the names that you define when creating a new user, either when logging on for the first time, or in the Users and Passwords control panel (Professional only). So, on some Windows 2000 PCs, you may find many copies of NTUSER.DAT on the machine.

If you work on a client/server network like Windows 2000 Server or Novell NetWare, Windows 2000 can store NTUSER.DAT in a user directory on the server. For example, you would typically store the file in the user's mail directory on a Novell 3.*x* server, in the user's home directory on a Novell 4.*x* or Windows NT server, or in whatever directory you like on a Windows 2000 server. When you log on, if the network copy is newer, Windows 2000 copies NTUSER.DAT (and some other stuff as well) from the network down to your PC. If your PC copy is newer, Windows 2000 copies NTUSER.DAT from your local PC to the network. When you log off, Windows 2000 copies NTUSER.DAT back to the network server, just in case you made any changes to your settings.

These multiple copies of NTUSER.DAT are not all the same! Whenever you log on to Windows 2000 with a particular name, Windows 2000 switches to the NTUSER.DAT file in the `C:\Documents and Settings\<username>` directory that matches your logon name. (When you log on as a new user for the first time, Windows 2000 copies `C:\Documents and Settings\Default User\NTUSER.DAT` into the newly created folder that's named after the new user. So all copies of NTUSER.DAT start out the same, but then they change as each user chooses different preferences and settings. If you ever need to restore an NTUSER.DAT file, you must make sure that you use the correct NTUSER.DAT for a particular user. Otherwise, you can create a situation in which Mark logs on and sees Janice's wallpaper (and all Janice's other user-specific settings).

Many Registry backup utilities, including Microsoft's own NTBACKUP, ignore the various NTUSER.DAT files in `C:\Documents and Settings`. I strongly suggest that you back up the individual user versions of NTUSER.DAT separately, as Chapter 2 discusses.

If you run Windows 2000 on a client/server network, you can create a special version of USER.DAT that users can't change — meaning that they can't modify any Windows 2000 or Windows 2000 program settings. This version is a *mandatory user profile,* which must have the special name NTUSER.MAN. NTUSER.MAN lives in the user's mail directory on a Novell server, and in a location you can specify on a Windows 2000 server.

USRCLASS.DAT

New to Windows 2000 is a feature called "per-user class registration." This has nothing to do with high school or college, despite the name. In Microspeak, "class registration" is the definition in the Registry of how a particular file type behaves. For example, a TXT file opens Notepad when you double-click it. TXT files form a "class," and the association with Notepad is part of the behavior that the Registry "registers."

In earlier versions of Windows, applications made all their class registrations in the SOFTWARE file. If one user installed a program that registers the file type *.XYZ and associates it with the program XYZ.EXE, for example, then all users would see that association. Now it is possible for an application to register a class in USRCLASS.DAT for the current user only. And so we have a new file to deal with, which becomes part of the user's profile. (For more details on how per-user class registration works, please see Chapter 6.)

USRCLASS.DAT can also contain per-user definitions for MIME types (similar to file associations but used with Internet software) and COM objects (Component Object Model, which defines how program modules can interact with each other). You can find the file buried in `C:\Documents and Settings\<username>\Local Settings\Application Data\Microsoft\Windows`.

The caveats in the previous section about including multiple copies of NTUSER.DAT in a complete Registry backup program also apply to the multiple copies of USRCLASS.DAT that may exist on a given PC.

DEFAULT

DEFAULT has a very limited purpose. You can think of this file as containing the user profile for the PC before anyone logs on. That is, when you see the Welcome to Windows dialog box, what you see is defined by `C:\WINNT\SYSTEM32\CONFIG\DEFAULT`. Even if you plan to share the PC with other people who will have their own accounts, everyone sees the same desktop before they log on, and DEFAULT defines it. So, it makes sense that this file live in the same folder as the other machine-specific Registry files.

USERDIFF

You can ignore both USERDIFF and USERDIFF.LOG. Windows 2000 uses them to upgrade old user profiles if Windows 2000 is upgrading an earlier version of Windows. These are not Registry hives and Windows 2000 doesn't use them after it has completed installing.

Transaction logs: *.LOG

Windows 2000 doesn't automatically back up your Registry files, but it does automatically create *.LOG files for every hive. These log files store information about Registry updates in progress. So, if you're changing a value in the Registry and the power fails and your PC shuts off just as Windows 2000 is modifying the Registry, Windows 2000 can recover when you restart the next time.

The Registry modification is either there or it isn't, but you never see a modification that only made it *partway* into the Registry. If you've ever seen a word processing document that was only partially saved to disk because of a power glitch or system crash, you'll appreciate how important this feature is! Such documents may look okay for the first few paragraphs, but they then turn into garbled junk. The Registry is *no place* for garbled junk.

Here's how the process works. Say a program needs to write a value to the Registry (that is, anyplace but the SYSTEM hive, which doesn't have a log file, as I explain in a minute). Windows 2000 doesn't modify the Registry right away. First, it writes the proposed new or changed Registry value to the LOG file for the particular hive to be modified. So, for example, a change destined for the SOFTWARE hive would first get saved into the file SOFTWARE.LOG.

After Windows 2000 has written the LOG file to disk, it puts a sort of digital tick mark at the beginning of the actual Registry hive file that is about to be modified. That's a flag that says, in effect, "Registry hive change in progress." Next, Windows 2000 starts applying the change or changes specified in the LOG file to the hive. When the hive modification is complete, Windows 2000 removes the tick mark from the hive. Now, if the system crashes in the middle of the hive update process, for whatever reason, Windows 2000 will notice on the next reboot that the hive is in transition — that's the sole purpose of the tick mark — and Windows will reapply the LOG file data.

Okay, you say, but what if the PC crashes when Windows 2000 is in the middle of creating the LOG file? In that case, the tick mark is never applied to the hive, because Windows 2000 only places the tick mark after the LOG file is successfully created. So, in this case, no recovery is possible, and the Registry doesn't get modified with the most recent change — but at least you don't have junk in there. You either get the most recent Registry change completely, or you get no change at all.

Incidentally, the *.LOG files are typically the only files in `C:\WINNT\SYSTEM32\CONFIG` that have the Hidden attribute set (see the section earlier in this chapter titled "File attributes in Windows 2000"). The one log file outside of `C:\WINNT\SYSTEM32\CONFIG` is NTUSER.DAT.LOG, and it's hidden, too (it lives in the same folder as NTUSER.DAT, under `C:\Documents and Settings\<username>`).

Now that you understand about the *.LOG files, you can pretty much forget about them. They work behind the scenes, and you'll never interact with them directly — except perhaps to back them up, which as you can now appreciate, is purely optional. However, I thought a brief explanation would be an interesting sidelight on the lengths to which Microsoft has gone in the NT platform to ensure the integrity of key system files. You don't see this sort of logging protection in Windows 95 or 98.

SYSTEM.ALT

The previous section mentions that the *.LOG safety blanket doesn't apply to the SYSTEM hive. The reason goes back to a point I made early in this chapter: SYSTEM comes into play earlier in the boot process than any other Registry hive — so early, in fact, that Windows 2000 isn't sufficiently conscious to be able to apply the log file trick.

So, Windows 2000 creates a full duplicate of SYSTEM in the form of SYSTEM.ALT (the ALT here stands for *alternate*). When you or a program makes a Registry change to the SYSTEM file, Windows 2000 puts a tick mark on SYSTEM, writes the change, and then removes the tick mark from SYSTEM. Then Windows puts a tick mark on SYSTEM.ALT, writes the change there, too, and removes the tick mark from SYSTEM.ALT as well.

In case Windows 2000 doesn't finish making a Registry change to SYSTEM, the operating system notices the tick mark at boot time and just switches over to SYSTEM.ALT. That's a simple enough change that Windows 2000 can handle it even at this early stage in the boot process.

In the normal course of events, SYSTEM.ALT is just a copy of SYSTEM. This information may be useful to know if you're designing a Registry backup script and your target media has limited free space. You don't really need to back up both SYSTEM and SYSTEM.ALT.

The original Registries: *.SAV and REPAIR

The .SAV files (DEFAULT.SAV, SAM.SAV, SECURITY.SAV, SOFTWARE.SAV, and SYSTEM.SAV) are snapshots of the baby Registry after the completion of the Windows 2000 setup program's *text mode,* but before completion of the setup program's *graphics mode*. The *.SAV files are basically there in case the graphical part of the setup program blows up, in which case setup can restart without having to build everything from scratch. Snapshots of the baby Registry *after* completion of setup's graphics mode may be found in C:\WINNT\REPAIR. These files (which do *not* have the SAV extension, but look just look the active Registry files) typically have time stamps around a half an hour to an hour later than the SAV files.

You can delete the SAV and REPAIR files without affecting the ability of Windows 2000 to run, but don't. If you're ever in a really terrible Registry bind, you can use these files to get your PC running again (although without all the customizations you've done since the day Windows 2000 was installed).

Backup files

If you use Microsoft Windows Backup, also known as NTBACKUP, to create an Emergency Repair Diskette (ERD), then you have the option of also making a backup copy of the Registry. This backup goes into the folder C:\WINNT\REPAIR\REGBACK, not onto the ERD. See Chapter 2 for details on NTBACKUP.

Registry-Related Files Not Part of the Registry

You find a certain number of Registry-related files floating around on your hard disk, and I mention them here even though they're not technically part of the Registry.

Bringing order to chaos, sort of: *.POL

Policy files (which have the suffix .POL) can modify the Registry on machines that use them. Although policies are more common in networked environments, you can set policies for a stand-alone Windows 2000 computer, too. Policy files can act as a sort of security layer, limiting what a user can do with Windows 2000, but often organizations use policies to ensure some consistency to the user environment by preventing users from changing certain settings for the desktop, network, Web browser, and so on.

Windows 2000 reads the settings in a policy file and applies them to the Registry. That is, a policy file can effectively modify the contents of any Registry hive. So although a policy file isn't a Registry file, it's certainly closely related.

You can't necessarily tell in advance what a policy file's full filename is. For one thing, you can create a policy file with just about any name (as long as it has the POL suffix) using the System Policy Editor utility on a stand-alone computer. For another thing, the names change on a network server, depending on whether you have Windows 2000 clients, Windows NT 4.0 Workstation clients, or Windows 95/98 clients.

- With Windows 2000 clients, you create policies with the Group Policy utility, and they reside in two files on the domain controller, each named REGISTRY.POL. One lives in `C:\WINNT\Sysvol\Sysvol\<domainname>\Policies\<classid>\GPT\Machine` and the other lives in `C:\WINNT\Sysvol\Sysvol\<domainname>\Policies\<classid>\GPT\User`, where *domainname* and *classid* may vary from one network and domain to another (see Figure 5-7). The first REGISTRY.POL file contains machine-specific Registry settings, and the second one contains user-specific Registry settings.

- If you're creating a network-based master policy file for Windows NT 4.0 clients, you use the Windows NT 4.0 System Policy Editor to create the policy filenamed NTCONFIG.POL, which lives in the domain controller's NETLOGON folder.

- If you're working with Windows 95 or 98 clients, the policy file for them must be CONFIG.POL, also in the domain controller's NETLOGON folder.

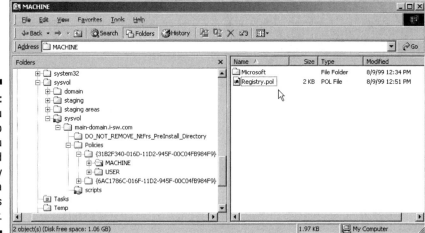

Figure 5-7:
If you
look deep
enough, you
can find
group policy
files on a
Windows
2000 Server.

Policy files can reside on non-Microsoft servers, for example, in the `PUBLIC` directory of a NetWare or IntranetWare server.

In addition to one or more of the previous network-based policy files, every Windows 2000 machine has *local group policy* files, which include `C:\WINNT\ SYSTEM32\GroupPolicy\Machine\REGISTRY.POL` and `C:\WINNT\SYSTEM32\ GroupPolicy\User\REGISTRY.POL` as well as `C:\Documents and Settings\All Users\NTUSER.POL` and (potentially) `C:\Documents and Settings\<username>\NTUSER.POL`. You may or may not see all these files on a given machine, depending on which policies have been activated.

If you're not even a little bit confused by now, you're unusual. Policy files can have lots of different names and locations, depending on specific circumstances. I won't gild the lily: Policies are complex, particularly because of the changes that Active Directory brings. However, they're well worth mastering if you run a network and want to minimize both user confusion and support costs. Check out Chapter 7 for the full lowdown on group and system policies.

NTUSER.INI

This little text file lives in the same place as NTUSER.DAT, that is, `C:\Documents and Settings\<username>`. If present, it typically contains a line that begins with the word "ExclusionList=" and then lists the various folders that should not "roam" around the network following users who may log on at different machines. (Here's more evidence that "INI" files aren't dead yet.) You can change the exclusion list through local or group policies, which Chapter 7 explores, and you can read more about roaming user profiles in Chapter 8.

GPEDIT.MSC

The Group Policy management console for creating or modifying the Local Group Policy file (which exists on every Windows 2000 computer) is GPEDIT.MSC. You can find it in the C:\WINNT\SYSTEM32 folder, along with its accompanying program module GPEDIT.DLL. The GPEDIT.CHM and GPEDIT.HLP files live in C:\WINNT\HELP.

POLEDIT.EXE

The System Policy Editor, POLEDIT.EXE, makes its usual home in C:\WINNT, although (unlike REGEDIT or REGEDT32) you have to install it yourself after a typical Windows 2000 setup. This program doesn't even come with Windows 2000 Professional; you need one of the server product versions to get it, and it installs via the ADMINPAK.MSI package. Chapter 7 deals with the System Policy Editor in a bit more detail.

*.REG

Files with the REG suffix may turn up in almost any Windows 2000 folder. These specially formatted text files usually contain partial or full Registry backups created with REGEDIT's export command, or application-specific instructions for modifying the Registry during a program installation. You can also use REG files as a convenient way to copy Registry changes to multiple computers. However, REG files are dangerous! If you double-click one by accident and blow by the warning screen, you modify the Registry.

Chapter 14 offers more meat on the subject of REG files.

*.INF

Files with the INF suffix, most of which reside in the Hidden directory C:\WINNT\INF, typically include instructions for installing new hardware devices and programs. These INF files can modify the Registry, and they do so when you install hardware and software. In one sense, INF files aren't quite as dangerous as REG files because the usual behavior after you double-click an INF file is for Windows Notepad to open the file for editing. Right-click an INF file and choose Install, however, and you're likely to modify the Registry as well as move some files around. In another sense, INF files are even more dangerous than REG files, because INF files can delete Registry keys and values while REG files can't.

*.MSI

MSI files are Microsoft Software Installer "packages" that may (and typically do) contain code to add and/or remove Registry entries. The new Windows Installer (as it is more often called) service uses a more structured approach to software installation and removal in order to increase the chances that you can undo all the changes that an application makes when it installs. Chapter 14 includes a tip on how you can view the contents of an MSI file.

These files can live just about anywhere on your system.

SECEVENT.EVT

This file, which lives in C:\WINNT\SYSTEM32\CONFIG, is the Security event log. If you enable auditing on any Registry keys so that the system records changes to those keys, then Windows 2000 records such changes to SECEVENT.EVT. You can view the contents of this file with Event Viewer.

REGEDIT.EXE

One of the Windows 2000 two Registry Editors, REGEDIT.EXE, typically resides in C:\WINNT. The Help files, REGEDIT.CHM and REGEDIT.HLP, reside in C:\WINNT\HELP. (For those readers not familiar with the new Windows 2000 Help system, the file extension CHM stands for *Compiled HTML* and is the proprietary Microsoft file format for the Windows 2000 browser-like HTML Help engine.) Chapter 4 deals with the Registry Editors from soup to nuts.

REGEDT32.EXE

The other Registry Editor, REGEDT32.EXE, lives in C:\WINNT\SYSTEM32. The Help files REGEDT32.CHM and REGEDT32.HLP live in C:\WINNT\HELP.

Profile files and folders

I deal with user profiles in depth in Chapter 8, but this chapter is supposed to be about where the files are, and it turns out that the Registry's user profiles feature duplicates a lot more than just NTUSER.DAT. Figure 5-8 shows a PC with two users, Administrator and Glenn E. Weadock. The Registry keeps track of which folders the current user gets a unique copy of in the key *HKCU\Software\Microsoft\Windows\CurrentVersion\Explorer\Shell Folders*.

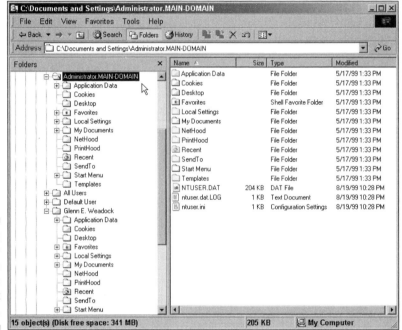

Figure 5-8:
User profiles clone more than just NTUSER.DAT.

Chapter 6

The Registry's Logical Structure

In This Chapter

▶ Understanding why some Registry branches point to other branches

▶ Unearthing the meaning of string, multi-string, and expandable-string values

▶ Using DWORD and binary values

▶ Finding out what you *don't* need to find out about Registry data types

▶ Getting comfortable with the Registry map

> *Blind hacking of the Windows Registry...is like peering into a gas tank by the light of a match.*
>
> —From *Computing Canada,* Lynn Greiner, January 15, 1999

*K*nowing where the Registry files are is important for backup and recovery purposes. However, if you want to drive cross-country with Microsoft's Registry Editor programs, you need to spend a little time with the maps that describe the Registry's internal structure.

In Chapter 5, I explain that the Registry is contained in several files, or *hives,* most of which live in `C:\WINNT\SYSTEM32\CONFIG`. These files represent the Registry's *physical structure* — files that you can back up or copy. However, you can't view or edit these files individually. They're stored in an encrypted binary format, and you need a special viewer to decode their contents. The viewers that Microsoft supplies are REGEDIT and REGEDT32.

Each of these Registry Editors integrates the files into a single "logical" structure — much as a typical e-mail program integrates its various data files and presents them in a logical structure (inbox, outbox, sent items, address book, and so on). You need to understand the e-mail program's physical structure (the files) in order to make backups for safekeeping, and you need to understand the logical structure to use the program.

The Basic Components

The Registry's organizational structure is like an upside-down tree (see Figure 6-1). Just like a real tree consists of branches, twigs, and leaves, the Registry consists of *branches, keys,* and *values.* The Registry tree becomes much more comprehensible after you look at the basic components, so that's a great place to start. I talk about how the branches and twigs actually fan out a little later in the chapter.

If you find only three different basic kinds of components, how many total components exist in a typical Registry? All Windows 2000 Registries have five branches, thousands of keys, and thousands more values. For a complete list of each of these keys and values, see Appendix A of this book. (Kidding!) Seriously, don't let the big numbers concern you. A botanist can understand everything important about a tree without knowing where every single branch and leaf goes.

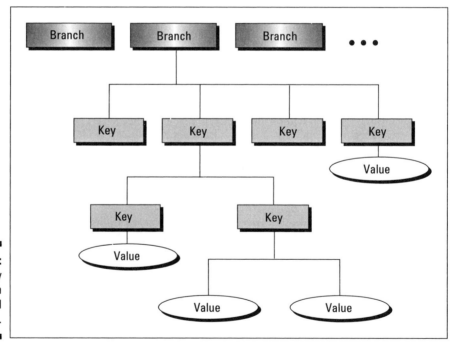

Figure 6-1:
The Registry
is an
inverted
tree.

Branching out

The Windows 2000 Registry has five *branches,* listed in Table 6-1, which are the main organizational structures at the top level of the Registry's inverted-tree layout. (Some Microsoft documents also call a branch a "root key," so don't be confused.) You can't delete a branch itself, although the Registry Editors typically let you delete most of a branch's contents.

These branches all start with the quirky notation "HKEY," which I pronounce "hickey" although I've heard it pronounced "high-key" also. The "H" stands for *handle*, and so these branch names act as *handles* to particular *keys* (specific Registry entries) that you need to view, change, or delete. People who program in C++ tell me that this notation makes perfect sense; I take their word for it.

Table 6-1	Windows 2000 Registry Branches	
Branch Name	*Is the Same As*	*Abbreviation*
HKEY_LOCAL_MACHINE		HKLM
HKEY_CURRENT_CONFIG	HKLM\SYSTEM\CurrentControlSet\ Hardware Profiles\Current	HKCC
HKEY_CLASSES_ROOT	HKLM\SOFTWARE\Classes plus HKCU\Software\Classes	HKCR
HKEY_USERS		HKU
HKEY_CURRENT_USER	HKU\<*security ID*>	HKCU

Unlike a real tree, where each main branch is completely separate and distinct from every other main branch, some of the Registry branches are really nothing more than *aliases,* or pointers, to specific keys located elsewhere. These particular keys are chosen because you use them frequently, so using a shorthand notation to refer to them is handy.

For example, *HKEY_CURRENT_USER* (abbreviated *HKCU*) contains all the user-specific Registry settings for the currently logged-on user. Saying (and writing) *HKCU* is easier than figuring out the current user's Security ID and specifying a key such as *HKU\S-1-5-21-448539723-842925246-2089417427-500*. Also, Windows 95/98 programs don't know about Security IDs and therefore need to see *HKCU* in order to run under Windows 2000.

You often spend time in *HKEY_CLASSES_ROOT* (abbreviated *HKCR*) because it contains information about how different file types behave. Saying (and writing) *HKCR* is easier than *HKLM\SOFTWARE\Classes*. The two locations contain pretty much the same information, though. Check it out yourself. If you're familiar with either Registry Editor, look at *HKCR\avifile* and compare it to *HKLM\SOFTWARE\Classes\avifile*.

HKCR and *HKLM\SOFTWARE\Classes* contain *pretty much* the same information because *HKCR* now contains a merged view of information in *HKLM\SOFTWARE\Classes* and *HKCU\Software\Classes*. Therefore, HKCR is actually an alias for the combination of those two keys, when in prior versions of Windows it was an alias for the *HKLM* key only. See the "HKEY_CLASSES_ROOT (HKCR)" section later in this chapter for more details.

HKCC, HKCR, and *HKCU* just point to other places in *HKLM* and *HKU.* The "core" branches *HKLM* and *HKU* actually contain the entire Registry contents. (For the curious, *HKLM* corresponds to the physical files SAM, SECURITY, SOFTWARE, and SYSTEM, while *HKU* corresponds to the physical files NTUSER.DAT, USRCLASS.DAT, and DEFAULT.)

The strategy of using aliases is confusing at first, but after a while, it gets even more confusing. Seriously, it's not so bad, really just a convenience that you'll come to appreciate as you begin spending some time with the Registry. Unfortunately, no visual clues tell you which branches are aliases and which aren't, and there's no catchy jingle you can use to remember the details, as students of human anatomy use ("the knee bone's connected to the thigh bone"). You just have to get familiar with Table 6-1 (or keep this book near your computer!). Also, the cheat sheet at the front of this book provides a cool fold-out Registry road map.

Figure 6-2 provides a more graphical way of looking at the Registry's branch organization.

All keyed up

A Registry *key* is nothing more complex than a location for storing data. A key is a container and can contain a *value* (see next section), another key, or any number of both. You can think of a key as similar to a directory or folder in Windows Explorer. In fact, the icon that the Registry Editor uses is the same for both keys and directories — a folder. Or, if you like the upside-down-tree analogy, a key is like a twig or a branch. (A Registry branch is just a key that happens to live at the top organizational layer.)

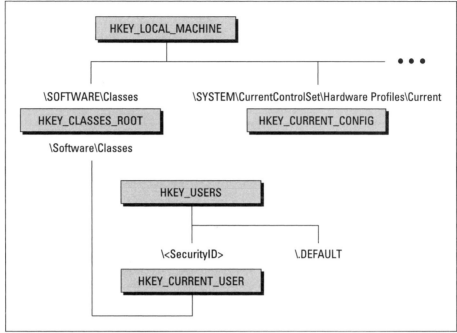

Many keys — the ones with a + sign either to their left (in REGEDIT) or on top of their folder icon (in REGEDT32) — contain other keys, or *subkeys*. You call a key a *subkey* in the same way that you call certain directories on your hard disk *subdirectories* if they reside inside another directory. In this book, *subkey* and *key* really mean the same thing, just in a slightly different context. If I talk about a subkey of Key X, I'm just emphasizing the subkey's location in the logical structure.

Complete key names can be fairly long because a key can reside several sub-keys deep in the Registry structure. In this book, I separate keys in a complete key name with the backslash character (\ ), and I usually abbreviate the branch name according to Table 6-1. Even so, I sometimes have to break complete key names across lines, in which case I try to make the break after a backslash so you don't have to worry about any invisible spaces at the end of the first line in which the key name appears.

Adding value

Most of the useful information in the Registry resides in values. A *value* is like a leaf on a tree branch: You can't have anything else hanging off a leaf. It's the end of the line in the organizational chain: "The sap stops here." Or, if you prefer to think of keys as directories in Windows Explorer, then think of values as individual files.

The Windows 2000 Registry uses three main types of values: *string*, *binary*, and *DWORD*. The string type has a couple of variations, *expandable string* and *multi-string*. A few other value types exist, although you'll rarely see them. (In the Registry Editors, value types appear using "Hungarian" notation beginning with the prefix REG, as in REG_BINARY.) In all cases, Microsoft says that the maximum size of a single value is about a megabyte, but in practice most values are just a few bytes in length.

Value names can contain letters, numbers, spaces, and underscores.

String

The *string* value type is indicated in both Registry Editors by the designation REG_SZ in the Type part of the value pane, and in REGEDIT by a tiny icon in the value pane's Name column containing the letters *ab*. Strings usually contain text, but may also contain numbers and dates. (As with many aspects of the Registry, the rules are sometimes soft and slow rather than hard and fast.) REG_SZ strings have a fixed length, as opposed to expandable strings, which have a variable length.

Here are some examples of the REG_SZ type, which occurs frequently in the Registry:

```
C:\WINNT\SYSTEM32
Temporary Internet Files
01/01/00
1024
```

Variations on a string theme

Two mutations of the string type exist in Windows 2000: expandable strings and multi-strings. You don't run into these often, but often enough that you should know about them.

Expandable string

The *expandable string* value type, REG_EXPAND_SZ, lets you create a string containing a system variable that Windows 2000 or a Windows 2000 program can fill in for you. For example, the value *LogPath* in the key *HKLM\ SOFTWARE\Microsoft\SchedulingAgent* contains a value such as this:

```
%SystemRoot%\SchedLgU.Txt
```

The part bracketed by percent signs, *%SystemRoot%*, is a variable that can change from one computer to the next, although it always appears in the Registry as *%SystemRoot%* and it's up to a program (or user!) reading the Registry to perform the substitution for what the variable means on any given PC. Here's an example: Usually, the *%SystemRoot%* is C:\WINNT, but it could have a different meaning. Someone could set up a Windows 2000 PC so that the operating system files live in C:\WIN2K, for example. The percent signs signify a replaceable parameter (the folder where Windows 2000 is installed) that is not written in stone. By using variables inside expandable strings, programs make their settings less vulnerable to nonstandard folder names and locations. The usual variables are:

✔ *%SystemRoot%* is usually C:\WINNT, the location of the operating system files.

✔ *%SystemDrive%* is usually C:, the system hard drive.

✔ *%ProgramFiles%* (a new variable for Windows 2000) is usually C:\Program Files, the application folder.

Although the above three are the most common, you can use any environment variable available to the system. View these by choosing Start⇨Run and entering **SET** at the command prompt.

Multi-string

The *multi-string* value type, REG_MULTI_SZ, is the other variation on the string theme. (Sounds like classical music!) It's very simple, just a collection of strings that the Registry treats as a single value. REGEDT32's multi-string editor lets you work with each string as one line in a list. (FYI, REGEDIT can't search on strings in a multi-string value past the first one.)

The multi-string value type is helpful whenever the Registry needs to keep track of a list. For example, Windows 2000 services sometimes depend on other services to be running before they can start. You can find values with the name *DependOnService* under certain subkeys of *HKLM\SYSTEM\CurrentControlSet\Services*, and these values are REG_MULTI_SZ because a given service may depend on two or more other services. (A *service* is just a program that Windows 2000 can start without a user being logged on to the computer.)

Second string

A backup Registry value that stands in when the primary value becomes damaged. (Kidding.)

Silly string

A value that, when opened, squirts streams of 0's and 1's all over your monitor, making a huge mess. (Kidding again. You have to have a *little* fun with this material.)

Binary

The binary value type (indicated by the REG_BINARY type in the value pane of either Registry Editor, and in REGEDIT by a tiny icon containing some 1's and 0's) is usually for numeric information. True binary numbers contain nothing but ones and zeroes, but binary values in the Registry show up as hexadecimal numbers (base sixteen) where each digit ranges from 0 to F. (A is the same as decimal 10, B is the same as 11, and so on.)

Sometimes you may want to convert quickly between hexadecimal and decimal values. For example, if you see in the Registry the hexadecimal value *d7 0a*, you probably don't immediately know that this value is the same number as decimal 55,050. Fortunately, you have a nifty conversion tool in the form of the Windows 2000 calculator! Open the calculator by choosing Start⇨ Programs⇨Accessories⇨Calculator and then choose View⇨Scientific to unveil the "hidden" calculator. You can enter a number in any format you like, and then instantly convert it by clicking the Hex, Dec, or Bin radio buttons (I skip Oct because the Registry doesn't use octal numbers).

(In REGEDT32, you can click the Binary radio button when editing a binary value if you want to see it in true binary format.)

It takes a two-digit hexadecimal number to make a *byte*. For example, *ff* represents a byte with the decimal equivalent of 255, and *00* represents a byte with the decimal equivalent of 0. Binary values appear in either Registry Editor's value pane as a succession of two-digit, single-byte hexadecimal numbers separated by spaces. A binary value in the Registry can be as small as 4 bytes long and as large as 65,536 bytes.

DWORD

The DWORD value type (which uses the same icon as the binary value type and appears as REG_DWORD) is also almost always for numeric information. You can think of DWORD as a special kind of binary value that's always the same size: four bytes. That translates to eight hexadecimal digits. (*DWORD* is short for *double word*. In computer lingo, two bytes make a word, so a double word is four bytes long.)

In practice, the Registry often uses the REG_DWORD type for a simple yes-or-no, 1-or-0 entry. This usage accounts for the prevalence of the double-word value type in the Registry.

The Registry format for a DWORD value is: 0x plus EightNumbersAllRunTogether plus the decimal equivalent of the number in parentheses — like this:

```
0x00000001(1)
```

Incidentally, REGEDT32 doesn't display any zeroes that appear immediately to the right of the x, but REGEDIT does.

Caveat Registry user: If a four-byte numerical Registry entry is supposed to have the DWORD format, you usually can't get away with creating the value in binary format, even though a four-byte binary number contains the same numerical data as a DWORD number. If Windows 2000 or a Windows 2000 program expect to see a DWORD value, you need a DWORD value.

Chapter 4 offers specific information on how to create, change, and delete Registry keys and values with the Registry Editors.

Other REGs you don't need to know

Here are a few other value types that you may or may not ever bump into, in alphabetical order:

REG_DWORD_BIG_ENDIAN

This variant on the DWORD concept is supposed to make Windows 2000 more usable on non-Intel platforms, some of which use a different method of organizing the bits in a byte (Intel processors are "little-endian" as in "one little, two little, three little-endians"). Now that Microsoft's support for DEC/Compaq Alpha processors is dead dead dead, the once vaunted multiple-processor support of the NT platform is pretty much history, and this value type needs no further attention here.

REG_FULL_RESOURCE_DESCRIPTOR

This value type describes a device's resource requirements in some detail. You typically find it in subkeys of *HKLM\HARDWARE\DESCRIPTION\System*. For example, Figure 6-3 shows a REG_FULL_RESOURCE_DESCRIPTOR value for the PC's parallel port, letting you know (among other things) that it uses interrupt 7 and base address 378. (The actual value is Configuration Data in the key *HKLM\HARDWARE\DESCRIPTION\System\MultifunctionAdapter\5\ ParallelController\0*, although that key may have a different name on your PC.)

REG_LINK

One place in the Registry can point to another place in the Registry, and this value type is the mechanism for doing so. However, you can't create or modify REG_LINK values with REGEDIT or REGEDT32.

REG_NONE

This type is just a placeholder and contains no actual data. You don't see it much at all.

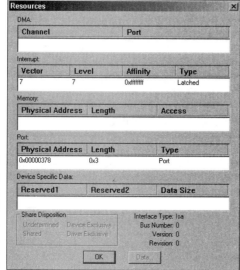

Figure 6-3:
An
example of
REG_FULL_
RESOURCE_
DESCRIPTOR.

REG_RESOURCE_LIST and REG_RESOURCE_REQUIREMENTS_LIST

These two types are so similar that I lump 'em together. You typically find
these value types in subkeys of *HKLM\SYSTEM\CurrentControlSet\Enum*.
Windows 2000 uses these value types internally to help keep track of the PC's
hardware resources — stuff like bus slots, interrupts, memory areas, and so
on — in a more concise fashion than with REG_FULL_RESOURCE_DESCRIP-
TOR. You should never have to interact with these value types.

Gross Registry Anatomy

This section presents an overview of the primary branches and the keys near
the upper levels of the Registry's inverted-tree organization. This overview is
just that — it doesn't try to present every subkey or key or value in the
Registry. That would be like a tour guide trying to discuss every shop in
Ghirardelli Square; you'd be bored because you don't need most of that information. My job here is to show you where Ghirardelli Square is, and also
where Coit Tower, the Golden Gate bridge, and Fisherman's Wharf are. Rest
assured that I'll zero in on particular Registry keys as necessary in chapters
where they're relevant.

Please do not read this section in its entirety unless (a) you are really, really
interested in this stuff, (b) you're writing a program that makes extensive use
of the Registry, or (c) you have a bad case of insomnia. This section is meant
as a reference for you to dip into and out of as events or curiosity dictate.

If you insist on reading this section straight through, then you may want to tear out the gatefold "cheat sheet" from the front of this book and place it where you can see it. It's a great visual aid.

HKEY_LOCAL_MACHINE (HKLM)

The *HKLM* branch stores all the Registry-resident configuration information that has to do with the computer, rather than any particular computer user. *HKLM* corresponds to the physical files SAM, SECURITY, SOFTWARE, and SYSTEM, which make up four of the five subkeys that appear in the *HKLM* branch. (The fifth key, *HARDWARE*, doesn't exist on disk. I explain in the next section.)

You might assume that because *HKLM* contains the word "machine," it's all about hardware information. Fact is, *HKLM* contains lots of software information, too. Whatever details about the computer that apply to every user of the computer go into this branch. These details include hardware devices, device drivers, installed programs, security settings, network connections, and user-independent program settings. You modify *HKLM* every time you install or remove a Plug and Play device, install hardware with the Add/Remove Hardware control panel, install or remove 32-bit Windows programs, or change the settings in the System control panel's Device Manager property sheet.

HKLM also contains the subkeys that form aliases to *HKCC* and *HKCR* (as you can see from Table 6-1). *HKLM* is definitely one of the two Big Kahunas of Registry branches, *HKEY_USERS* being the other.

HKLM contains five major subkeys, as described in the following sections.

HARDWARE

The *HARDWARE* key is the Registry's honest politician — that is, it's a bit of an aberration. Unlike the other four keys under *HKLM*, *HARDWARE* doesn't have a corresponding disk file, or *hive*. Windows 2000 builds the *HARDWARE* key anew at each reboot and stores its information completely in memory. When Windows 2000 is figuring out what hardware exists on the PC, Windows may not yet even know what sort of disk drive the PC has, or how to find it. RAM, however, is easy to find. So Windows notes the results of its initial hardware detection phase in RAM, specifically, the *HARDWARE* key.

Don't make changes to the *HARDWARE* key. You could freeze up your machine.

If you view the information in the *HARDWARE* key, you'll see three subkeys, as follows:

- ✔ **The *DESCRIPTION* key** records the Windows 2000 hardware detection process during the boot phase, and is built by the program NTDETECT.COM. The hardware picture here is incomplete, because the boot phase doesn't detect all possible connected hardware. However, this key does contain resource assignments (interrupts, memory addresses, and so on) for detected hardware, under the *System\ MultifunctionAdapter* subkey. These are boot-time resource assignments and may change when Windows 2000 finishes booting; for example, this key may show the parallel port to use interrupt 7, but Windows 2000 typically deallocates this interrupt later in the boot process. (Parallel ports in Windows 2000 don't generally need an interrupt in order to work.)

- ✔ **The *DEVICEMAP* key** correlates device drivers to devices, for device drivers that load successfully. Most values in this key point to keys in *HKLM\SYSTEM\ControlSetxxx\Services*, where the actual driver filenames appear. (The "xxx" is a number that can vary from PC to PC.) Note that like *DESCRIPTION*, this key is incomplete; you won't see device driver information for network cards or printers here, for example.

- ✔ **The *RESOURCEMAP* key** used to correlate devices to resources (interrupts and such) back in Windows NT 4.0. In Windows 2000, however, this key contains much less information, as the *DESCRIPTION* key contains boot-time resource assignments. The *PnP Manager\PnPManager* key contains references to currently active hardware, although they're so obscurely fashioned that you have to be quite a detective to track them down.

Although the *HARDWARE* key contains a fair amount of information, you can get a much friendlier display of the same information (plus some) by right-clicking the My Computer icon, choosing Manage, and expanding the System Information node in the left windowpane. (For you Windows NT 4.0 users, this feature replaces the Windows NT Diagnostics utility you may have used in the past.)

SAM and SECURITY

These keys aren't normally accessible in either Registry Editor, so we don't need to spend much time with them here. The Security Accounts Manager (SAM) contains a list of all local or "workstation" users and groups, as well as user permissions for accessing resources such as folders, files, and printers. The SAM may also contain details for domain users and groups on a network, but the new Active Directory database — which is separate from the Registry — is now the main storage area for such information.

For more information on the SAM and SECURITY Registry data, see Chapter 5. Chapter 7 includes lots of security-related material that (indirectly, at least) involves these keys.

SOFTWARE

This megakey contains user-independent settings for Windows 2000 and Windows applications installed on your machine.

General layout

The general layout of the *HKLM\SOFTWARE* key is as follows: The software vendor's name appears under *HKLM\SOFTWARE*, the vendor's products appear in subkeys of the vendor's key, and program-specific keys (such as product version keys) appear in subkeys of the individual product keys.

- ✔ One exception to the above rule is the key *HKLM\SOFTWARE\Classes,* which contains information about different file types (*.TXT, *.BMP, and so on) and which forms the bulk of the alias branch *HKEY_CLASSES _ROOT* (see the section by the same name later in this chapter).

- ✔ Another exception is *HKLM\SOFTWARE\Policies*, one of four approved Registry locations for policies — settings that restrict what the user can do on a Windows 2000 PC and that customize the system's configuration. (More on this in Chapter 7.)

When you install a new application program, the installation procedure typically creates new Registry entries in *HKLM\SOFTWARE* as well as in *HKCU\Software*. The latter location is for user-specific and user-modifiable settings. Not all software vendors adhere to this scheme religiously, but you can generally expect machine-specific settings for new programs to live in *HKLM\SOFTWARE* and user settings for those programs to live in *HKCU\Software*.

Windows settings

The Windows 2000 machine-specific settings mostly reside in *HKLM\ SOFTWARE\Microsoft\Windows\CurrentVersion* and *HKLM\SOFTWARE\ Microsoft\Windows NT\CurrentVersion*.

Why two keys with nearly identical names? Tradition over logic. Windows 2000 has a dual heritage; the Windows 9x Registry uses the *Windows* key, and the Windows NT platform has mainly used the *Windows NT* key in the past.

Various other keys under *HKLM\SOFTWARE\Microsoft* relate to bundled applications that can be considered separately from Windows 2000, such as Internet Explorer, NetShow, Outlook Express, and so on. Unfortunately, Microsoft isn't very consistent here.

- ✔ *HKLM\SOFTWARE\Microsoft\DeviceManager* doesn't have to do with a separate application, but rather with the Device Manager display of the System control panel, which is very much a Windows 2000 component.

- ✔ A number of DirectX keys live under *HKLM\SOFTWARE\Microsoft*, even though DirectX is fundamentally a class of device driver interfaces and, again, not a separate component from Windows 2000.

Just remember that even if a key in *HKLM\SOFTWARE\Microsoft* doesn't live in *Windows* or *Windows NT*, it still may pertain to a Windows component or module.

Here's a smattering of the subkeys of *HKLM\SOFTWARE\Microsoft\Windows\ CurrentVersion* that you may be interested in knowing about:

- ✔ The **Explorer** key contains a plethora of settings for the Windows 2000 user interface, or shell.

- ✔ **Policies** is another of the four "approved" Registry locations for local and group policies.

- ✔ **Run, RunOnce,** and **RunOnceEx** list programs to run when Windows 2000 starts up.

- ✔ **Uninstall** lists programs that you can activate via the Add/Remove Programs wizard to remove software you no longer want. (Programs installed with the new Windows Installer appear as keys with long alphanumeric ID codes.)

And here's a sampling *of HKLM\SOFTWARE\Microsoft\Windows NT\ CurrentVersion* subkeys:

- ✔ **Compatibility, Compatibility2,** and **Compatibility32** contain information that Windows 2000 uses to handle older programs that may have compatibility problems.

- ✔ **Fonts** lists all the TrueType fonts installed on the system, while the *Type 1 Installer\Type 1 Fonts* key lists PostScript fonts.

- ✔ **IniFileMapping** contains settings that formerly lived in *.INI files in earlier versions of Windows, so that older applications can still find these settings on the system.

- ✔ **WinLogon** has lots of settings about what should happen when a user logs on.

SYSTEM

This key is huge, in both importance and size. Here's where you find Registry-based collections of hardware and startup configuration details, which are called *control sets*. Control sets guide Windows 2000 as to how to start the computer, as the following section explains.

Control sets

Whenever Windows 2000 starts, it looks to the Registry for a control set that tells the operating system about the hardware that's installed on the PC, as well as the operating system services (programs) that are necessary to boot.

The process is not much different from the one you go through when you hop into a strange rental car. You find the brake, door lock switch, and shifter; you adjust your seat and rearview mirrors; you plug your radar detector into the cigarette lighter (not because you plan to violate the law, of course, but because you staunchly defend your unalienable right to listen to the radio at whatever frequency you prefer); and so on.

Now, if you change the PC's hardware setup, for example by adding a new device driver, the revised hardware setup may not work. In a similar fashion, you may have activated a new service that effectively jams a potato in the tailpipe of your PC. Windows 2000 lets you revert to the *last known good* hardware setup at boot time in such cases. So in any Windows 2000 PC, you're guaranteed to see at least two control sets: the one that booted the machine for the present work session (*CurrentControlSet*) and the one that successfully started the machine on the previous work session (one of the other SYSTEM subkeys labeled *ControlSet00x*, where *x* is some number).

The *HKLM\SYSTEM\Select* key contains values that tell you which control set is the current one and which is the last known good one, as well as the default control set (that is, the one Windows will use for the next boot) and the last control set that failed to boot.

CurrentControlSet

The *CurrentControlSet* key is identical to the numbered control set that Windows 2000 used to boot the machine for the current session. Why the duplication? Programs can simply look here for control set details, instead of trying to figure out the right numbered control set.

This key contains the subkeys *Control, Enum, Hardware Profiles,* and *Services.*

- ✔ **The *Control* key** contains a wide variety of startup information, including your computer's network name, the order in which to look for types of network connections, what multimedia resources your PC has to offer, printer settings, startup and shutdown information, what time zone to use, which applications have problems running under Windows, and so on ad nauseam. For Windows 2000 Server, this key contains lots of details on which network services are installed (DHCP, DNS, Terminal Server, and so on). New to this key since Windows NT 4.0 are keys (under *SafeBoot*) that define precisely which drivers and services load during a "safe mode" boot. *Control* also contains the important subkey *Class*, which includes driver details for system hardware (such as which INF file Windows 2000 used originally to install a given device).

- ✔ **The *Enum* key** is quite different from Windows NT 4.0, thanks to Windows 2000's new Plug and Play capabilities. This key contains lots of hardware details, including hardware that doesn't appear in

HKLM\HARDWARE. Enum is short for *enumerator*, which is software that sniffs around your PC, assigns each installed device a unique identifier, and notes each device's settings. Much of this information feeds the Plug and Play "hardware tree" that you see in the Device Manager window of the System control panel (see "The 'Enum Tree' and Plug and Play" sidebar in this chapter).

Some keys under Enum may appear dimmed, or grayed out, because of their default permission settings; *DISPLAY* and *LPTENUM* are typical examples. If you really want to peek inside these keys, you can change the permissions using REGEDT32; see Chapter 7 for details.

✓ **The *Hardware Profiles* key** contains details on multiple hardware configurations, as you may have, for example, if you use a notebook PC that can have either a diskette drive or a CD drive in the same drive bay. (Another example is a notebook PC that could run in a docking station or on its own.) For more details, see the "HKEY_CURRENT_CONFIG (HKCC)" section later in this chapter.

If you drill down into the subkeys of *HKLM\SYSTEM\CurrentControlSet\ Hardware Profiles*, you'll see keys named *Control*, *Enum*, and maybe *SERVICES*. Before you start feeling too much like you're on a hamster wheel going in perpetual circles, I should explain that these subkeys present any *differences* that the given hardware profile may have from the details in the *Control*, *Enum*, and *Services* keys just under *HKLM\SYSTEM\ CurrentControlSet*.

✓ *Services* contains details about programs that Windows 2000 runs even if you're not logged onto the computer, and this key lists them and their configurations. If you look at the subkeys under *Services*, you can find keys pertaining to device drivers (such as *ATAPI*, which controls storage devices), network modules (such as *TCP/IP*, Windows 2000's preferred networking language), and operating system programs (such as *Schedule*, which manages recurring tasks). Different though they are, all these things are "services" to Windows 2000. So this is a very important subkey.

When you modify Registry data in *HKLM\System*, be sure you have a current Registry backup. One wrong move when trucking through this key and Windows could refuse to restart.

The contents of the *CurrentControlSet* subkey follow the same structure as *ControlSet001*, *ControlSet002*, and so on.

Control set structure gets fairly complicated, but just remember the control set equals everything Windows 2000 must know to boot successfully. That's a minor oversimplification, but close enough to the truth to help keep you on the right road.

Other keys under SYSTEM

The *SYSTEM* subkey also contains a key named *Setup*, which Windows 2000 only uses during installation and which I now encourage you to forget.

You'll also find a key named *MountedDevices*, which lists the storage devices on your system using the same drive letters that you would see by right-clicking My Computer, choosing Manage, and clicking the Logical Drives icon. (*Mount* in computer parlance means "to make available for use.")

The "Enum Tree" and Plug and Play

Although focusing on its role as a software settings database is perfectly natural, the Registry also stores all your PC's hardware information. Whenever you use the System control panel's powerful Device Manager to fine-tune or troubleshoot hardware settings, you're actually using a Registry Editor. The Registry also makes possible one of Windows 2000's key advantages over NT 4.0: *Plug and Play*.

The ambitious Plug and Play specification, introduced in 1994, tries to set up computer hardware automatically, using the Windows 2000 Registry as a central hardware database. It's a broad hardware and software specification that requires support at all hardware and software levels within a PC — not just the operating system, but also the BIOS (Basic Input/Output System), device driver software, and device hardware. Plug and Play's two main goals are to make setting up your PC hardware as painless and automatic as possible, and to reduce support costs for company PCs. The specification achieves these goals by automatically managing PC hardware resources — such as IRQs, upper-memory addresses, and base I/O addresses.

Plug and Play tries to shift the responsibility for assigning computer resources from you to your operating system. When you add a new device, Windows 2000 looks at all devices connected to the machine (a process called *enumeration*) and notices the newcomer. After recognizing new hardware, Windows 2000 displays the New Hardware Found dialog box, which asks you whether you want to install software for the device. Normally, you click Yes and insert the diskette or CD-ROM that contains the manufacturer-supplied device driver software. Windows 2000 then installs the device driver software onto your hard drive, assigns any necessary resources to the device based on what the Registry says is available, and updates the Registry's *HKLM* key to contain essential device information. Everything happens behind the scenes.

Programs called *enumerators* do most of the work by automatically identifying Plug and Play devices, and you see the results in *HKLM\ SYSTEM\CurrentControlSet\Enum*. The organization of the subkeys under that key is a little hard to follow, but it roughly parallels the computer's *bus structure* — that is, the layout of slots and device connectors inside the PC. This makes sense, because each enumerator program only handles one bus type. A special subkey, *Root*, contains references to "legacy" devices that don't follow the Plug and Play spec.

The precise fields the Registry stores for each device varies by device and manufacturer, but you can expect to see the manufacturer's name, product model number, and certain configuration options. Driver information under *Enum* generally refers to a key in *HKLM\SYSTEM\ CurrentControlSet\Control\Class*, which in turn provides the details of which INF file (and which section within that INF file) was used to install the device in the first place. (Manufacturers provide INF files to guide Windows 2000 in the details of installing new hardware; Microsoft itself provides many INF files with Windows 2000.)

HKEY_CURRENT_CONFIG (HKCC)

This key is an alias, or pointer, to *HKLM\SYSTEM\CurrentControlSet\Hardware Profiles\Current*, and contains any changes that the current hardware configuration may have compared to the *default hardware configuration*, in terms of device drivers to load, display settings, and so on. (That default hardware configuration, by the way, consists of settings in *HKLM\SYSTEM* and *HKLM\ SOFTWARE*. Note that *HKCC's* first-level subkeys are *System* and *Software*, reflecting their relationship to *HKLM\SYSTEM* and *HKLM\SOFTWARE*.)

Hardware configurations or *hardware profiles* (you see both terms in Microsoft documentation) allow you to define multiple sets of devices for use in different circumstances. The classic example is the notebook user who has a docking station at the office. Such a user would typically define two hardware configurations in the System control panel's Hardware Profiles property sheet (shown in Figure 6-4): *docked* and *undocked*. (You have to hit the Copy button to create a new hardware profile, incidentally.) The docked configuration can specify a different display adapter, printer, and network connection than the undocked configuration. Using the System control panel's Device Manager tab, you can navigate through the *hardware tree* on a device-by-device basis and specify which hardware configurations any given device should belong to.

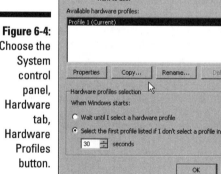

Figure 6-4:
Choose the System control panel, Hardware tab, Hardware Profiles button.

So how does Windows 2000 choose a hardware configuration at startup? You set the options in the Hardware Profiles dialog box: Either you make Windows wait for you to choose from the list, or you let Windows pick the top profile in the list after a fixed delay period.

This selection method is less sophisticated than that of Windows 98, where the operating system tries to figure out the correct profile automatically at boot time. In this respect, the support for Plug and Play in Windows 2000 isn't as mature as in Windows 98.

Rarely, if ever, do you need to modify *HKCC* directly, so this branch doesn't merit any more of our time here.

HKEY_CLASSES_ROOT (HKCR)

HKCR not only matches up data file suffixes with their associated programs (TXT with Notepad, BMP with Paintbrush, and so on). *HKCR* also defines the drag-and-drop behavior for those file types, what icons the different file types use, what commands you can apply to file types by right-clicking; what the files' property sheets look like. *HKCR* even keeps track of the unique numbers that identify each different file type under Windows 2000: *the Class IDs*.

Class IDs pop up all throughout the Registry, especially in *HKCR*. A *Class ID*, or CLSID for short, is a unique number that identifies an ActiveX object in Windows 2000. *ActiveX objects* include data file types (such as a PowerPoint slide show) and program modules (such as the code that displays and processes dialog box radio buttons). Class IDs take the form of a 16-byte number enclosed in curly braces; each byte is expressed by a two-digit hexadecimal number, arranged in a 4-2-2-2-6 byte grouping, for example {25336920-03f9-11cf-8fd0-00aa00686f13}.

Lately, Microsoft often refers to CLSIDs as *GUIDs (Globally Unique IDs)*, although the difference between these two terms escapes me. You might see GUID two or three times in the Registry, while CLSID appears several hundred times, but GUID appears in many company publications. You also see "ClassGUID" sometimes.

Figure 6-5 shows a big-picture view of *HKCR*'s structure, which the following sections explore in more detail.

New with 2000: Per-user class registration

In a departure from earlier versions of Windows, *HKCR* is no longer merely a pointer to *HKLM\SOFTWARE\Classes*. *HKCR* now shows a merged view of that key along with *HKCU\Software\Classes*. In case you're not a programmer and you haven't read Microsoft's "Software Development Kit for Windows 2000" (which is the only document I've found that discusses this new merged view), here's what this new urge to merge is all about.

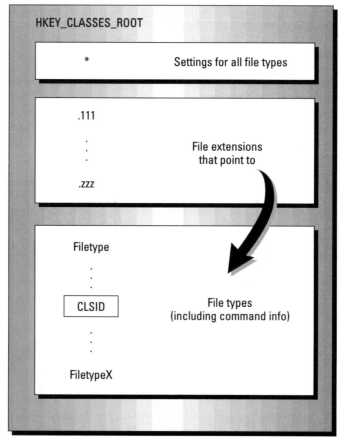

HKEY_CLASSES_ROOT

*   Settings for all file types

.111
.
.
.zzz

File extensions
that point to

Filetype
.
.
.

CLSID

File types
(including command info)

.
.
.

FiletypeX

Figure 6-5:
An aerial
view of
HKCR
shows its
basic
structure.

The *HKCU* branch includes file association details that apply to the current user only. Formerly, programs had to register their *class information* in *HKLM* only, meaning that all users on the PC saw the same ActiveX object information. Now, a program can place class registration information into *HKCU* and not *HKLM*. The *HKCU* settings always "win" in a duel with conflicting *HKLM* settings for the same file type.

One implication of this change is that you can now have Mario log on to a Windows 2000 PC and see Internet Explorer run when he double-clicks a JPG file, while when Emerson logs on to the very same PC later in the day and double-clicks a JPG file, he sees Photoshop run. That's pretty cool if Mario only wants to view JPG images, but Emerson sometimes needs to edit them. So what Microsoft has done here is to make it possible for users to have their own personal file type associations as part of their user profiles, instead of imposing the same file type associations for every user of a given PC.

I really like this new capability. In the real world, different users often really do want to use different tools with their files. The only drawback, and it's significant, is that you must use a Registry Editor to customize user-specific file associations. The File Types tab of the Folder Options dialog box only applies to *HKLM\SOFTWARE\Classes*, and Microsoft hasn't given us a separate tool for editing per-user class registrations — reserving the feature instead for application developers. I think it's too cool a feature to let Microsoft keep it hidden from us nonprogrammers, so in Chapter 9 I show you how to put it to constructive use without learning C++.

Ignore the first key? You'd be an asterisk it

The asterisk key *HKCR** contains ActiveX object settings for every sort of Windows 2000 file, regardless of type. (You may have guessed this from the common use of the asterisk as a wildcard character in file specifications like *.* and so on.) *HKCR** typically contains the single subkey *shellex,* which stands for *shell extensions*.

The user interface, or *shell,* presents the operating system to you and defines how Windows 2000 looks and acts. A shell *extension* is an add-on that defines how the shell deals with a certain file type. That definition appears in the Registry key *shellex,* through its two subkeys, *ContextMenu-Handlers* and *PropertySheetHandlers. Context menus* are the pop-up menus that appear when you right-click files, and *property sheets* are the tabbed windows that appear when you right-click files and choose Properties.

When you add programs that can work with every file on your computer, such as WinZip or Novell NetWare, *HKCR*\shellex* may receive new entries. These new entries are Class IDs that usually point to a chunk of program code. The program code handles the job of providing context menu and property sheet choices. (Note the existing entries for "Open With" and "Offline Files," the first of which lets you right-click a file and open it with a nonstandard program, the second of which lets you select network files that you can work on when not connected to the network.)

Top half (filename extensions)

After the *HKCR** key, roughly the top half of all the entries under *HKCR* are *filename extension* keys (see Figure 6-6). An entry appears here for every filename extension (or suffix, like TXT or BMP) that Windows 2000 or a Windows 2000 program has defined on the PC.

Many of these filename extension keys contain nothing more than a single string value defining the related file type key, which appears in the bottom half of *HKCR.* For example, if you look at the *HKCR\.bmp* key, it contains a single value with the data *Paint.Picture* that refers to a later key, *HKCR\ Paint.Picture,* which has all the details on how Windows 2000 handles such a file type.

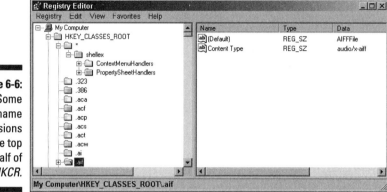

Figure 6-6:
Some
filename
extensions
in the top
half of
HKCR.

Why divide up *HKCR* into two halves with extension keys in the top half that point to file type keys in the bottom half — why not just put all the relevant details in the filename extension key instead of creating an additional file type entry in the bottom half? For example, why not just put all the information under *HKCR\.bmp* instead of having that key just point to *HKCR\Paint.Picture*?

There's a good reason. What if you want the same program to handle a file type that has two different extensions? For example, you want JPG and JPEG files to open the same program, as well as HTM and HTML files to open another program. Using *HKCR's* organizational structure, you can have two entries in the filename extension key group (the top half) both point to a single entry in the class definition group (bottom half). For example, *HKCR\.JPG* and *HKCR\.JPEG* both point to *HKCR\jpegfile,* and *HKCR\.HTM* and *HKCR\.HTML* both point to *HKCR\htmlfile.*

One detail about file types must appear in the top half, though, and that's what to do if you right-click the desktop and choose New⇨*<filetype>*. Windows 2000 needs to create the file with the proper filename extension, so you may find a subkey called *ShellNew* under the filename extension key in *HKCR.*

Bottom half (class definitions)

The bottom half or so of *HKCR* contains *class definition* keys, such as *HKCR\ Paint.Picture* or *HKCR\jpegfile,* to which the filename extension keys in the top half of *HKCR* point. The class definition keys are where all the action is in terms of defining how different file types behave. Figure 6-7 shows an example of the bottom half of *HKCR.*

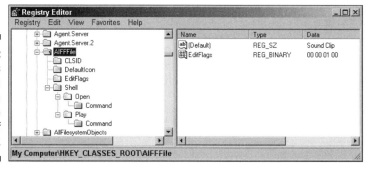

Figure 6-7:
Class
definition
information
in the
bottom half
of *HKCR*.

A few of the subkeys you may find beneath a class definition key include the following:

- ✔ **Shell.** Here's where context menu actions unique to a file type appear. For example, *HKCR\<filetype>\Shell\Open\Command* contains the actual command to run (usually a program on disk) when you double-click a file of the specified file type. In this example, "open" is called the *verb*. Other common verbs are "play," "print," and "edit."

- ✔ **Shellex.** If the file type's property sheet is to display special choices not included on the generic property sheet, here's where the Registry references the Class ID for the program code that provides the property sheet enhancements. The Registry may also include references to a special *ContextMenuHandler, PropertySheetHandler,* or *DropHandler* if special software is required to handle context menus and drag-and-drop desktop behavior.

- ✔ **DefaultIcon.** Here's the location of the icon that Windows 2000 displays for files of a specified type.

A special key in *HKCR*'s bottom half, *HKCR\CLSID*, contains a comprehensive list of every CLSID on the system. Each subkey under CLSID is a unique 16-byte identifier and typically contains a default string value describing the object type (such as "Video Clip" or "MS Conference Manager Object"). Beneath each specific CLSID key, you typically find a subkey named *InProcServer32,* which (again typically) contains the path and filename for the chunk of program code that Windows 2000 associates with that CLSID. *HKCR\CLSID* is important to know about if you're troubleshooting problems with a certain kind of file, because this key can point you to the DLL file on disk that handles that kind of file.

HKEY_USERS (HKU)

Any Windows 2000 operating system or application setting that can conceivably vary from one user to another goes into the *HKU* branch. *HKU* contains user-related Windows settings such as desktop wallpaper and network connections. The application-related settings depend on the software, but could include user preferences such as toolbar placement and data file storage locations. *HKU* corresponds to the files NTUSER.DAT, USRCLASS.DAT, and DEFAULT.

This key contains at least one primary subkey, *.DEFAULT*, and it may contain two additional subkeys, both of which are named after the currently logged-on user's Security ID (SID for short). *HKU* normally never shows more than that, although the number of different users that can have Registry accounts is practically unlimited. For example, if you set up a PC for users Bob and Ray, when Bob logs on, *HKU* contains the subkeys *.DEFAULT, <Bob's SID>,* and *<Bob's SID>_Classes.* When Ray logs on, *HKU* contains the subkeys *.DEFAULT, <Ray's SID>,* and *<Ray's SID>_Classes.* (Just to be real clear, you wouldn't actually see the literal text *<Bob's SID>* but rather the long sequence of numbers that is unique to Bob's account.) The key that ends with "_Classes" may be empty; if it has contents, they reflect any per-user class registrations that programs have made. (See the earlier section in this chapter titled "New with 2000: Per-user class registration.")

The *.DEFAULT* key contains the desktop settings (wallpaper, screen saver, and so on) that Windows 2000 applies to the PC before a user logs on.

The contents of each subkey immediately under *HKU* share the same organization and include the following keys, among others.

- ✔ **AppEvents.** Here's where the Registry stores locations and filenames of the sounds that play when specific Windows 2000 events occur.

- ✔ **Console.** This is where Windows 2000 keeps your command-line session settings (yes, you can customize these! — just click Start⇨Run, type **CMD**, click the little icon in the upper right, and choose Properties). You can even define separate settings for different programs that you run at the command prompt, and these appear as separate subkeys under *Console.*

- ✔ **Control panel.** Many user-specific control panel settings live here, but watch out. Not all control panel settings can vary from user to user. Remember that modifying control panel settings from a control panel or MMC (Microsoft Management Console) is always better than using the Registry Editor.

✔ *Printers.* This subkey names any printers that the current user has set up. (The actual printer settings live in *HKLM\SYSTEM\ CurrentControlSet\Control\Print\Printers*.) You can also find user-specific settings for the Add Printer wizard in this HKU subkey.

✔ *RemoteAccess.* Here's where Windows 2000 stores the names of Dial-Up Networking connections for remote network access sessions. (The actual details of the connections typically live in the RASPHONE.PBK file in the `C:\Documents and Settings\All Users\Application Data\ Microsoft\Network\Connections\PBK` folder.)

✔ *Software.* Here's where all the user-settable and user-specific preferences for installed software applications (including Windows 2000 itself) reside. When you install a new application, it makes entries here and in *HKLM\ SOFTWARE* (where settings exist that don't vary from user to user).

HKEY_CURRENT_USER (HKCU)

HKCU contains the subset of settings in *HKU* that pertain to whoever logged on at the Windows 2000 startup prompt. *HKCU* is an alias that points to *HKU\<SID>*, where *<SID>* is the security ID for the logged-on user.

If the current user logs on for the very first time, then Windows 2000 creates *HKCU* from the file `C:\Documents and Settings\Default User\ NTUSER.DAT`, and the current user looks just like the default user — until the new user starts changing his or her settings and preferences. The subkeys for *HKCU* are the same as those defined for *HKU* in the previous section.

If the same desktop or application setting exists in both *HKLM* and *HKCU*, as happens occasionally, the setting in *HKCU* usually wins.

Part III

Mag Wheels and Pinstripes: Customizing the Registry

The 5th Wave   By Rich Tennant

@RICHTENNANT

"Jeez-I thought the Registry just defined the wallpaper on the screen."

In this part . . .

You've probably seen those "custom" paint jobs on amateur racing cars — and some of them are amazingly elaborate. Tongues of multicolored flame licking the car body from headlight to taillight, beautifully stenciled sentiments like "For Trisha, the gas in the engine of my life" — that sort of thing. I was in a body shop once where the office *refrigerator* had one of those custom paint jobs. (Flames on a 'frige didn't make much sense to me, but the owner was a very large man, so I kept my thoughts to myself.)

Of course, few car nuts stop at customizing the paint. I outfitted my little street racer with custom air intakes, custom exhausts, high-lift camshafts, big anti-sway bars, and anything else that made the car run faster on straights or in turns. This had nothing to do with turning the car into a Babe Magnet. It was all about personalizing that car so that it took on the stamp of my own personality and simultaneously became a more perfect example of the car its designers intended it to be, just as a piece of art in a house not only reflects the taste of its owner but also makes its own esthetic statement. (Okay, I wanted it to be a Babe Magnet.)

This part of the book is where you discover how to customize your PC vehicle using the Registry. The only real difference between customizing Windows 2000 and customizing your street racer are that with Windows, you don't have to sign over your paycheck to your mechanic every two weeks.

Chapter 7

Customizing Security with the Registry

- -

In This Chapter

▶ Getting the skinny on Windows 2000 security

▶ Setting Registry key permissions

▶ Auditing Registry activities

▶ Finding out what policies can do for both stand-alone and networked PCs

- -

> *When you are passing, or being passed, or when you're crossing a main road, you are exposed to danger. The time spent exposed to danger is what you want to reduce.*
>
> —From *High Performance Driving*, Paul Petersen,
> Simon & Schuster, 1974

*O*ne of the big attractions of Windows 2000, and of Windows NT 4.0 before it, is security. Unlike the Windows 9*x* product line, the NT product line has its own facilities for keeping track of users and groups, and for designating just what those users and groups are allowed to do. Windows 2000 also offers NTFS, the NT File System, which lets you control access to files as well as folders. Add the Windows 2000 ability to track system events with auditing, and you have a computer environment that can be made much more secure from mishaps, both intentional and unintentional, than Windows 9*x*.

So, what does that have to do with the Registry? Two things, mainly, and both apply (although to differing degrees) whether you have a single stand-alone Windows 2000 Professional PC or a huge network of Windows 2000 Servers.

First, you may want to use the Windows 2000 access control and auditing features to protect the Registry itself, to a greater degree than Microsoft has done "out of the box." Second, you may want to apply *policies*, special files that place restrictive or customizing settings into the Registry to enhance security, consistency, or both. This chapter provides some background and suggestions for both Registry-related security areas.

As with securing your car, a lot depends on your neighborhood. You probably live in a perfectly safe neighborhood (computer-wise) if:

- ✔ You're using Windows 2000 at home.
- ✔ You never connect to information services or other computers.
- ✔ You never install software other than shrink-wrapped commercial applications.

If all these are true, then you live in a small, friendly community in a sleepy semi-rural town, where you can leave your car unlocked in your driveway. There's no point having more security than you need, because every additional layer of security can make the system a little more complex to use.

On the other hand, if you're a network manager for a Silicon Valley startup company whose lifeblood is its intellectual property, then you need all the information in this chapter, and that's just for starters. (*You* live in a high-density, high-crime urban community, and you need the Club, a car alarm, and maybe a Doberman in your back seat.)

Whatever your situation, security is a big part of Windows 2000, and the Registry, as usual, is intimately involved.

If you haven't read Chapters 4 and 6 covering Registry Editors and the Registry structure, now is a good time to get out your trusty map and take a look. Also, if you need more information on security and the Registry than this chapter provides, check out *Deploying Windows 2000 Policies* by Mark Wilkins (McGraw-Hill).

Windows 2000 Security in Six Pages or Less

Because many ways exist to compromise the security of a Windows 2000 machine, many different types of security exist as features of the operating system. This section introduces the main layers of the Windows 2000 security onion: computer accounts, logon security, user and group rights, permissions, security for stored data, security for transmitted data, policies, and auditing. (Internet security, which Microsoft provides with the Internet Information Server bundled with Windows 2000 Server, borrows concepts from these main security areas and adds a few of its own — but that's another book.)

I can only introduce each of these subjects concisely here, but you need at least to be aware of each of them to appreciate how they tie in with the Registry. By the way, if you're not already familiar with Windows NT 4.0, please don't worry if you don't understand each of these security mechanisms after a single read-through. Windows 2000 security can get pretty complicated!

Computer accounts: Pre-logon security

If your Windows 2000 machine is on a network, then before you even log on, the computer has already "checked in" with a Windows 2000 server by means of a *computer account*. That is, regardless of who logs on to that PC, the server can apply some restrictions to the machine, through the use of Registry-modifying *policies* (one of this chapter's main topics). Think of this security layer as a locked gate in front of your house. (Incidentally, Windows 95 and 98 don't have computer accounts.)

Logon security: Getting in the door

The default behavior for Windows 2000 is to require a username and password before you can log on. (You can change that behavior for a stand-alone Windows 2000 PC, but think twice before you do.) Logon security is the second line of defense, after computer accounts, against both intentional and unintentional harm.

Windows 2000 uses various technologies to authenticate a network user: Kerberos, certificates, and smart cards. I won't go into the details here. You can think of logon security and user authentication as a locked front door on your house, with a peephole for you to identify a visitor before you unlock the door.

Logon security depends on passwords. The problem with passwords is the same as with lottery tickets: Most of them are no darned good. That is, they're too easily guessed or not complex enough to foil crackers. On a networked computer, you can apply some policies (see "Securing Computers and Users with Policies" later in this chapter) to enforce better passwords and better password maintenance.

Another problem with logon security is that many Windows 2000 users either never change the name of their Administrator account, or they do their everyday work when logged on as an Administrator. The latter is especially risky, because a user with Administrator privileges on the local machine has the widest latitude when it comes to making Registry changes (or any other changes, for that matter).

Do most of your work when logged on as a User, Power User, Domain User, and so on — not as an Administrator.

User and group rights

You can grant different people different *rights* after you let them in your house. In the winter, for example, you may let adult visitors throw additional logs into your wood-burning fireplace when the fuel runs low, but you probably won't let little children attempt to do the same, out of a concern that they will burn themselves and/or your house down. The generic "group" of children has limited rights in your house; the group of adults has a different set of rights.

In a similar way, Windows 2000 lets you assign different rights on the PC and on the network by user and by group. (Note that groups exist even on a non-networked Windows 2000 Professional system.) For example, some users should have the right to back up and restore the system, but other users shouldn't have those rights. By default, Windows 2000 Professional has three user groups: *Administrators* have all the power, *Users* have lots of restrictions, and *Power Users* (the default assignment for newly created users) fall in the middle. Windows 2000 Server has many more predefined groups, such as *Domain Administrators, Authenticated Users, Backup Operators,* and so on.

Time was, all user and group rights lived in the Registry, in the SAM (Security Accounts Manager). They still live there for "local" users and groups, that is, those defined on the logon machine; but user and group rights on a Windows 2000 network now live in the Active Directory database rather than the Registry.

Permissions

Windows 2000 includes several types of *permissions.* You can think of rights as "actions that users and groups can or can't take" and permissions as "objects that users and groups can or can't modify." The distinction is a subtle one, but it should become clearer as you read on.

Users have rights. Objects have permissions.

To continue the homeowner analogy, you may allow your adult neighbors to help themselves to a bottle of wine from your refrigerator when they come over to watch a Formula I race on TV, but you probably won't extend that permission to their 8-year-old child, unless you live in France. In fact, it's likely that you won't allow *any* children to have a glass of wine. You may forbid it to your crazy uncle Harry, also, who gets silly after a glass or two. Your wine is an object, and you control which users and groups can access it.

I should mention in passing that Windows 2000 includes the concept of an object's *owner*. If you own the wine bottle, you can change the permissions that specify who can drink from it (and whether they can drink directly from the bottle). Likewise, in Windows 2000, if you own an object (such as a file folder or Registry key), you can change the permissions for that object. Hiccup.

Share permissions

When you share a resource (typically, a file folder) for use by other computer users, you can specify which users and groups you want to have access to that resource, and how much access you want them to have. The basic share permissions in Windows 2000 are *full control*, *read*, and *change*. These permissions work on FAT as well as NTFS disks, and you set them in Windows Explorer using the Sharing dialog box, which you get to by right-clicking the shared folder or drive and clicking the Sharing menu choice.

NTFS permissions

If you format a disk using the NT File System, or NTFS (now in Version 5 for Windows 2000), then you have additional permissions available to you beyond share permissions. Microsoft sometimes calls NTFS permissions "file and folder permissions." The basic ones are *full control*, *read*, *read+execute*, *modify*, *write*, and (for folders only) *list folder contents*. View and set NTFS permissions in Windows Explorer by right-clicking the shared file or folder, clicking the Security tab, and making the relevant changes.

Registry permissions

The Registry is a shared resource in the sense that various applications on the machine use it, much like various users on a network use shared folders on a server. So, it makes sense that the Registry should use permissions, too, which you can assign on a key-by-key basis using REGEDT32. The section "Securing the Registry Itself" a little later in this chapter explains how to view and set Registry key permissions.

Others

Permissions also exist in Windows 2000 for Active Directory objects, printers, and services, but those areas get a bit esoteric for this overview, so you have my permission not to worry about them. (As if you need it.)

Security for stored data

If you have a safe in your house, only those who know the combination can get to the valuables. Similarly, when mere access controls aren't good enough, Windows 2000 offers another level of protection for data sitting around on storage devices: *encryption*. This feature only exists on disks formatted with NTFS, and you access it in Windows Explorer via the file or folder's property sheet.

When it comes to device drivers and system files, Windows 2000 provides an additional level of authentication called *driver signing*. Microsoft brands a *digital signature* into the core operating system files and drivers that it ships with Windows 2000. That way, Windows 2000 can "tell" when a program installation tries to replace one of those core files with a version not "signed" by Microsoft.

The Registry contains settings that govern how Windows 2000 behaves with respect to driver signing: *See Unsigned driver installation behavior* and *Unsigned non-driver installation behavior* in the Group Policy utility under Computer Configuration\Windows Settings\Security Settings\Local Policies\Security Options. (The "Securing Computers and Users with Policies" section later in this chapter shows you how to get there.)

Security for transmitted data

Encryption may be fine for data that's sitting around, but you may want to protect files that *aren't* encrypted on disk when you decide to send those files across a communications link. Windows 2000 offers a variety of methods to secure data in transit, including callback security for dial-up links, PPTP, and IPsec for secure network transmissions, and a bunch of other stuff that doesn't directly relate to the Registry and that you and I can therefore happily dismiss for now.

System and group policies

Policies, which can be local or network-based (or both), are really more of a mechanism for implementing and controlling the various other types of Windows 2000 security than a new type of security themselves. You can think of policies as the "rules of the house" that set forth all the security restrictions you've chosen to implement from the areas discussed so far.

Policies work differently depending on whether you're running a stand-alone machine, a computer in a "pure" Windows 2000 network, or a computer in a "mixed-mode" network with NT 4.0 clients. However, although the details vary, the concept is basically the same: After an Administrator sets them, policies automatically modify the Registry (applying security, user interface consistency, or both) at boot time, logon time, and periodic refresh intervals.

Auditing

The last main area of security is *auditing*, that is, keeping track of events that may reflect on system security. Think of auditing like a security camera pointing at your front door: The camera itself doesn't present any physical impediment to entry, but it creates a recorded document that you can use later on to prove a security breach (and maybe nab the breacher!). Windows 2000 "videotapes" are the event logs, most of which live in C:\WINNT\SYSTEM32\ CONFIG and have the suffix EVT. You view these with the Event Viewer, one of the Windows 2000 administrative tools.

The next section tells you (among other things) how you can enable auditing on Registry accesses, but keep in mind that Windows 2000 lets you audit lots of other events as well.

Securing the Registry

When you wear a helmet while bicycling, you're using your brain to protect your brain. In this section, you can use the Registry to protect the Registry (and therefore most of the rest of your system as well). This section looks at how you can assign permissions to Registry keys and set up auditing for Registry events.

The concept of securing the Registry never got the press it deserved until the first Registry-related viruses hit the scene. If you hang out on the Internet or download software from online sources, read on — and make sure that you're *not* logged on as an Administrator when you're connected to remote computer systems. Administrators have unlimited access to the Registry, which makes your system more vulnerable when you're online.

In addition to the measures the following section discusses, you may consider removing the REGEDT32.EXE file from your hard drive and from the hard drive of any other machines for which you're responsible, after you have the Registry the way you want it. REGEDT32 is a small program that easily fits on a diskette. Alternatively, consider putting it on a network drive with limited access. You need to leave REGEDIT.EXE so that program installations will work, but at least you'll know that no one can easily modify Registry key permissions or auditing settings without REGEDT32. (You can't edit key permissions or auditing settings with REGEDIT.)

Registry key permissions

Before delving into the details of viewing and setting Registry key permissions, a brief caveat:

Carelessly changing the permissions on certain Registry keys can render your machine unbootable, unable to load certain services, or unable to properly run some programs that may need access to the keys you've restricted. When fiddling with permissions, therefore, take it slow and steady. Be especially wary of modifying permissions for the SYSTEM or CREATOR OWNER entities.

Protecting Registry keys

REGEDT32 lets you assign different permissions to every Registry key. The basic permissions are *read* and *full control*. These two, which are actually convenience groupings, or composites, of ten more fine-grained permissions (see the "Technical stuff" icon with the next paragraph), handle 99 percent of the situations that come up. A user or group with the Read permission can read but not modify a Registry key; a user or group with the Full Control permission can read, take ownership of, change, or delete the key.

You can assign a third permission type, *Special*, to have pretty much any combination of the more "atomic" Registry key permissions, which are *query value, set value, create subkey, enumerate subkeys, notify, create link, delete, write DAC, write owner*, and *read control*. (DAC stands for Discretionary Access Control, which basically means "a permission that Windows 2000 lets you change.") The likelihood of your ever needing to use these fine-grained permissions is low, but check out the *Microsoft Windows 2000 Resource Kit* if you need more detail. As a brief FYI, the basic Read permission is a composite of the *query value, enumerate subkeys, notify, and read control* permissions, while the Full Control permission, as you may expect, is a grouping of all ten.

When you assign or change permissions on a Registry key, you can grant Read or Full Control permissions to any users and groups defined on that system, including domain users and groups if you're on a Windows 2000 network. Windows 2000 maintains each user or group's permissions separately; that is, you can grant user *X* Full Control permission to a particular key, if you like, but restrict user *Y* to Read permission only.

You must be the owner of a key to be able to assign or change its permissions. (If you're logged on as an Administrator, then you can take ownership of any key that you don't already own.) You must also be running REGEDT32 in Read-and-Write mode as opposed to Read-Only mode.

At this point, you may be asking yourself, "Doesn't Windows 2000 automatically apply the appropriate permissions to Registry keys?" The answer is "pretty much yes," but one size doesn't necessarily fit all. The Windows 2000 installation program doesn't know what level of security you may need, so it assigns Registry permissions that should work well for a broad audience but that may not work well for more security-conscious customers.

For a pretty good rundown on Registry permissions, check Microsoft's Web site for the white paper titled "Windows 2000 Security — Default Access Control Settings."

Protecting against viruses

Here's an example that demonstrates why you may need to know this stuff and, as a bonus, illustrates the main principles of setting Registry key permissions. A number of recent viruses insert a value in one of the Registry keys *HKLM\SOFTWARE\Microsoft\Windows\CurrentVersion\Run, . . .\RunOnce, . . .\RunOnceEx, . . .\App Paths,* or *. . .\Uninstall*. These keys specify software to run at the next restart (the first three), when a program is run by a user (*. . .\App Paths*), or when software is removed (*. . .\Uninstall*).

Now, many organizations routinely apply security settings to NT PCs using predefined templates. As some companies have already discovered, applying the basic NT workstation template to Windows 2000 lets the Everyone group have full control over these sensitive Registry keys. (What actually happens is the Everyone group gets its Full Control permission at *HKLM\SOFT-WARE\Microsoft\ Windows,* which then propagates downward to subkeys of that key through permission *inheritance*.)

The only drawback to the following procedure, which protects your Registry from virus attacks, is that you may need to be logged on as Administrator to install certain software applications in the future. The reason is that some installer programs legitimately need to access one or more of these five keys. If you're comfortable with such a limitation, proceed. I think it's a good trade-off for most situations.

Here's how to change this situation to better protect your system from a virus attack if an NT template was applied to your system.

1. **Open REGEDT32 by choosing Start⇨Run and then typing** REGEDT32.

2. **Navigate to *HKLM\SOFTWARE\Microsoft\Windows\ CurrentVersion\Run* and select this key in the left windowpane.**

3. **Choose Security⇨Permissions.**

   This command displays the Access Control List Editor window, here called Permissions for Run, as shown in Figure 7-1. Notice that the Allow check boxes toward the bottom of the window are grayed out, a problem that the next step fixes.

4. **Deselect the check box labeled** Allow Inheritable Permissions from Parent to Propagate to Phis Object.

The normal behavior is for each Registry key to inherit the same permissions as its parent key. We need to change the permissions, though, so we have to disable the inheritance feature first.

5. **In the Security dialog box, click the Copy button.**

   This dialog box, shown in Figure 7-2, tells Windows 2000 to copy the permissions from the parent key into the present key (that is, *Run*), but to then let you modify them. After you click Copy, notice that the check boxes under Permissions are no longer grayed out.

6. **Click Everyone under the Name column toward the top of the Permissions for Run dialog box.**

7. **Deselect the Full Control check box under the Allow column in the Permissions area.**

   You have now removed the Full Control permission from the Everyone group and secured your Registry against some kinds of virus attacks.

8. **Lather, rinse, and repeat Steps 1 through 7 for the keys . . .\RunOnce, . . .\RunOnceEx, . . .\App Paths, and . . .\Uninstall.**

9. **Click OK and then close the Registry Editor.**

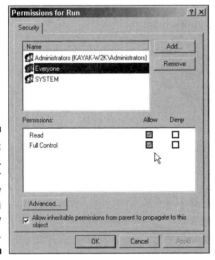

Figure 7-1:
The ACL
Editor
window
lets you
change key
permissions.

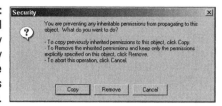

Figure 7-2:
You'll
normally
click Copy
to select the
parent key's
permissions.

Controlling remote Registry access

You can use Registry key permissions to control who can and can't edit a given Windows 2000 PC's Registry remotely (that is, across a network or dial-up link). If you add or remove users or groups from the permission list of a special Registry key, you simultaneously enable or disable those users or groups from accessing that machine's Registry remotely.

The special key in question is *HKLM\SYSTEM\CurrentControlSet\Control\ SecurePipeServers\winreg.* By default, only administrators can modify this key. Backup operators have Read permission, which gives them the ability to back up the Registries of remote PCs.

You should leave the *Machine* value under the *AllowedPaths* subkey alone; it specifies Registry paths that Windows 2000 services may need to access from anywhere on the network, and that are exempt from the remote-access restrictions that you set with the *winreg* key.

Controlling remote Performance Monitor access

Set permissions on the *HKLM\SOFTWARE\Microsoft\Windows NT\ CurrentVersion\Perflib* key to govern which users and groups have permission to run Performance Monitor (PERFMON.MSC) over a network or dial-up link. Removing permissions for INTERACTIVE is not a bad idea (this special predefined group includes any user logged on interactively). If you add users or groups here, also make sure you add them in the *winreg* key permissions (see the previous section).

Auditing Registry events

You can use Registry *auditing* to monitor certain activities that require Registry access. You can specify the type of activities that Windows 2000 will audit, as well as which Registry keys. For example, you could enable auditing for successful *Create Subkey* events on the *HKLM\SOFTWARE* and *HKCU\ Software* keys in order to track users who may be installing their own programs.

Audited activities appear in the Security event log, which you can view by choosing Start➪Settings➪Control Panel➪Administrative Tools➪Event Viewer.

Turning auditing on

To enable auditing of Registry events, you first have to enable auditing generally. Windows 2000 ships with auditing turned off. To turn it on, you have to log on with Administrator privileges.

You can enable auditing through a domain-based policy (see the "Securing Computers and Users with Policies" section later in this chapter) on a domain controller running Windows 2000 Server. Or, you can enable auditing on a stand-alone computer (that is, a Windows 2000 Professional PC or a non-domain-controller Windows 2000 Server PC) using the local Group Policy editor (choose Start➪Run, type **GPEDIT.MSC,** and navigate to Computer Configuration\Windows Settings\Security Settings\Local Policies\Audit Policy). Using the check boxes, enable success and failure for the "object access" category (see Figure 7-3), or, on a Windows 2000 Server acting as a domain controller, "directory service access."

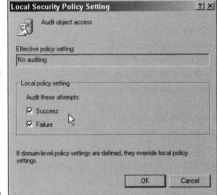

Figure 7-3: Activating "object" auditing for a stand-alone machine.

Telling Windows what to audit

After you turn on the auditing feature for the PC, you can run REGEDT32 to specify which keys and which Registry-related actions you want to audit. In the following example, you can set *HKLM\SOFTWARE* and its child keys to log Create Subkey events and thereby track software installations.

1. **Choose Start➪Run and type** REGEDT32 **to start the Registry Editor.**

   (You can't enable auditing with REGEDIT.)

2. **Highlight *HKLM\SOFTWARE* and choose Security➪Permissions.**

3. **Click the Advanced button and then the Auditing tab.**

4. **Click the Add button, select Everyone, and click OK.**

   You've just specified that you want to audit every user on the system who may access *HKLM\SOFTWARE*. You should now see the dialog box in Figure 7-4.

5. **Click the check box in the Create Subkey row and the Successful column of the Auditing Entry for SOFTWARE dialog box.**

   You've just specified that you want to audit successful attempts to create new subkeys under *HKLM\SOFTWARE*. If you wanted to audit failed attempts to perform a given action, you'd select a box in the Failed column.

6. **Click OK three times to close the dialog boxes, and exit REGEDT32.**

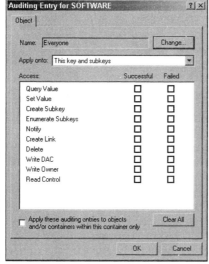

Figure 7-4:
Telling
Windows
what
Registry
actions to
audit.

If you want to add your own subkey manually to *HKLM\SOFTWARE* and then check the Event Viewer's Security log, you can see the sort of entry that Windows 2000 creates for you.

Don't go overboard on auditing. In particular, if you audit failures for read operations (such as "read" and "query value"), you'll get way too much information, because Windows 2000 and lots of Windows programs normally read the Registry to see whether some particular data is there. (If the read fails, then the program knows the data isn't there.) Also, excessive auditing can bog down your system's performance.

Securing Computers and Users with Policies

Policies in Windows 2000 provide a way of enforcing many of the security measures that I discuss in the "Windows 2000 Security in Six Pages or Less" section earlier in this chapter. (If you haven't read that section yet, you should do so now.) Policies aren't the only way of enforcing security; see the sidebar "Tool time" for a few words on the Security Configuration Tool Set. However, generally speaking, policies are the preferred and Microsoft-recommended method for implementing Registry-based security. They are the security guards at the gates to your house, with responsibility for applying the guidelines that you, the homeowner, have set ("Don't let anyone through if they're selling magazine subscriptions so that they can spend two weeks in Bermuda").

Companies also use policies to bring consistency to a network and thereby reduce both training and support costs, but the focus in this chapter is on the security angle. And for those of you who aren't using a network and are just about to skip this section, you can use policies on a stand-alone PC, too, so please don't flip forward just yet!

Policies work by automagically modifying the Registry whenever you boot the PC, whenever you log on, and even periodically *while* you're logged on, so that a predefined set of Registry settings (the policies) is always in place on your PC. The core concept is just that simple, even if the implementation details can get a bit complicated.

Windows NT 4.0 veterans will want to know that Microsoft has moved the policies feature around so that it's now intimately tied in with the new Active Directory database. If you're familiar with policies under NT 4.0, you may still need that knowledge if you work on a network that still has NT 4.0 clients, because such clients don't understand Windows 2000-style policies. (They can still use NT 4.0-style policies on a Windows 2000 server, however, and Windows 9x clients can use 9x-style policies as well.) But if you're working in a pure Windows 2000 network, you can pretty much forget most of what you knew in the past about "system policies," because the tools and terms and files and settings are different now.

To keep things simple, or at least *simpler,* this section doesn't deal much with Windows NT 4.0-style system policies or with the old System Policy Editor tool. Those technologies still work basically as they did in Windows NT 4.0; for example, NT-style policies don't apply until a user logs on (whereas some Windows 2000 policies apply during startup). You may also be interested to know that the System Policy Editor doesn't even come with Windows 2000 Professional anymore; you need one of the Server versions to get it, and it installs with the administrative tools package (ADMINPAK.MSI on the CD). That's sort of a shame, because the System Policy Editor still makes a user-friendly Registry Editor for some settings, but Microsoft really wants you to use Windows 2000-style policies now. The *Microsoft Windows NT 4.0 Resource Kit* is a good source if you need details on NT 4.0-style policies.

Accessing the Group Policy snap-in

You modify policies in Windows 2000 using one of several tools. For local policies, which are the ones I look at here, you use the Local Group Policy snap-in, which you can start by choosing Start⇨Run and then entering **GPEDIT.MSC**. (The MSC suffix, as explained in Chapter 3, denotes a Microsoft Management Console [MMC] program, which works a lot like a control panel.) Expand the hierarchies a little and you see something like Figure 7-5.

Tool time

Policies aren't the only way that you can apply security-related Registry settings in Windows 2000. You can also use the *Security Configuration Tool Set*, which consists of various Microsoft Management Console snap-ins that act sort of like control panels, as well as a command-prompt tool called SECEDIT.

You can use the Security Configuration Tool Set to create *security templates* (text-based INF files) and then apply the settings those INF files contain to specific machines. The security templates can specify Registry settings to create or change; they can even modify Registry key access control lists (ACLs). (Sample templates live in the folder C:\WINNT\SECURITY\ TEMPLATES; you can view them in Notepad, but they're pretty cryptic. You're better off viewing them with the Security Templates snap-in, which you can see by running **MMC /S** from the Run dialog box, choosing Console⇨ Add/Remove Snap-In, clicking Add, and adding the snap-in from the list.)

The unattractive aspect of using the Security Configuration Tool Set on a network is that change isn't automatic. That is, if you want to modify security on one or more PCs, you have to fire up these tools again, make your changes, and reapply them to the PCs. On the other hand, Windows 2000 applies policies to each PC at every logon and at periodic intervals between logons. So you can change the policies later and let Windows 2000 worry about reapplying them to each PC.

If you're using a stand-alone PC, then you may want to look into the Security Configuration Tool Set more deeply (I still suggest you try using local policies to accomplish your security goals, however). The Tool Set is complex, but Microsoft has published a helpful technical document on its Web site. Search www.microsoft.com (or TechNet, if you have it) for "Using the Security Configuration Tool Set" and work through the examples in that document.

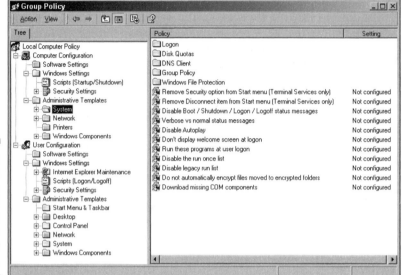

Figure 7-5:
Getting
ready to
set local
policies in
Windows
2000
Professional.

I don't know who names Microsoft's software utilities, but whoever came up with the name "Group Policy" should be stripped of a couple million dollars' worth of stock options. This utility should have a name like "Group Policy Editor" or "Group Policy Tool," but it's just "Group Policy."

You can change various local policies from this console. Your changes end up in the folder `C:\WINNT\SYSTEM32\GROUPPOLICY`, and Windows 2000 applies them from that location before processing any network-based policies (if any).

If you're working on a network and want to create policies to apply to, say, every user in a particular domain, then you would use the Active Directory Users and Computers console on a domain controller, instead of the Local Group Policy console on a workstation. (Much less work that way! Windows 2000 handles the distribution of network-based policy settings behind the scenes.)

Computer and user policies

Right away, you notice that the left windowpane of the Group Policy management console has two main divisions: Computer Configuration and User Configuration. The first category makes modifications to *HKLM,* which occur when the computer starts, and the second makes modifications to *HKCU,* which occur when a user logs on. This division ensures the ongoing separation in the Registry between machine-specific settings and user-specific settings, enabling users to "roam" from PC to PC if they so choose and having their preferences and settings follow them around.

Each big category has three smaller categories under it: Software Settings, Windows Settings, and Administrative Templates.

- ✔ **Software Settings** has to do with the Group Policy tool's ability to publish and assign programs to network users.

- ✔ **Windows Settings** has to do with scripts that you can write to take place at startup and shutdown, and security settings (many of which affect the Registry, some of which only affect Active Directory).

- ✔ **Administrative Templates** has to do entirely with Registry-based policies. Some of these settings are security-related, too, which can be a little confusing. Windows NT 4.0-style templates can work with this category, as the next section explains.

As you expand the Group Policy tree structure, you eventually see entries labeled Policy in the right-hand windowpane. Although it would take about two hundred pages to describe all of these, doing so would be a serious waste of paper, because Microsoft has done a great job providing some online help here. Double-click any policy in the right windowpane and click the Explain tab to get copious details on the effects of that particular policy.

Microsoft takes some lumps in this book, but these new policy explanations are greatly helpful, and Microsoft deserves a round of applause. Nicely done.

Templates

A couple of words now on the subject of the Administrative Templates feature, which allows the Group Policy console to work with Windows NT 4.0-style *.ADM template files. This simply means that you can import sets of Registry settings from a predefined text file having the suffix ADM, and define how you want those Registry settings to look. ADM files let you make a wider variety of Registry settings part of your policy structure. A template file is nothing more than a list of policies that you can set; the template provides the choices and knows which Registry keys to change as a result.

Try this experiment: Right-click the Administrative Templates node in the left windowpane and choose Add/Remove Templates. Click the Add button and you see a list of additional templates, all with the ADM suffix (they live in C:\WINNT\INF). Using the Add/Remove Templates command, you could specify an ADM file that would let you customize Registry settings for, say, Office 2000, or any other application software that ships with an ADM template. (You can even write your own template files, but that's beyond the scope of this book!)

Policies on the network

On a Windows 2000 Server network, group policies can do more than "merely" modify the Registry. They can also control software distribution (through the Windows Installer service), folder redirection (such as pointing the My Documents folder to a network location), and startup and shutdown scripts (such as those you might write with VBScript or JavaScript).

Network-based policies become part of the Active Directory database, rather than the Registry, but network-based policies can still modify computer and user Registry settings when clients power up and log on. In fact, network-based policies still do all the things that the Local Group Policy console can do when it comes to modifying the Registry.

The big difference with network-based policies is that you can set them up to apply to an entire network site, domain, or organizational unit. (These three terms have very specific meanings in the context of Active Directory; look into *Active Directory For Dummies* by Marcia Loughry [published by IDG Books Worldwide, Inc.] for details.) You can then create access control lists, similar to the ones REGEDT32 uses to assign key permissions that filter policies by group membership. Being able to assign policies in this way is a fantastic time-saver, because you don't have to run around to every PC on the network. Windows 2000 handles the policy "propagation" for you — but remember, only Windows 2000 clients can see Windows 2000 network-based policies!

Figure 7-6 shows the Group Policy tab of the property sheet for the domain named `main-domain.isi.com`. To get there, I right-clicked the domain's icon in the Active Directory Users and Computers management console on a Windows 2000 Server domain controller. Clicking the Edit button brings up a window very similar to the Local Group Policy console.

When you apply network-based policies in Windows 2000, remember the pecking order. Local policies are applied first, then site, domain, and organizational unit policies. Therefore, local policies are the weakest, because they can get overridden at three subsequent levels. If a policy doesn't seem to be working, a higher-level policy may be coutermanding it.

Group Policy modifies the Registry keys *HKLM\SOFTWARE\Policies*, *HKLM\SOFTWARE\Microsoft\Windows\CurrentVersion\Policies*, *HKCU\Software\Policies*, and *HKCU\Software\Microsoft\CurrentVersion\Policies*. (Note that by default, non-administrators do not have write access to these keys.) The Group Policy utility cleans these keys out if, for example, a user's group membership changes. This behavior is an improvement over how Windows NT 4.0 handled policies, in that in NT 4.0, policy settings could be scattered throughout the Registry and weren't always cleaned out when users changed a group affiliation. (Registry settings that don't get cleaned up are called "tattoos," in that they don't come off without a certain degree of pain.)

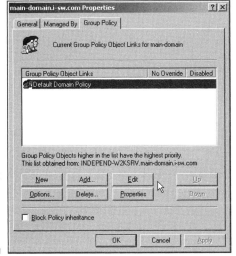

Another difference is that with the Windows 2000 Group Policy tools, it is somewhat of a pain to set policies for specific users — something that Windows NT 4.0 made relatively easy to do. Microsoft really wants you to assign policies by site, domain, organizational unit, or group.

The best bit of advice I can offer regarding network-based policies that don't seem to be working is to make sure you've set up DNS (Domain Name Services) properly. The Group Policy feature is mighty sensitive to DNS problems, such as the lack of a properly set reverse-lookup zone on the DNS server. The online help for Windows 2000 Server has a lot of details on setting up Microsoft DNS. Once you follow those guidelines and get DNS working right, I'm betting your Group Policy problems go away. If they don't, please call me at home, anytime. I'm at 212-555-1212.

Chapter 8

Customizing User Profiles

• •

In This Chapter

▶ Finding out what user profiles can do for you

▶ Discovering what user profiles do to your Registry and your PC

▶ Setting up local and roaming user profiles

▶ Customizing the default user profile

▶ Removing and copying user profiles

• •

> *I am very fussy about the little things that matter in my workplace. The*
> *pedals have to be positioned just right, and so do the footrests, the steering*
> *wheel and gear lever as otherwise I just cannot concentrate on driving.*
>
> —From *The Art and Science of Grand Prix Driving,*
> Niki Lauda, Motorbooks International, 1977

*I*n Microsoft's public pronouncements about Windows 2000 and why the
world should move to it, something called *IntelliMirror* inevitably comes
up. This term is very broad, but the general idea behind IntelliMirror is providing increased mobility, flexibility, and fault tolerance for people who work
on a network. The network contains a mirror image of all that is important on
your own workstation.

As is so often the case when you start studying a new buzzword, the underlying technology isn't all that new. A big part of the IntelliMirror technology set
is none other than the *user profiles* feature that has been around in earlier
versions of Windows (both 9*x* and NT) for some time now. User profiles in
Windows 2000 still do what they've always done; that is, let different users
share one or more PCs while maintaining their own individual settings and
preferences — desktop icons, Start menu, application settings, network connections, and so on. (I think of user profiles like those electrically adjustable
car seats with memory, where you can push one button and the seat changes
in 49 different directions to fit the contours of your body.)

But user profiles now fit into a broader set of technologies. Windows 2000 provides options for you to have not only your Registry-based user preferences follow you from one PC to another, but your data files and programs, too. True, in the past you could always achieve pretty much the same benefits by simply keeping documents and applications on network servers, either in addition to or instead of keeping them on local hard drives. Windows 2000 adds some mechanisms for keeping local copies of preferences, data files, and programs synchronized, more or less automatically, with network copies. The downside is twofold: You have to have a pure Windows 2000 network for many IntelliMirror features to work, and the performance demands on the network can be draining.

As this is a Registry book, this chapter's focus is on one very specific spoke on the IntelliMirror wheel: the ways that Windows 2000 keeps user-specific Registry settings separate. But even though user profiles are a key enabler of IntelliMirror, this chapter is definitely not just for network workers. User profiles have their most obvious appeal in the network situation, but they also have important uses on stand-alone machines. So even if IntelliMirror doesn't rev your engine, user profiles may nevertheless come in handy.

What's a User Profile?

Okay, so a user profile is a set of "user-specific preferences and settings." What does that mean in English? I can't tell you . . . I'm a technical writer! Seriously, you can think of a user profile as containing two big categories of information: Registry information and non-Registry information.

- **Registry stuff:** This is basically everything in the *HKCU* branch: Windows customizations such as control panel settings, Explorer viewing options, printer connections, Dial-Up Networking connections, command prompt window settings, and any user-specific settings for Windows applications — stuff like whether your word processor checks your spelling as you type, whether you like your spreadsheets to print with gridlines, and so on. (See the "What Profiles Do to the Registry" section a little later in this chapter for a more complete list.)

- **Non-Registry stuff:** This is everything in the subfolders under `C:\Documents and Settings\<username>`, as shown in Figure 8-1. (If you upgraded from Windows NT 4.0, your profile folders live in `C:\WINNT\PROFILES`.) You mostly see shortcuts in these folders, but some of 'em contain actual data files, most notably the My Documents folder. Non-Registry stuff includes the recently used documents list, user-specific Start menu shortcuts, Internet Explorer *cookies,* contents of the Network Neighborhood and Printers folders, lists of favorite documents or Web sites, history lists, and so on.

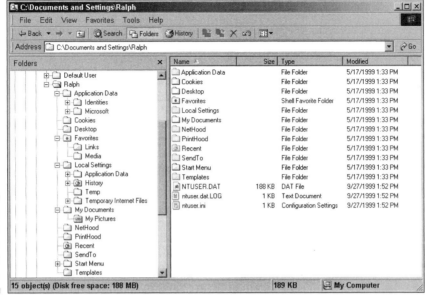

Figure 8-1:
Typical user
profile
folder
structure.

One point needs clarification. You should see an "All Users" folder in the main profile folder of your machine. The contents of this folder — usually some Start menu shortcuts and other scattered miscellany — *combine* with the contents of a user's individual profile folders to create the actual user profile. So, for example, the actual Start menu that you see is really the sum of all the shortcuts in `C:\Documents and Settings\<username>\Start Menu`, plus all the "community" shortcuts in `C:\Documents and Settings\All Users\Start Menu`. Only administrators can add, change, or delete contents of the `All Users` folder.

On a related note, if you're wanting to make a particular program available to every user on the system, just log on as an Administrator and put the appropriate shortcut into the All Users folder. (You can also right-click the Start menu and choose "Open All Users" to achieve the same result.)

When to Use Profiles

One of the cleverer things about the Registry is the way it separates user-specific settings from machine-specific settings. This need to split is the whole idea behind putting user-specific stuff in NTUSER.DAT and USRCLASS.DAT. These two files don't have to come from the same location as the other Registry files in `C:\WINNT\SYSTEM32\CONFIG` — unlike the situation with

Windows 3.*x*, where all your core INI files have to exist in the same directory on your disk. Furthermore, although you can only have one SYSTEM file, one SOFTWARE file, one SECURITY file, and so on, on any given PC, you can have an unlimited number of NTUSER.DAT and USRCLASS.DAT files.

Many drivers, one car

User profiles make it possible for different users to share the same computer and for each to keep his own settings. This capability comes in handy three ways:

- ✓ **Some companies still don't buy every employee a computer.** Have you ever seen a residential real estate office that has a single community PC for the agents to use when the need arises? In a situation like this, Broker A doesn't want to log on to the PC and deal with all the rearranging that Broker B did while using the PC previously.

- ✓ **Many families share the same PC at home.** Adults may enjoy occasionally visiting certain dimly lit alleyways off the information superhighway that they don't want their kids to be able to see. Or the adults in the house may want access to the household finances but don't want their teenagers copying their credit card numbers and ordering up designer snowboard equipment by mail.

- ✓ **Windows 2000 predefines different kinds of users for different situations.** Running Windows 2000 as an Administrator for daily use is a bad idea, because your system is most vulnerable to errors and attacks when you're logged on with maximum rights. So you want an Administrator account for certain occasions but a User or Power User account for routine work.

If you use a notebook PC, you may even want to set up different software configurations for when you're using your notebook at work and at home. You can log on as BobWork and see all the serious stuff; log on as BobPlay and see your fun programs and icons.

For desktop users who must all share the same computer, road warriors who use the same computer in different settings, and security-conscious users who don't want to put their system at needless risk, user profiles can come to the rescue. That is, *local* user profiles, the kind that live on a single PC.

Nomad's LAN

Nowadays, most PCs in medium-to-large businesses connect in networks. One of the benefits of networking is that you can (theoretically, at least) sit down at any PC, wherever you happen to be at the time, and work as efficiently as though you were at your regular PC.

The ability to log on to any PC is handy for technical support people who have to hoof it around the office working on different users' computers. You can also find networking handy when your usual computer is a slacker of a first-generation Pentium, but the woman in the neighboring cubicle has a zippy Pentium III (or is it ///?), and she's off on vacation for a week. Finally, if you work in a company that frequently reorganizes people and teams, you'll be happy that you don't have to lug your PC to your new workplace in order to get working again.

Bringing the theory of roaming users into the real world takes a bit of doing, however. For example, Richard may go to some lengths to get his Windows 2000 desktop the way he wants it:

- Richard has crummy eyesight, so he likes larger than normal icon titles.
- Richard digs Porsches, and he puts a picture of the 944S2 that he will never be able to afford onto his system as wallpaper.
- Richard uses five or six programs on a regular basis, so he customizes his Start menu and his desktop shortcut icons so that he can launch those programs fast.
- Richard works with a dozen or so data files routinely, too, so they get convenient desktop icons, as well.

After all, PCs aren't called *personal* computers for nothing. Now, when Richard moves over to Jeanine's fast Pentium III machine, he doesn't want to have to live with small icon titles, a picture of Jeanine's Chrysler minivan for wallpaper, and a different set of desktop icons and Start menu options that don't pertain to what Richard does for a living. He darned sure doesn't want to muck around with Jeanine's PC so that it looks the way he wants, only to have her jump down his throat when she comes back from the Paris-Dakar rally two days early. Richard's situation is a job for . . . *user profiles.* Specifically, *roaming* user profiles, the kind that follow a user around across a network.

Setting Up User Profiles

The procedure for setting up user profiles depends on whether you're working with local profiles or roaming profiles. This section takes the simpler case first.

Local profiles

Local profiles are user profiles that live on a particular PC as opposed to a network location. To clarify, a *local* profile doesn't mean that the user account must be on a stand-alone, non-networked PC. You can have a local profile for a network user account as well as for a stand-alone user account.

The thing to remember is that regardless of the type of user and regardless of the version of Windows 2000 (Professional or Server), a local profile stays on the local hard drive of a single PC. If you take a local profile for a network user account and then give it a new home so that it lives on the network instead of solely on the local hard drive, then it becomes a "roaming" profile, as described in the next section.

With Windows 2000, unlike Windows 95/98, you don't have to take a separate step to activate user profiles; the feature is already "on," you just have to create the user accounts and log on with them. Unlike Windows 95/98, however, you can't necessarily just log on with a new username and have Windows 2000 create an account for you automatically. You have to create the account ahead of time and then log on.

Which tool you must use and which procedure you must follow to create a local profile depends on your circumstances, as follows:

- ✔ On a Windows 2000 Professional machine that's *not* on a network domain, fire up the Users and Passwords control panel. The detailed example right after this bulleted list shows you how.

- ✔ On a Windows 2000 Professional machine that *is* on a network domain where you want to add a user who's already defined on the domain, run the Users and Passwords control panel, or simply log on to Windows 2000 Professional as that user.

- ✔ On a Windows 2000 Professional machine that *is* on a network domain where you want to add a local (non-domain) user, run the Users and Passwords control panel and use the Advanced tab.

- ✔ On a Windows 2000 Server acting as a domain controller, use the Active Directory Users and Computers snap-in. (It's normally in the Administrative Tools folder in the control panel window.)

- ✔ On a Windows 2000 Server *not* acting as a domain controller, use the Computer Management snap-in (which also normally lives in the Administrative Tools folder).

To run the Users and Passwords control panel, the Active Directory Users and Computers snap-in, or the Computer Management snap-in, you must log on as Administrator. Windows 2000 cares about security, so only an Administrator can create a new user account.

The following example runs through the procedure for setting up a new local user profile on a Windows 2000 Professional system that's not part of a domain-based network — the first of the four scenarios just mentioned. (For advice on setting up a new local nondomain user on a PC that *is* part of a domain, see the Tip icon at the end of the example.)

1. **Choose Start⇨Settings⇨Control Panel and double-click the Users and Passwords icon.**

   The existing user accounts appear on the Users tab (see Figure 8-2).

2. **Click the Add button on the Users tab and type in a username and other optional account info.**

   The full name and description are optional.

3. **Click the Next button and type in the user's password.**

   You have to type it twice in order to confirm it — a good safeguard if you type like I do.

4. **Click the Next button and specify the user's group membership (see Figure 8-3).**

   The default choice of Standard User makes the new user a member of the predefined Power Users group, which has lots of privileges on the system but not as many as an Administrator. To secure the account more tightly, choose Restricted User, which makes the new user a member of the predefined Users group. Or you can pick a group of your choosing from the drop-down list box. (If you want the user to belong to more than one group, set that up later, using the Users and Passwords control panel's Advanced tab and Advanced button.)

5. **Click the Finish button to create the account and redisplay the Users and Passwords dialog box.**

   The new user should now appear. You can come back to this control panel later to change the user's account password, change its group membership, or remove the account. (The Users and Passwords control panel can't do those things with a domain account on a networked PC, though.)

6. **Click OK to close the control panel.**

7. **Choose Start⇨Shut Down and then select the Log Off <username> check box and then log on as the new user.**

   Windows 2000 then builds the new local user profile on the hard disk. This set of folders and Registry files lives under `C:\Documents and Settings\<username>`, or under `C:\WINNT\PROFILES\<username>` if you updated your PC from Windows NT 4.0. The main user profile folder should contain a fresh copy of the hidden files NTUSER.DAT and NTUSER.DAT.LOG, and if you ferret down to the subfolder `C:\Documents and Settings\<username>\Local Settings\Application Data\Microsoft\Windows`, you'll see the other Registry files USRCLASS.DAT and USRCLASS.DAT.LOG. Your Registry has been cloned!

Figure 8-2:
Start here to
create a
new local
user profile.

Figure 8-3:
Put the new
user into a
predefined
local group.

When you create your new local user account, you create a password, too. You can use the Local Group Policy utility (choose Start⇨Run and enter **GPEDIT.MSC** and then navigate to Computer Configuration\Windows Settings\Security Settings\Account Policies\Password Policy) to place various Registry-based restrictions on the machine and make user passwords more secure for all accounts on that machine.

Roaming profiles

Creating a roaming profile allows a user to log on to any PC on the domain and have a server download his settings to that PC immediately after logon.

So, the basic procedure for creating a roaming profile is to create a folder on the server for storing profile data, point the specific user's account to that profile folder, and (optionally) load that server-based folder with customized profile information that Windows 2000 will download the next time the user logs on at any PC. Here's a bit more detail (this example assumes the user's domain account already exists):

1. **Log on to a domain controller as** Administrator.

2. **Using Windows Explorer, create a new profiles folder (such as** C:\PROFILES**).**

3. **Right-click the new folder, choose Sharing, share the folder as "PROFILES," and give the Everyone group the Full Control permission.**

   Each user's individual profile folder will live beneath the main C:\PROFILES folder.

4. **Run the Active Directory Users and Computers plug-in from the control panel's Administrative Tools folder.**

5. **Navigate to the user's icon, right-click it, and choose Properties.**

6. **On the Profile tab (see Figure 8-4), type the path to the user's profile folder, such as** \\server\profiles\bob.

7. **Optionally, run the System control panel, click User Profiles, and copy a template profile to the user's profile folder to "preload" it.**

Creating a local profile on a Windows 2000 domain

What if you want to add a local user profile, but your PC is part of a Windows 2000 domain? Here's the procedure:

1. **Make sure the user account that you want to add to the PC already exists as a domain user account.**

   Create it on a Windows 2000 domain controller if you need to; the "Users and Passwords" control panel won't let you create a new local user account that doesn't already exist on the domain.

2. **Open the Users and Passwords control panel, click the Advanced tab, click the**

Advanced button, and then right-click the Users folder and choose New User from the context menu.

You might guess (as I did) that clicking the Add button on the Users tab of the control panel would accomplish the same result, but it doesn't.

3. **Fill in the new user's information in the dialog box and close out.**

If this procedure seems needlessly complex to you, I agree, but Microsoft recommends against adding local users to domain computers; maybe this is its way of discouraging the practice.

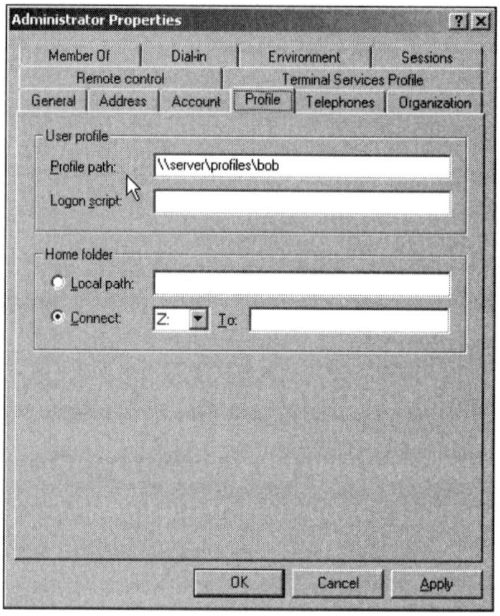

Figure 8-4:
Modifying a
user's
Active
Directory
properties.

By default, the folders History, Local Settings, Temp, and Temporary Internet Files do not "roam" with the user. (They typically contain too much stuff; having these files roam would bog down the network.) You can specify additional files that you'd like to exclude from the roaming profile. Run the Group Policy utility (see Chapter 7 for details) and modify the Exclude Directories in Roaming Profile policy. You can find it under User Configuration\Administrative Templates\System\Logon-Logoff. This policy modifies the text file C:\Documents and Settings\<*username*>\NTUSER.INI.

If you want to change a roaming profile back to a nonroaming profile, or (for that matter) vice versa, run the System control panel's User Profiles tab and click the Change Type button to display the Change Profile Type dialog box (see Figure 8-5). If the "roaming profile" choice appears dimmed, as in the figure, then the user account is probably not a domain account — or no profile directory has been set up for it yet.

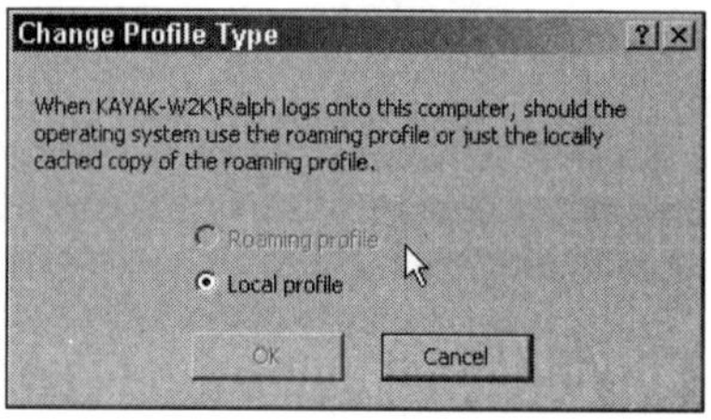

Figure 8-5:
Changing a
profile's
type.

What Profiles Do to the Registry

Here's a brief list of the Registry-based settings that Windows 2000 user profiles keep separate for each user:

- ✔ User interface settings, such as color schemes, desktop icons, icon spacing and titles, wallpaper, sounds, and so on
- ✔ Most control panel settings, including the display size and color depth
- ✔ Printer settings
- ✔ Dial-Up Networking connections
- ✔ Application-specific settings (as long as the applications support user profiles), such as menu layouts and window customization
- ✔ Network-related information such as preferred logon server, shared resources, and so on
- ✔ Taskbar settings
- ✔ What kind of doughnuts you like in the morning (*HKCU\ FatteningFoods\ Morning\PreferredType*)
- ✔ Per-user object class information (such as file type associations, like BMP and Paint)

You can look at the effect of user profiles on the Registry from two angles: the files (physical structure) and the keys (logical structure).

Now where's that file?

User-specific settings live in the NTUSER.DAT and USRCLASS.DAT Registry files. When you log on, you tell Windows 2000 that it needs to look in a particular place for your particular NTUSER.DAT and USRCLASS.DAT files. Exactly *where* Windows 2000 looks depends on whether you're in a multiple-user-per-PC situation or a roaming-network-user situation.

Local profile files

On a non-networked PC, Windows 2000 doesn't bother checking a network server because one doesn't exist. If a PC is networked but you haven't enabled roaming profiles, then Windows 2000 looks up user profile information in much the same way that it does on a non-networked PC.

Here's what happens. When you start Windows 2000, it activates the DEFAULT file in C:\WINNT\SYSTEM32\CONFIG as a sort of "system" user profile whose sole purpose in life is to display the Welcome to Windows screen. Then, as soon as you press Ctrl+Alt+Del and log on with a username, Windows 2000 proceeds directly to a new, user-specific NTUSER.DAT file in a special location.

The special location of the NTUSER.DAT file is under the master profile directory C:\Documents and Settings (it's C:\WINNT\PROFILES if you upgraded from Windows NT 4.0), in a subdirectory that's the same as your username. The NTUSER.DAT and USRCLASS.DAT files in C:\Documents and Settings\ *<username>* override the settings for the DEFAULT file in C:\WINNT\SYSTEM32\ CONFIG, which Windows 2000 loaded just moments earlier.

Every time you add a user to a Windows 2000 system (for example, with the Users and Passwords control panel), Windows 2000 creates a new subdirectory under C:\Documents and Settings and puts a new NTUSER.DAT in that subdirectory, based on the default user information in C:\Documents and Settings\Default User\NTUSER.DAT. Windows 2000 also creates a new USRCLASS.DAT file, which is buried in C:\Documents and Settings\ *<username>*\Local Settings\Application Data\Microsoft\Windows. This file contains any per-user object class information, such as the fact that Emily wants to run Photoshop and not Internet Explorer when she double-clicks a JPG file.

Associated with both NTUSER.DAT and USRCLASS.DAT are LOG files that Windows 2000 uses to recover a Registry change if that change doesn't finish because of a crash or power glitch. And that's all you need to know about those files.

If Windows 2000 has a limit to the number of user profiles that you can define on a single machine, I haven't bumped into it yet.

Roaming profile files

On a networked PC with roaming profiles enabled, Windows 2000 maintains a user-specific copy of NTUSER.DAT under C:\Documents and Settings\ *<username>* just as it does with local profiles, but Windows 2000 keeps a copy on the network, too.

Here's what happens on the network. When you log on, Windows 2000 checks for an NTUSER.DAT file on your local hard drive in C:\Documents and Settings*<username>*, and it also checks for an NTUSER.DAT file in the user's profile directory on the server. (The user's profile directory where NTUSER.DAT resides used to be the *home directory* in Windows NT 4.0 Server, but in Windows 2000 Server, you can specify NTUSER.DAT to be anywhere you want.) If either copy of NTUSER.DAT is newer than the other, Windows 2000 updates the older version and then starts up. Ditto with USRCLASS.DAT.

Incidentally, Windows 2000 performs a similar comparison with all the non-Registry user profile stuff, too, including the My Documents and My Pictures folders. If a file hasn't changed, Windows 2000 doesn't download it — and that's a good thing, because otherwise network performance would really suffer from all the unnecessary file transfers.

When you log off, Windows 2000 copies any changed profile settings back to your profile folder on the network, so the latest settings and documents are available next time you log on — wherever you log on. (If this Registry shell game has you crosseyed and dizzy, see the sidebar, "Follow the bouncing Registry.")

Location data in the Registry

The Registry tries to keep track of itself. If you want to see where the Registry stores the location of user profile folders for all the different users defined on the PC, peek at *HKLM\SOFTWARE\Microsoft\Windows NT\CurrentVersion\ ProfileList*. Each user appears under a subkey named for that user's Security ID (SID). Under each SID subkey is a string value *ProfileImagePath,* which shows the path to the user's profile folder.

Follow the bouncing Registry

Windows 2000 compares the versions of NTUSER.DAT and USRCLASS.DAT on the server and on your local hard drive. Stop and think for a minute about why this is necessary. You may have logged onto Windows 2000 at your last work session when the network server was unavailable, in which case the files in `C:\Documents and Settings\<user-name>` are newer than the ones in your network profile directory. On the other hand, if you're roaming, then Windows 2000 must use the profile files in your network directory because your own NTUSER.DAT, USRCLASS.DAT, My Documents folder, and so on may not exist under `C:\Documents and Settings` on a particular PC's hard drive. Even if you've used a specific PC before, your user profile folders and files on that PC are bound to be stale.

If you change settings during a work session, Windows 2000 copies your local profile up to the network at shutdown to keep everything in synch (that's one reason why shutting down a networked PC can take longer than a stand-alone PC). Remember, you may log on to a different PC later, in which case Windows 2000 needs your updated profile data from your profile directory on the network.

This information can be a little confusing, so read this sidebar again a couple of times until you get the idea. If you think about it, this system is the only way roaming user profiles *could* work. And the design feature that makes this system possible is the ability to sling NTUSER.DAT and USRCLASS.DAT files around the network and onto different directories on the PC's hard drive, while leaving SYSTEM and the other machine-specific HKLM hives serenely nestled in `C:\WINNT\ SYSTEM32\CONFIG.`

Because that path includes the user's logon name, the *ProfileList* key is a quick way to correlate SIDs with users. Handy!

If you want to see the location of the currently logged-on user's profile files and folders in detail, look at the key *HKCU\Software\Microsoft\Windows\CurrentVersion\Explorer\Shell Folders,* shown in Figure 8-6.

Backups

What about backups? The main thing to note on this subject is that unless you're backing up the entire contents of the `C:\Documents and Settings` folder, you're not backing up all the user profiles on the machine. Even backing up the "System State" in NTBACKUP only copies the currently active NTUSER.DAT file, not all the other copies in other profile folders.

If you enable roaming profiles, then you always have a backup of sorts, because the user profile always exists on at least one PC and at least one server — at least, if you haven't excluded any profile folders from roaming, using the Group Policy tool. So you can breathe a little easier in this situation.

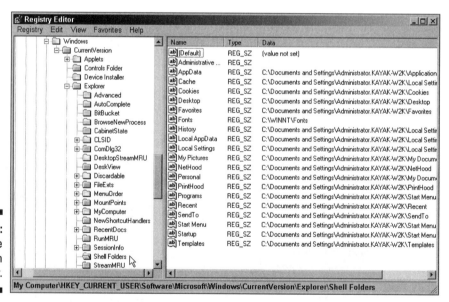

Figure 8-6:
Profile
locations in
the Registry.

Chapter 2 gives you some ideas for creating your own custom Registry backup solutions that can include user profile files.

A spare set of keys

The view from the Registry Editor changes when you activate user profiles, but things are a bit simpler from the standpoint of the Registry's logical structure. *HKU* contains two significant subkeys: *.DEFAULT,* plus a subkey named after the current user's Security ID (see Figure 8-7). (A third subkey, much smaller than the other two, has the name of the current user's Security ID plus the suffix "_Classes" and contains per-user object class information.)

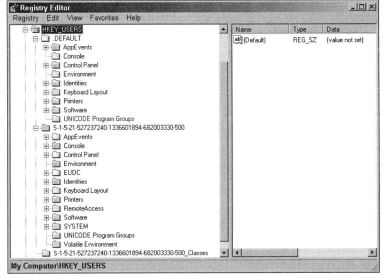

Figure 8-7:
The *HKU*
branch
shows the
default and
current user
profiles.

Even if you've created many different user profiles on a given Windows 2000 PC, only two users show up in *HKU* at any one time: *.DEFAULT* and the currently logged-on user. Any Registry changes that affect user settings, such as a user-specific control panel change, get logged to the subkey for the current user and don't affect the *.DEFAULT* subkey.

Now, you may reasonably assume that Windows 2000 uses the contents of *HKU\.DEFAULT* to create a new subkey with the user's name (corresponding to the new NTUSER.DAT file under `C:\Documents and Settings\<username>`) because that's how it works with Windows 9*x*. But that's just not the case in Windows 2000! The contents of *HKU\ .DEFAULT* are only used by Windows 2000 for defining the "prelogon" desktop, or, as Microsoft sometimes calls it, the *system user profile*. The actual starting point for creating a new user profile is the file `C:\Documents and Settings\Default User\NTUSER.DAT`. However, this file's contents don't show up in the Registry Editor.

What if you want to modify the NTUSER.DAT file in `C:\Documents and Settings\Default User`? You may want to modify the default user profile before creating other user profiles that base themselves on that default profile. Even though Windows 2000 doesn't load the default user profile in *HKU*, you can load it yourself. Just use REGEDT32 to open *HKU*, make sure *HKEY_USERS* is highlighted in the key pane, and choose Registry⇨Load Hive. In the Load Hive dialog box, navigate to `C:\Documents and Settings\Default User\NTUSER.DAT` and double-click it. Give the hive a temporary name, like *DEFUSER,* and then proceed to modify the key at will. For example, you could put a special wallpaper setting in *HKU\DEFUSER\Control Panel\Desktop.* When you're done, choose Registry⇨Unload Hive. From that point forward, any new user profile created on that PC reflects your custom settings.

Mandatory User Profiles

You can replace the NTUSER.DAT file that resides in the user's network directory with an NTUSER.DAT file that you want to make mandatory and unchangeable. Create a roaming profile folder as you would normally, copy the NTUSER.DAT file you want to use into that folder, rename it NTUSER.MAN, and you've created a mandatory user profile.

In the case of NTUSER.MAN, Windows 2000 never copies an NTUSER.DAT on the user's PC hard drive back to the network location, as it does with regular user profiles. Instead, Windows 2000 always uses the NTUSER.MAN file. It's as though you've made the file read-only.

If you're planning to use this feature, I suggest that you point a whole group of users to the same roaming profile folder, so you only have to manage one copy of NTUSER.MAN for the entire group. (For example, you could make periodic changes to the mandatory profile by modifying the profile settings on a test PC, logging off, logging on again as an Administrator, copying the profile back up to the network location using the User Profiles tab on the System control panel, and renaming the file NTUSER.MAN.)

Mandatory user profiles don't provide any control over the settings in the other Registry hives. You may be able to use group policies (see Chapter 7) in combination with mandatory user profiles, but doing so creates a security environment that's so complex that not many organizations would want to manage it. So, organizations typically choose group policies to impose restrictions on users, rather than mandatory user profiles. However, if you want to freeze user settings for application programs and if those programs don't come with policy templates that let you use group policies to impose restrictions, then you may need to consider mandatory user profiles.

Managing User Profiles

On a Windows 2000 Professional machine, you manage user profiles with the Users and Passwords control panel described earlier in this chapter, and with the System control panel's User Profiles tab (see Figure 8-8). Use the latter to delete a user profile, copy a profile from one location to another (you can't use Windows Explorer for this task), and change the type of profile from local to roaming or vice versa.

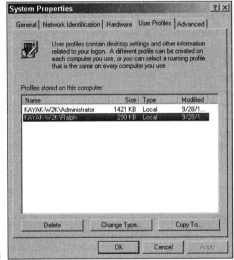

Figure 8-8:
The System control panel's User Profiles tab.

 Why did Microsoft confusingly put some profile commands on the System control panel and some on the Users and Passwords control panel? Maybe because unlike Windows 2000 Professional, Windows 2000 Server doesn't have the Users and Passwords control panel. Too bad Microsoft didn't create a unified User Profiles control panel that would appear on the Server and Professional versions and offer the appropriate options for each.

Profile Downsides

You pay a price for the convenience of user profiles. Well, actually, *three* prices. Just think of them as luxury taxes, and include them in your configuration planning so they don't surprise you.

Luxury tax 1: Performance

Local user profiles don't hurt you much in terms of performance (and, anyway, you can't turn 'em off!). However, roaming user profiles can hurt quite a bit. When users log on and off, Windows 2000 can heat up the LAN cables quite a bit downloading and uploading profile data — depending on how many folders are excluded from the roaming profile and how many changes to profile data have occurred since the last logon.

If you use Windows 2000's *folder redirection* capability to point the My Documents folder to a network location, then you lighten the performance burden that roaming profiles impose, because Windows 2000 doesn't copy the entire contents of the folder when synchronizing a user profile — just a shortcut to it. However, in a sense, you're robbing Peter to pay Paul, because the user will be putting more traffic onto the network in the normal course of using the My Documents folder than if the folder lived on the user's local hard drive. As the wise man said, there is no free lunch.

Luxury tax 2: Convenience

The second tax is on convenience. Managing your PC gets more complicated when you have a lot of user profiles. For one thing, backing up the Registry gets more involved because you have to worry about those individual NTUSER.DAT and USRCLASS.DAT files under C:\Documents and Settings\ <username>. If you don't back 'em all up when you back up your Registry and if you're unlucky enough to encounter a hard drive problem bad enough to affect several files, you may be up the creek. And even if you do back up the individual NTUSER.DAT and USRCLASS.DAT files, you have to make sure you restore them to the right places.

The Microsoft-supplied NTBACKUP program doesn't include user profile information when you create an Emergency Repair Diskette and opt to back up the Registry at the same time.

The complexity of user profiles also carries a convenience cost when you perform nifty user-oriented Registry edits such as some of the ones that I discuss in this book. If you make a Registry modification that affects NTUSER.DAT or USRCLASS.DAT (that is, in the logical structure, the *HKCU* branch), that modification doesn't apply to all users on the PC — just the one currently logged on. So you find yourself logging on as different users and making your Registry modifications multiple times. You can ease the inconvenience by exporting a Registry key to a REG file and then importing that file when logged on as a different user, but the process is still drudgery.

Luxury tax 3: Size

The third tax is on the size of the files on your hard drive. The size of the
profile and associated folders easily can be in the megabytes. If you plan on
having a PC host lots of profiles, buy larger disk drives. (This concern may
be more of an issue for network servers, where disk space is typically more
expensive.)

Chapter 9

Customizing the Desktop

. . . .

In This Chapter

▶ Using the Registry to wring more speed out of your PC

▶ Streamlining common activities

▶ Dressing up Windows a little bit

▶ Filling Windows 2000 security holes with a nifty VBScript file

. . . .

Automation has led us away from the manual transmission and the technique of shifting has been lost to many drivers. The pleasures in shifting, the fun and the craft, more than make up for the extra work.

—From *High Performance Driving,*
Paul Petersen, Simon & Schuster, 1974

*A*lmost everyone has an interest in tuning up the Windows desktop to make it faster, prettier, and more useful — hence the subject of this chapter. The surgical procedures presented here range from cosmetic to structural, so there's something for everyone.

Many of the tips in this chapter require the use of a Registry Editor to execute. Some tips you can achieve in other ways — for example, with the TweakUI control panel that comes with the *Windows 2000 Resource Kit.* (The *tweak* in TweakUI is nerdspeak for "fiddle with," while *UI* stands for "User Interface.") If the past is any guide, Microsoft will eventually put a downloadable TweakUI on its Web site for those of you who don't buy the Resource Kit. Why do I give you some tips that you can achieve with TweakUI?

✔ You may work in a company that doesn't permit unsupported software such as TweakUI. (Not a bad policy, incidentally.)

✔ If you know exactly which keys and values to export, you can share the customizations you make with others via REG files, logon scripts, setup scripts, and so on. You can't do that with TweakUI.

✔ You can't run control panels remotely — at least, not without Terminal Server — but you can run the Registry Editors remotely, so you can make user interface settings over a network (carefully!) with REGEDIT or REGEDT32.

Use the right tool for the job. If you have a single PC and you want to make settings that a standard control panel or management console can make, use the control panel or console. If you have a single PC and TweakUI, use TweakUI. And if you do use a Registry Editor, which is the *only* way to make some of the changes I mention in this chapter and which is more convenient than a control panel or TweakUI when you're on a network, always back up the key or value you're about to change.

This chapter assumes that you already know your way around the Registry and the Registry Editors. If not, please take a look at Chapters 4 and 6.

Customizing for Speed

Even if you're running Windows 2000 on a 10,000 MHz Pentium XVII system, it can still "feel" sluggish because of several Registry settings that Microsoft didn't set for speed.

Depersonalizing menus

Windows 2000 introduces the concept of personalized menus with the intention of reducing desktop clutter. The idea is that after you work with the operating system for awhile, it automatically hides Start menu choices that you haven't used. You can still get to those choices via a chevron character at the bottom of the menu.

At first I liked this feature, but later I decided it was just one more source of delays — one more place you had to click to see everything you might want to see. If you agree, you can turn personalized menus off like so:

1. **Choose Start⇨Settings⇨Taskbar & Start Menu.**

2. **Deselect the Use Personalized Menus check box.**

Note: If you want to make the change via the Registry, modify the string value *IntelliMenus* from Yes to No in *HKCU\Software\Microsoft\Windows\CurrentVersion\Explorer\Advanced*. One network manager I know put this change into a REG file to be executed after every user runs the Windows 2000 upgrade program. For information on such upgrade trickery, see Chapter 12.

You can set personalized menus on or off via group policies, as well. The setting is "Disable Personalized Menus" in User Configuration\Administrative Templates\Start Menu & Taskbar.

Slippin' and slidin' around the road

Windows 2000 uses various forms of animation on the desktop, such as:

- **Window animation.** When you minimize or maximize a window, Windows 2000 displays a zoom effect: Any window shrinks down toward the taskbar when you minimize it and expands up from the taskbar when you maximize or restore it.

- **Menu animation.** When you choose a drop-down menu, it no longer drops down, it fades in (the default behavior) or, if you modify the transition effect in the Display control panel, slides down from one corner to the opposite one. When you choose a submenu off the Start menu, it also fades or slides into place.

- **Smooth scrolling.** When you use the scroll bar to click through a long list, say the *HKCR* key in REGEDIT, Windows 2000 slides the new items into place instead of snapping directly to them. Also, when you expand or contract a folder in Windows Explorer, you see a sliding effect.

If you would prefer that your Active Desktop wasn't quite this active, for example so that your desktop responds more quickly, you can turn animation off for windows, menus, and scrolling lists in one fell swoop using the following procedure:

1. **Right-click any empty spot on the desktop and choose Properties.**

    The Display control panel appears.

2. **Select the Effects tab.**

3. **Deselect the Use Transition Effects for Menus and Tooltips check box.**

4. **Click OK.**

The problem with the Display control panel method is that it doesn't let you pick and choose which animation effects you want or don't want: It's all or nothing. Here's how to set each of the animation effects separately. The changes take effect on the next system reboot:

- To turn off the window animation effect, run REGEDIT and set the string value *MinAnimate* in the key *HKCU\Control Panel\Desktop\ WindowMetrics* to "0."

✔ Turn off sliding menu animation by subtracting 2 from the leftmost hexa-decimal number in the value *HKCU\Control Panel\Desktop\ UserPreferencesMask*. For example, if the value is 9E 3E 00 80, change it to 9C 3E 00 80. (9E–2 = 9C in hexadecimal notation; use the Scientific view of the Windows calculator to do math like this. Chapter 6 has a bit more on the subject of hex math.)

✔ Turn off fading menu animation by subtracting 2 from the leftmost hex number in *HKCU\Control Panel\Desktop\UserPreferencesMask, and* sub-tract 2 from the second-from-the-left value. For example, 1E 1E 00 80 would become 1C 1C 00 80.

✔ Turn the smooth scrolling animations off by changing the DWORD value *HKCU\Control Panel\Desktop\SmoothScroll* from "1" to "0." (Note that this setting doesn't affect smooth scrolling in an Internet Explorer window. IE's setting is controlled by the DWORD value *SmoothScroll* in *HKCU\Software\Microsoft\Internet Explorer\Main*. Integrated interface? Well, not quite!)

Fun fact: When you change one or two of the above three settings, the transi-tion effects check box in the Display control panel goes gray with a check in it, indicating that it's neither completely on nor completely off.

The *UserPreferencesMask* value in *HKCU\Control Panel\Desktop* controls sev-eral other effects, most of which you cannot control individually with the Display control panel. For example:

✔ To turn off "hot tracking," or the little animated text boxes that appear when you point the cursor at one of the small buttons (minimize, restore, maximize, or close) on the far right of an application's title bar, subtract 80 from the leftmost hex number in *UserPreferencesMask*. (Remember to use the hex mode of Windows Calculator!)

✔ To turn off the display of underlined characters, or "*hot keys,*" on menu bars and menus (File, Edit, and so on), subtract 20 from the leftmost hex number.

✔ To turn off the way drop-down lists slide into place in a dialog box such as the Run dialog box (choose Start⇨Run and click the little arrow), sub-tract 4 from the leftmost number.

✔ To turn off the mouse cursor's shadow, a new Windows 2000 default set-ting that some people love and others hate, subtract 20 from the second-from-the-left hex number. (The mouse control panel's Pointers tab has a check box for the shadow setting.)

If any of the above features is off, add the specified number instead of sub-tracting it, and you'll turn the feature back on. The trick to all this is that you must perform these additions and subtractions with a base-16, or *hexadeci-mal,* calculator. Fortunately, you have one in the Windows 2000 Calculator; choose View⇨Scientific and click the Hex button.

Why Microsoft chose to lump so many settings into the single *UserPreferencemask* value is a bit of a mystery. The straightforward approach would have been to use a different Registry value for each individual setting and then give the user the option to control each one independently on the Display control panel. But that's just my opinion, I could be wrong (which I say as sincerely as Dennis Miller).

Taking fast laps around your menus

If you've ever wished that those cascading menus that branch off the Start button would pop up just a little faster than the default four-tenths of a second, run REGEDIT and change *HKCU\Control Panel\Desktop\ MenuShowDelay* to the number of milliseconds (one millisecond = one-thousandth of a second) delay you prefer. The default is 400 milliseconds. (If the value doesn't exist, add it; it's a string type.) I like to change this setting to 100 or 200. For maximum speed, set it to 0, although you do have to get out of the habit of leisurely moving the mouse diagonally across cascading menus if you eliminate the delay entirely.

If you prefer your menus to be *sticky* rather than fast, set *MenuShowDelay* to the maximum value, which is 65534. With this setting, you have to click a menu item to see its submenus, and clicked menus don't follow the mouse cursor as you navigate the Start menu. You click it; it stays put. What you give up is the automatic menu-opening feature as you pass your cursor over menu entries that have subsidiary menus. Try it both ways and see whether you like your menus better fast or sticky.

Turbocharging your keyboard

The keyboard control panel's Speed tab enables you to modify the delay period before a key begins repeating, as well as the repeat rate (the speed with which a key repeats after it starts repeating). Experienced typists appreciate the responsiveness that Windows 2000 suddenly gains when they set the delay period as short as possible and the repeat rate as fast as possible. For one thing, scrolling around a document with the arrow keys becomes much faster.

The relevant Registry keys are *HKCU\Control Panel\Keyboard\KeyboardDelay,* which ranges from 0 (short) to 3 (long), and (in the same key) *KeyboardSpeed,* which ranges from 0 (slow) to 31 (fast). Changing the keyboard settings at Windows 2000 installation by modifying the Run Once command in Setup Manager (see Chapter 12) is handy.

Disabling folder memory

Ever wonder how Windows 2000 manages to remember your view settings for each and every folder on the system? When you set C:\WINNT\FONTS to display large icons, for example, and C:\WINNT\SYSTEM32 to display files in detail view, Windows keeps track of those settings for you. The next time you visit those folders, you see the same view settings that you made the last time you visited them.

It turns out that these folder-by-folder view settings live in the Registry, specifically in *HKCU\Software\Microsoft\Windows\CurrentVersion\Explorer\UserAssist*. Now, the ability to have individualized folder settings is a capability that you may enjoy, but frankly, it's one that I never use. I use Details view everywhere. (But then I also like gauges, as opposed to on-off "idiot" lights, on a car's instrument panel. If a gauge breaks, you discover the problem instantly and you replace the gauge. If an idiot light breaks, you discover the problem a little later, when you have to replace your engine.)

Anyway, if you turn off Explorer's *folder memory,* then Explorer no longer has to consult the Registry to find out what its particular view settings are. Skipping this Registry lookup lets the user interface become a bit snappier. Simply run the Folder Options control panel, click the View tab, and deselect the Remember Each Folder's View Settings check box. You can always select the check box later if you find that you prefer things the original way.

Streamlining Common Activities

A good way to make Windows 2000 faster in your day-to-day work is to put some of the common activities that are usually buried under a series of keystrokes and mouse clicks up onto the Start menu or the desktop, where you can get to them pronto. Examples may include your Dial-Up Networking connections, various control panels, and even Windows Explorer itself.

Expanding the Start menu

In Chapter 3, I show you two ways to put the control panel onto your Start menu. You can use similar methods to force the cascade effect with My Documents, Printers, and Network and Dial-Up Connections.

To expand these folders using Microsoft's prewired locations, choose Start⇨Settings⇨Taskbar & Start Menu, click Advanced, and check the appropriate box for the menu you want to expand. Doing so modifies the Registry values *CascadeMyDocuments*, *CascadePrinters*, and *CascadeNetworkConnections* in the *HKCU\Software\Microsoft\Windows\CurrentVersion\Explorer\Advanced* key.

To place these folders anywhere in the Start menu structure you want, follow the procedure in Chapter 3's section, "An even better answer." (I probably don't need to say this, but you should replace the folder name "My Control Panel" with "Printers" or "Network and Dial-Up Connections" as appropriate, followed by the period and CLSID.) Use the following CLSID codes from the Registry:

- ✔ For Printers, use {2227A280-3AEA-1069-A2DE-08002B30309D}.
- ✔ For Network and Dial-Up Connections, use {7007ACC7-3202-11D1-AAD2-00805FC1270E}.

For the My Documents folder, don't use a CLSID. Just drag-and-drop the folder from `C:\Documents and Settings\<username>` onto the desired place on the Start menu.

Pruning the search tree

The Start menu's Find submenu has not only changed its name to "Search" in Windows 2000, it has grown to include two new commands:

- ✔ **Search⇨On the Internet:** This option takes you to a Web-based search engine of Microsoft's choosing.
- ✔ **Search⇨For People:** This option fires up your address book and also lets you search various Internet-based address books.

Unlike some Start menu entries on the Active Desktop, you can't right-click these options to delete them. Furthermore, although you can use the Local Group Policy tool (GPEDIT.MSC) or its Active Directory counterpart to get rid of the Search menu entirely, you may prefer to leave the original Search command (For Files or Folders) intact.

Removing either or both of the two new Search items from the Start menu requires a Registry edit. Start either Registry Editor and navigate to *HKLM\SOFTWARE\Microsoft\Windows\CurrentVersion\Explorer\FindExtensions\Static*. Before going on, back up (export) this key for safekeeping (or in case you change your mind later). Then, delete the *WebSearch* key to remove the Internet search option from the Search menu. Delete the *WabFind* key to remove the People search option. (FYI, "*Wab*" is short for "Windows address book.")

If you want to keep the Search⇨On the Internet command but change its default search page, follow these steps:

1. **Choose Start⇨Search⇨On the Internet.**

2. **Click the Customize button above the search window.**

   The Customize Search Settings dialog box appears.

3. **Click the Use One Search Service For All Searches radio button and select your search engine of choice.**

   This procedure sets the DWORD Registry value *Use Custom Search URL* to 1 in the key *HKCU\Software\Microsoft\Internet Explorer\Main*, and it adds the actual Web address to the string value Search Bar in the same key. These are user-specific values that you can set separately for different users. Note that Internet Explorer's Search button pulls up the same search page that you specify for the Search⇨On the Internet command.

More convenient encryption

Encryption lets a Windows 2000 user encode a file or folder so that only that user can access the file later. (The buzzword acronym here is *EFS*, for Encrypting File System.) A cool thing to do with NTFS disks (and EFS requires NTFS) is to add the Encrypt/Decrypt command to the standard file and folder context menu. This saves you having to right-click a file or folder, choose Properties, click Advanced, then check the Encrypt check box. Add the DWORD value *EncryptionContextMenu* to *HKLM\SOFTWARE\Microsoft\Windows\CurrentVersion\Explorer\Advanced* and give it a value of **1**. Restart the computer and try it out.

Making desktop icons for control panels

Chapter 3 gives you the procedure for adding the control panel to the Start menu. You can also make desktop icons for specific control panels that you tend to use more often than others. You can even specify which particular *tab* of a particular control panel you want to open up automatically! Here's the procedure:

1. **Right-click any open area on the desktop and choose New⇨Shortcut.**

2. **In the Command Line field, type the following:**

```
C:\WINDOWS\CONTROL.EXE cplfile,iconname,tab
```

Replace *cplfile* with the name of the actual control panel file, *iconname* with the control panel's icon name, and *tab* with the number (starting at zero for the leftmost one) of the tab you want to open automatically. For example,

```
C:\WINDOWS\CONTROL.EXE SYSDM.CPL,SYSTEM,3
```

opens the System control panel to the fourth tab, Performance.

3. **Click Next and give your shortcut a suitable name.**

4. **Click the Finish button.**

You can get the control panel filenames from Table 3-1 in Chapter 3. And incidentally, if you want to place desktop icons for a Microsoft Management Console, you can just right-click and drag from the control panel's Administrative Tools folder and choose Copy Here from the context menu. These are all shortcuts to begin with. Or, you can right-click and drag files with the *.MSC extension from C:\WINNT\SYSTEM32 onto the desktop and choose Create Shortcut Here from the context menu. Just be aware that the SYSTEM32 folder may contain some MSC files that aren't active or functional on your PC.

Opening My Computer in Explorer view

When managing files, the dual-pane Windows Explorer view is the one most folks actually use because it's more convenient than the single-pane My Computer view. However, right-clicking My Computer and choosing Explore is a two-step process. Using a bit of Registry magic, you can reduce the process to a single step so that every time you choose My Computer, you see an Explorer-style dual-pane window. Here's how:

1. **Fire up REGEDIT, choose Edit⇨Find, and enter** "Displays the files and folders on your computer" **into the Find dialog box.**

   That search text is actually the infotip for "My Computer," and looking for it is a quick way to get to the right place in *HKCR\CLSID*. The actual CLSID is {20D04FE0-3AEA-1069-A2D8-08002B30309D} if you prefer to go there directly.

2. **Open the "shell" key immediately under the {20D04...} folder and change the (Default) value to** open_ex.

   This stands for "Open in Explorer view," but you can choose something else as long as it matches the key name in Step 3. Whatever you put into the (Default) value here becomes the default action when you double-click My Computer.

3. **In the key pane, right-click the key named "shell" immediately under the {20D04...} folder and choose New⇨Key. Name the new key** open_ex.

4. **Right-click the just-created open key and select New⇨Key once more. Name this new key command.**

5. **With the new command key highlighted, double-click the (Default) value in the value pane and type EXPLORER.EXE for the value data.**

   The default behavior for EXPLORER.EXE is to open at the My Documents folder. You could type **EXPLORER.EXE /e,c:** for the value data if you want your Explorer window to open at the C: drive root instead of at the My Documents folder. Substitute d:\ for c:\ if you want to see drive D: by default, and so on. (See Figure 9-1.)

6. **Close REGEDIT.**

Figure 9-1:
Making My Computer run Explorer via the Registry.

Adjusting file type associations

The three-letter suffix after the period in a filename unlocks a whole set of instructions that help Windows 2000 understand how to deal with each particular kind of file. Those instructions all live in the Registry — specifically, the *HKCR* branch, and even more specifically, the lower half of that branch. This section presents three tips for adjusting file type associations so that your data files act the way you want them to.

The basics: Adding to the context menu

You can add programs to the right-click menu (that is, the *context menu*) of a data file that you may not always want to open with the same program. As it turns out, a directory, or file folder, is a file type, too — at least, as far as the Registry is concerned. In this example, you add a context menu option to print directory contents — a command Microsoft apparently is never going to supply in the standard user interface! (The only caveat is that you can't use this trick with PostScript printers that can't handle plain text files.)

First, run Notepad and create a *batch file* (call it PD.BAT) that changes to the current directory and then runs the DIR command with a software switch to send the output to the printer. PD.BAT could be as simple as the following, which sends the print job to a printer on the first parallel port:

```
CD %1
DIR > LPT1:
```

Modify the DIR command line if you like, for example by adding **/O**, which forces an alphabetical sort, or **/S**, which forces the inclusion of subdirectories (typing **DIR /?** at the command prompt shows your choices).

If, when you run PD.BAT, you have to touch your printer's "flush buffer" button to force an incomplete page to print, create a text file FORMFEED.TXT containing a single form feed character (Ctrl+L, which is ASCII 12) and add a command like `COPY FORMFEED.TXT LPT1:` as the last line of PD.BAT (you should specify the appropriate path where you store FORMFEED.TXT).

Now that you've created the "program" that the new context menu option will run, you have to add it to the context menu for the File Folder type. Here's how:

1. **Choose Start⇨Settings⇨Control Panel and double-click the Folder Options icon.**

2. **Click the File Types tab.**

   You may see an animated flashlight for a moment or two, while Windows 2000 consults the Registry to build the list of known file types.

3. **Scroll down to File Folder, click it, and click the Advanced button to display the Edit File Type dialog box.**

4. **Click the New button to display the New Action dialog box.**

5. **In the Action area, type** Print **and in the Application Used to Perform Action, type**

   ```
   C:\PD.BAT
   ```

   (or whatever the correct full pathname should be on your system.)

6. **Click OK, OK, and Close.**

Now, when you right-click a folder in Explorer, you see a new command on the context menu to print the directory listing. To see the effect that the preceding steps have on the Registry, look up the new keys *HKCR\Directory\ shell\print* and *HKCR\Directory\shell\print\command*. You can export the entire *HKCR\Directory* key as a REG file and share this change with other computers. You can also apply the preceding technique (minus the batch file stuff!) to any file type that you may want to use multiple applications with: BMP with Windows Paint and Adobe Photoshop, HTM with Internet Explorer and Netscape Navigator, and so on.

A little fancier: Adding an extension to a file type

You may want to activate a particular program when you select data files
having one of two or more possible extensions. A good example is the *.1ST
file type, which typically denotes a text file (such as README.1ST). In this situation, you want to run Notepad whenever you select either a TXT or 1ST
file. Now, in previous versions of Windows, there was no option to merely add
an extension to an existing file type class; you had to use a Registry Editor. In
Windows 2000, you can use the Folder Options control panel, as follows:

1. **Choose Start⇨Settings⇨Control Panel and double-click the Folder
   Options icon.**

2. **Click the File Types tab.**

3. **Click the New button to display the Create New Extension dialog box.**

4. **Type 1ST in the File extension: area.**

5. **Click the Advanced button.**

6. **Click the down arrow by the Associated File Type list box, scroll
   down to Text Document, and click OK.**

   Guess where this list comes from?

7. **Click the Close button.**

Now, when you select either a 1ST file or a TXT file, Notepad runs. You have
just created the new key *HKCR\.1st* in the Registry; take a look at it.

Registry trickery: Opening unknown file types

After you've seen how the Folder Options control panel works to modify
HKCR (as discussed in the previous section), it's time to graduate from file
association school with a trick that you can *only* accomplish with the
Registry. The goal is to modify Windows 2000 so that if you double-click a file
with an unknown file extension, Windows 2000 automatically runs Notepad
(or Wordpad or whatever other text editor you like). Here's the procedure:

1. **Run REGEDIT (for example, by choosing Start⇨Run⇨REGEDIT).**

2. **Scroll to *HKCR\Unknown* and expand the subkeys.**

   HKCR\Unknown is in the bottom half of the HKCR structure; that is, it's a
   file type class, not a file extension. (See Chapter 6 for more on the organization of the *HKCR* branch.) The subkey expands out to *HKCR\
   Unknown\shell\openas\command,* where you see the code that displays
   the usual Open With context menu option.

3. **Add the new key *HKCR\Unknown\shell\open\command* containing
   the (Default) string value**

```
C:\WINNT\NOTEPAD.EXE "%1"
```

You can substitute the path name for any preferred text editor. The *%1* is a stand-in for the actual filename that you want to open. You can often get by without specifying *%1* when defining open commands, but I include it here as a matter of good practice.

4. **Change the (Default) value of *HKCR\Unknown\shell* from** openas **to** open.

This is your way of telling the Registry you want *open* to be the default command.

5. **Close REGEDIT.**

Now, when you double-click a file with an undefined extension, Windows 2000 automatically opens the file in Notepad. (Try creating a text file and naming it READ.ME, for example.) Obviously, if you try this trick with a binary file that isn't a simple text file, you just see a lot of gibberish — but no harm's done.

The one drawback to this trick is that it disables the little-used "Open With" feature in the user interface. If you find that you miss it, reverse Step 4 and the feature magically returns.

Window Dressing

And now for a couple of cosmetic tweaks, just for fun.

Changing application-related icons

Programs that register a particular file type have the option to define a special icon for that file type, too. The relevant Registry key is *HKCR\<filetype>\DefaultIcon,* where *<filetype>* is a file type entry in the bottom half of the *HKCR* branch, such as *TIFImage.Document.* Figure 9-2 shows an example associating the TIF file type with an icon in the Kodak Imaging program. The value data `"C:\Program Files\Windows NT\Accessories\ImageVue\KodakImg.exe",1` indicates that the icon is the second one (0 being the first) stored within the program KODAKIMG.EXE. (Yep, EXE files can store icons!)

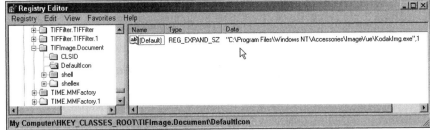

Figure 9-2:
The Registry stores default icon information.

The easiest way to change an icon for a particular file type is not to use the Registry Editor at all because REGEDIT doesn't give you any visual feedback about the alternative icons available. Instead, follow this procedure:

1. **Start Windows Explorer by right-clicking the My Computer icon and choosing Explore.**

2. **Click Tools⇨Folder Options to display the Folder Options dialog box.**

   You can also get here via the Folder Options control panel.

3. **Click the File Types tab to display the File Types dialog box.**

4. **Choose the file type you want to change and click the Advanced button.**

5. **Click Change Icon, type in (or browse to) a filename, and make a selection for the current icon in the scrolling window.**

   The currently displayed filename may have multiple choices; if you want different ones, specify a filename of C:\WINNT\SYSTEM32\MORICONS. DLL or C:\WINNT\SYSTEM32\SHELL32.DLL. It turns out that DLL files aren't just for programs, after all!

6. **Click OK, Close, and Close again; then close Windows Explorer by clicking the close box in the upper-right corner.**

If you want to go icon hunting in REGEDIT, look in *HKCR* and *HKCR\CLSID* for keys named *DefaultIcon*.

Adding info to your tips

Windows 2000 includes pop-up *infotips* that appear as if by magic if you allow your cursor to hover over particular icons (My Computer, My Documents, Control Panel, and so on). You can customize these infotips by searching for them in the Registry and then changing the string values. Each tip has the name *"InfoTip,"* so you can just search for that string if you like. (Use REGEDIT here rather than REGEDT32, because only REGEDIT can search for value names.)

Figure 9-3 gives an example of a modified infotip for the Administrative Tools icon in the control panel. The Registry key modified here is *HKCR\CLSID\ {D20EA4E1-3957-11d2-A40B-0C5020524153}*.

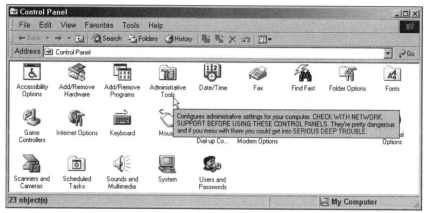

Figure 9-3:
A more informative customized infotip, courtesy of REGEDIT.

To turn infotips off entirely, open My Computer, choose Tools➪Folder Options➪View, and clear the check box labeled Show Pop-Up Description for Folder and Desktop Items. If you want to put the setting into a REG file, the relevant DWORD value is *HKCU\Software\Microsoft\Windows\ CurrentVersion\Explorer\Advanced\ShowInfoTip*. Zero is off, while one (the default) is on.

Sorting the Start menu

Here's a customization tip that illustrates the use of the REG.EXE utility. Install this critter from the \SUPPORT\TOOLS folder of your Windows 2000 CD by running SETUP.EXE in that folder. The setup program installs the Windows 2000 Resource Kit Tools sampler onto your system, and REG.EXE is one of the programs you get.

In Windows 2000, you can change the order in which programs appear on your Start menu's Programs submenu (and all of its submenus) by simply dragging and dropping program entries to the place you want them. However, if you're like me, over time you end up with a seriously nonalphabetical listing that just slows you down when you want to run a particular program (or that slows someone else down when they're using your machine).

Oh, sure, you can choose the command Start➪Settings➪Taskbar & Start Menu, click the Advanced tab, and click the Re-Sort button. That alphabetizes your Programs menus on a one-time basis. Wouldn't it be cooler, though, to have Windows 2000 realphabetize those menus at each restart? You can set this up with the following simple little batch file, SORTMENU.BAT:

```
@ECHO OFF
REG DELETE
        HKCU\Software\Microsoft\Windows\CurrentVersion\
        Explorer\MenuOrder /F
```

Note that the batch file only has two lines; we had to wrap the second line to make it fit on the page. The "/F" on the REG command line tells REG not to bother asking you for confirmation of the delete operation.

Create this batch file in Notepad, store it wherever you like, and then drop a shortcut to it into your Startup group (off the Programs menu) so that SORTMENU.BAT runs every time you start Windows 2000. You can now mess up your menus in any given computing session, but when you restart, they fall back into alphabetical order. SORTMENU.BAT nukes the Registry keys that contain the order information, forcing Windows 2000 to rebuild the lists. When it does so, it does so in alphabetical order.

Incidentally, the reason I don't use a REG file to make this change is that REG files can't delete Registry keys, and the reason I don't use a script is that the RegDelete command doesn't work with non-empty keys. Moral: REG.EXE is darned handy when you need to delete a key that may have subkeys under it.

Filling Security Holes

Windows 2000 maintains several different records of your activities, mainly for your convenience if you want to work later with documents or programs that you recently used. However, these *history lists* do create several security holes. Anyone can easily see what documents you've been working on by examining the history lists.

Windows 2000 lets you clear these history lists by choosing Start⇨Settings⇨ Taskbar & Start Menu, clicking the Advanced tab, and clicking the Clear button. 'This command is a fairly laborious procedure; a desktop icon that you can just double-click would be worlds easier. Fortunately, your Registry knowledge (and a little guidance from me) is all you need. First, I need to identify the various lists. Here are the main ones (unfortunately, many indi-vidual programs maintain their own history lists, scattered around *HKCU\Software*):

✔ **The recent documents list (Start⇨Documents).** Contains the most recent 15 data files that you've opened in a 32-bit Windows program; doesn't list documents that you open in 16-bit Windows programs.

✔ **The Run MRU list (MRU = Most Recently Used).** This list appears after you choose Start⇨Run and click the list display arrow; you see a history of program command lines that you've typed via Start⇨Run.

✔ **The Open/Save MRU lists.** These lists, which Windows 2000 maintains by file type, appear when you choose to open or save a file and click the list display arrow in the filename field. Not all programs use the main Windows 2000 lists; for example, Microsoft's Windows Media Player stores its own open MRU list in a separate Registry location.

✔ **The Typed URLs list (URL = Uniform Resource Locator).** This list keeps track of Web addresses you've typed in the address field of Internet Explorer, as well as file locations you've typed in the address field of Windows Explorer.

The recent documents list is not stored entirely in the Registry; it's also in your profile folder, typically `C:\Documents and Settings\<username>\ Recent`. The other three lists exist entirely in the Registry. So, you can use a one-two punch to take care of all three lists. The first punch, a little VBScript file called SECURE.VBS, deletes the Run MRU, OpenSaveMRU, and Typed URLs lists. Note that you have to create a separate RegDelete command for each subkey of OpenSaveMRU; I'm including the * and *txt* subkeys for an example. (RegDelete won't delete a key like *OpenSaveMRU* that has subkeys in it.)

```
Dim WSHShell
On Error Resume Next
Set WSHShell = WScript.CreateObject("WScript.Shell")
WSHShell.RegDelete "HKCU\Software\Microsoft\Windows\
CurrentVersion\Explorer\RunMRU\"
WSHShell.RegDelete "HKCU\Software\Microsoft\Windows\
CurrentVersion\Explorer\ComDlg32\OpenSaveMRU\*\"
WSHShell.RegDelete "HKCU\Software\Microsoft\Windows\
CurrentVersion\Explorer\ComDlg32\OpenSaveMRU\txt\"
'Continue as needed for OpenSaveMRU
subkeysWSHShell.RegDelete "HKCU\Software\Microsoft\Internet
Explorer\TypedURLs\"
```

Due to the fact that this book doesn't use foot-wide pages, I had to break some of the lines in the preceding program. When you enter them into Notepad, don't break them!

That's a pretty small and simple program! Now that Windows 2000 includes the Windows Scripting Host capability, I find VBScript a little easier to work with than INF files, which can also delete Registry keys and values but that are not well documented in the Windows 2000 help files. You could also use JavaScript, if you are more comfortable with that scripting language; the Windows 2000 CD contains help files for both scripting languages in the `\VALUEADD\MSFT\XTRADOCS` folder. If you're wondering why you need to use any scripting language here at all, remember that you can't use a REG file here. REG files don't delete stuff; they can only change or add stuff in the Registry.

Note that Windows 2000 rebuilds the *RunMRU, OpenSaveMRU,* and *TypedURLs* keys (and their subkeys) automatically the next time you perform an action that normally creates an entry in these lists, so you're not doing any irreversible damage in SECURE.VBS.

Just when you thought you knew about all the history lists: Internet Explorer 5 maintains history lists for the fields in every Web-based form that you fill out! These history lists live in the Registry, too, under *HKCU\Software\ Microsoft\ Protected Storage System Provider\<user SID>\Data.* (The *<user SID>* part is the user's security ID.) Microsoft hasn't documented this Registry location as I write this, so deleting its contents could be risky. You may find it safer simply to turn the Web form autocomplete feature off, so that the history lists don't appear. Go to the Internet Options control panel's Content tab, click the Autocomplete button, and deselect the Forms check box. Or, in the Registry, set *HKCU\Software\Microsoft\Internet Explorer\Main\Use FormSuggest* to **no**.

The second part of the one-two punch is a little batch file, call it SECURE.BAT, that first runs the VBScript program (via CSCRIPT.EXE, the command-line version of the new Windows Scripting Host) and then deletes the contents of the Recent folder, while answering the "Are you sure?" prompt with an echoed "Y":

```
@ECHO OFF
CSCRIPT SECURE.VBS
ECHO Y | DEL %USERPROFILE%\RECENT\*.*
```

The third line uses the environment variable *%userprofile%* as a handy way of referencing a path that changes depending on the user's logon name. All you have to do now is create a desktop icon to run SECURE.BAT (for example, by dragging and dropping the file to the desktop). Double-click the icon whenever you want to clear the various history lists. (Note that the Run MRU list doesn't clear until you restart.)

Part IV
Flat Repair: Troubleshooting the Registry

The 5th Wave   By Rich Tennant

"Hold on there boy! You think you're gonna set Windows 2000 profiles on an old Pentium all by yourself? Well you'd better hope to high heaven she's in a good mood today."

In this part . . .

1 was living in Dallas when the city hosted its first (and very probably last, due to the heat) Grand Prix race. The race itself was a lot of fun to watch — especially when an exhausted Nigel Mansell clambered out and pushed his crippled Formula I car toward the finish line in the merci-less Texas heat. But it was even more fun going down to the track at 3:00 a.m. a couple of days later (as some friends and I did) to take our street cars for a few illicit laps around the circuit before the city tore it up. (Those orange cones warning the public off the tarmac, it turned out, were not bolted down.)

None of us planned for the huge garbage truck lumbering across the track just as we were rounding a curve around lap 4. No one got hurt, and we decided to make that our last lap. But it was a sobering experience that taught us all a valuable life lesson: You never know when a garbage truck is going to cross the race track of your life. Therefore, it helps to know of a good body shop for those cases when you just can't avoid wrinkling the sheet metal. Think of this Part of the book as your Registry repair center. It will help you fix your Registry if possible, and if it's totaled, these chapters will help you start over. In no event will you receive an insurance check, however. There's a reason nobody insures software!

Chapter 10

A Dozen Registry Problems (And Solutions!)

● ●

In This Chapter

▶ Dealing with Registry Editor error messages

▶ Discovering how to fix broken system and group policies

▶ Solving REG file problems

▶ Finding out how to increase Registry size

▶ Manually applying Windows Installer Registry settings

● ●

> *Nobody knows how transmissions work, or even where they come from... So if something goes wrong with your transmission, your best bet is to just give your car to the poor and claim a tax deduction.*
>
> —From *The Taming of the Screw,*
> Dave Barry, Rodale Press, 1983

*A*s with car transmissions, there are two categories of Registry problems: serious, and extremely serious. This chapter looks at some of the more common examples of the first category: problems that can definitely cramp your computing style, but that probably don't require major time and effort to correct. (Chapter 11 deals with the truly dire situations that may require restoring all or part of the Registry.)

Much as I would like it to be, this chapter can't be comprehensive. Here's proof: If you install the Resource Kit Tools from the \SUPPORT\TOOLS folder of your Windows 2000 CD, and consult the Windows 2000 Error and Event Messages help file, you can find *over 300* error messages that include the word Registry. Clearly, even though I've tried to pick problems that a typical user may actually encounter, the dirty dozen issues in this chapter are only a small subset of all the potential Registry potholes lurking around the next bend.

That Resource Kit help file isn't a bad resource and I'm glad Microsoft provides it, but it shouldn't be your only reference. Sometimes the help file's recommended course of action in response to a specific error message is to "report this to your network administrator." That doesn't help those of us who use Windows at home and are not cohabitating with a network administrator. I guess you could always call up a big local company, ask for the network administrator, and say your name is Bob or Susan in Accounting. If you ever really do get help this way, send the network administrator some doughnuts by way of thanks. Or send a copy of this book, which incidentally makes a great gift for almost any occasion.

A second source to know about if you encounter a Registry-related pothole not described here, or in the error messages help file, is Microsoft TechNet. TechNet includes Microsoft's knowledge base of problems and solutions. You can subscribe to the CDs for about $300 a year, or access much of its content on the Web for free at `http://support.microsoft.com/search`. Finally, check into `http://msdn.microsoft.com`, home of the free and useful Microsoft Developer Network Web site. (If you are not *really* a software developer, go ahead and use this site anyway, I won't tell anyone.)

Registry Editors Display Error Messages

Here are a few of the more common error messages that the Registry Editors may display. Note that error message wording is inconsistent between REGEDIT and REGEDT32, even for the exact same situation:

- ✔ `The specified file is not a Registry script. You can import only Registry files.` (REGEDIT) The only way REGEDIT can tell whether a file is truly a Registry script or not is by looking at the very beginning of the file for the line `Windows Registry Editor Version 5.00`. If this line is missing, you get this error. If it's there but the version number is wrong, you see `The specified file is not intended for use with this version of Windows`. You don't see these messages in REGEDT32 because that program doesn't deal with REG files.

- ✔ `Unable to delete all specified values.` (REGEDIT) REGEDIT doesn't let you delete the (Default) value in the value pane (right window). If you want to get rid of a key, delete it in REGEDIT's key pane (left window).

- ✔ `Unable to rename <key name>. The specified key name contains illegal characters.` (REGEDIT) or `The key name specified is not valid.` (REGEDT32) You see this message if you try to use the backslash character in a key name, which is *verboten.*

- ✔ `The specified key name already exists.` (REGEDIT) or `Registry Editor could not create the key.` (REGEDT32) Key names have to be unique, at least within a particular group.

✔ Cannot rename New Value #1: The specified value name already exists. Type another name and try again. (REGEDIT) or Registry Editor could not create the value entry. The value entry already exists. Please enter a new name. (REGEDT32) Value names have to be unique, too, within a particular key. However, the two editors treat the situation differently. REGEDIT leaves a value with the name *New Value #1*; REGEDT32 behaves more sensibly and doesn't create the value until you specify a unique name. REGEDIT's error message is also much more cryptic.

✔ Registry Editor is operating in the Read Only Mode. Changes made to this value entry will not be saved in the Registry. (REGEDT32) You see this message every time you double-click a value when you've set the Read Only option on the Options menu. You often have to double-click a value to see its entire contents, so this is especially maddening. I don't know of any way to turn it off, though. This message has no parallel in REGEDIT because REGEDIT has no Read-Only mode.

In certain error situations, REGEDIT and REGEDT32 don't bother to communicate with you. For example, you can try to delete subkeys of *HKLM\ HARDWARE* in REGEDT32, and nothing happens — no deletions, no error messages, no nothing. (Curiously, if you try the same drill in REGEDIT, the program happily deletes all the subkeys without complaint. Thankfully, Windows 2000 seems to run just fine with no contents in *HKLM\HARDWARE* — the memory-resident key is mainly used at boot time — but don't try this on your system!)

I Get Errors When Backing Up the Registry

You may be more likely to bump into this problem with Windows 2000 compared to Windows NT 4.0, partly because the newer operating system uses a lot more disk space and partly because the new NTBACKUP wants to back up all your protected operating system files (200MB+) as well as your Registry, when you choose to back up the "system state" (Microsoft's term for essential operating system files). The problem is more likely to occur with:

✔ Notebook computers that have small hard drives

✔ Drives that you've partitioned to use multiple drive letters

✔ Systems with lots of applications

✔ Systems where Internet caches build up to large sizes

✔ Systems with very large data files (such as digital video)

The Windows 2000 Disk Cleanup wizard (which you can run by right-clicking a drive icon in My Computer, choosing Properties, and clicking the Disk Cleanup button on the General tab) is a handy utility for freeing up space. You can also take some of the following steps:

✔ Reduce your Web browser cache size (see your browser's online help)

✔ Reduce your Recycle Bin size (modify its property page)

✔ Consider converting a FAT disk to the more efficient FAT32 disk format

When backing up the System State interactively, follow the instructions in Chapter 2 for excluding the system protected files if you only want to back up the Registry. Unfortunately, this option is not available to you if you schedule a backup job using the Windows 2000 Scheduled Tasks utility. You should use a different backup program if you want to schedule regular Registry backups that don't include all those system DLLs.

System Policies Aren't Working

Many organizations can't convert over to Windows 2000 overnight. If you work in a company that is migrating from Windows NT 4.0, you may have developed NT-style "system policies" that for some reason don't work any-more when you start installing Windows 2000 clients.

The reason is that the new Windows 2000 "group policies" are Microsoft's preferred alternative to NT 4.0 system policies. Group policies work with Active Directory and they do a better job of cleaning up old settings when, for example, a user's group membership changes. So Microsoft turns off the older system policies.

However, you can flip the Registry switch that disables system policies. Modify the DWORD value *DisableNT4Policy* in *HKLM\SOFTWARE\Microsoft\Windows\CurrentVersion\policies\system* so that it's 0 instead of 1.

Windows 2000 clients always look for a Windows 2000 domain controller at logon time, and if they find one, they use Windows 2000-style group policies. If a Windows 2000 client can't find a Windows 2000 domain controller, and instead finds a Windows NT 4.0 domain controller to validate the logon, then the NT machine can apply NT-style system policies to the Windows 2000 client as long as you've set the *DisableNT4Policy* Registry value to 0.

I Can't Reverse Restrictive Policies

The Group Policy utility allows you to set a policy for the current Registry that disables the Registry Editors (run GPEDIT.MSC and expand the branches User Configuration\Administrative Templates\System and select the Disable Registry Editing Tools policy). Later, you can run the Group Policy program again to reverse this setting if you want to run REGEDIT or REGEDT32.

However, you may not be able to run GPEDIT.MSC if you've also added restrictions to the programs that Windows 2000 is allowed to run (by selecting the Run Only Allowed Windows Applications policy in the same location). If GPEDIT (or the earlier POLEDIT, if you've installed it from the Windows 2000 Server CD) isn't on the list of allowed Windows applications, then you can't run the program to remove the restrictions on itself and on the Registry Editors. A vicious circle!

You're not really trapped, though. The easiest escape hatch is to run a command prompt (choose Start⇨Run and type **CMD**) and type **GPEDIT.MSC** at the command prompt. The Run Only Allowed Windows Applications policy doesn't apply to programs you run from a command prompt. If you've set the Disable The Command Prompt capability also and if you're on a Windows 2000 network domain, you can set a domain policy reversing the local policy restricting program access. Domain policies always take priority over local policies.

If you can't get to the command prompt and if you're not on a network, then what you need to do is create a REG file that looks like the following:

```
Windows Registry Editor Version 5.00

[HKEY_CURRENT_USER\Software\Microsoft\Windows\CurrentVersion
Policies\Explorer]
"RestrictRun"=dword:00000000
```

You can even create this text file on another computer and bring the file over on diskette, if you find that you can't run any programs at all. This REG file — call it UNLOCK.REG or something similar — resets the *RestrictRun* value to zero, effectively switching off the policy that restricts you to only running certain applications.

Now, log on as an Administrator. You can't run REGEDIT directly in order to import this REG file because you've disabled Registry editing tools. However, this situation is no sweat for those in the know. Use Windows Explorer to locate the REG file, right-click it, choose Merge, and the program restrictions disappear. You can now run the Group Policy utility and fine-tune the restrictions until they're the way you *really* want them.

The Registry Editor Policy Doesn't Restrict Other Editors

The Disable Registry Editing Tools system policy that I discuss in the preceding problem is effective in restricting the Registry Editors REGEDIT and REGEDT32, but it does nothing to restrict other Registry editing tools you may use, such as (for example) Norton Registry Editor. If you want to limit access to such programs, either put 'em on a network server where you can make them available only to certain users or groups, or hide their application directories on the local disk so other users aren't tempted to find and run them.

Group Policies Aren't Working

Here's an interesting quirk that had me pounding my head against the wall during the beta testing of Windows 2000: Local group policies don't get processed if your computer is part of a domain and no domain controller is available. They *do* get processed if your computer is not part of a domain (for example, it's a stand-alone computer, or part of a workgroup network rather than a domain network).

The way to tell whether a given PC is on a domain or workgroup is to look at the Network Identification tab on the System control panel.

This is something of a hole in policy-based security. A user can simply disconnect a network cable and bypass policy changes, even policy changes made on the local machine with the Local Group Policy utility. (The precise behavior is that Windows 2000 uses the most recently applied policies when it can't find a domain controller.) So you can't just assume that policy changes you make on a local PC with the Local Group Policy program, or on a server via the Active Directory Users and Groups tool, are going to take effect for every user. Policies depend on valid network connections taking place — even local policies, which seems a little strange!

You can't do much for people who unplug their LAN link, and that's not too likely a scenario anyway. One of the things that you *can* do is make sure that you've configured DNS properly on your network. Users may be able to log on to a server, but if the DNS service isn't set up right, group policies may still not be able to work. Check out the *Microsoft Windows 2000 Resource Kit* and the Windows 2000 Server online help (choose Start⇨Help to find this) for all the gory details on DNS configuration. And if you change a local group policy on a PC, reboot, and make sure it takes effect!

Of policies and permissions

Another possible policy processing problem pertains to permissions. (Say *that* ten times fast!) Even after creating a group policy object and linking it to an organizational unit (*OU* in Active Directory lingo), domain, or site, Windows 2000 doesn't actually apply the policy object until you add the user or group to the policy's access control list, or *ACL*. So if you've made a new policy object but it doesn't seem to be modifying user Registries, follow these steps:

1. **Go to your Windows 2000 Server and fire up the Active Directory Users and Computers tool.**

2. **Right-click the OU, domain, or site for which you've created a policy.**

3. **Choose Properties from the context menu.**

4. **Click the Group Policy tab, highlight the policy object in the list, click the Properties button, and click the Security tab.**

5. **Use the Add button to add any appropriate users and groups, and click OK multiple times to get all the way out.**

Your policy object should now work.

User Profiles Load Slowly Over a Modem

Chapter 8 discusses how users can store the user-specific parts of the Registry on a network server, along with various other files (such as the contents of the My Documents folder), so that whenever the user logs on from any PC, she sees her own individual settings and preferences. However, when users dial into a server from home or the road, they typically use a comparatively slow modem connection — and downloading that profile information can result in a loooong delay.

Correct this problem by taking the following steps, both of which refer to the Local Group Policy tool's Computer Configuration\Administrative Templates\System\Logon area:

- Define what you consider to be a "slow" connection by specifying a speed in the Slow Network Connection Timeout for User Profiles policy.
- Enable the Prompt User When Slow Link Is Detected policy.

When the user dials in and makes a connection that meets your criteria for "slow," such as anything less than 40 Kbps for example, Windows 2000 prompts the user to specify whether to wait for the roaming user profile to download, or use the locally cached copy of the profile on the user's PC.

Importing a REG File Doesn't Work

A number of reasons can prevent REG files from properly merging into the Registry. Here are the more common ones.

Missing keys

Symptom: You perform an import (or merge) of a REG file (maybe a REG file that you wrote yourself), but some or all the keys in the REG file don't appear in the actual Registry.

Windows 2000 is very nitpicky about the punctuation in REG files. The most common problems are as follows:

- ✔ The file doesn't start with a separate line containing the words *Windows Registry Editor Version 5.00.* In this case, REGEDIT displays the message in Figure 10-1. Note that this header line has changed since Windows NT 4.0.
- ✔ The file includes keys or values that are missing a curly bracket ({ or }).
- ✔ The file includes string values that are missing the enclosing double quotes.
- ✔ The file includes path names that use single backslashes instead of the required double backslashes.

Figure 10-1:
If you see this message, your REG file doesn't have the correct first line.

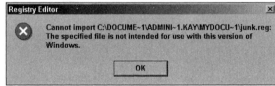

Registry Editor

Cannot import C:\DOCUME~1\ADMINI~1.KAY\MYDOCU~1\junk.reg: The specified file is not intended for use with this version of Windows.

OK

Rather than creating the REG file from scratch, it's much easier to export a REG file of the key you want to modify and then change the REG file to your liking by using Notepad.

REGEDIT gives you no indication whether it finds invalid statements in a REG file after it finds the header line at the beginning of the file. Because you don't see an error message, the only way you know your REG file works is to run REGEDIT and check the keys and values manually. To illustrate, take a look at Figure 10-2. I merged this utterly bogus REG file into the Registry (after making a backup first!), and the result was the cheery message that the information in JUNK.REG had been "successfully entered into the Registry." Yecch. (Incidentally, Windows 2000 still ran perfectly normally.)

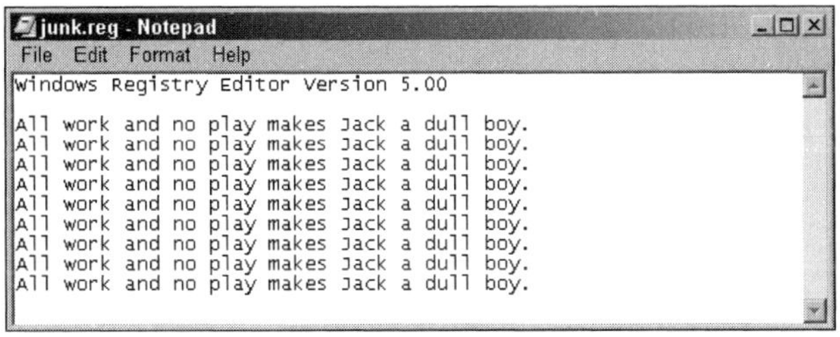

Figure 10-2:
This bogus
REG file
imports
without
an error
message!

```
junk.reg - Notepad                                        _□×
File  Edit  Format  Help
Windows Registry Editor Version 5.00

All work and no play makes Jack a dull boy.
All work and no play makes Jack a dull boy.
All work and no play makes Jack a dull boy.
All work and no play makes Jack a dull boy.
All work and no play makes Jack a dull boy.
All work and no play makes Jack a dull boy.
All work and no play makes Jack a dull boy.
All work and no play makes Jack a dull boy.
All work and no play makes Jack a dull boy.
```

Unwanted duplicates

This problem is a subtle variation on the preceding one. When Windows 2000 processes a REG file, instead of changing the value of a particular key or value, REGEDIT seems to add a new key or value with the same name.

The most likely cause of this strange problem is a space at the end of the key name in your REG file. If such a *trailing space* exists, then REGEDIT interprets the key or value as new and different and adds it to the Registry, instead of changing the existing entry. *Solution:* If you write your REG files from scratch, make sure your key and value names have no trailing spaces.

REG and INF files aren't working on other PCs

The most likely reason for this problem is that your PC uses different folders for program directories than the PC that you're sending your REG or INF file to. Find out what folder names the target PCs use and edit the REG or INF file with Notepad to point to those folder names. Or use the expandable string value type with variables like *%SystemRoot%* (see Chapter 6, "Variations on a string theme").

This sort of problem is one more argument for using the default folder names when installing new software. It's just too bad that some software vendors still haven't bought into the notion that all application files should go into subfolders beneath `C:\Program Files`.

I Can't Find Stuff in the Registry that I Know Is There

This problem breaks out into four common situations. It's bad enough when you can't find your car keys, but it's worse when you can't find your Registry keys.

REGEDT32 doesn't find value names or data

An old joke in the medical profession: A patient tells a doctor "My arm hurts when I do this," and the doctor responds "Don't do that." The computer industry has borrowed this "DDT" response to user "bugs." While I usually don't like that answer in real life, here, DDT fits the bill. Don't use REGEDT32 to find stuff in the Registry. It only finds strings in key names, not value names or value data fields. Use REGEDIT for searching instead. And even then, recognize that REGEDIT's search facility can't see strings past the first in a list for values of type REG_MULTI_SZ.

Context menu search strings

When you're using the Registry Editor's Find command (or a third-party Registry search tool) to locate text that you've seen in a *context menu* (a menu that appears when you right-click a desktop object), you come up empty. The Registry defines how context menus look and act. So what's the story here?

The context menu command might live in a separate file that the Registry merely references, in which case your Registry search can't succeed. However, it could also be that the context menu command that you're looking for contains an underlined character, which the Registry marks with a leading ampersand (&). For example, if the *t* in *Properties* appears underlined, then a search for *Properties* will fail, but a search for *Proper&ties* will succeed.

Incidentally, if you've become used to those underlines, which allow you to choose menu commands from the keyboard, you may be surprised to see them missing from the Windows 2000 user interface. You can turn 'em back on easily enough. In the Display control panel's Effects tab, deselect the check box that says `Hide keyboard navigation indicators until I use the Alt key`. This check box modifies the Registry value *HKCU\ Control Panel\Desktop\UserPreferencesMask*.

Find command follies

A very common reason that a Find operation fails in REGEDIT is that the My Computer icon isn't highlighted in the key pane (the one on the left). The Registry Editor's Find command starts with the highlighted key, works downward, and stops when it gets to the bottom. REGEDIT doesn't wrap around to the top of the file and search the area above the highlighted key like most good word processors do. So, if you don't remember to click My Computer, it could be that the item you're searching for is located above the currently highlighted key.

The short and long of it

You may be hunting for a particular file reference in the Registry. The secret here is to remember to try both the regular long filename version, and the truncated short filename equivalent. (Some programs create Registry entries using the truncated filenames for backward compatibility with Windows 3.*x*, DOS, and other applications that don't implement long filename capability.) If your search for `C:\Program Files\Internet Explorer\iexplore.exe` comes up empty, try `C:\Progra~1\Intern~1\iexplore.exe`.

I'm Low on Registry Quota . . . Whatever That Is

You may get an error message that says

```
Registry Editor is unable to complete the requested operation
```

or something similar, when you attempt a "Load Hive" operation in REGEDT32. You may also see an error message stating that your system is running low on Registry quota. Or, when you log on, Windows 2000 may tell you that it wasn't able to load the locally stored user profile or that the operating system has insufficient resources. All these messages, some of which may only be visible via the Event Viewer utility, can appear when your Registry size limit is too low.

Those readers new to Windows NT technology may be surprised to learn that the operating system expects you to manage the Registry's size limit, or RSL, but it does. The RSL is buried several layers deep in the user interface; ferret it out by choosing the System control panel and then clicking the Advanced tab, the Performance Options button, and the Change button. You should see the dialog box in Figure 10-3; the RSL is on the bottom line of that dialog box.

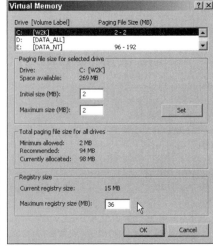

Figure 10-3: The Windows 2000 Registry Size Limit.

You have to log on as an administrator to change this number. Microsoft recommends setting it to 2.4 times the current Registry size. So, a Registry that's 15MB should have a ceiling of 36MB. Randomly choosing a huge number can adversely affect the memory and hard drive space available to the system and other programs.

"Another Installation Is in Progress"

The new Microsoft Windows Installer uses the Registry to track whether an installation is in progress or has completed successfully. However, several users have reported problems with Windows Installer claiming another installation is in progress when, in fact, the second installation either hasn't started yet, or has already finished successfully. The specific error message is as follows:

```
Error 1500. Another installation is in progress. You must
complete that installation before continuing this one.
```

The fix that seems to work in most of these problem situations is to run REGEDIT or REGEDT32, navigate to the key *HKLM\SOFTWARE\Microsoft\ Windows\CurrentVersion\Installer*, and delete the *InProgress* subkey. That disables the flag from that point forward, at least until you perform another software installation that uses Windows Installer.

As a side note on Windows Installer, you can rebuild a program installation's Registry entries by opening a command-prompt window and typing **MSIEXEC /fm *file.MSI*** and **MSIEXEC /fu *file.MSI***, where *file.MSI* is the Microsoft Software Installer file containing the new program. The first command rebuilds machine-specific Registry settings that the installation puts into *HKLM,* and the second command rebuilds user-specific settings that go into *HKCU.* This tip may come in handy if you accidentally overwrite a program's Registry settings, but be aware that it is also likely to reset all the program's Registry entries to the default values.

Office 2000 Programs Quit after Launch

Chapter 7 on Registry security warns that if you monkey around with the permissions settings on certain Registry keys, you may run into problems with applications that need and expect access to those keys. Office 2000 provides a perfect example.

If the key *HKLM\SOFTWARE\Microsoft\Office* doesn't have the correct minimum permissions, Office programs may start, wait a few seconds, and then quit. I sometimes like to take a nap after launch, but this is ridiculous. (Thanks, you've been a great audience.)

Set the permissions on this key using REGEDT32's Security⇨Permissions command. The minimums that Office 2000 expects to see are as follows:

- ✔ Creator Owner: Full Control
- ✔ Everyone: Special Access (which in this case includes Query Value, Set Value, Create Subkey, Enumerate Subkeys, Notify, Delete, and Read Control)
- ✔ *‹Machine Name›*Administrators: Full Control
- ✔ System: Full Control

Chapter 11

Restoring the Registry

. . . .

In This Chapter

▶ Understanding partial Registry restores

▶ Discovering what the Last Known Good boot option does to the Registry

▶ Finding out how to restore your entire Registry from backups

▶ Secrets of the new Recovery Console

. . . .

Don't fool yourself into thinking you are Emerson Fittipaldi because you once controlled a skid that was the result of an error you committed in the first place.

—From *High Performance Driving,*
Paul Petersen, Simon & Schuster, 1974

*R*estoring a classic car is usually a labor of love. Restoring a Windows 2000 Registry is usually a labor of frantic, last-ditch desperation. Your system is refusing to boot properly; it is relaying dire error messages about a corrupted Registry; your user settings don't take effect; or, most serious of all, you can't play the latest computer game anymore.

Fear not. Desperate measures taken by a well-informed Registry power user are far more likely to succeed than those taken by a Registry ignoramus. This chapter gives you the knowledge you need to restore all or part of the Registry from those backups you made when you read Chapter 2.

You can probably fix whatever problem is ailing your machine by restoring your Registry from an earlier backup, but you may sacrifice some recent settings by doing so, which is why a Registry restore is your last resort before you reinstall Windows 2000 itself (something that's almost never truly necessary). I like trying to perform a partial Registry restore before resigning myself to restoring the whole dadblasted database.

Depending on how diligent you've been about making periodic backups, restoring the Registry may not turn out to be a big time drain. I had to restore from a backup more than a few times in the course of nearly two years of beta-testing Windows 2000, and the restoration process never took more than half an hour once I learned the ropes. Just remember that even though a good surgeon can perform a routine appendectomy quickly, maybe even while listening to Dire Straits in the operating room, *it's still surgery.* Approach a Registry restore seriously, read this chapter at least twice before performing your first one, and try to have another knowledgeable person on hand during the procedure, just as a surgeon would.

If you're reading this book backwards, as I sometimes do with technical books (just for a change), at least skim over Chapter 2 before you read this chapter. Chapter 2 explains that you can back up your Registry with several different tools and techniques, and this chapter is a mirror image of Chapter 2, providing the restore procedures that match up with the various backup procedures. Also, please check out Chapter 10's dozen common Registry problems before taking the more radical steps in this chapter. It may be that your problem doesn't require major surgery.

This chapter doesn't tell you every possible method for restoring the Registry, nor does it cover every possible situation. My goal here is to present the most common restore methods for the most common problem situations.

Partial Restores

If you're in an off-road rally and you take a sharp rock in the oil pan, you may not need to replace your whole engine. A new oil pan (and a bit of fresh oil) may be enough to get you four-wheeling again. Similarly, with the Registry, you can usually get away with restoring just part of it — a good tactic, because the less you have to restore, the fewer settings you lose that have changed since your last Registry backup.

As a general rule, you want to restore as little of the Registry as you can and still fix your problem. It's okay to save some time and restore the whole Registry if you have a very recent backup, and you're therefore certain that you won't lose many settings by doing so.

Last Known Good = Smart First Step

You Windows NT 4.0 veterans probably know about the *Last Known Good* (LKG) boot option, and you'll be pleased to know it's still around in Windows 2000. For the rest of you, a couple of words on this slick subject — and a note of caution, too.

Chapter 6 explains the concept of a *control set:* a set of Registry keys and values that tells the operating system about the hardware that's installed on the PC, as well as the operating system services (programs) that are necessary to boot. Windows 2000 maintains a copy of the last known good control

set in the Registry. If you restart Windows 2000 and it doesn't boot successfully, then you can restart it again, press F8 at the text-mode Starting
Windows boot prompt, choose Last Known Good Configuration (see
screen excerpt below, which may look a little different from your PC), and
continue booting. Doing this instructs Windows 2000 to copy the last known
good control set into the Registry's current control set (*HKLM\SYSTEM\
CurrentControlSet*), so that the system can (knock wood) boot normally.

```
Windows 2000 Advanced Options Menu
Please select an option:
     Safe Mode
     Safe Mode with Networking
     Safe Mode with Command Prompt

     Enable Boot Logging
     Enable VGA Mode
     Last Known Good Configuration
     Directory services restore mode
     Debugging mode

     Boot Normally
     Return to OS choices menu
```

So, booting to LKG is a way of restoring part of the Registry, specifically, the
current control set. When does this procedure bail you out of trouble? Well,
the LKG is mostly useful when you've added a device driver that won't let
your system boot properly. LKG will not help you with Registry problems outside of the control set keys, but it can be a lifesaver with boot-time blues.

If you enable your Windows 2000 Professional system for automatic logon, you
could get into a situation where the LKG feature doesn't work for you. Here's
why: When Windows 2000 senses a user logon, it thinks that it's completed a
successful boot, and it writes the current control set contents into the last
known good control set. However, if you've installed a driver that affects your
ability to use the mouse or keyboard, the next time you reboot, trouble's
afoot. Your PC logs on automatically, copies the current control set to the LKG
because Windows thinks the system has booted successfully, and to your
chagrin you find that you can't type or point anymore. At this point, you no
longer have a fallback position because your LKG is the same as your current
control set. This is one reason I don't like automatic logon. (Note that since
Windows NT 4.0, Microsoft has disabled automatic logon for PCs in a domain-
based network, but you can still use it on stand-alone and workgroup PCs.)

Restoring a key, or two, or three

If you created a partial Registry backup by using the export technique
(method five in Chapter 2), you can import that export and perform a partial
restore.

Restoring keys with REGEDIT

If you can boot to Windows 2000 normally and if you created your export file using REGEDIT, you must use REGEDIT (not REGEDT32) to restore it, as follows:

1. **Close all Windows programs and then run REGEDIT.**

2. **Click Registry⊏>Import Registry File to display the dialog box in Figure 11-1.**

Figure 11-1:
Merging a
REG file into
the current
Registry
with
REGEDIT.

3. **Specify the directory in the Look In field and name the file in the File Name field.**

   REGEDIT defaults to showing files with the suffix .REG.

4. **Click the Open button to restore the data.**

If you don't already have REGEDIT open and you know where your REG file is, you can save a few mouse clicks and import your REG file by right-clicking it in Explorer and choosing Merge. The results are identical. The REG file contains all the location information for every exported key and value, so REGEDIT knows exactly where to put it during the import.

A REGEDIT import operation isn't a complete replacement of an existing Registry key. Importing with this program can only change or add keys — it can't delete keys. If you feel that you need an exact image of the earlier backup, you must first delete the current key in REGEDIT (back it up first for safety) and then perform the import. Or, use the REGEDT32 import procedure if you have a REGEDT32 export file (segue to next section).

Restoring keys with REGEDT32

Use REGEDT32's Registry⊏>Restore command to import keys that you saved with the same program's Registry⊏>Save Key command.

Unlike with REG files, the binary files that REGEDT32 creates don't include location information. So it's up to you to ensure that the correct key is highlighted before you use the Restore Key command, because REGEDT32 will wipe out whatever you've highlighted before bringing in the saved file's information. The best advice I can give is to use REGEDIT for exporting and importing rather than REGEDT32.

Restoring keys with REG

The little REG.EXE tool that you can install as part of the Resource Kit Tools in the Windows 2000 CD's SUPPORT folder can restore keys that you used it to back up in the first place. The syntax is

```
REG RESTORE keyname filename
```

where *keyname* is something like *HKLM\SOFTWARE\XYZCo\Prog1* and *filename* is whatever you named the backup file when you created it.

You can't always restore keys with REG. If you try restoring keys that Windows 2000 is using or that the operating system has protected, then you'll get an `Access is denied` error message. In such a case, you may have to restore an entire hive, as explained in the following section.

Restoring a whole hive

If you can't get away with just restoring a Registry key or handful of keys, then your next step should be to try restoring a single Registry hive. (Remember, the hives are the Registry files on disk.) You're usually better off if you can fix a problem by restoring a single hive than if you have to restore the entire Registry. If you have a really recent backup of the whole Registry, though, you may want to just restore the whole shebang, because that procedure's often simpler and quicker. See the "Full Restores" section later in this chapter for details.

Restoring a hive with Recovery Console

Microsoft added the *Recovery Console* since Windows NT 4.0, and it can come in mighty handy — especially on a system with an NTFS boot disk. You can't use the full breadth of programs and commands in the Recovery Console that you can use in a normal command prompt session, but you do have access to the RENAME and COPY commands, and those are all you need to restore a particular Registry hive.

You can add the Recovery Console to your text-mode boot menu by running Windows 2000 setup with the command **WINNT32 /CMDCONS** from the \I386 folder of your original Windows 2000 CD. That's handy in that it lets you boot the Recovery Console a lot faster than booting from the CD or from the startup diskettes, as described in the rest of this section.

The following example restores the SYSTEM hive from a backup created with the NTBACKUP program's Emergency Repair Diskette *(ERD)* procedure (method two in Chapter 2).

1. **Set your PC's BIOS to boot from the CD-ROM and boot from the Windows 2000 installation CD.**

   If that option doesn't exist, you can boot your PC with the four diskettes you created with MAKEBOOT or MAKEBT32, as described in Chapter 2.

2. **At the Welcome to Setup screen, press** R **to repair.**

3. **Press C at the next screen to enter the Recovery Console.**

4. **Press a number (usually 1) to specify a Windows 2000 installation to modify, and press Enter.**

5. **Log on with the administrative password.**

   Here's the Achilles' heel of the Recovery Console: If your SECURITY or SAM hives are really messed up, Windows 2000 won't recognize your administrative password and you'll have to use a different method to restore a Registry hive. The rest of this example assumes that you can log on successfully.

6. **Change to the** C:\WINNT\SYSTEM32\CONFIG **folder and rename SYSTEM to** SYSTEM.BAD**.**

   This way, if you're wrong about needing to restore the SYSTEM hive, you can come back here and undo the restore operation later, so as not to lose any settings you may have made since the last backup.

7. **Copy** C:\WINNT\REPAIR\REGBACK\SYSTEM **to the** C:\WINNT\SYSTEM32\CONFIG **folder.**

8. **Type** EXIT **and press Enter to leave the Recovery Console; then restart the PC.**

When Windows 2000 restarts, it uses the restored SYSTEM hive.

For security reasons, Recovery Console doesn't let you copy files to or from removable media, so you can't use this method to restore a hive from a Zip disk or floppy. Also, you can't run REG, REGEDIT, or REGEDT32 in the Recovery Console.

Restoring a hive with DOS

If you use backup method four in Chapter 2, whereby you boot to a DOS diskette and run a batch file to copy your Registry files to a backup location, you can boot to the same DOS diskette and copy a hive file into the active Registry from your backup location.

Full Restores

You can perform a full restore of the Registry if any of the following applies:

✔ You've got a very recent backup of the full Registry and you want to get back up and running as quickly as possible.

✔ The partial restore methods discussed in the first part of this chapter don't fix your problem, but you still think it's a Registry-related problem. You've already tried booting into Safe Mode and removing any new device driver (via the System control panel) or software program (via the Add/Remove Programs control panel).

Safe Mode (accessible by pressing F8 at the text-mode Starting Windows boot prompt) uses default drivers for the mouse, keyboard, display, disk, and so on, to boot your system when one of those device's normal drivers is acting up.

✔ Your Registry is so horribly mangled that you can't even perform any of the partial restore methods discussed earlier.

✔ Your Registry is fine, but you want to compress it to its minimum possible size by using NTBACKUP.

You can restore the entire Registry various different ways, depending on how you backed it up originally and on whether you can boot Windows 2000 normally or not. This section presents the more common methods, all of which presume that you're restoring onto the same machine from which you created your backups earlier. The "Restore or rebuild?" sidebar discusses the perils of restoring a Registry to a machine with different hardware than the original one.

Restore or rebuild?

Sometimes, you have a Registry backup (either by itself, or as part of a full disk backup) and you need to restore it to a machine with different hardware — either the same machine with, say, a new disk controller and drive, or maybe an entirely different machine.

If you want to take on a project like this, I won't tell you it's impossible, but it can be mighty tricky. Many computer professionals won't even try it; they'd rather reinstall Windows 2000 and any application programs and then restore only the user's data files from a backup medium. That's the route I generally recommend, especially when you're talking about restoring to a wholly different computer. For example, Windows 2000 looks at the motherboard during setup and determines what sort of power management it can use. Lots of other file and Registry decisions later in the setup process depend on that early

judgment as to motherboard type. If you just restore all the files from one Windows 2000 PC to another with a different kind of motherboard, Windows may not work properly with the new PC's power management features (or its Plug and Play features, either).

If you have a really strong reason for trying to fully restore a Windows 2000 machine onto hardware that's different from the backed-up system's hardware, then Microsoft has published some tech notes (Q112019 and Q139822) that address Windows NT 4.0 but that may work with Windows 2000. Q112019 gives details for just changing the disk and controller, Q139822 discusses changing the whole computer. You can find these notes on TechNet (if you subscribe) or on Microsoft's Web site (key in the document numbers at http://support.microsoft.com/search).

Restoring the Registry with Microsoft Windows Backup

As long as you can boot Windows 2000, either in regular mode or safe mode (see the "Backup à la mode" sidebar in Chapter 2), you can probably run Microsoft Windows Backup to restore your full Registry.

This tool is actually method one in Chapter 2. As a quick reminder for those of you who read that chapter, this program (NTBACKUP.EXE) can back up and restore the Registry even with the operating system up and running. It ain't perfect by any means. For example, you don't get a verify-after-restore option. You can't restore from a batch file. Also, NTBACKUP's tape management commands are wondrously complex. I could go on. But NTBACKUP is serviceable for doing disk-to-disk backups, which is how I usually use the program.

Here's a typical sequence of steps in order to restore the Registry on a Windows 2000 Professional machine.

1. **Run NTBACKUP by choosing Start⇨Programs⇨Accessories⇨System Tools⇨Backup.**

   You can also choose Start⇨Run and type **NTBACKUP** to activate the utility.

2. **Click the Restore tab.**

3. **Click the + sign next to the System State backup you created earlier.**

   This will have a name like "Media created 10/3/99 at 9:08 PM" to help you identify the correct backup set to restore.

4. **Select the appropriate check boxes, such as the C: drive and the System State, as shown in Figure 11-2.**

   If you used Chapter 2's procedure for backing up the whole Registry, including the individual user profiles, then you'll see these two choices.

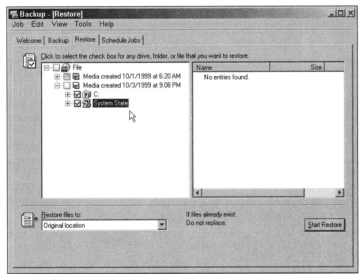

Figure 11-2:
Selecting
what to
restore.

5. **Choose Tools⇨Options to display the Options dialog box.**

6. **On the Restore tab, click** Always replace the file on my computer.

   Note the lack of an option to prompt the user if a file already exists, which is a useful choice that was present in the Windows NT 4.0 version of this program. Here, you're restoring files that you know already exist, so you have to choose this option.

7. **On the Backup Log tab, choose Detailed.**

8. **Click OK to close the Options dialog box.**

9. **Make sure the Restore Files To field at the lower left says** `Original location`.

10. **Click the Start Restore button.**

11. **Click OK after reading the warning.**

12. **Click OK in the Confirm Restore dialog box.**

13. **Click OK in the Enter Backup File Name dialog box.**

    Yes, this is redundant. You took care of this in Steps 3 and 4. Just make sure that the information is correct and click OK. When the restore is complete, you can either close out, or take a look at the report that NTBACKUP made for you.

14. **Click Yes to the message prompting you to restart the computer.**

One nice side benefit of restoring the Registry (oops, excuse me, the *system state*) with NTBACKUP is that the program gets rid of wasted space in your Registry hives. For example, on a test PC with just a few programs installed, this backup-and-restore cycle scrunched my SOFTWARE hive from 11 megabytes to around 7MB. The other hives stayed about the same size.

All other things being equal, a smaller Registry is faster and better than a bloated Registry.

NTBACKUP does not restore a select few Registry keys (mostly in *HKLM\SYSTEM\CurrentControlSet*) that might interfere with the functioning of your PC. You can view a list of these at *HKLM\SYSTEM\CurrentControlSet\Control\BackupRestore\KeysNotToRestore*. Use REGEDT32, as the values are multi-string.

A note for restoring the system state on a Windows 2000 Server machine acting as a domain controller: You must choose F8 at the text-mode Starting Windows boot prompt and select the Directory Services Restore Mode option. Follow the prompts and Windows 2000 boots you into safe mode, from which you can run NTBACKUP as described in the preceding steps. The reason for the different procedure: On a domain controller, the system state includes the Active Directory database as well as the Registry database.

Restoring the Registry with REGEDIT — Not!

You used to be able to use REGEDIT with the /C qualifier to re-create the Registry from a previously exported REG file. This procedure was always a bit risky, as it was up to the user to make sure that the REG file contained a complete Registry backup. Now, in Windows 2000, REGEDIT /C doesn't seem to work at all. You can try it, but you get an error message stating that REGEDIT cannot import the REG file because some keys are open by the system, or by another process. You get the same error if you try running REGEDIT /C in safe mode, and Windows 2000 won't allow you to run REGEDIT at all from the Recovery Console.

Restoring the Registry with the Emergency Recovery Diskette

The Emergency Repair Process is good for repairing boot sector problems, for repairing your startup environment, and for checking and repairing critical system files (using the SETUP.LOG file on the Emergency Recovery Diskette). But because this method sometimes restores the Registry and sometimes doesn't, and because it doesn't look for the most recent Registry backup, it's not the best way to authoritatively restore the Registry.

When you run the Windows 2000 setup program by booting from CD or diskette, the Emergency Repair Process (Fast option) restores the original version of your Registry. (At the Welcome to Setup text screen, press **R** to repair, **R** again for the Emergency Repair Process, and **F** for Fast repair. The manual repair option, **M**, doesn't touch the Registry.)

The Emergency Repair process only restores Registry hives that are missing or badly messed up. I can't tell you exactly what constitutes serious enough Registry corruption to trigger a restore. You may very well want to restore a Registry that the Emergency Repair Process thinks is okay.

The Emergency Repair process only looks in C:\WINNT\REPAIR, which contains your PC's original Registry. You may have made backups using NTBACKUP's Emergency Repair Disk feature, which puts Registry hives into C:\WINNT\REPAIR\REGBACK, but the Emergency Repair Process ignores them. (You could certainly make a practice of copying the REGBACK files into the REPAIR folder, but I'm not ready to recommend that. It's nice to know you can fall back to your PC's original Registry in dire situations.)

Restoring the Registry with the Recovery Console

The Recovery Console lets you restore the Registry even if you can't boot Windows 2000 normally, or in safe mode.

✔ If you've made a backup of the Registry via NTBACKUP's Emergency Repair Diskette procedure (method two in Chapter 2), then you can restore that backup (in C:\WINNT\REPAIR\REGBACK) using the Recovery Console.

✔ If you *haven't* backed up the Registry with NTBACKUP's ERD procedure, you can still restore the PC's original Registry from the C:\WINNT\REPAIR folder, although you'll lose any customizations and settings you've made since you originally installed Windows 2000.

Either way, you may be able to get your PC up and running again with this method so that you can then run NTBACKUP to restore a more recent Registry backup (as described in the "Restoring the Registry with Microsoft Windows Backup" section earlier in this chapter).

The procedure here is basically the same as in the "Restoring a hive with Recovery Console" section earlier in this chapter. The difference is that instead of renaming and copying a single hive file, you rename and copy *all* the Registry hives in the C:\WINNT\REPAIR or C:\WINNT\REPAIR\REGBACK folder.

You can't run REGEDIT or REG in the Recovery Console, which offers a very limited list of allowed commands.

Restoring the Registry with a batch file

Chapter 2 describes backup method four: booting to a DOS diskette and running a batch file to copy your Registry files to a backup location. If you use this method to back up the Registry, all you need to do to restore the Registry is to create a second batch file that simply copies all those backup files back to their original locations.

I recommend that you rename your existing Registry files with the suffix *.BAD, however, instead of overwriting them. The problem that you're having with your system may not be Registry-related, in which case you can go back to the *.BAD files (either by rebooting to DOS, or by starting the Recovery Console) and get to a more recent Registry.

Part V
For Rally Masters Only: The Networked Registry

The 5th Wave   By Rich Tennant

"I DON'T KNOW - SOME PARTS OF THE NETWORK SEEM JUST FINE, AND OTHER PARTS SEEM TO BE COMPLETELY OUT OF CONTROL."

In this part . . .

*W*hen you watch a professional auto race, you focus on the driver, but many people have a hand in that driver's ultimate success or failure: mechanics, crew, sponsors, families. The great Formula I driver from Austria, Niki Lauda, raced for Ferrari throughout his career largely because he thought that Ferrari's support network of designers, technicians, and facilities was the best around. Plus getting paid in lire made it sound like a lot more money. ("Good race, Niki! Here's your check for nine hundred million lire!")

Business is like car racing in that most successful ventures require a network of individuals working together, at least most of the time. Coordinating a network of people often depends on coordinating the network of computers they use. And the Registry is a big part of building, tuning, and managing a Windows 2000 network — as this part demonstrates.

Chapter 12

Network Management and the Registry

In This Chapter

▶ Putting a network server to work as a Windows 2000 installation device

▶ Creating a custom script to control how a user's first Registry is built

▶ Troubleshooting remote PCs by using remote Registry editing

> We have come a long, long way from the days when prehistoric humans would write crude numbers on cave walls. How would these ancient ancestors react if we were to show them a modern computer? Probably they would beat it into submission with rocks. They were a lot smarter than we realize.
>
> —From *Dave Barry In Cyberspace,*
> Dave Barry, Crown, 1996

*W*indows 2000 comes in various server flavors as well as the Professional (what Microsoft used to call *Workstation*) flavor. Nearly everything in this book up to now applies equally to all versions, but some of you have a special interest in the Server product, possibly because if you don't take a special interest in the Server product, you will get fired.

Managing a Windows 2000 network starts with beating it into submission with rocks, or, at least, network management tools. Windows 2000 includes enough network management features to fill the cargo bay of a Ford Expedition. Most of these features relate in one way or another to the new Active Directory service: IntelliMirror, Windows Installer, Group Policies, and so on. Some of these features relate to the new version of the NTFS file system, such as Windows 2000's long-requested *disk quota* capability, which lets you restrict how much disk space users can have. Most of these features interact with the Registry on a fairly intimate level in ways that don't affect users of stand-alone Windows 2000 Professional workstations.

This chapter takes two aspects of network management — rolling out Windows 2000 and troubleshooting remote PCs — to illustrate how an understanding of the Registry can make life easier for the network manager. (Another Registry-related aspect of network management, backing up a remote PC's Registry across the network, appears in Chapter 2 alongside other backup methods and techniques.) By putting the Registry to good use, you can save both time and shoe leather, taking strides towards that holy grail of network management: a happy, productive user community. (Or at least a user community that doesn't throw stale doughnuts at you when you walk by.)

The Registry and the Rollout

You can customize the Registry many ways, but one of the slickest is by creating your own custom Windows 2000 installation program. In this way, you can modify the Registry's initial contents when a new user installs Windows 2000 over a network or even from a local hard drive. Getting the Registry to look more like you want it to as part of the Windows 2000 setup program sure beats running around to a lot of PCs and making dozens of customizations after the fact. Consistent settings make life easier for those who must support and troubleshoot systems long after they're installed.

As it turns out, you can preset every one of the Registry changes that this book discusses. So how can you customize the Windows 2000 setup program to create a Registry that's closer to the way you want it from day one? I'm glad you asked.

LAN-based installation methods

First, a quick primer on the main methods available for installing Windows 2000 over a network:

✓ **Scripting:** This method involves running the setup program from a central network server under control of a script — a method that works really well in situations where you have a hodgepodge of PC makes, models, and components. The setup program can still autodetect PC hardware and make adjustments for the fact (for example) that Carina has a 3Com network card while Cecily has a Madge network card. The customized script that you create to guide the setup program doesn't mandate that everyone's initial Registry look identical — that doesn't work, for example, with the two different network cards. The script mandates only that *certain* settings such as the time zone, standard networking language, and so on are identical on each PC.

✔ **Disk Cloning:** If you're lucky enough to work in a network where everyone has pretty much the same hardware, you may want to consider *disk cloning* as an alternative to a scripted, network-based setup. Microsoft provides the SysPrep utility for this situation. What you basically do with disk cloning is to crank out carbon-copy hard drives that include not only Windows 2000 but also any desired Windows 2000 applications. This technique works *only* if all the PCs have the same basic hardware (Hardware Abstraction Layer, power management, hard disk controller, and number of processors); other hardware can vary, because of the new Windows 2000 Plug and Play detection capabilities. If your network PCs are all very similar, disk cloning may be faster and easier than setting up a network-based setup with a custom script. Cloning a hard drive over a network can take as little as ten minutes.

✔ **Remote Installation Service (RIS):** You can set up a Windows 2000 Server with RIS, which enables you to install Windows 2000 onto PCs that don't even have an existing operating system on their hard drives. Such PCs can boot to a special diskette or they may have a network card with remote-boot capabilities.

The next section takes a closer look at the first of these three methods and how you can use it to create a customized initial Registry. (You can customize the initial Registry with the other two setup methods, also, but the process is more involved; check out the *Windows 2000 Server Resource Kit* for details.)

Tales from the script

The cool part of a custom installation — and the part where you can start tinkering with the prenatal Registry — is creating a special text file known as the *answer file*. This is the script for the installation, and it kicks in whenever a user runs the Windows 2000 setup program (that is, WINNT32.EXE for upgrades from Windows NT or Windows 9*x,* WINNT.EXE for upgrades from Windows 3.*x* or DOS) from the server directory.

If you've ever installed any version of Windows, you know that the setup program asks you a number of questions, such as "What's your computer name? What time zone do you live in? If Bill Gates ran for president, would you vote for him?" and so on. The *answer file* in Windows 2000 is like a virtual user that automatically answers each of the setup program's questions as they come up. Because the answers come from a file instead of an interactive user, the installation is termed *unattended,* hence the typical name of the answer file: UNATTEND.TXT. Figure 12-1 shows an example of an answer file, and Figure 12-2 shows an example of an UNATTEND.BAT file that would actually start a Windows 2000 installation.

Figure 12-1:
A fairly
brief, simple
answer file.

```
unattend.txt - Notepad                              _ |□| x|
File  Edit  Format  Help
;SetupMgrTag
[Data]
    AutoPartition=1

[Unattended]
    UnattendMode=ProvideDefault
    OemPreinstall=Yes
    TargetPath=\WINNT

[GuiUnattended]
    OEMSkipRegional=0
    TimeZone=10

[UserData]
    FullName=AnyUser
    OrgName=Acme Cognac, Inc.
    ComputerName="

[Display]
    BitsPerPel=24
    Xresolution=800
    YResolution=600

[TapiLocation]
    CountryCode=593

[RegionalSettings]
    LanguageGroup=3

[SetupMgr]
    DistFolder=E:\DIST
    DistShare=win2000dist

[GuiRunOnce]
    Command0="regedit stuff.reg"
```

Figure 12-2:
An auto-
generated
batch file to
run setup
with the
answer file.

```
unattend.bat - Notepad                              _ |□| x|
File  Edit  Format  Help
@rem SetupMgrTag
@echo off

rem
rem This is a SAMPLE batch script generated by the Setup Manager wizard.
rem If this script is moved from the location where it was generated, it
may have to be modified.
rem

set AnswerFile=.\unattend.txt
set SetupFiles=\\KAYAK-W2K\win2000dist

\\KAYAK-W2K\win2000dist\winnt32 /s:%SetupFiles% /unattend:%AnswerFile%
```

Microsoft provides a very long document (UNATTEND.DOC, located in the DEPLOY.CAB file on the Windows 2000 CD's \SUPPORT\TOOLS folder) explaining all the details of creating an answer file. Happily, the company also provides a friendly, graphical utility called Setup Manager (SETUPMGR.EXE) that does a pretty good job of building an answer file for you. The UNATTEND.DOC file is handy to know about in case you want to fine-tune your answer file by hand, but you may never need it.

Installing Setup Manager

Windows 2000 doesn't automatically install Setup Manager, so you have to install it yourself. As of this writing, the tool lives in a "cabinet" file named DEPLOY.CAB on the Windows 2000 CD in the \SUPPORT\TOOLS folder. The installation procedure is as follows:

1. **Slide the Windows 2000 CD-ROM into the drive.**

   You can use either the Professional or Server version.

2. **Open Windows Explorer.**

3. **Create a new folder for the Setup Manager program.**

   I'm partial to `C:\Program Files\Deploy`, but pick any name that you like.

4. **Double-click the CD file** `\SUPPORT\TOOLS\DEPLOY.CAB`**.**

   Windows 2000 automatically opens up compressed CAB, or *cabinet*, files within the Explorer window. You don't have to extract the files one by one, as you do with some other Windows versions.

5. **Drag and drop all the contents of DEPLOY.CAB into the folder you created in Step 2.**

6. **Right-click-and-drag SETUPMGR.EXE onto the desktop and choose Create Shortcut Here.**

   Alternatively or additionally, you can drag and drop this file to a position on your Start menu.

After you install Setup Manager, running it is simply a matter of double-clicking the icon you created, or selecting the Start menu option you made. You then see the manager's main screen, as shown in Figure 12-3.

Figure 12-3:
Setup
Manager's
main
screen.

Setting script options via "Run Once"

As you go through the various screens in Setup Manager — a laborious procedure, by the way, compared to the tabbed Batch 98 utility that provides similar functionality in Windows 98 — you provide the answers to as many setup questions as you want. I'm not going to go through every one of those screens here. Instead, I'd like to focus on the screens that you can use to modify the Registry with your own custom settings. The first such screen has the name Run Once, as shown in Figure 12-4.

To see the Run Once screen, you must click Yes when asked whether you want to specify "additional settings" after you've created the basic answer file.

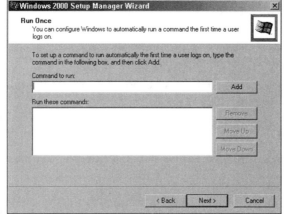

Figure 12-4:
Setup
Manager's
Run Once
screen.

The commands that you enter here run automatically the first time a user logs onto Windows 2000 after setup has finished. You can include here, for example, a command such as **REGEDIT BLAH.REG** if you want to merge the contents of BLAH.REG into the user's Registry. (BLAH.REG could be a file with Registry keys that you exported from a test PC, or it could be a file that you created yourself, using REGEDIT export files as a guide; see Chapter 14 for more on creating REG files.)

The commands that you enter in Setup Manager's Run Once screen appear in the [GUIRunOnce] section of UNATTEND.TXT, by the way, in case you want to use Notepad to edit them after you run Setup Manager.

Even though virtually every "answer" that you provide to Setup Manager affects the Registry of the installing user, the Run Once screen offers a chance for you to modify Registry entries directly. You can also specify other Registry-related commands, such as the REG.EXE program (which comes with the Windows 2000 Resource Kit Tools), NTBACKUP, or pretty much anything you want, Registry-related or not.

Three very important points merit your attention if you plan to use the Run Once feature:

- **Number 1:** If your user is upgrading from a previous version of Windows, the Run Once feature doesn't work. (It seems illogical to me, too. Changing network settings doesn't work in this scenario, either, so be forewarned.)

- **Number B:** Because the Run Once commands execute after the first user logon, any user-related settings affect the *HKCU* branch, rather than the default user.

- **Number III:** The Run Once commands are subject to any permissions restrictions that may apply to the logged-on user. If you want to make Registry changes that will not be restricted by any potential permissions issues, you should use the CMDLINES.TXT file, described in the titled "Setting script options via CMDLINES.TXT" section later in this chapter.

Creating the distribution point

An essential step in creating a network-based setup procedure is to install a complete copy of the Windows 2000 source files onto a server, called a *distribution server,* from which a new user can install Windows 2000 across the network onto the workstation. (The server "distributes" Windows 2000 to the network users, who use the server as the source for their Windows 2000 files instead of the Windows 2000 CD-ROM.)

Setup Manager offers to create a distribution point for you as its final act; this is an offer you should generally accept, because it saves you the trouble of manually copying over the necessary files to your network server and ensures that all the right files make the trip. Creating a distribution point is also a necessary step if you want to run a CMDLINES.TXT file, which won't run from a CD-ROM even if you burn your own.

If you want to include your own custom help files, application files, or any other sort of files in the Windows 2000 distribution folder, Setup Manager lets you do so in the Additional Files or Folders window toward the end of the procedure. Those additional files go into the folder named OEM in recognition of the fact that Original Equipment Manufacturers (*OEMs*) make heavy use of this feature. (That doesn't mean that you can't, too!)

Setting script options via CMDLINES.TXT

After you tell Setup Manager where you want your distribution point to be, and after you answer a few more questions, you get to the Additional Commands screen, as shown in Figure 12-5.

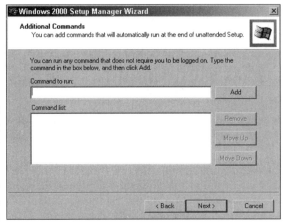

Figure 12-5:
Setup
Manager's
Additional
Commands
screen.

Any additional commands that you type into this window ultimately go into the text file CMDLINES.TXT, which Setup Manager places into the OEM folder of your distribution point. The simple CMDLINES.TXT file has a section labeled [Commands] under which you can see the command or commands you created in the Additional Commands screen. As with the "Run Once" section, these commands can include instructions to load REG files of your own devising. And if you want to get fancy, they can also include VBScript or JavaScript programs that you create.

Unlike the Run Once commands, commands in CMDLINES.TXT execute at the end of the setup procedure but *before* the user logs on to Windows 2000 for the first time. These commands basically run with system privileges, so they aren't subject to any user-specific access control restrictions. Furthermore, CMDLINES.TXT runs whether the user is performing an upgrade from a previous version of Windows, or from a fresh install. However, because no user is logged on, no access to protected network resources is available.

Figure 12-6 shows a fairly typical example of a distribution point created by Setup Manager. Note the presence of CMDLINES.TXT in the OEM folder.

You may notice a few files in the distribution folder with names like HIVE*xxx*.INF, where "*xxx*" varies from one file to the next; these are, in fact, seed files that Windows 2000 uses to create the baby Registry. *Don't modify them!* Make your Registry changes via the Run Once or CMDLINES.TXT methods outlined previously. Windows 2000 performs some integrity checks on the HIVE*xxx*.INF files and if you monkey with them, the operating system may refuse to install.

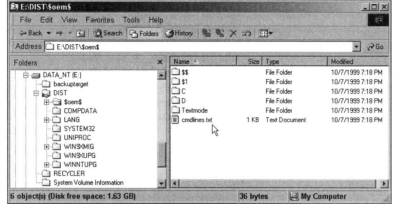

Figure 12-6:
A distribution server, ready for action.

Implementing the scripted setup

Your final step would be to include the setup command file (typically UNATTEND.BAT) in a network logon script. Here's a typical procedure:

1. **Set up a special user account (say, UPGRADE) for the user who wants to install Windows 2000 to log on to.**

2. **Define appropriate security for the UPGRADE account (no changing passwords, rights to the server with Windows 2000 on it, and so on).**

3. **Create a logon script and associate it with the UPGRADE user.**

When a user wants to install Windows 2000, she can log on to the UPGRADE account and sit back, answering only the questions that you left for users to decide on their own (if any).

Editing Remote Registries

Say you're using Windows 2000 on a network and, because of your skills, your job description, or both, other network users look to you for technical support. Now, say a novice Windows user calls you for help, and it becomes clear that some Registry editing is necessary — but you would no more trust that user with REGEDIT or REGEDT32 than give a 13-year-old the keys to a Corvette.

You can always walk over to the user's PC, but if you do a lot of technical support work, you don't want to spend your life walking around the building — besides, all your handy reference books are in your own office. Plus, you may prefer that the user doesn't see what you're doing, so he won't be tempted to try it himself after you leave! Good news: You can run either Registry Editor on your machine and edit the distressed user's Registry remotely over the network.

If you need to modify everyone's Registry and not just a single user's, consider writing a script that executes at logon and modifies the Registry. The Group Policy property sheet for Active Directory objects lets you specify the name and location of logon and logoff scripts, and Chapter 9 provides a short example of a VBScript file that modifies the Registry. (JavaScript works fine, too.) Microsoft has also published a TechNet paper titled "Windows 2000 Professional in a Novell NetWare Environment" that provides details for using logon scripts on Novell networks; track it down using `www.microsoft.com/search`.

Getting set up for remote Registry editing

You can use a Registry Editor remotely only if all of the following conditions are met:

- ✔ Your network is a *client/server* type, that is, you have a dedicated central server running a network operating system like Novell NetWare or Windows 2000 Server. In other words, you can't run REGEDIT over a peer-to-peer network like LANtastic or the workgroup networking built into Windows 2000, NT, and 9x.

- ✔ You log on with an account that has administrative privileges both on the local PC and on the remote PC you're attempting to connect to. (Note that the remote PC just has to be on and at the "Welcome to Windows" screen in order for you to connect to it over the network and edit its Registry; a user doesn't have to be logged onto it locally.) It may seem weird that you can effectively log on to a remote machine over the network, but with the appropriate software support, you can do almost anything over a network or dial-up link that you can do from a local keyboard. Products like PCAnywhere take such capabilities much further than the Registry Editors.

- ✔ The Windows 2000 PCs you want to connect over the network share at least one common *protocol* or network language (usually TCP/IP, IPX, or NetBEUI).

Running REGEDIT remotely

After satisfying the requirements in the previous section, using REGEDIT to modify a remote user's Registry is a piece o' cake:

1. **Run REGEDIT.**

2. **Choose Registry⇨Connect Network Registry.**

   The Connect Network Registry dialog box appears.

3. **Type in the name of the computer you want to connect to in the Computer Name field, or select the computer you want from a list by clicking the Browse button.**

4. **Click OK in the Connect Network Registry dialog box.**

   A screen like Figure 12-7 appears, showing your local machine's Registry at the top of the left windowpane and the remote machine's Registry at the bottom.

Figure 12-7:
Viewing a
remote
user's
Registry in
REGEDIT.

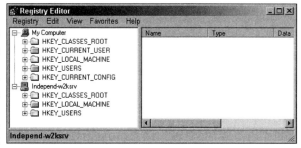

Notice that you can only see the *HKLM*, *HKU*, and *HKCR* branches of the remote Registry. This makes sense, because you're not really logged on to the remote machine as a user, so your "current configuration" and your "current user" status don't really exist. However, you have access to keys for all users via *HKU* and to keys for all configurations via *HKLM*. So, in effect, the entire remote Registry is available to you for editing.

Running REGEDT32 remotely

Using REGEDT32 to modify a remote user's Registry is just as easy as it is using REGEDIT. The same three prerequisites discussed earlier apply with REGEDT32, too. The commands are slightly different, however:

1. **Run REGEDT32.**

2. **Choose Registry▷Select Computer.**

   The Select Computer dialog box appears.

3. **Type in the computer's network name or pick a computer from the list and click OK.**

In REGEDT32 you can only see *HKLM* and *HKU*, not *HKCR* — but because *HKCR* is just an alias to other keys within *HKLM* and *HKU,* this limitation isn't really limiting, just a bit of an inconvenience.

Limiting remote Registry access

You can control who can and can't edit a given Windows 2000 PC's Registry remotely. If you add or remove users or groups from the permission list of the special Registry key *HKLM\SYSTEM\CurrentControlSet\Control\ SecurePipeServers\winreg*, you simultaneously enable or disable those users or groups from accessing that machine's Registry remotely. By default, only administrators can modify this key. Backup operators can read it, which gives them the ability to back up the Registry on remote PCs.

Chapter 13

Network Services and the Registry

In This Chapter

▶ Finding out where network services store their settings in the Registry

▶ Discovering the stop-and-restart rule for making Registry changes

▶ Picking up some Registry-based performance pointers

*A*lthough the Windows 2000 Active Directory certainly steals some of the Registry's thunder when it comes to centralizing network configuration, many network-related settings still live in Ye Olde Registry. In fact, the Registry's split user/machine design makes certain network services possible — such as Terminal Server, now included with Windows 2000 Server, which lets you set up *dumb PCs* to run Windows and Windows programs without any local storage.

My goals in this little chapter are to suggest a few areas that may merit your attention and to identify some of the more important Registry locations for network service configuration data. Those of you who have configuration responsibility for your network may want to probe more deeply into these Registry settings than I can here; for example, by delving into Microsoft white papers and technical notes available on the Web. Point your browser to http://www.microsoft.com/search and go crazy.

TCP/IP

The network language of choice for Windows started as NetBEUI, changed to IPX/SPX, and has now become TCP/IP (Transmission Control Protocol/Internet Protocol). The evolution has certainly moved from simple to complex: TCP/IP has more configurable parameters than Hollywood has Porsches. You can modify many TCP/IP parameters via the Network and Dial-Up Connections folder, but some hide in the Registry, where you can only tune them up with REGEDIT or REGEDT32.

Registry-based TCP/IP settings live in *HKLM\SYSTEM\CurrentControlSet\ Services\Tcpip\Parameters.* This section provides a few examples of how you can use the Registry to control TCP/IP.

TCP/IP Registry settings are described in detail in the *Windows 2000 Server Resource Kit* and in a technical paper titled "MS Windows 2000 TCP/IP Implementation Details," which you can find on TechNet as well as on Microsoft's Web site.

Automatic IP addressing

Automatic IP addressing, introduced with Windows 98, allows Windows PCs to assign themselves IP addresses if no address server exists on the network. You can turn this feature off by flipping the DWORD value *IPAutoconfigurationEnabled* from 1 to 0 in the key *HKLM\SYSTEM\ CurrentControlSet\Services\Tcpip\Parameters\Interfaces\<adaptername>.* If the value doesn't already exist, add it. You can also disable automatic IP addressing for *all* network adapters on the system by setting *IPAutoconfigurationEnabled* to 0 in *HKLM\SYSTEM\CurrentControlSet\Services\ Tcpip\Parameters.*

Novell recommends turning off automatic IP addressing on clients of NetWare networks.

IP security

IP security features are much enhanced in Windows 2000. Monitoring and troubleshooting secure IP becomes easier with a Registry Editor, because you can turn on logging as follows:

- ✔ **Policy agent logging:** Set the DWORD value *Debug* to 1 in the *HKLM\SYSTEM\CurrentControlSet\Services\PolicyAgent* subkey. Policy agent logging records data to IPSECPA.LOG in `C:\WINNT\DEBUG`.

- ✔ **Security association logging:** Set the DWORD value *Debug* to 1 in the *HKLM\SYSTEM\CurrentControlSet\Services\PolicyAgent\Oakley* subkey. Security association logging records data to OAKLEY.LOG in `C:\WINNT\DEBUG`.

TCP/IP tuning

One of the key performance variables for the TCP/IP protocol is the transmission packet *window size.* (And the correct value is *not* "2000.") The larger the window size, the less overhead your network must endure. However, at some point (which varies depending on the connection speed), too large a window size produces looong delays. Believe me, you'll know when you hit that point!

The setting to tweak is the DWORD value *TcpWindowSize* in the *HKLM\System\CurrentControlSet\Services\Tcpip\Parameters* key. Add it if it doesn't already exist. The setting's decimal value is typically 64240, 32120, or 16060. Try the larger numbers first and if you don't suffer bad delays, you're in good shape.

Removing and reinstalling TCP/IP

When you remove the TCP/IP protocol from a Windows 2000 PC, remnants of it remain in the Registry. This fact is a PITA (Internet-ese for *pain in the . . . abdomen*). If you install TCP/IP again later, or if you install some other service that needs to install TCP/IP as a prerequisite, then you are highly likely to encounter the error `The registry subkey already exists.`

The way around this problem is to use either REGEDIT or REGEDT32 to manually and completely exorcise TCP/IP from your system before you reinstall it. The keys to delete (and some may not appear on your system) are:

- *HKLM\SYSTEM\CurrentControlSet\Services\<adapter>\Parameters\Tcpip* (where *<adapter>* is the network adapter's ClassID)
- *HKLM\SYSTEM\CurrentControlSet\Services\Dhcp*
- *HKLM\SYSTEM\CurrentControlSet\Services\LmHosts*
- *HKLM\SYSTEM\CurrentControlSet\Services\NetBT*
- *HKLM\SYSTEM\CurrentControlSet\Services\Tcpip*
- *HKLM\SYSTEM\CurrentControlSet\Services\TcpipCU*

TCP/IP Applications and Services

Applications and services intimately related to TCP/IP — software such as Telnet, DHCP, DNS, and so forth — also make pretty extensive use of the Registry. This section offers a few tips for these rascals.

DHCP

Dynamic Host Configuration Protocol, or DHCP, is a boon for reducing the administrative overhead of a Windows network. DHCP assigns IP addresses to clients as they join the network and permits automatic assignment of various other TCP/IP settings as well.

Most of the Registry-based DHCP server settings live in *HKLM\SYSTEM\ CurrentControlSet\Services\DHCPServer\Parameters*. For example:

- ✔ If you want to change the default value of 15 minutes for the DHCP database backup interval, change the *BackupInterval* value in this key.

- ✔ Specify the full path to the folder where you want the DHCP log file to live in the *DhcpLogFilePath* string value.

- ✔ Tell Windows 2000 to stop DHCP logging when the server is about to run out of disk space by specifying the threshold free space value, in megabytes, in the *DhcpLogMinSpaceOnDisk* DWORD value.

As with removing TCP/IP and then reinstalling it later, when you remove DHCP, you should also fire up a Registry Editor and delete the following keys, which Windows 2000 is likely to leave lying around:

- ✔ *HKLM\SOFTWARE\Microsoft\DhcpMibAgent*

- ✔ *HKLM\SOFTWARE\Microsoft\DhcpServer*

- ✔ *HKLM\SYSTEM\CurrentControlSet\Services\DhcpServer*

DNS

Domain Name Services, or DNS, lives at the heart of the new Windows 2000 networking model. Active Directory requires DNS, which manages computer domain names such as W2KSRV1.MAIN-DOMAIN.I-SW.COM and correlates those names with numeric IP addresses.

The default behavior for the DNS service on a Windows 2000 Server domain controller is for DNS to use settings in both the Registry and the Active Directory database for controlling its operation. As Active Directory matures, I expect future versions of the Server product to use the Active Directory more and the Registry less.

You can change DNS's behavior so that it uses the Registry only, or, so that it doesn't use the Registry but uses a text file (BOOT.DNS) to control all settings. Choose Start➪Programs➪Administrative Tools➪DNS, right-click the server, choose Properties, and click the Advanced tab. Then modify the Load Zone Data on Startup field by selecting the option you want from the drop-down list box.

Most of the Registry-based DNS settings live in *HKLM\SYSTEM\ CurrentControlSet\Services\Dns\Parameters*. These are described in detail in the Windows 2000 Server Resource Kit. After you make a change to one of these settings, you must stop and restart the DNS service before they take effect.

If you want to preset DNS server locations for network clients that dial up over a remote connection, the Registry value to modify is *DNSNameServers* in the *HKLM\SYSTEM\CurrentControlSet\Services\RemoteAccess\Parameters\IP* key. This is a REG_MULTI_SZ value, so use REGEDT32 and give it the dotted IP addresses of the primary and backup DNS server machines.

When you remove DNS, run REGEDT32 or REGEDIT and delete the following leftover keys:

- ✔ *HKLM\SOFTWARE\Microsoft\Dns*
- ✔ *HKLM\SYSTEM\CurrentControlSet\Services\Dns*

Telnet

The Telnet Server settings live in the *HKLM\SOFTWARE\Microsoft\TelnetServer\1.0* key. For example, you may need to adjust the authentication method. You can set the DWORD value *NTLM* to 0 for no NTLM authentication, 1 to try NTLM first and then try without it, and 2 to use NTLM only. You must stop and restart the Telnet Server service for any change in this key to take effect.

The Telnet Server Admin utility's option 3 lets you change Telnet-related Registry settings. Run the utility by opening a command prompt and typing **TLNTADMN**. Refer to the Windows Help system for details on each setting; search on "telnet server admin."

WINS

The death of Windows Internet Naming Service, or WINS, in Windows 2000 has been (as Mark Twain might say) greatly exaggerated. In a pure Windows 2000 network, you may not need WINS anymore, but it's still handy for mixed networks with "downlevel" clients such as Windows NT 4.0 and Windows 98. Those older operating systems use NetBIOS names to identify computers instead of the DNS names favored by Windows 2000. WINS helps correlate NetBIOS names to IP addresses for such systems.

If you want to preset WINS settings for network clients that dial up over a remote connection, enter the dotted IP address of the WINS server machine (or machines) into the following values under the *HKLM\SYSTEM\CurrentControlSet\Services\RemoteAccess\Paramaters\IP* key:

- ✔ *WINSNameServer*
- ✔ *WINSNameServerBackup*

When you remove WINS, you should also fire up a Registry Editor and delete the following keys, which Windows 2000 is likely to leave lying around:

- ✔ *HKLM\SOFTWARE\Microsoft\Wins*
- ✔ *HKLM\SOFTWARE\Microsoft\WinsMibAgent*
- ✔ *HKLM\SYSTEM\CurrentControlSet\Services\Wins*

Internet Information Server

Internet Information Server, or IIS, comes with Windows 2000 Server and allows you to host World Wide Web and FTP sites on an intranet or Internet server.

The version of IIS that ships with Windows 2000 (that is, 5.0) doesn't require you to make as many manual Registry settings as previous versions of IIS. The IIS snap-in for the Microsoft Management Console allows you to set nearly all IIS options.

Many of those settings live in the metabase, which you can think of as Active Directory for IIS. The *metabase* is a hierarchical database that lets you make IIS settings for a specific computer, Web site, file, folder, or virtual folder. The metabase is faster, more flexible, and more expandable than the Registry.

Having said that, IIS 5.0 still uses the Registry for some things. Here are the relevant locations.

- ✔ "Global" IIS settings in the Registry live in the *HKLM\SYSTEM\ CurrentControlSet\Services\InetInfo\Parameters* key. If you change any of these, you must stop and restart all IIS services for them to take effect.
- ✔ The WWW service keeps its Registry settings in *HKLM\SYSTEM\ CurrentControlSet\Services\W3SVC\Parameters*. If you change any of these, you must stop and restart the WWW service.
- ✔ The FTP service keeps its Registry settings in *HKLM\SYSTEM\ CurrentControlSet\Services\MSFTPSVC\Parameters*. If you change any of these, you must stop and restart the FTP service.

If you want to move the metabase to a different location, as you may (for example) to help balance the disk activity load on a busy server, you can do so with the Registry's help by following these steps:

1. **Stop IIS.**

2. **Move METABASE.BIN from its default location in the INETSRV folder to wherever you want its new home to be.**

3. **Add a string value named** *MetadataFile* **to the** *HKLM\SOFTWARE* *Microsoft\INetMgr\Parameters* **key. Assign this value the complete path (including drive letter) to the new metabase location.**

4. **Restart IIS.**

   That's it; you're done!

Improving Server Performance

You can use the Registry in various ways to improve server performance, as well as set configuration options. Here are three examples.

Just browsing

One way to tune up a Windows network is to tinker with the *browsemaster,* or browser server, settings. A browsemaster is a machine that services other PCs' requests to find computers on the network. With the default settings, PCs on a Windows network negotiate with each other to figure out who should perform browsemastering. Computers running more recent versions of Windows always win this election.

However, that default behavior may not always be appropriate. For example:

- You may have Windows 2000 running on a relatively slow machine. Windows 2000 is likely to win a browsemaster election if the other computers on the network are all running Windows NT 4.0 or Windows 98. But you'd rather disable browsemastering on that Windows 2000 computer because other, faster computers are better able to handle the chore.

- You may have a single Windows 2000 Professional machine on a network with a couple of Windows NT 4.0 servers. You want the servers to do server-type stuff (such as browsemastering), but the Windows 2000 workstation will take on that job because it's the most recent flavor of Windows on the network.

- You may take into consideration how heavily used a given machine is. A lightly used PC at a reception desk, for example, may be the most logical candidate to handle browsing services.

You can change the value *MaintainServerList* in the *HKLM\SYSTEM* *CurrentControlSet\Services\Browser\Parameters* key and modify the default browsemaster behavior. Changing the default value "Auto" to "No" disables browsemastering on that computer. Stop and restart the browser service to make the change take effect.

Give me all your cache

The tip I'm about to give you is secret and highly unrecommended by Microsoft, and so it's time for one of those scary icons:

You are probably making Windows 2000 Server more vulnerable to Active Directory database corruption by making the change in this section. I mention this change mainly for those of you running Windows 2000 Server in nonserver mode (for example, programmers) and for those of you running noncritical network servers that have highly reliable hardware, battery backup, and frequently backed up disks. You must be over 21 to try this technique. Do not try this technique while in the bathtub or shower, or while taking medication.

One of the things I found out fairly early in the Windows 2000 product development cycle was that the Server version disables write caching if you've set up the machine as an Active Directory domain controller. (*Write caching* simply means that Windows can delay hard-drive write operations for a few tenths of a second and wait for a moment when the system isn't all that busy with other tasks.) The party line is that turning write caching off makes it less likely that the Active Directory database will get mangled in a power interruption. (Non–domain controllers don't manage the Active Directory database, so write caching isn't such a big deal with them.)

Write caching has a pretty noticeable impact on system performance, though, so I pestered Microsoft until I found out how to turn it back on. (They love me over there, as you can imagine.) The string value name is *DSA Heuristics* and it lives in *HKLM\SYSTEM\CurrentControlSet\Services\NTDS\Parameters,* along with most of the other Active Directory settings. (NTDS is short for NT Directory Services, which is in turn an alias for Active Directory.) Give the string a value of "1" and you prevent NTDS from disabling write caching. Be prepared to see a lot of fussy messages in the File Replication Service event log after you make this change, but your system should run measurably faster. If you don't notice much difference, then delete the *DSA Heuristics* value; this risk is only worth taking if you gain speed — sort of like the lightweight bumpers I put on one of my old sports cars when I was a younger, less mortal man.

While you're looking in the NTDS key, take a look at some of the other parameters that live there. The Active Directory database itself lives in the NTDS.DIT file, and Windows 2000 manipulates it with the Microsoft "Jet" database engine. This database can hold millions of objects, it's extensible, and performance doesn't degrade with size as fast as a flat-file database (such as the Registry).

A Terminal Server tweak

Windows 2000 Server now comes with Terminal Server, a product formerly known by the catchy moniker "Windows NT Server 4.0 Terminal Server Edition." Terminal Server lets you use old, slow PCs much like mainframe terminals: The PCs connect to a Windows 2000 Server where the lion's share of the processing occurs, and the local PCs only handle keyboard and display chores. I recommend this approach to organizations that need to run modern software but don't want to throw out dozens or hundreds of perfectly functional older machines. (You do need a pretty powerful machine for your Windows 2000 Server, though, if you're going to run Terminal Server on it.)

To make Terminal Server seem faster to the user, you can increase the size of the *bitmap cache*, a chunk of disk space on the local PC that's devoted to storing image files so the PC doesn't have to get these from the server over and over. Beef up the size of the DWORD value *BitmapCache Size* in the key *HKCU\Software\Microsoft\Terminal Server Client\Default*. (Add the value if it isn't already there.)

Part VI
The Part of Tens

The 5th Wave   By Rich Tennant

"Oddly enough, the Windows 2000 Add New Hardware
wizard recognized it immediately."

In this part . . .

When you race cross-country, you need every edge you can get. Often, that means you know a little trick that other drivers don't know: rolling your window down if you start feeling drowsy, rechecking your tire pressure when you change elevation, not reminding the highway patrolman who pulls you over for doing 120 miles per hour, that your taxes pay his salary, and so on.

This Part, a traditional aspect of the *...For Dummies* series, offers a trunkful of such tips that may come in handy as you drive off into the sunset.

Chapter 14

Ten (Or So) Registry Tricks

In This Chapter

▶ Unlocking the Registry secrets of Windows Installer files

▶ Controlling what programs Windows 2000 can run with Start⇨Run

▶ Hiding selected Control Panels

▶ Customizing the logon screen

▶ Telling Windows 2000 where to find its own files

> *When you do go off the road the most important thing to do is to turn the wheels straight the instant just before you leave the road so you don't dig a wheel into the dirt and flip over. The next most important thing is to not hit anything.*
>
> —From *Bob Bondurant on High Performance Driving*,
> Bob Bondurant with John Blakemore, Motorbooks International, 1982

*Y*ou can't have too many helpful tips and tricks up your sleeve, whether you're driving your car or driving your computer. This chapter contains some miscellaneous Windows 2000 Registry tricks that I couldn't figure out where else to put. Most of these are potentially very convenient and useful, others are just cool.

Some of these tips I derived from Microsoft's technical notes, others have been shared with me by students and colleagues, and a few I discovered myself (no doubt simultaneously with dozens of other Registry hackers!). In all cases, I've tried the tips, and they haven't caused any problems that I've noticed on my machines. However, to quote two of those Internet acronyms, YMMV (Your Mileage May Vary) and SAYOR (Swim At Your Own Risk). So, the standard grandmotherly caution applies here, as everywhere:

Back up your Registry before making *any* of the changes in this chapter. And if you never listened to your grandmother, then *at least* back up the specific Registry key that you're about to change.

The tricks in this chapter typically involve using one or both Registry Editors, so if you haven't looked over Chapter 4, you may want to do so. I assume here that you're familiar enough with REGEDIT and REGEDT32 to know how to add, delete, and change keys and values. Also, you need to log on as an Administrator to perform some of the Registry magic in this chapter. Now on to the tips.

Peek Inside a Windows Installer Package

One of the truly good new goodies in Windows 2000 is the *Windows Installer,* a combination of utilities and specifications that I mention in Chapter 14.

If you haven't read that chapter yet, I should start by explaining that Microsoft's new Windows Installer guidelines specify the structure of an *.MSI file, which you can double-click to install a program. The *.MSI file contains not only a list of files to copy, shortcuts to create, INI files to build or modify, services to run, and so on, but also an organized list of Registry changes that the installation performs when activated.

Now, one of the great things about such a scheme is that it makes a proper rollback not only feasible, but practical. When you remove a program that uses Windows Installer, any Registry changes unique to that program should go away. That keeps the Registry leaner and meaner and makes Registry troubleshooting simpler.

In the past, the technology was available for such a "clean" rollback, but many application software vendors (Microsoft included!) didn't take full advantage of it. Now that the technology for a clean rollback ships with Windows 2000, it seems fair to predict that more programs will use it. So, raise a glass with me and say a toast to Windows Installer: Late though ye have arrived, glad we are ye are here.

One price for the new Windows Installer technology, however, is that for the power user or the system administrator, figuring out what a given program does upon installation is not nearly so obvious. Many of us "in the business" grew adept at reading and understanding *.INF files, the text files that many programs use to direct what happens during setup. However, the *.MSI file (which stands for Microsoft Software Installer) is inscrutable. It's a database package of a special format, not suitable for viewing in Notepad or WordPad. So does any way exist to "peek inside" an MSI file and see what a given application is about to do to your Registry before it does it?

Yes indeed, but the secret utility lies buried several folders deep on your Windows 2000 CD-ROM. Look in the folder \VALUADD\3RDPARTY\ MGMT\WINSTLE and you should see, together with a couple of "read me" documents that are worth reading, the file SWIADMLE.MSI (pronounced "swee-add-millie-dot-imzee").

By now, you recognize the MSI suffix as a Windows Installer database. But this is a special one. Double-click the file, and Windows Installer puts the Veritas program WinINSTALL LE onto your PC. (The "LE" stands for "Limited Edition," meaning that this is a somewhat feature-shy, freebie version of a bigger program that you can pay money for.) The best news is that WinINSTALL LE lets you open any *.MSI file on your hard drive (or any other read/write drive) and check out its contents. For example, you can run WinINSTALL LE and open the file SWIADMLE.MSI and take a look at the installation details for Winstall LE itself.

However, if you try to open SWIADMLE.MSI while it's sitting out there on the CD-ROM, you'll get the error message in Figure 14-1, because Winstall LE is an action-oriented program that wants to be able to modify an installer package as well as just read it. So use Windows Explorer to copy the file to your hard drive. Then, right-click it, choose Properties, and clear the "Read-Only" check box. Now you can open it in WinINSTALL LE by simply right-clicking the filename and choosing the Edit with WinINSTALL LE command.

Figure 14-1:
WinINSTALL
LE won't
open a
read-only
file.

The WinINSTALL LE window can get pretty complicated, but I'd like to keep things simple here. If you click the + sign by the WinINSTALL LE package icon in the upper-left windowpane, you can expand the tree to see the WinINSTALL LE feature icon right below it. The terminology of Windows Installer is fairly straightforward:

✔ A *package* is basically a program.

✔ A *feature* is a module of a program that benefits from being installable separately.

For example, a database program might constitute a package, and a report-writer module that ships with that database program might constitute a feature. Some people may want the database program, but without the report writer feature. Alternatively, it may be possible to use the report writer feature with some other vendor's database program, although that scenario is probably more theoretical than practical. Anyway, one program can contain lots of features, which is typical of larger programs, or (as with WinINSTALL LE) only one feature.

If you now click directly on the WinINSTALL LE feature icon, all of a sudden the lower-left window displays several categories. These are the various elements that go together to define precisely what happens when you install that feature. These elements are pretty much what you'd expect: files to copy, shortcuts to create, Registry entries to make, and so on.

Click the Registry listing in that lower-left windowpane, and the right-hand windowpane shows a My Computer icon. Expand that, and lo and behold, you can see all the Registry entries that the SWIADMLE.MSI database will add to your system when the WinINSTALL LE feature gets installed (see Figure 14-2).

Now for something fun. If you look closely at Figure 14-2, you can see the Registry key *HKCR\Msi.Package\shell\leedit*, which contains the string value *&Edit with WinINSTALL LE*. Recognize that? It's the right-click command that you chose to start WinINSTALL LE in the first place! So this is the Registry entry that puts the "Edit with WinINSTALL LE" command on the context menu for *.MSI files. If you want to fire up REGEDIT and verify that this entry actually exists in your Registry, you'll see for yourself that it does.

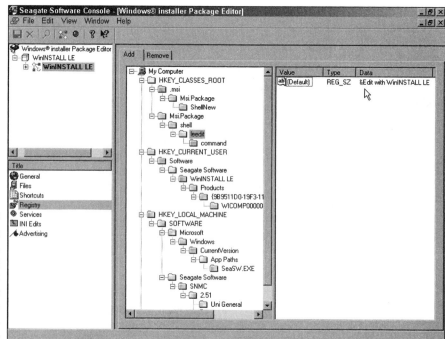

Figure 14-2: WinINSTALL LE lets you see what an *.MSI file does to the Registry.

Now that you know the tricks for sticking your nose into Windows Installer packages, you can educate yourself in advance about the effects on your Registry of installing any program that comes with an *.MSI file. That knowledge may come in mighty handy if a program installation ever breaks something else on your system — or if you ever need to remove a program that won't uninstall properly via the Add/Remove Programs wizard. In addition, seeing the contents of an *.MSI file is a good way to achieve a deeper understanding of the various Registry keys, as the previous paragraph illustrates.

If you *really* want to get into WinINSTALL LE, check out its Discover capability; it lets you install a pre–Windows 2000 program (that is, one that wasn't designed for Windows 2000 and doesn't come with an MSI file) and then build an MSI file based on what the installation does to your system. You can then roll out that MSI file to other users or to a whole network. Spiffy.

Remove Programs from the Install/Uninstall List

Scenario: A user (not you!) who isn't familiar with the Add/Remove Programs control panel tries to delete a program by simply running Explorer and deleting the program folder. In this situation, the program may still show up as an installed application, even though the uninstall program doesn't work because the files aren't there anymore. If the uninstall program fails, the program doesn't remove itself from the list of installed programs.

Another possibility is that you update a program by installing a new version over an old one, but the uninstall program for the old version is still hanging around on the Install/Uninstall tab. You can often avoid this problem by uninstalling the old version before installing the new version, but most programs don't require this step and you probably don't know which ones do. (They don't always tell you in their documentation.)

Fortunately, you can use the Registry Editor to remove those annoying holdovers from the Install/Uninstall list. Slide on over to *HKLM\SOFTWARE\ Microsoft\Windows\CurrentVersion\Uninstall.* A screen like Figure 14-3 appears. Scroll around the list until you find the key corresponding to the program entry that you want to delete and delete the key. Voilà — the program no longer appears when you run the Add/Remove Programs wizard from the control panel.

Note that programs that use the Windows Installer method for installation and removal may appear in the *Uninstall* key using their Class ID for an identifier, as is the case with the first three subkeys in Figure 14-3. You can easily determine which programs those CLSIDs go with by looking at the *DisplayName* subkey.

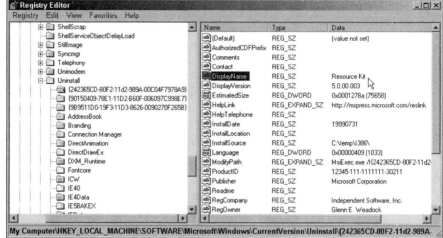

Figure 14-3:
The Registry
location of
the installed
programs
list.

Be careful when deleting items from the Registry's uninstall list. Some of these items appear on the Windows Components portion of the Add/Remove control panel; you probably don't want to remove those Registry keys. Also, the items don't necessarily appear in the same order in the Registry as they do in the control panel.

Let Windows "Run" Amok

Ever wonder when you run a program via the Start⇨Run command just how Windows 2000 knows where to *find* the program if you don't key in a complete path? These programs aren't all in the same folder, you know. Just look at REGEDIT and REGEDT32 as an example. Both run from the Start⇨Run dialog box, but normally one is in `C:\WINNT` and one is in `C:\WINNT\SYSTEM32`.

Ah, some of you may be thinking, it probably has to do with the PATH setting. In the olden days, when DOS ruled the PC landscape, you would set a PATH variable in your AUTOEXEC.BAT file to tell DOS where to look for programs. Specifically, you'd list a series of directory paths, separated by semicolons.

Good suspicion. Take a look at the PATH on your computer. (You can see it on the System control panel; click the Advanced tab and then click the Environment Variables button, as in Figure 14-4.) You'll probably see something like the following (you can click the Edit button and scroll with your left and right arrow keys, if you can't see the whole PATH variable in the dialog box):

```
%SystemRoot%\system32;%SystemRoot%
```

If you've installed some applications onto your PC, you may see other folder names, too. (The "%SystemRoot%" notation just means "the folder where Windows 2000 system files live," normally C:\WINNT.)

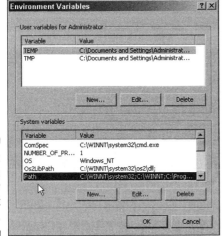

Figure 14-4:
Checking
on your
environment
variables.

So that's the end of the story, right? *Wrong.* Try this experiment: Choose Start⇨Run, type **WORDPAD** in at the command prompt, and then click OK. The WordPad program runs. But — here's the mysterious part — WORDPAD.EXE isn't in C:\WINNT or C:\WINNT\SYSTEM32. It's in C:\PROGRAM FILES\WINDOWS NT\ACCESSORIES, a folder that most definitely is not in the path.

So, as the bum asked his friend after hearing that the Thermos bottle keeps hot liquids hot and cold liquids cold, how does it *know?* Take a look at the key *HKLM\SOFTWARE\Microsoft\Windows\CurrentVersion\App Paths.* Underneath the *App Paths* key live a bunch of subkeys that contain location information for specific programs. If Windows 2000 doesn't find a program you want to run via the Run dialog box in the path folders, it consults this Registry location to see whether it can match up the program name with a preset location. If it finds such a preset location, it can run the program — as it does in the preceding example with WordPad, as shown in Figure 14-5.

So what's the tip? Here it is, in three parts:

✔ You can add any program that you want to be able to run quickly from the Run dialog box to the Registry and specify its location. The advantage of this method versus editing the Path variable is that it's faster: The longer the Path variable, the more time Windows 2000 has to spend before consulting the Registry for the specific program you've typed.

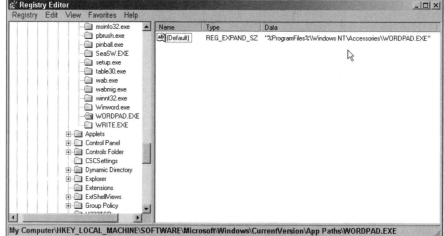

Figure 14-5:
How the
Run dialog
box finds
WordPad.

✔ On the flip side, any program that doesn't live in the Path folders and that you *don't* want to run from the Run dialog box, you can delete from the *App Paths* key. (For example, try saving and deleting the PINBALL.EXE subkey, and then try to run Pinball from the Run dialog box. Restore the key if you're a Pinball junkie. If you didn't *know* about the Pinball game, then now is a good time to have a little fun amidst all this Registry seriousness.)

✔ Network managers can take this tip still further and create a REG file that modifies the Registry to add several program names and locations to the *App Paths* key. Some of these programs may be administrative or troubleshooting utilities that you don't necessarily want on user desktops or Start menus, but that you do want to be readily accessible when you're doing some on-site support work.

If you really look closely, you can see that the path for WordPad is an expandable string that uses the variable *%ProgramFiles%* instead of `C:\Program Files`. That's because your main hard drive may not have drive letter C:, and it would be good if the Registry would work properly in that case. So, I encourage you to use expandable strings if you're going to add paths to this or any other Registry key, because it's good housekeeping. (The expandable string is a great example of a cool Windows 2000 Registry feature that the Windows 9x Registry doesn't have.) Alas, Microsoft undermines this great idea with spotty execution. The company's own software ignores the REG_EXPAND_SZ value type so often that you'll probably never see a completely clean Registry, that is, one with no hardcoded drive letters. For example, the *App Path* for WINWORD.EXE on my test PC is `C:\Program Files\ Microsoft Office\Office\Winword.exe`.

Recover a Lost Internet Explorer Password

As computer programs add more and more security capabilities, we're bound to forget a password at some point. If you forget the supervisor password for the content advisor ratings in Internet Explorer 5 (see Figure 14-6), with which you can prevent little Johnny from browsing www.back-seat-love.com on your home PC, you're in luck: The Registry can help.

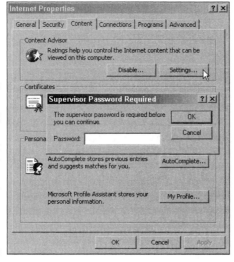

Figure 14-6:
Internet
Explorer's
content
advisor
requires a
supervisor
password
to make
changes.

Log in with administrator privileges, run your favorite Registry Editor, and drive over to *HKLM\SOFTWARE\Microsoft\Windows\CurrentVersion\Policies*. Delete the entire *Ratings* subkey, and the password restriction goes away immediately — no need to even reboot. (You're not allowed to delete this subkey unless you log on as an administrator.) You can now go to Internet Explorer and create a new supervisor password.

Hiding Selected Control Panels

After you get your rally car tuned and ready for action, you don't want anyone else messing with the settings (seat position, mirror angles, cup holder location, and so on). Similarly, you may want to make sure no one else in your (pick one: home, office, home office) messes with your control panel settings.

If you use group policies, you can set the Hide Specified Control Panel Applets policy under User Configuration\Administrative Templates\Control Panel. If you don't, the Registry provides a slick way of hiding individual control panels without your having to delete or rename the *.CPL files that live in C:\WINNT. Check out the key *HKCU\Control Panel\Don't Load.* (If it doesn't exist already, go ahead and create it.) The values in this key should have value names that correspond to the filename of the control panel you wish to suppress.

For example, to suppress the Display control panel, create a value named *desk.cpl* and give it the word "No" for its data field (see Figure 14-7). Now choose Start⇨Settings⇨Control Panel. The Display control panel no longer appears, as is evident in Figure 14-8. This little trick gives you greater control than the System Policy Editor (if you have the Windows 2000 Server CD) or the Group Policy utility permit.

Of course, when you need to change a display setting, you know where to go in the Registry to bring the control panel back. Alternately, you can just double-click the relevant *.CPL file. (For more about the *.CPL files and what they do, see Chapter 3.)

This tip does *not* apply to the Microsoft Management Console shortcuts that appear in the Administrative Tools folder inside the Control Panel window.

Figure 14-7: Hiding the Display control panel in the Registry.

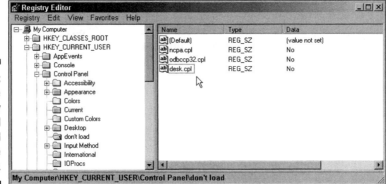

Figure 14-8:
The Display
control
panel
"don't load"
anymore.

Set the DUN Logon Option

When you see the logon screen for Windows 2000, you get an option to Log on using dial-up connection — even if you don't have a modem in your PC! That's because Windows 2000 installs Remote-Access Services (RAS, or what Microsoft now calls DUN, for Dial-Up Networking) with the operating system, no matter what. Heck, even if you do have a modem, you still may not need this option if you're a desktop user who doesn't participate in a network.

On the theory that anything you don't use shouldn't show up, you can use the Registry to get rid of the DUN logon check box . . . almost. (It doesn't completely disappear, but it does go dim so that it's less likely to distract you, and the check box can't be checked anymore.) Here's how: Create the REG_SZ value *RasDisable* in the key *HKLM\SOFTWARE\Microsoft\Windows NT\CurrentVersion\Winlogon* and set it to 1, as shown in Figure 14-9.

On the flip side of this coin, you may want to force a Dial Up Networking logon for a notebook computer user who's always going to be connecting to the network from a remote location. In that case, create the string value *RasForce* in the key *HKLM\Software\Microsoft\Windows NT\CurrentVersion\Winlogon* and set it to 1.

Be very careful forcing a DUN logon — if you can't log on this way, you're sunk! You'll probably have to restore an earlier version of your Registry to reenable a normal logon.

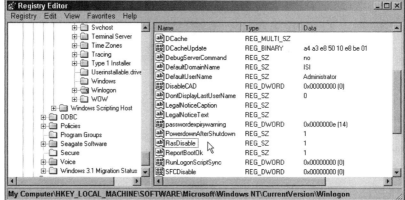

Figure 14-9:
Turning off
the DUN
logon
option.

Set NumLock for the Logon Screen

You may have discovered that the Keyboard control panel contains no setting for whether you want the NumLock key to be on or off after you log on to the computer. That's an oversight, but if you call Microsoft to complain, they'll politely advise you to keep your shirt on, because Windows 2000 remembers your NumLock setting when you log off and will continue to use that setting next time you log on.

It turns out that one of the nineteen zillion things that Windows 2000 does when you log off or restart is to write the current state of the NumLock key into — where else? — the Registry, specifically, into the value *InitialKeyboardIndicators* under the key *HKCU\Control Panel\Keyboard*. Windows 2000 writes 2 into this string value if the NumLock setting is on, and 0 if it's off. (No, the 2 doesn't make any sense to me, either, but trust me, that's not a misprint.)

The *gotcha* here is that Windows 2000 only sets the NumLock key on or off *after* you log on. What if you, like me, have created a good and proper password that uses numbers as well as letters? It's a bit of a pain to have to type those numbers off the top row of the keyboard instead of the keypad, and to have to remember to hit the NumLock key at every logon, before typing in your password. And if you happen to manage other Windows 2000 machines, you can bet that users will gripe about this inconvenience. It seems minor, but when you consider how many times a year you log on to your PC, it's one of those annoyances whose importance grows by repetition.

The secret solution (which also works in NT 4.0 by the way) is as follows: Crank up your Registry Editor of choice and modify the value *InitialKeyboardIndicators* under the key *HKU\.DEFAULT\Control Panel\Keyboard*. It turns out that Windows 2000 uses the default user profile to present the welcome screen to you. (Makes sense, eh? If you don't know which user is sitting at the keyboard, assume the default settings.) So, if you modify the default profile in the Registry, you can turn NumLock on for your logon sequence. (Note that your logon sequence setting doesn't have to be the same as your per-user setting. That is, you can have NumLock on for typing your password, and then have it turned off after that.)

Set Background for the Logon Screen

If you're actually reading these tips in order, then the previous tip may have caused you to think, "Hey, wait a minute, if the default user profile controls the logon screen's NumLock setting, maybe it controls other stuff also?" in which case you are absolutely right. Foremost among such "other stuff" is the display background.

Here's an example of what you can do. Create a wallpaper file at the appropriate size (800 x 600, 1024 x 768, or what have you) using a paint or image creation program like Photoshop. Place some text at the top of that image file that says something like "Authorized users of Yoyodyne Propulsion Systems ONLY" or "Darren, if you touch this computer while I'm out of the house, you are DEAD MEAT." Then, run your favorite Registry Editor and point to that file in the value *Wallpaper* under the key *HKU\.DEFAULT\Control Panel Desktop*. Your welcome screen will look something like Figure 14-10.

Of course, if you have some other cool wallpaper that is part of your individual user profile and you just want that to appear at the logon screen for consistency's sake, then that's fine, too. Just point to it in the Registry for the default user profile. You may find it aesthetically pleasing to see the same wallpaper at the logon screen that you see after you've logged on.

You may also need to modify the Registry values *WallpaperStyle* (0 = centered or tiled, 2 = stretched) and *TileWallpaper* (0 = not tiled, 1 = tiled) In *HKU\ .DEFAULT\Control Panel Desktop* to get an exact match with your post-logon settings.

Figure 14-10:
Darren is
forewarned.

On a related subject, you can display a custom dialog box between the Welcome to Windows dialog box and the Log On to Windows dialog box (see Figure 14-11). Because big companies can use this capability to remind their employees of all the things they'd better not do with their computers, Microsoft has given this message the value name *LegalNoticeText* in the key *HKLM\SOFTWARE\Microsoft\Windows NT\CurrentVersion\Winlogon*. (The window title gets the value *LegalNoticeCaption* in the same key.)

Figure 14-11:
Just in case
Darren
missed the
wallpaper
message
and pressed
Ctrl+Alt+Del
anyway.

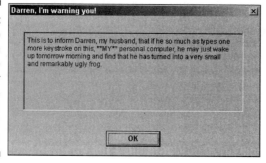

If you have the System Policy Editor program, which only comes with Windows 2000 Server but which you can install on a Windows 2000 Professional system (see Chapter 7), then you can use this tool in its Registry-editing mode to create the Registry logon message, as shown in Figure 14-12 (note the references to Windows NT in the figure; POLEDIT is really an NT leftover). If you're a Windows 2000 network administrator, you can set these strings with the Group Policy utility and apply them to every-one in a given organizational unit, domain, or group. The relevant policies are under Computer Configuration\Windows Settings\Security Settings\Local Policies\Security Options.

Figure 14-12:
Use the System Policy Editor to set the logon message and window title.

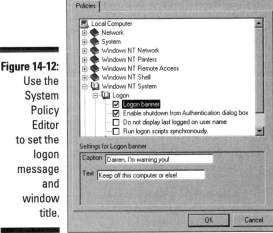

Change the Default Setup Location

When you buy a new computer, the default setup directory often points to an area on the hard disk where the computer manufacturer has copied the Windows 2000 installation files. These files can occupy a myriad of megabytes, however, and they duplicate the files on the Windows 2000 installation CD-ROM. So you delete them, saving all sorts of disk space. However, the next time you do something that makes Windows 2000 look for the original files — such as adding new software via the Network control panel — Windows looks for the original files in the original location, doesn't find them, and asks you to locate them.

Doing so isn't usually a big deal (the normal answer is X:\I386, where X is the drive letter that your computer assigns to the CD-ROM drive), but if you make a lot of changes to your system, retyping the correct location becomes a tad tedious. This retyping gets even more tedious if you use System File Protection, which looks to the original location to restore system files that (for example) a new program installation may brazenly replace.

Fortunately, with the Registry you can tell Windows 2000 to stop looking in the old location and automatically look in a new one. Run your favorite Registry Editor and shuffle over to *HKLM\SOFTWARE\Microsoft\Windows\CurrentVersion\Setup*. Modify the *SourcePath* string value to point to your CD-ROM drive (or a network drive or wherever the Windows 2000 setup files reside). You should also set the DWORD value *CDInstall* to 1 if you're specifying a CD-ROM drive; add the value if it isn't present.

If you have lots of hard disk space (around 300MB) and you want to copy the files from the CD to a directory on your hard disk, you can do that, too, and use the same procedure to reset the location in the Registry. Putting the setup files on a hard disk makes a lot of sense for notebook computer users who either don't have built-in CD-ROM drives or don't want to worry about leaving the Windows 2000 CD behind.

Annotate the Registry

Documenting the changes that you make to your computer ranks right up there with flossing your teeth on the list of things you know you should do more often. You have two options open to you:

- ✔ Become more disciplined about documenting Registry changes in a text or word processing file somewhere on the computer.
- ✔ Find an easier method.

I, being essentially lazy, prefer the second option. Happily, it exists. Just make your own special Registry keys next to the ones that you've added or changed, or one level up from the ones you've deleted. Give the keys a consistent name, such as *TechTip,* and put a single string value in each key with a note about what you modified.

Figure 14-13 shows an example. In this way, if you're ever surfing the Registry and you come across something that strikes you as odd, you can look for the relevant TechTip. Or, if you're troubleshooting a Registry problem, you can search for all the TechTips (hence the desirability of a consistent name) to see what Registry entries you've changed and that may be causing the problem. You don't have to hunt down a separate document — and because adding notes this way is so easy, you're more likely to do it.

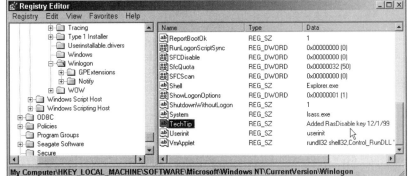

Figure 14-13:
Documenting
your
Registry
changes in
the Registry
itself.

Photo Finishes

How can you find out exactly what happens to the Registry after you change a control panel setting, install a new program, or modify an object's property sheet? Actually, you have several options, including snapshotting and using REGMON.

Snapshotting

One way to track Registry changes is to take a snapshot before you do something that you think will alter the Registry, take another snapshot afterward, and compare the before and after pictures to see what changed. You can compare Registry snapshots without any fancy special-purpose software; just create an export REG file by using REGEDIT's Registry➪Export Registry File command. Name your "before" snapshot BEFORE.REG and your "after" snapshot AFTER.REG.

If you have a pretty good idea of which key an action is likely to affect, export that key only. Comparing very long files, such as an entire export of *HKLM,* can take several minutes even on a fast PC.

To compare the differences between snapshots, Microsoft offers a freebie program called WinDiff with the Windows Resource Kit tools on the Windows 2000 CD (you can find WinDiff in the \SUPPORT\TOOLS folder). Load the "before" file, then load the "after" file, and WinDiff highlights the differences.

REGMON

Snapshotting isn't the only way to track Registry changes. One of my favorite Registry utilities — and thus one I include on the enclosed CD-ROM — is a freebie: REGMON from Mark Russinovich and Bryce Cogswell. REGMON tracks Registry accesses in *real time,* or as they occur.

The data REGMON produces can be overwhelming, but you get a complete picture of every Registry access — reads as well as writes and edits. (REGMON lets you filter events, so that you can choose, for example, to see only successful Registry writes.) You'll be amazed at how many Registry accesses even a seemingly simple act like opening My Network Places generates. And if you want to jump from a REGMON display to REGEDIT, just double-click an entry in the REGMON log window, and REGMON takes you to the precise location in the Registry Editor. Very handy indeed.

Keep up-to-date with the latest version of REGMON by checking Mark and Bryce's Internet site, www.sysinternals.com.

Rules and REGs

After a bit of practice, you master the arts of snapshotting and real-time Registry monitoring (see previous tip) and discover some nifty Registry hacks by tracking what happens when you perform different Windows 2000 tasks. Now you want to share those hacks with other people at the office, in your local computer users group, or even on the public Internet. Or, maybe you're a network manager and see the convenience of grouping a bunch of control panel settings or other system settings together into a single file that you can run on each PC with one fell swoop. Whatever the reason, you can share your Registry tweaks with REG files.

REG files are easy if you don't have to create them yourself from scratch. Just run REGEDIT, highlight the key in the key pane that you want to export, and choose Registry⇨Export Registry File. Give the thing a name and that's it.

If making a Registry error on your own PC is a misdemeanor, propagating a Registry error to others is a felony. REG files are powerful tools. Be very careful with their design and test them yourself before distributing them to others. And guard against exporting Registry values that don't pertain to the change you want to distribute to others. Accidentally exporting too many values or keys is easy to do. You can always trim the REG file in Notepad after you create it, if you find that you exported too much.

If you want to create your own REG file from scratch, using a text editor such as Notepad rather than just modifying the current Registry and performing an export — and I can't think of too many cases where you'd prefer doing so — then you must pay close attention to the rules of REG file construction. Here they are, in brief:

- ✔ Begin your REG file with a single line that reads **Windows Registry Editor Version 5.00** or the REG file won't load.

- ✔ For every key in which you want to add or change a value, create a new REG file section with the key name in square brackets.

- ✔ Remember that REG files can't delete keys or values, they can only add or change keys and values.

- ✔ To enter a Default value, use the format @="valuedata".

- ✔ If a backslash appears in a Registry value, it appears as a double back-slash in the REG file.

- ✔ You can use a single backslash as a line separator character for really long lines that you need to wrap across two or more lines in your text editor.

- ✔ You must end your REG file with a carriage return (press Enter at the end of the last line) or REGEDIT doesn't process the final entry.

The best way to get familiar with these rules is to export a good-sized REG file from the current Registry and then open the REG file with Notepad or a word processor. Compare the lines in the REG file that identify specific keys and values with how the keys and values appear in REGEDIT.

A common problem with shared REG files occurs when your machine uses different folder or filenames than the machine or machines to which you're distributing the REG file. Say you want to share a REG file that makes a change to a word processor that we'll call SuperWord, and you have the application installed in C:\PROGRAM FILES\SUPERWORD. Now you export a Registry key that references a file in that directory. A user who has the program installed in the C:\SUPERWORD folder may not be able to use your REG file successfully. This sort of situation is one more reason to use the application's default installation folder when adding programs to your PC. However, if you don't, you may want to advise whomever you're sending the REG file to that a little editing with Notepad may be necessary.

Chapter 15

Ten (Or So) More Registry Tricks

• •

In This Chapter

▶ Saving keystrokes in command windows

▶ Fine-tuning the new System File Protection feature

▶ Relocating event logs for better performance

▶ Adding sounds to programs that don't provide sound schemes

▶ Changing your name without going to court

• •

1 thought about putting all twenty-four of my Windows 2000 Registry tricks into one chapter, but then we would have had to retitle this part "The Part of Twenty-Fours," and that doesn't have a good ring to it. Besides which, I'm not allowed to have only one chapter in a Part. (That would be sort of like having only one option on a drop-down menu. Not that I'm hinting about the design of REGEDT32 or anything.)

So I would have had to come up with another chapter with twenty-four things in it, like "Twenty-Four Ways the Registry Can Improve Your Sex Life." That chapter would have been very difficult to write, however, because there's only one way to use the Registry to improve your sex life, although I won't go into that here, as this book is certainly not the proper place to disclose that. For male readers of this book, reviewing the Registry structure in your head ("*HKCR* is a pointer to *HKLM\SOFTWARE\Classes. . . .*") is just as effective as thinking about taxes or state capitals or elderly heads of state, if you need a temporary distraction for some reason.

So, the previous chapter contains a dozen tricks, and so does this chapter. Now for the obligatory exhortation to back up your Registry, or at least the specific Registry key that you're about to change, before making any of the changes mentioned here. It also helps a lot if you're familiar with Chapter 4 on using the Registry Editors.

As you ride off into the sunset

This is the last chapter in the book, so here's a quick parting comment. My editors and I have tried to make everything in this book accurate. (I started collecting these Registry tidbits back at the Beta 2 stage, over a year before Windows 2000 actually came out.) However, if I've slipped up somewhere, I'd be grateful if you'd please let me know so that the proper correction can be made in subsequent printings. I would also love to hear from you if you see a way that the book can be improved, if you found something here that you really liked, or if you have a slick Registry tip that you think should find its way into these pages. You can e-mail me at gweadock@i-sw.com, or write to me via "snail mail" care of IDG Books Worldwide, 10475 Crosspoint Boulevard, Indianapolis, IN 46256. I can't guarantee that I'll respond to every message right away, but I'll do my best to answer each inquiry. Finally, thanks for reading this book, and I sincerely hope you've found some fun and interesting stuff in it.

Enable AutoComplete in Command Windows

You've almost certainly bumped into the AutoComplete feature of Internet Explorer by now. The browser maintains a list of URLs (Uniform Resource Locators, or Internet locations) that you've visited recently, and when Internet Explorer sees you starting to type one of those URLs, it fills it in for you. That saves keystrokes and time and is an advance that just about everyone likes.

Microsoft labels the AutoComplete feature part of its IntelliSense technologies. One day, these technologies will probably start finishing our sentences for us, based on similar sentences we've typed in the past.

Yet another reason not to use your office word processing program to write love letters. You start to write "Dear Mr. Thudpucker" but as soon as you write the word "Dear," Word 2020 will remember your previous document and fill it in to read "Dear Annabelle, I've been thinking all day about last night, and I just can't get you out of my head." That would be out of place, however, in an interoffice memo about next year's budget. So we should all hope that Microsoft doesn't take this IntelliSense thing too far.

Microsoft has, however, already extended the AutoComplete concept to the command prompt. You can test this feature easily by typing **CMD /F:ON** in the Start⇨Run dialog box. Now, let's say you want to see a directory of the WINNT folder. Without AutoComplete, you'd type

```
DIR WINNT
```

But with AutoComplete, you can type

```
DIR W
```

and then press Ctrl+D. (Try it.) Windows looks for the first directory that begins with W, and fills it in. If you have several folders that start with W, repeating the Ctrl+D combination shows them each in turn.

Ctrl+D is the completion character for directory listings, and Ctrl+F is the completion character for file listings. However, Ctrl+F actually works for both files and directories. So if you wanted to type a command like **EDIT BOOT.INI** you would need to use Ctrl+F rather than Ctrl+D.

Okay, I hear some of you saying, "Oooh, Glenn, *neat* tip, I can save *two whole keystrokes* when getting a directory listing of C:\WINNT. You should get a Pulitzer prize for this." Well, this brings up several issues:

✔ What if the folder you want to look at is Documents and Settings? Then you're saving lots more than two keystrokes.

✔ I have to agree that Ctrl+D isn't the easiest thing to type (or remember), so that aspect needs some attention.

✔ Who wants to type **CMD /F:ON** every time you open a command prompt? Not this cowboy, so that could stand some streamlining as well.

✔ I agree with you about the Pulitzer, but I suspect that the committee members wouldn't know an operating system if it bit them on the nose. Plus I use a lot of informal words like *plus,* so a prize is probably a long shot here.

Naturally, a better way to implement command-prompt AutoComplete exists, but you have to fire up a Registry Editor (either one will do) to enjoy the benefit. The specific hack varies depending on whether you want to make it machine-specific or user-specific.

✔ If you want to make command-prompt AutoComplete the default behavior for the computer, regardless of who logs on to it, then add the DWORD values *CompletionChar* and *PathCompletionChar* to the key *HKLM\SOFTWARE\Microsoft\Command Processor*.

✔ If you want to make command-prompt AutoComplete the default behavior for the *current user only,* then add the same values to *HKCU\SOFTWARE\Microsoft\Command Processor* instead. (Note that the *HKCU* setting takes precedence over the *HKLM* setting, if the latter exists.)

CompletionChar is the file completion hotkey, and *PathCompletionChar* is the directory completion hotkey. (I usually just specify *CompletionChar* because it handles both files and directories, but you can certainly specify both if you want.)

The values that you add to these new keys are the codes corresponding to the hotkeys. For example, 0x4 is Ctrl+D and 0x6 is Ctrl+F, if you want to mimic the behavior of **CMD /F:ON**. My own preference, shared by many power users on the Internet who have debated the issue, is the Tab key, because it's easy to type and never used in the normal course of command-prompt business. The code for the Tab key is 0x9. Figure 15-1 shows you how I set up my PC.

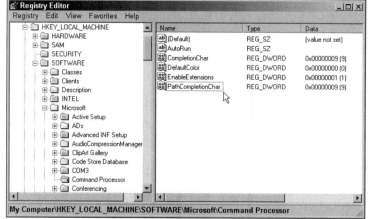

Figure 15-1:
Enabling command-prompt AutoComplete with the Tab key.

What's New on the Menu?

When you right-click any open space on the desktop and choose New, a submenu (see Figure 15-2) opens that lets you create a new file of that type on the desktop. After giving the new file a name, you can select it and run the program in which you normally create files of that type. For example, the bitmap image type opens Microsoft Paint.

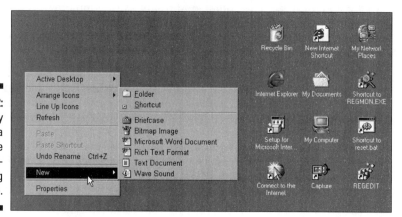

Figure 15-2:
Quickly create a new file by right-clicking the desktop.

After a few months' worth of using Windows 2000, the New menu becomes cluttered with programs that you're not likely to use to create desktop icons. The flip side of the coin is that there may be file types you'd like to add to the New menu.

Removing a file type

If you have the TweakUI control panel (which comes with the separately available *Windows 2000 Resource Kit*), run it, go to the New tab, and clear the check boxes for any existing file types that you want to remove.

If you don't have TweakUI on your PC, fire up either Registry Editor and go to the file extension key under *HKCR* for the file type you want to remove from the New menu. (For example, if you want to remove "Bitmap Image," go to *HKCR\.bmp*.) In case you change your mind later, first export the *ShellNew* key underneath the file extension key (see Figure 15-3) for safekeeping. Then, delete it. No more listing on the New menu!

Figure 15-3: Putting the New menu on a diet.

Adding a file type

To add a file type by using TweakUI, create a blank file as a template, using the desired software application (this is what your new file will look like when you create it), and drag-and-drop it into the window on the New tab of TweakUI.

There's often a slicker way to add a file type, however, using the Registry Editor. Run REGEDIT or REGEDT32, go to the file extension key under *HKCR*, and create the *ShellNew* key beneath it. Now, in the *ShellNew* key, add a string value named *NullFile* containing an empty string (" "). Many applications can open an empty file, and you don't have to create a separate template file with this method. If this method doesn't work with a particular program, use the TweakUI method.

Customize System File Protection

One of the big advances in Windows 2000 compared to Windows NT 4.0 is *System File Protection (SFP)*, a feature that Microsoft introduced over a year prior to Windows 2000 with Windows 98. The idea here is to try to bring some order to the chaotic state of Windows version control. You need to understand the problem that System File Protection tries to solve to appreciate the value of the feature, so let me explain this before I tell you how to customize SFP with the Registry.

It's never really been possible to say with certainty what versions of important Windows system files (such as *.DLL and *.EXE files) are on a given PC. Application vendors have been allowed, and even encouraged, to package updates of Microsoft files for redistribution with their programs. Microsoft itself updates system files with some of its own applications. With Windows 98 (and now Windows 2000), the Windows Update feature lets a user connect to the Internet at any time and perform system software updates. This uncontrolled file-update frenzy has contributed to a lack of stability in Windows when running multiple applications. System files that were never tested together as a group find themselves trying to work together, sometimes successfully and sometimes unsuccessfully. This malaise has become so famous it has its own nickname, "DLL hell."

The Windows 2000 approach is to run a file system "guardian angel" in the background, watching over system files (that is, the files that come with Windows 2000 and have the extensions DLL, EXE, FON, OCX, SYS, and TTF). When this guardian angel detects that a program has updated (or, in some cases, backdated!) one of these files, it tries to automatically restore the original version of the file, typically from the folder C:\WINNT\SYSTEM32\ DLLCACHE. If the file isn't in DLLCACHE, then the guardian angel pops up a window asking you to supply the original Windows 2000 installation media.

Try this experiment: Run Windows Explorer, open C:\WINNT, and rename NOTEPAD.EXE to NOTEPAD.SAV. Say Yes to the confirmation question. If you try this trick on a machine with a small hard drive, you'll probably see a message telling you to pop in the Windows 2000 CD so that the guardian angel can restore the proper NOTEPAD.EXE, which it thinks no longer exists in your C:\WINNT folder. If you try the trick on a machine with a large hard drive, then most likely you won't see any message, but if you take another look at the Explorer window, you'll see that the operating system has quietly placed another copy of NOTEPAD.EXE into C:\WINNT from the DLLCACHE folder. (If neither of these things happens, then someone has disabled system file protection on your PC, but don't worry — in a couple of paragraphs you'll be able to reset it if you want.)

The guardian angel isn't bulletproof, however, because a user can hit the Cancel button and tell the angel that the new file is okay to keep. So Microsoft also gives you a command-line version (SFC.EXE) of the System File Checker utility (this utility has an attractive graphical face in Windows 98, but that part didn't make it into Windows 2000). You can use SFC to scan system files and/or to rebuild the contents of the DLLCACHE folder if it becomes damaged — type **SFC /?** at a command prompt for more details. It turns out that the SFC utility modifies the Registry, as detailed in Table 15-1. (The Registry values in the table all live in the key *HKLM\SOFTWARE\Microsoft\ Windows NT\CurrentVersion\Winlogon.*)

Table 15-1	System File Checker and the Registry	
Command	*Action*	*Change to Registry*
SFC /SCANONCE	Perform a file scan once at next reboot	SFCScan = 2
SFC /SCANBOOT	Perform a file scan at each boot	SFCScan = 1
SFC /CANCEL	Don't perform a file scan	SFCScan = 0

The SFC utility doesn't give you total control over the System File Protection feature, however; for that, you need the Registry (or the Group Policy utility, which is the preferable way to change these settings if you run a Windows 2000 Server-based network). Here are the values you can change and what they do. (Again, all values reside in *HKLM\SOFTWARE\Microsoft\ Windows NT\CurrentVersion\Winlogon*, as you can see in Figure 15-4.)

✔ **SFCShowProgress** (DWORD) is 1 if you want to see a progress bar when SFC is doing its check, 0 if you don't.

✔ **SFCQuota** (DWORD) specifies the maximum size of the DLLCACHE folder, in megabytes. Typical values are 0x32 (hex), or 50MB (decimal), for Windows 2000 Professional, and 0xffffffff (unlimited size) for Windows 2000 Server. If you run Windows 2000 Professional, have lots of disk space, and don't like being prompted for the original CD-ROM every time System File Protection notices that it needs to restore a file, then you may want to change this value to 0xffffffff. Your DLLCACHE folder should grow to around 200MB.

✔ **SFCDisable** (DWORD) is 0 by default, which means that System File Protection is on. If you set this value to 1, you disable SFP, but you get a nag window at every reboot. Microsoft really wants you to leave the guardian angel active. A value of 2 disables SFP at the next boot only, and 4 enables SFP but suppresses the popup windows (the default for Windows 2000 Server and its variants).

✔ **SFCDllCacheDir** (REG_SZ) specifies the location of the DLLCACHE folder. You can change this to a second hard drive, for example, or even to a network drive for more convenient space allocation.

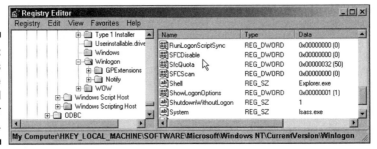

Figure 15-4:
SFC settings
in the
Registry all
live under
one subkey.

Move Those Event Logs

In professional road rallies, manufacturers test the heck out of their cars before unleashing them on a brutal journey such as the famous Paris-to-Dakar race. As part of that testing, car builders put all sorts of sensors in the engine and at key suspension points. In a similar vein, Windows 2000, like Windows NT 4.0 before it, is heavily instrumented. The operating system is constantly checking its own oil temperature, engine rpm, and other vital signs, and recording them to disk in the form of *event logs*.

You can view these logs with the logically named Event Viewer, in the Administrative Tools folder of your control panels. (This design is in marked contrast to Windows 9*x*, which logs hardly anything unless you tell it to — and even then doesn't give you many choices.) The main event logs are the Security, Application, and System logs, but you may see a number of others, depending on which programs are installed on your system. (If you're running Windows 2000 Server, for example, you could see a DNS Server event log and a Directory Service event log, as shown in Figure 15-5.)

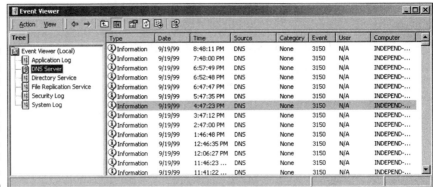

Figure 15-5:
Windows
2000 Server
shows the
usual three
event logs,
and then
some.

The extensive event logging in Windows 2000 is evidence of the debt that Windows 2000 owes to the VAX/VMS operating system. I remember from my early consulting days (pre-PC) that VAX/VMS created extensive logs also, which were very helpful in troubleshooting problems and tuning systems for performance. I doubt it's any coincidence that Dave Cutler, one of the brains behind VMS, is now a driving force at Microsoft behind Windows NT and 2000.

For all its virtues, event logging is disk-intensive activity. Your C: drive is probably already pretty darned busy even without event logging. You may be tempted to turn event logging off in order to enjoy better disk performance, and you can do so in some cases through the Windows 2000 user interface. For example, if you click Start➪Settings➪Printers and then choose File➪Server Properties, you can adjust some logging options on the Advanced tab. Deselecting the top three check boxes tells Windows 2000 to stop logging print events altogether.

The three logging check boxes modify the DWORD Registry value *EventLog* in the key *HKLM\System\CurrentControlSet\Control\Print\Providers.*

You also have control over what goes into the Security log, by virtue of the audit policy settings you've made, for example, by right-clicking a folder on an NTFS disk and choosing Properties➪Security➪Advanced➪Auditing. The Registry auditing choices you make also affect what goes into the Security log, as Chapter 7 discusses. The default is for Windows 2000 to audit hardly any security activity, so you have wide latitude here.

You generally do *not* have control over what goes into the Application log (which contains alerts that your program developers thought were appropriate to record), or into the System log (which contains alerts that Windows 2000 thinks are appropriate). However, you do have control over *where* those event logs live, and that brings me to the meat of this tip. (I know, you'd thought I'd never get there.)

A good way to reduce the performance impact of event logging is simply to move the event logs to a second hard drive, if you have one. (If you don't, you may want to consider getting one. A second hard drive is cheap and provides a great way to perform quick Registry and data backups. It also enables clever performance-enhancing tricks like this one.) Note that you have to restart your system for the move to take effect.

Normally, the Security, Application, and System event logs (SECEVENT.EVT, APPEVENT.EVT, and SYSEVENT.EVT, respectively) live in the same folder with the Registry hives — that is, C:\WINNT\SYSTEM32\CONFIG. However, you can change these locations by modifying the location specified by the *File* value in the following Registry keys:

✔ *HKLM\SYSTEM\CurrentControlSet\Services\Eventlog\Security*

✔ *HKLM\SYSTEM\CurrentControlSet\Services\Eventlog\Application*

✔ *HKLM\SYSTEM\CurrentControlSet\Services\Eventlog\System*

Log Some New Stuff

On the subject of event logging (see previous tip), you may want to have your PC log some activities that it doesn't normally log — for example, to help you troubleshoot a challenging problem. You take a certain risk that the log file itself may confuse you even worse than you are already, but if you're prepared to assume that risk, the Registry (as usual!) can help.

This tip is actually two tips in one:

✔ To enable logging of user profile and policy events, create the DWORD value *UserEnvDebugLevel* in the key *HKLM\SOFTWARE\Microsoft\Windows NT\CurrentVersion\Winlogon*. Assign *UserEnvDebugLevel* the number 0x10002 (hex) to activate logging. The log has the name `C:\WINNT\DEBUG\USERMODE\USERENV.LOG` and you can view it with a text editor like Notepad (see Figure 15-6).

✔ To log what happens when you install a program using the new Windows Installer technology, create (assuming it doesn't already exist) the string value *Logging* in the key *HKLM\SOFTWARE\Policies\Microsoft\Windows\Installer*. Assign *Logging* the string **vicewarmup**. Then, install your program. Windows 2000 creates the log file MSI*nnnnn*.LOG in the current user's Temp folder, where *nnnnn* is a random number. Again, the log file may be viewed with Notepad.

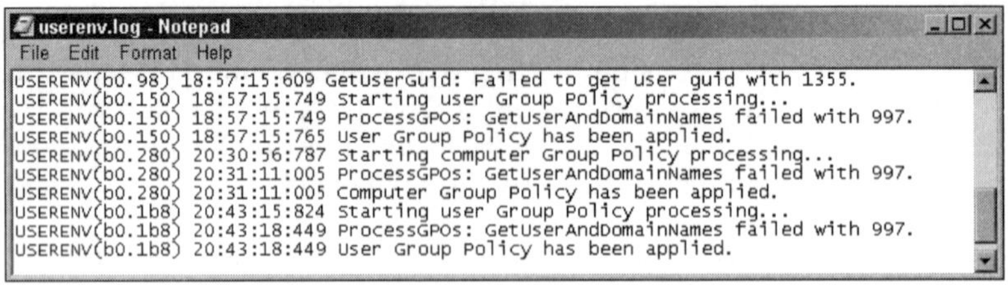

Figure 15-6:
Logging
user profile
and policy
details may
help in trou-
bleshooting.

```
userenv.log - Notepad                                                    _|□|×|
File  Edit  Format  Help
USERENV(b0.98) 18:57:15:609 GetUserGuid: Failed to get user guid with 1355.
USERENV(b0.150) 18:57:15:749 Starting user Group Policy processing...
USERENV(b0.150) 18:57:15:749 ProcessGPOs: GetUserAndDomainNames failed with 997.
USERENV(b0.150) 18:57:15:765 User Group Policy has been applied.
USERENV(b0.280) 20:30:56:787 Starting computer Group Policy processing...
USERENV(b0.280) 20:31:11:005 ProcessGPOs: GetUserAndDomainNames failed with 997.
USERENV(b0.280) 20:31:11:005 Computer Group Policy has been applied.
USERENV(b0.1b8) 20:43:15:824 Starting user Group Policy processing...
USERENV(b0.1b8) 20:43:18:449 ProcessGPOs: GetUserAndDomainNames failed with 997.
USERENV(b0.1b8) 20:43:18:449 User Group Policy has been applied.
```

For the curious, logging for Dial-Up Networking is on by default if you're running Windows 2000 Professional. You can't turn it off, either, as far as I've been
able to tell. All you can do is control whether a new log gets created every
time a DUN connection occurs, or the logging info appends to the existing
DUN log via the Telephone and Modem Options control panel, on the property
sheet for the modem. (The log file, by the way, is typically in C:\WINNT and
has a name that begins with MODEMLOG and ends in .TXT. The precise filename depends on the make and model of your modem, for some weird
reason.) If you're running Windows 2000 Server, on the other hand, then the
default behavior is for DUN logging to be off, unless you turn it on.

Create Application-Specific Sound Schemes

You probably already know that you can use the Windows 2000 Sounds control panel to assign sounds to system events, such as the Windows 2000
startup or a critical error message.

Some application programs make Registry entries that enable you to assign
sounds to those programs, too. However, most don't. If you want to assign
sounds on a program-by-program basis to programs that don't already offer
the capability in the Sounds control panel, you can do so with a Registry
Editor and a little patience. Here's the procedure:

1. **Find out the name of the program.**

   The easy way to do this is to take a look at the property sheet for the
   shortcut on the desktop, or on the Start menu, that points to the program. What you want is the name of the main EXE file that the shortcut
   runs. You can also just use Windows Explorer to open the program's primary subdirectory and look for the EXE files. Sometimes, however, you
   see more than one EXE file, so you have to double-click each one until
   you get the right one. I take an easy example here: REGEDT32!

2. **Run your favorite Registry Editor and navigate to** *HKCU\AppEvents\
   Schemes\Apps.*

3. **Add a new key underneath the Apps key and give it the same name as
   the program to which you want to add sounds.**

   In this example, I name the new key REGEDT32.

4. **Make the (Default) value a descriptive string.**

   Double-click the (Default) value and name it "Registry Editor, NT Style"
   if you're setting up REGEDT32 as I did.

5. **Add keys underneath the key you added in Step 3 and name them
   according to the events that you'd like to associate with sounds.**

The possibilities include Close, Open, RestoreUp, RestoreDown, Minimize, Maximize, MenuCommand, MenuPopup, SystemAsterisk, SystemExclamation, and SystemQuestion.

6. **Close the Registry Editor and open the Sounds and Multimedia control panel.**

   Technically, you can continue using the Registry Editor to finish the job, but I try to live by my rule to use control panels rather than Registry Editors wherever possible. Besides, the Sounds and Multimedia control panel enables you to browse for sound files and test them ahead of time.

7. **Scroll down the list until you see your newly added program, and assign sounds to events in the usual way.**

That's it! Your changes take effect immediately, so you can test them straight-away. To find the sound files that are floating around on your PC, do a search for files ending in .WAV, .MID, or .RMI. A lot of these will be in C:\WINNT\MEDIA. One last hint: Your PC may suspend other processing duties while playing a sound clip, so keep the clips on the brief side.

Lock Out File Type Changes

Chapter 9 talks about the file type settings that you can make from the new Folder Options control panel. What if you get these settings just the way you want, and you don't want anyone else to be able to change them?

The secret lies in an obscure Registry setting called *EditFlags*. When you get a particular file type set up the way you want it via the File Types screen, you can lock out future changes by running either Registry Editor. The general procedure is to navigate to the relevant file type key in *HKCR's* lower half and add the EditFlags binary value (if it isn't already there), which you then set to 01 00 00 00. As an example, here's how to lock out changes to the REG file type.

1. **Run a Registry Editor, for example by choosing Start⇨Run⇨REGEDIT.**

2. **Navigate to *HKCR\regfile* in the key pane and click it.**

3. **Double-click in the value pane on the value** EditFlags.

   However, if the value is already present as a DWORD, then delete it and re-create it as a binary value.

4. **Type in** 01 00 00 00 **for the value data and click OK.**

   Your screen should look like Figure 15-7.

5. **Close the Registry Editor.**

   Now, when you choose the Folder Options control panel, you don't even see a listing for Registration Entries. You can't change what you can't see.

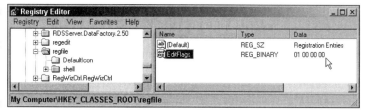

Figure 15-7:
Lock out
changes to
the REG
file type.

You can regain the ability to make file type changes by deleting the *EditFlags* key that you created.

Sometimes you want to go in the reverse direction and enable file type editing for types that normally don't permit editing at all, or that Windows 2000 has restricted your ability to edit to some degree. To do this, just replace the existing *EditFlags* value with 00 00 00 00. That value turns on all editing capabilities.

Lots of intermediate *EditFlags* values can turn specific buttons in the File Types screen on and off, but 99 percent of the time you either want all editing options on or all options off. You can perform those two actions without having to learn the nuances of binary addition. That's good, because I haven't learned the nuances of binary addition, nor do I want to.

Telling DUN When to Be Done

The DUN (Dial-Up Networking) "deadman timer" controls how long a period of inactivity DUN tolerates before hanging up the line. The DWORD value is *AutoDisconnect* under the key *HKLM\SYSTEM\CurrentControlSet\Services\RemoteAccess\Parameters.* The value is expressed in minutes and the default is 20.

I generally cut this setting down to five minutes to save on long distance charges for connections that don't have a local number. Set it to 0 if you don't want DUN to hang up the phone after *any* period of inactivity, but only do so if you only dial up local numbers.

Another timer setting in DUN may be of interest, too, and that's the time DUN allows for a user to successfully enter a correct username and password. The default is 120 seconds, but I generally find that 60 seconds is plenty, and the shorter you make this time period the more secure your dial-up connections are. The DWORD value is *AuthenticateTime* under the key *HKLM\SYSTEM\CurrentControlSet\Services\RemoteAccess\Parameters.*

Less Power to You

You may notice that your PC doesn't turn itself off when you exit Windows 2000, as for example it may have done under Windows NT 4.0 or Windows 9*x*. Instead, you see a message saying that it's now safe to turn off your computer. Now, I sometimes have to leave the office in a hurry, such as when I'm late with a manuscript and an editor is trying to find me. In those cases, I don't really want to wait around for two or three minutes just so I can tap the power switch on my workstation.

Try setting the REG_SZ value *PowerdownAfterShutdown* in the key *HKLM\ SOFTWARE\Microsoft\Windows NT\CurrentVersion\Winlogon* to **1**, which means "yes" to the Registry.

Although this tip is cool when it works, don't be surprised if it doesn't. Getting this tip to work is an iffy proposition because it involves hardware power management, one of the traditional bugbears of Windows NT (Windows 98 does a much better job in this area). Here are the "gotchas" that may interfere with your ability to automatically power down a Windows 2000 PC. (These factors also have a lot to do with how well Plug and Play works on your system.)

✔ If your computer doesn't support *ACPI* (Advanced Configuration and Power Interface), a newish power management standard, then this trick probably won't work. (You can tell whether Windows 2000 thinks your PC fully supports ACPI by choosing Start⇨Settings⇨Control Panel⇨System⇨Hardware⇨Device Manager, and expanding the Computer icon. If the computer's label says `Advanced Configuration and Power Interface (ACPI) PC`, `ACPI Uniprocessor PC`, or `ACPI Multiprocessor PC`, then you have ACPI support. If it says `Standard PC`, `MPS Uniprocessor PC`, or `MPS Multiprocessor PC`, then you don't. (See Figure 15-8.)

Figure 15-8: This computer doesn't support the ACPI standard.

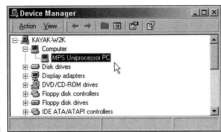

✔ If your computer doesn't fully support *APM* (Advanced Power Management), an oldish power management standard, then this trick may not work. (You can tell whether Windows 2000 thinks your PC fully supports APM by choosing the Power Options control panel and looking for the APM tab. If it's there, then enable APM if it isn't already enabled. If it's not there, then Windows 2000 doesn't perceive your PC as APM-capable.)

✔ If your computer supports APM and if you're running Windows 2000 Server, then you'll never, ever be able to enable shutdown power-off, because Microsoft turned this option off late in the beta testing process. Turns out that some APM PCs with SCSI hard drives can shut themselves down even though a lot of server activity is going on, and Microsoft decided not to give users the option to live dangerously. That's a pity for notebook computer users who run the Server product for reasons other than to act as a server (for example, as an instructional or software development machine).

✔ If your BIOS setup program lets you switch between these two power management standards, don't try doing so after Windows 2000 is already installed (unless you want to reinstall the operating system!). Windows 2000 installs a *Hardware Abstraction Layer*, or *HAL* (no reference to *2001: A Space Odyssey* — at least I don't *think*), based on what power management standard Windows "sees" in the BIOS at installation time. You can't change the HAL without reinstalling Windows.

Change the Registered Organization and Owner Names

People change their names all the time. Sometimes they do it when they get married, in which case they may even add punctuation to their names in the form of hyphens. Other times, they may decide to stop using that middle initial. (Although I generally do use it, so that the reading public can distinguish me from the other Glenn Weadocks out there.) Or sometimes a Windows 2000 user may just wish to hide his true identity by recording his registered PC name as Bjorn B. Bjorkman or some other "nom de PC." He might do so, for example, if he plans on spending lots of time on the Internet in the alt.cigar.afficionado newsgroup and is worried what would happen if a hacker discovered that his true identity is C. Everett Koop.

And that's just people; companies change their names all the time, say, from Acme Cognac, Inc. to Bargain Bourbon, Ltd. The tricky thing is that Windows 2000 maintains your old name and organization name internally, where they're not easy to change, and displays both names on the System control panel's General tab. This bugs me. It can actually become slightly inconvenient, too: Often, when you install new software, the installation program consults these internal owner and organization names and pops them up by default.

Change these names with the Registry Editor by skipping over to *HKLM\SOFTWARE\Microsoft\Windows NT\CurrentVersion*. Here, you can modify the values of *RegisteredOrganization* and *RegisteredOwner*. To change either value as recorded by specific applications, use REGEDIT's Edit⇨Find command. Just be aware that you may need to explain the change or changes when you call the vendor for technical support.

Run a Program Automatically

You can use a REG file to specify that a particular program should run at the next Windows 2000 restart by adding an entry to the Registry's RunOnce key, which specifies a program to be run one time and one time only. The program can be an EXE, COM, or BAT file. For example, you could use a batch file that calls a script written in VBScript or JavaScript. Follow these steps to use this technique:

1. **Run REGEDIT and navigate to *HKLM\SOFTWARE\Microsoft\ Windows\CurrentVersion\RunOnce*.**

   The key should be empty; Windows 2000 clears it after each reboot.

2. **Add a new string value specifying the program you want to run.**

   The name can be whatever you want, but the data should be the full path name to the program. Using long filenames is okay, but don't put the path name in double quotes.

   If you plan to distribute the REG file to multiple computers, and the program to be run lives on a server, use the server's name rather than a drive letter. Different PCs may use different drive letters to refer to the specific server.

3. **Export the *RunOnce* key.**

Now you can distribute the REG file to other computers. Note, however, that if you've secured your Windows 2000 environment to protect the *RunOnce* key with access controls, users have to be logged on as an Administrator to modify that key via your REG file. Which leads me to the last tip of this chapter.

Run Registry Editor as Administrator without Restarting

Many of the actions this book describes require that you run the Registry Editor with Administrator privileges. (In Windows 2000, the Administrator account can do pretty much anything on the system, whereas Users, Power Users, Domain Users, and other accounts may bump into access restrictions — for example, when deleting or modifying a Registry key.)

What if you're running Windows 2000 logged in as, say, a Power User, and you need to perform a Registry edit that only an Administrator can perform? Well, you can log off and log back on, but a faster way exists. For example, hold down the Shift key and right-click REGEDT32.EXE. Then, choose the "Run <u>A</u>s" option, which lets you enter the Administrator's name and password so you can run REGEDT32 as the Administrator! You can use this nifty capability to run any program, not just REGEDT32 and REGEDIT. Sure beats logging off and back on, especially if you have a lot of software that loads at logon time.

Appendix

About the CD

*H*ere's some of what you can find on the *Windows 2000 Registry For Dummies* CD-ROM:

- Registry Monitor, which tracks Registry activity in real time as it occurs
- Multi-Remote Registry Change, which lets you edit multiple Registries on a network
- InstallWatch, which lets you track Registry changes during software installation

System Requirements

Make sure that your computer meets the minimum system requirements listed below. If your computer doesn't match up to most of these requirements, you may have problems using the contents of the CD.

- A PC with a Pentium 166 or faster processor.
- Microsoft Windows 2000 (any version).
- At least 32MB of total RAM installed on your computer for Windows 2000 Professional, and at least 64MB for Windows 2000 Server (any version).
- At least 70MB of hard drive space available to install all the software from this CD. (You need less space if you don't install every program.)
- A CD-ROM drive — quad-speed (4x) or faster.

If you need more information on the basics, check out *PCs For Dummies,* 6th Edition, by Dan Gookin, published by IDG Books Worldwide, Inc.

Using the CD

To install the items from the CD to your hard drive, follow these steps.

1. **Insert the CD into your computer's CD-ROM drive.**

2. **Click Start⇨Run.**

3. **In the dialog box that appears, type** D:\SETUP.EXE.

   Replace *D* with the proper drive letter if your CD-ROM drive uses a different letter. (If you don't know the letter, see how your CD-ROM drive is listed under My Computer.)

4. **Click OK.**

   A license agreement window appears.

5. **Read through the license agreement, nod your head, and then click the Accept button if you want to use the CD — after you click Accept, you'll never be bothered by the License Agreement window again.**

   The CD interface Welcome screen appears. The interface is a little program that shows you what's on the CD and coordinates installing the programs and running the demos. The interface basically enables you to click a button or two to make things happen.

6. **Click anywhere on the Welcome screen to enter the interface.**

   Now you are getting to the action. This next screen lists categories for the software on the CD.

7. **To view the items within a category, just click the category's name.**

   A list of programs in the category appears.

8. **For more information about a program, click the program's name.**

   Be sure to read the information that appears. Sometimes a program has its own system requirements or requires you to do a few tricks on your computer before you can install or run the program, and this screen tells you what you might need to do, if necessary.

9. **If you don't want to install the program, click the Go Back button to return to the previous screen.**

   You can always return to the previous screen by clicking the Go Back button. This feature allows you to browse the different categories and products and decide what you want to install.

10. **To install a program, click the appropriate Install button.**

    The CD interface drops to the background while the CD installs the program you chose.

11. **To install other items, repeat Steps 7 – 10.**

12. **When you've finished installing programs, click the Quit button to close the interface.**

    You can eject the CD now. Carefully place it back in the plastic jacket of the book for safekeeping.

In order to run some of the programs on the _Windows 2000 Registry For Dummies_ CD-ROM, you may need to keep the CD inside your CD-ROM drive. This is a Good Thing. Otherwise, the installed program would have required you to install a very large chunk of the program to your hard drive, which may have kept you from installing other software.

What You'll Find

Here's a summary of the software on this CD arranged by category. The CD interface helps you install software easily. (If you have no idea what I'm talking about when I say "CD interface," flip back a page or two to find the section, "Using the CD.")

Registry Editors and managers

KVManager 3.1, from KVLabs, Inc., www.keyvision.com

30-day trial. This industrial-strength desktop configuration tool manages application components and multiple Registries on a network. Also check out the vendor's Registry education Web site, www.winMD.com.

Multi-Remote Registry Change 3.1, from Eytcheson Software, www.eytcheson.com

Functional demo with limit on number of PCs you can access at once. For those readers on a network, this program is a whole lot handier than using the Windows 2000 built-in remote Registry editing capabilities. Make a Registry change to several PCs at one time with this tool.

Registry monitors

FileMon 4.0, from Bryce Cogswell and Mark Russinovich, www.sysinternals.com

Freeware. This handy utility monitors file activity as it occurs. It tracks reads as well as writes, and after a monitoring session you can save a FileMon log to disk as a plain text file. You can also set filters to control which types of events Filemon logs. If you're doing something that you think modifies the Registry, run FileMon as well as RegMon to see whether files are changing as well as the Registry.

InstallWatch Basic 1.1, from Epsilon Squared, Inc., `www.installwatch.com`

Freeware. Not all Windows 2000 programs adhere to the Windows Installer specification, and for those that don't, this utility makes it easier to remove a program — not just its files, but also the Registry modifications that the vendor-supplied removal programs often leave behind.

RegMon 4.13, from Bryce Cogswell and Mark Russinovich, `www.sysinternals.com`

Freeware. This cool program monitors Registry activity as it occurs. You get a listing of every variety of Registry access (read, write, create key, delete key, and so on) and you can save that listing as a text file after a monitoring session. You can also set filters to control which types of events RegMon logs. A slick new feature lets you double-click a log entry and jump to that location in REGEDIT! Highly recommended if you want to see what happens when you change a control panel setting, install or uninstall an application, or just perform an everyday task like logging on to a network.

If you've previously installed RegMon, you may see a message similar to `Unable to copy REGMON to C:\WINNT\System32\drivers\REGSYS.SYS`. To fix this problem, delete the existing REGSYS.SYS file from the `C:\WINNT\System32\Drivers` directory and repeat the installation.

Handy utilities

NovaBackup 6.0 (SCSI and IDE versions), from Novastor Corporation, `www.novastor.com`

30-day trial. This full-featured commercial backup utility supports full and partial backups, including the Registry. The program offers virus protection, automatic backup scheduling, multilanguage support, automatic log files, and more.

PerfectDisk 2000, from Raxco Software, Inc., `www.raxco.com`

Evaluation version. This disk defragmenter optimizes the Master File Table along with the "usual" files, and is an improvement on the built-in Windows 2000 defragmenter.

PKZIP for Windows 2.70, PKZIP Command Line 2.50, from PKWare, Inc., www.pkware.com

Shareware. Here's a file compression and decompression utility that's handy for moving files over modem links, saving space by archiving little-used files, and compressing your Registry backups, too.

WinHacker, from Wedge Software, www.wedgesoftware.com.

Shareware. A shareware remake of TweakUI, with various extended capabilities to modify the Registry and tune up the user interface.

WinZip 7, from Nico Mak Computing, Inc., www.winzip.com

Shareware. WinZip offers a step-by-step wizard mode for those who want to fiddle with the program as little as possible, or a "classic" mode for users who want access to all the program's features.

ZipMagic 2000, from Mijenix, www.mijenix.com

Shareware. Another compression tool, with the ability to let you "see" partially downloaded ZIP files.

If You Have Problems (Of the CD Kind)

I tried my best to compile programs that work on most computers with the minimum system requirements. Alas, your computer may differ, and some programs may not work properly for some reason.

The two likeliest problems are that you don't have enough memory (RAM) for the programs you want to use, or you have other programs running that are affecting installation or running of a program. If you get error messages like Not enough memory or Setup cannot continue, try one or more of these methods and then try using the software again:

- ✔ **Turn off any anti-virus software that you have on your computer.** Installers sometimes mimic virus activity and may make your computer incorrectly believe that it is being infected by a virus.

- ✔ **Close all running programs.** The more programs you're running, the less memory is available to other programs. Installers also typically update files and programs; if you keep other programs running, installation may not work properly.

- ✔ **Close the CD interface and run demos or installations directly from Windows Explorer.** The interface itself can tie up system memory, or even conflict with certain kinds of interactive demos. Use Windows Explorer to browse the files on the CD and launch installers or demos.

> ✔ **Have your local computer store add more RAM to your computer.** This is, admittedly, a drastic and somewhat expensive step. However, adding more memory can really help the speed of your computer and enable more programs to run at the same time.

> ✔ **Download a newer version of the software from the vendor's Web site.** It could be that you're seeing a compatibility problem involving your hardware or software that a newer version fixes.

If you still have trouble installing the items from the CD, please call the IDG Books Worldwide Customer Service phone number: 800-762-2974 (outside the U.S.: 317-596-5430).

Index

• *Numbers & Symbols* •

& (ampersand), 248
* (asterisk), 171
\ (backslash), 155, 246, 309
: (colon), 113
{} (curly braces), 81, 246
$ (dollar sign), 41, 51
" (double quotes), 246
/ (forward slash), 134
% (percent sign), 157
. (period), 81
[] (square brackets), 17
_ (underscore), 65, 101, 156
16-bit programs, 15–16, 18 – 19
32-bit programs, 15–16
32-Bit ODBC control panel, 77

• *A* •

Access Control Lists (ACLs). *See* ACL
   (Access Control Lists)
Access Control Settings dialog box,
   121–122
Accessories folder, 98
ACL Editor, 187–188
ACLs (Access Control Lists), 121, 138
   changing key permissions in, 187–188
   editing, 187–188
   security templates and, 193
   troubleshooting, 245
ACPI (Advanced Configuration Power
   Interface), 324
ACROREAD.INI, 15
Active Desktop, 22, 24–25. *See also*
   desktop
Active Directory (AD) database, 14–15,
   32, 47
   basic description of, 14, 25–26
   corruption of, 286

   disabling animation effects for, 221
   learning more about, 196
   network management and, 267
   permissions and, 183
   SAM file and, 138–139
   security and, 182, 183, 196–197
   user groups and, 182
   write caching and, 286
Active Directory For Dummies
   (Loughry), 196
Active Directory Group Policy utility, 31
Active Directory Users and Computers
   tool, 207, 245
ActiveX controls (Microsoft), 169, 171
AD (Active Directory). *See* Active Directory
   (AD) database
Add Key command, 118
Add Value command, 118
Add Value dialog box, 118
Add/Remove Hardware control panel, 72
Add/Remove Hardware wizard, 28, 55
Add/Remove Programs control panel, 72
Add/Remove Snap-in option, 68
Add/Remove Templates command, 195
ADM files, 195–196
administrative shares, 51
Administrative templates, 195–196
Administrative Tools control panel, 72
Administrative Tools folder, 69, 70
Administrator rights, 51, 190
   basic description of, 182
   logon security and, 181–182
   running Registry Editors with, without
      restarting, 327
   user profiles and, 204–205, 207
administrators, reporting configuration
   data to, 22–23
ADMINPAK.MSI, 70, 86

Adobe Systems
  Acrobat Reader, 15
  Photoshop, 30
Advanced Backup Options dialog box, 51
Advanced Configuration Power Interface
    (ACPI). *See* ACPI (Advanced
    Configuration Power Interface)
Advanced Power Management (APM). *See*
    APM (Advanced Power Management)
aliases, 153, 154
AllowedPaths key, 189
ALT files, 40–41
Always use this program to open these
    files option, 85
ampersand (&), 248
animation
  effects for menus, 221–222
  enabling/disabling, 109, 221–223
  zoom effect, 109, 221–222
annotations, 306
answer files, 269–270
APM (Advanced Power Management),
    24, 325
App Paths key, 298
Appearance tab, 65–66
AppEvents key, 174
application(s)
  16-bit, 15–16, 18–19
  32-bit, 15–16
  adding, to context menus, 228–229
  minor, installation of, 28, 36
  opening, with other applications, 84–86
  software, editing, 88–90
Application tab, 83
APPWIZ.CPL, 72. *See also* Add/Remove
    Programs control panel
Archive attribute, 132
associations, 15, 30, 83–84, 228–231
asterisk (*), 171
AT.EXE, 36, 37, 139
ATTRIB command, 133–134, 136
attributes
  Archive attribute, 132
  basic description of, 132–134
  Hidden attribute, 132, 134, 140, 143
  Read-only attribute, 132, 133, 134
  System attribute, 132, 133, 134

auditing, 185, 189–191
  basic description of, 120–122
  enabling, 190
  selecting keys for, 190–191
Auditing tab, 121
authentication, 184
Auto Refresh option, 115
AutoComplete feature, 312–314
AUTOEXEC.BAT, 55–56
AUTOEXEC.NT, 16
Automatically Backup System Protected
    Files with the System State option, 50
AutoShareServer value, 51
AutoShareWks value, 51

• B •

backslash (/), 155, 246, 309
backup(s). *See also* ERD (Emergency
    Repair Disk); restore operations
  basic description of, 26–60
  bootin'-and-batchin' solution, 54–56
  destinations for, 37–38
  difficulties involved with, 42–43, 241–242
  distant Registry, 51
  errors during, 241–242
  export and import method, 56–58
  files, location of, 130
  how to make, 42–43
  importance of, 3, 6, 33–35, 92
  job files, 46
  landmark, 35–36
  NTUSER.DAT and, 41, 48, 53, 56, 58,
    141, 142
  overwriting older, 37, 53
  REG method, 53–54, 58
  scheduled (recurring), 36–37
  selecting files for, 38–41
  SYSTEM file and, 144
  "tricks and traps" for, 46–48
  USRCLASS.DAT and, 48, 53, 56, 58
  when to make, 28
Backup Files and Folders right, 54
Backup Job Information dialog box, 50, 51

Backup Log tab, 50, 261
Backup Operator right, 51
Backup tab, 48, 51
Backup Type tab, 50
Basic Input/Output System (BIOS). *See*
    BIOS (Basic Input/Output System)
batch files
  backups and, 54–56, 58
  customizing the desktop and, 229,
    233–234
  customizing the Start menu and, 233–234
  restoring the Registry with, 264
Batched 98 utility, 271–272
Binary Editor dialog box, 116–117
binary file format, saving/restoring data in,
    120. *See also* binary (REG_BINARY)
    value type
binary (REG_BINARY) value type, 99–100,
    106, 114, 156, 158
BIOS (Basic Input/Output System), 325
bitmap caches, 287
BMP files, 30, 83
.bmp key, 171–172
bookmarks, to keys, 96
boot (startup) diskettes, 44, 55, 58.
    See also booting; ERD (Emergency
    Repair Disk)
boot menu, 35
BOOTDISK folder, 43–44
booting. *See also* safe mode boot; startup
  backup methods using, 54–56
  diskettes for, 44, 55, 58
  LKG (last know good) options for, 35, 82,
    165, 254–255
  SYSTEM file and, 136–137
  system state and, 47
BOOT.INI, 17, 18, 66
branches. *See also* branches (listed by
    name)
  basic description of, 152–154
  primary, overview, 160–175
branches (listed by name). *See also*
    branches
  HKCC (HKEY_CURRENT_CONFIG)
    branch, 153–155, 168–169
  HKCR (HKEY_CLASSES_ROOT) branch,
    153–155, 169–173, 228–231

HKCU (HKEY_CURRENT_USER) branch,
    153–155, 170, 175, 189–191, 200,
    194–196
HKLM (HKEY_LOCAL MACHINE) branch,
    153–155, 161–167, 170, 189–191,
    194–196
HKU (HKEY_USERS) branch, 53, 118, 120,
    153–155, 174–175
browsemaster, 285
browsers. *See* Internet Explorer browser
    (Microsoft)
bugs, 28–29, 34. *See also* errors
bus structure, 167

• *C* •

/C option, 110, 262–263
caches. *See also* memory
  bitmap, 287
  browser, 242
  write, 286
Calculator, 28, 36, 222
cartridge (removable) drives, 28–29, 58
  backups and, 37, 42, 44, 54
  Iomega drives, 37, 42, 44, 54–55
CascadeControlPanel value, 78
cascading menus, 77–81. *See also* menus
CD (Windows 2000)
  backups and, 43–44, 53
  creating startup diskettes using, 43–44
  Registry Editors on, 93
  Resource Kit Tools on, 36, 239–240, 257
CD (Windows 2000 Server), 70, 86
CD-R drives, 37
CD-R/W drives, 37
Certificate Services database, 47
change permissions, 183
characters, illegal, 65
CHM file extension, 148
Choose Program option, 85
class definition keys, 172–173
Class IDs (CLSIDs). *See* CLSIDs (Class IDs)
class registration, 47, 141–142, 170
client/server networks, 22, 140, 276. *See
    also* networking
Clipboard, 80–81, 100

Close command, 112
CLSIDs (Class IDs), 79–80, 169–173
CMDLINES.TXT, 273–274
colon (:), 113
color schemes, customizing, 21, 65–66, 73
Colors key, 65
COM (Component Object Model), 21–22, 47, 142
COM+ Class Registration Database, 47
command(s). *See also* commands (listed by name)
  -line mode, 109–110, 126
  in the Run Once screen, 272–273
  used in this book, syntax for, 4
commands (listed by name). *See also* commands
  Add Key command, 118
  Add Value command, 118
  Add/Remove Templates command, 195
  ATTRIB command, 133–134, 136
  Close command, 112
  COPY command, 34, 42, 44, 257
  Copy Key Name command, 100
  DIR command, 134, 229
  Export Registry command, 107
  Export Registry File command, 104
  Find command, 105–106, 248–249
  Import Registry File command, 108
  Load Hive command, 118, 120
  Load Selections command, 46
  Modify command, 101
  NET SHARE command, 51
  On the Internet command, 225–226
  Open Registry command, 86
  Options command, 88
  Print Subtree command, 119
  Printer Setup command, 119
  REG RESTORE command, 53
  REG SAVE command, 53
  RegDelete command, 235
  Rename command, 100, 257
  Restore command, 120
  Run command, 44, 48, 56, 296–297
  Save command, 62
  Save Key command, 118, 120
  Save Selections command, 46

  Save Subtree As command, 120
  Unload Hive command, 120
  XCOPY command, 34, 44, 55–56
Compatibility key, 164
Compatibility2 key, 164
Compatibility32 key, 164
Compiled HTML (.CHM) format, 148
component behavior, determining, 21–22
Component Object Model (COM). *See* COM (Component Object Model)
computer(s)
  accounts, 181
  network names of, 20, 64–65
Computer Management snap-in, 204
Computer Name field, 64, 65
CONFIG.NT, 16
CONFIG.POL, 145
CONFIG.SYS
  backup batch files and, 55–56
  device drivers and, 16
configuration data, reporting, 22–23
Confirm on Delete option, 116
Connect Network Registry dialog box, 277
Console key, 174
conspiracy theories, 23
context menu(s). *See also* right-clicking
  adding programs to, 228–229
  basic description of, 171
  customizing, 22, 30, 84–86, 171, 228–229
  in Registry Editors, 95
  search strings, 248–249
ContextMenu-Handlers key, 171
control panel(s). *See also* specific control panels
  adding, to the Start menu, 224–225
  basic description of, 67–81
  cascading menus for, 77–81
  customizing, 3, 77–81, 224–227, 300–301
  effects of, on the system and the Registry, 72–77
  hiding, 69, 300–301
  icons, 69, 226–227
  making changes to, backups after, 28, 36
  precautions for modifying, 3
  primary, 69–76
  secondary, 77

Control panel key, 174
control sets, 164–167, 254–255
COPY command, 34, 42, 44, 257
Copy Key Name command, 100
copying. *See also* backups
  with the COPY command, 34, 42, 44, 257
  with drag-and-drop, problems with, 42
  key names, 100
CPL files, 68, 69
crashes, 20, 29, 143. *See also* backups;
    restore operations
create link permission, 186
Create New Extension dialog box, 230
create subkey permission, 186
curly braces ({}), 81, 246
CurrentControlSet key, 165–166
cursor shadow effects, 222
customizing
  color schemes, 21, 65–66, 73
  context menus, 22, 30, 84–86, 171,
    228–229
  control panels, 3, 77–81, 224–227,
    300–301
  the desktop, 21, 30, 82, 219–236, 303–305
  double-clicking, 22, 77–78
  fonts, 21, 73, 164
  icons, 21, 69, 77–81, 231–232
  menus, 220–223
  MMC, 68, 227
  REGEDT32 behavior, 115–116
  right-clicking, 22, 30, 84–86
  security, 179–198
  sound schemes, 76, 321–322
  Start menu, 220–226, 233–234
  user profiles, 199–218, 320

• 𝔇 •

data
  problems searching for,
    troubleshooting, 248
  stored, security for, 183–184
  transmitted, security for, 184
  types, special, 95
Data field, 99

date stamps, 27, 52
Date/Time control panel, 72
DCOM (Distributed COM), 21–22
DEFAULT file
  basic description of, 40, 132, 142
  HKU settings and, 174–175
  user profiles and, 210
.DEFAULT key, 174, 213
Default string value, 103
DefaultIcon key, 173
deleting
  keys, 104–105, 118–119
  permissions for, 186
  SAV and REPAIR files, 144
  values, 102, 104–105
  warnings, 63
DEPLOY.CAB, 270–281
Deploying Windows 2000 Policies
    (Wilkins), 180
DESCRIPTION key, 162
DESK.CPL, 73. *See also* Display
    control panel
desktop
  Active Desktop, 22, 24–25
  adding REGEDIT to, 97
  animation effects, enabling/disabling, 109,
    221–223
  cosmetic changes to, 231–234
  creating new files by clicking on, 314–315
  customizing, 21, 30, 82, 219–236, 303–305
  history lists, 234–236
  HKU settings for, 175–176
  icons, 226–227, 231–232
  security features, 31, 234–236
  shell, 83
  wallpaper, 21, 303–305
Detailed option, 50
device drivers, 167, 168–169
  16-bit, 16
  32-bit, 16
  backups and, 54
  basic description of, 20
  loading, into memory, 20
  signing, 184
Device Manager, 68, 167–168
Device Manager tab, 168

DEVICEMAP key, 162
DHCP (Dynamic Host Configuration Protocol), 281–282
Dial-Up Networking (DUN). *See* DUN (Dial-Up Networking)
digital certificates, 181
digital signatures, 184
DIR command, 134, 229
directories. *See also* folders
  backups to different, 38
  setup, changing the default location for, 305–306
Disable Registry Editing Tools option, 88, 243–244
Disable Registry Editing Tools system policy, 243–244
DisableNT4Policy value, 242
disk cloning installation method, 268
Disk Operating System (DOS). *See* DOS (Disk Operating System)
diskette(s). *See also* ERD (Emergency Repair Disk)
  boot (startup), 44, 55, 58
  drives, backups with, 38, 43–44, 58
Display control panel, 65–66, 249
  animation settings, 109, 221–223
  basic description of, 73
  hiding, 300
Display List of Operating Systems for x Seconds option, 66
DisplayName key, 295
Distributed COM (DCOM). *See* DCOM (Distributed COM)
distribution servers, 273–274
DLLs (Dynamic Link Libraries), 316
DNS (Domain Name Services), 197, 244, 282–283
documentation, 23
Documents and Settings folder, 48, 140, 146
dollar sign ($), 41, 51
domain controllers, creating user profiles on, 207
Domain Name Services (DNS). *See* DNS (Domain Name Services)
DOS (Disk Operating System)
  attributes, 132
  backups and, 44, 54–55

boot (startup) diskettes, 44, 55
  device drivers, 54
  programs, 16
  prompt, 97, 109, 110
  restore operations and, 259, 264
double quotes ("), 246
double-clicking
  customizing, 22, 77–78
  in Registry Editors, 96
  use of the term, 4
drag-and-drop
  backups and, 44
  copying Registry files with, 42
  customizing, 22
drivers, device, 167, 168–169
  16-bit, 16
  32-bit, 16
  backups and, 54
  basic description of, 20
  loading, into memory, 20
  signing, 184
DSA Heuristics value, 286
DUN (Dial-Up Networking), 301–302, 321, 323
DWORD Editor dialog box, 116–117
DWORD (REG_DWORD) value type, 99–103, 114
  basic description of, 156, 158–159
  searching for data in, 106
Dynamic Host Configuration Protocol (DHCP). *See* DHCP (Dynamic Host Configuration Protocol)
Dynamic Link Libraries (DLLs). *See* DLLs (Dynamic Link Libraries)

• *E* •

/E option, 110
Edit Binary Value dialog box, 101–103
Edit DWORD Value dialog box, 101–103
Edit File Type dialog box, 229
Edit menu
  Add Key command, 118
  Add Value command, 118
  basic description of, 114
  Find command, 105–106
  Modify command, 101

Edit String dialog box, 101–103
EditFlags value, 322–323
editing. *See also* Registry Editors
   real-mode, 110
   simplifying complex changes when, 65–66
   without a Registry Editor, 61–90, 92–93
Effects tab, 109, 249
EFS (Encrypting File System), 226
Emergency Repair Disk (ERD). *See* ERD
      (Emergency Repair Disk)
Encrypting File System (EFS). *See* EFS
      (Encrypting File System)
encryption, 184, 226
end users, use of the term, 20
Enum key, 165–167
Enum tree, 167
enumerate subkeys permission, 186
enumerators, 167, 186
ERD (Emergency Repair Disk)
   creating, 26–27, 29, 52
   restore operations and, 29, 258, 263, 264
   user profiles and, 216
ERD wizard, 27, 29
error messages. *See also* bugs
   "Another installation is in progress,"
      250–251
   during backups, 241–242
   troubleshooting, 239–242, 249–252
   "unable to complete requested
      operation," 249–250
event(s). *See also* Event Viewer
   auditing, 189–191
   logs, 318–321
Event Viewer, 68, 148, 250, 317–318. *See
   also* events
EXCEL.INI, 17
Expand Control Panel option, 78–79
Explorer (EXPLORER.EXE)
   checking date stamps with, 27, 52
   copying Registry files with, 42
   editing the Registry with, 82–84
   executable file for, 83, 228
   folder memory, 224
   handling Class IDs with, 80–81
   opening My Computer with, 227–228

opening REG files with, 108
   scrolling effects with, 221
   setting permissions with, 183
   use of the term, 83
   viewing hidden files with, 38
Explorer (Windows 2000 shell), 83
Explorer key, 164
Export Range panel, 57
Export Registry command, 107
Export Registry File command, 104
Export Registry File dialog box, 107–108
Export Registry File option, 56–57
exporting/importing, 107–110, 119–120
   data for restore operations, 255–257
   keys, 107–109
   older Windows versions, and, 108
   REG file construction rules and, 308–309
   "snapshotting" when, 307
   troubleshooting, 246–248

• *F* •

FAT (File Allocation Table), 54–55, 183,
      133, 242
FAT32, 54, 242
Favorites folder, 41
Favorites menu, 96, 100, 113
feature, use of the term, 293
file(s). *See also* filenames; file types
   attributes, 132–134
   creating new, by clicking on the desktop,
      314–315
   date stamps, 27, 52
   double-clicking, 22
   listings of, printing, 136
   Registry-related, which are not part of the
      Registry, 145–150
   viewing, 38–39, 132–136
File Allocation Table (FAT). *See* FAT (File
      Allocation Table)
File Checker, 82
File menu
   Open Registry command, 86
   Save command, 62
File Name field, 57, 108

file type(s)
  adding, 315–316
  associations, 15, 30, 83–84, 228–231
  icons for specific, changing, 231–232
  locking out changes to, 322–323
  opening specific or unknown, 84–86, 230–231
  registered, 83–84
  removing, 315
File value, 319–320
filename(s)
  extensions, 135, 171–172, 230–231
  searching for, 246, 249
Find command, 105–106, 248–249
Find dialog box, 79, 105–106, 125, 227
Find Fast control panel, 77
Find What field, 80, 105
FINDFAST.CPL, 77
FindFlags value, 125
flat structure, of INI files, 18
folder(s). *See also* directories; Folder Options control panel
  memory, disabling, 224
  redirection capabilities for, 216
Folder Options control panel, 38, 83–84
  adding extensions to file types with, 230
  basic description of, 73
  customizing icons with, 232
  disabling folder memory with, 224
  locking settings in, 322–323
Folder Options dialog box, 171
fonts
  customizing, 21, 73, 164
  used in this book, 4
Fonts control panel, 73
Fonts key, 164
For People command, 225–226
forward slash (/), 134
FTP (File Transfer Protocol), 284
full control permission, 183, 186, 188, 251

• *G* •

Game Controllers control panel, 73
General tab, 50, 133

Globally Unique IDs (GUIDs). *See* GUIDs (Globally Unique IDs)
GPEDIT.MSC (Group Policy management console), 69, 147
Graphical User Interface (GUI). *See* GUI (Graphical User Interface)
graphics mode, 40
Group Policy Editor, 24–25, 145
  backup procedures before using, 28
  configuration changes with, 194–197
  console, accessing, 193–194
  controlling access to control panels with, 69
  driver signing and, 184
  reversing settings with, 243
Group Policy management console (GPEDIT.MSC), 69, 147
GUEST program, 54
GUI (Graphical User Interface), 97
GUIDs (Globally Unique IDs), 169

• *H* •

handles, to keys, 153
hard drive(s)
  failures, 34
  partitions, 55, 56
  reformatting, 82
  second local, 38
  space, taken up by user profiles, 217
hardware
  Plug and Play feature for, 24, 29, 167, 169
  profiles, 16, 20, 161–162, 166, 168–169
HARDWARE key, 161–162
Hardware Profiles dialog box, 168
Hardware Profiles key, 166
HDWWIZ.CPL, 72. *See also* Add/Remove Hardware control panel
help. *See also* Help menu
  for Internet Explorer, 96
  for naming computers, 64–65
  for NTBACKUP, 37
  for Registry Editors, 63, 96, 112, 115, 148
  for Windows 2000 Server, 244
Help menu, 101, 115. *See also* Help

hidden files
  attributes for, 131–135
  displaying, 38, 134–135
  Hidden attribute for, 132, 134, 140, 143
Hidden Files Extensions for Known File
    Types option, 135
Hide Protected Operating System Files
    (Recommended) option, 38, 135
Hide Specific Control Panel Applets
    option, 69
history lists, 234–236
hives
  basic description of, 131
  loading/unloading, 118, 120, 249–250,
    257–259
  *.LOG files for, 142–143
  restoring, 257–259
HKCC (HKEY_CURRENT_CONFIG) branch,
    153–155, 168–169
HKCR (HKEY_CLASSES_ROOT) branch,
    153–155, 169–173, 228–231
HKCU (HKEY_CURRENT_USER) branch,
    153–155, 170, 200
  auditing and, 189–191
  information in, overview of, 175
  policies and, 194–196
HKLM (HKEY_LOCAL MACHINE) branch,
    153–155, 161–167, 170, 189–191,
    194–196
HKU (HKEY_USERS) branch, 53, 118, 120,
    153–155, 174–175
hot keys, 222
hot tracking, 222
HTML (HyperText Markup Language)
    files, 172
Hungarian notation, 156
HyperText Markup Language (HTML) files.
    See HTML (HyperText Markup
    Language) files

• 1 •

icons
  application-related, changing, 231–232
  control panel, 69, 226–227
  customizing, 21, 69, 77–81, 231–232
  desktop, 97, 111, 226–227, 231–232
  hiding/displaying, 69, 77–81
  for keys, 154

Start menu, 69, 77–81
  used in this book, 9
IIS (Microsoft Internet Information Server),
    19, 180, 284–285
Import Registry File command, 108
Import Registry File dialog box, 108
importing/exporting, 107–110, 119–120
  data for restore operations, 255–257
  keys, 107–109
  REG file construction rules and, 308–309
  "snapshotting" when, 307
  troubleshooting, 246–248
INF files
  basic description of, 147
  troubleshooting, 247–248
INI files. See also specific files
  64K size limitations and, 17, 18
  basic description of, 17
  changes in, with Windows 2000, 13
  editing, 66–67
  mapping, 19
  private, 15–16, 17, 19, 89
  role of, in Windows 2000, 17–19
  shortcomings of, 17–19
infotips, 232–233
IniFileMapping key, 164
initialization. See INI files
InProcServer 32 key, 173
installation. See also setup programs
  backups after, 28, 35
  backups before, 36
  Calculator, 28, 36
  choices, recording, 20
  device drivers and, 184
  error messages, 250–251
  incomplete, 41
  LAN-based, 268–269
  network management and, 268–271
  over previous versions of Windows, 19
  re-, 34, 82
  security and, 184
  Setup Manager, 270–271
  System Policy Editor, 86
  TCP/IP, 281
  of Windows 3.x applications, 19
  of Windows 2000, 19–21, 28, 35, 184,
    250–251
Install/Uninstall list, 295–296
intellectual property, 180

IntelliMirror, 41, 199–200

IntelliSense, 312

Internet
control panel options for, 73, 236
transmissions, security for, 184

Internet Connection Wizard (Microsoft), 89

Internet Explorer browser (Microsoft)
accessing unknown sites with, 89–90
Active Desktop and, 24–25
AutoComplete feature, 312–314
help system, 96
history lists, 234–236
passwords, recovering lost, 299

Internet Options control panel, 73, 236

Internet Protocol (IP). *See* IP (Internet Protocol)

interrupts, 20

INTL, 75. *See also* Regional Options control panel

IntranetWare, 146

IP (Internet Protocol), 280–281, 283

• J •

Job menu
Load Selections command, 46
Save Selections command, 46

JOY.CPL, 73. *See also* Game Controllers control panel

JPEG images, 170, 172–173

jpegfile key, 172–173

• K •

Kerberos, 181

key(s). *See also specific keys*
abbreviations for, 110
active, 99, 101, 113
adding, 102–104
basic description of, 95, 98, 152, 154–155
bookmarks to, 96
creating, 117–119
deleting, 104–105, 117–119
duplicate, unwanted, 247
finding, 105–106

icons for, 154
importing/exporting, 110, 119–120
last-key-memory feature for, 123–124
missing, when importing REG files, 246–247
names, 53, 95, 100, 110, 155
primary, overview of, 160–175
restoring, 255–257
root/top-level, 100
security settings for, 120–122, 183, 185–191
sub- (descendant), 98, 155
troubleshooting, 246–247

key pane
adding values in, 103
basic description of, 97–99
expanding, 113

Keyboard control panel, 74, 223

• L •

landmark backups, 35–36. *See also* backups

LANs (local-area networks), 202–203, 216, 244, 268–269

last known good (LKG) boot option. *See* LKG (last know good) boot option

LastKey value, 123–125

Licensing control panel, 74

list folder contents permission, 183

LKG (last know good) boot option, 35, 82, 165, 254–255

Load Hive command, 118, 120

Load Hive operation, 249–250

Load Selections command, 46

Local Group Policy Tool, 31, 206
bypassing changes made with, 244
console, accessing, 193–194
controlling access to control panels with, 69
troubleshooting changes made with, 245

local-area networks (LANs). *See* LANs (local-area networks)

LOG files (transaction logs), 39, 40, 142–143

logical structure, of the Registry, 130,
  151–176
logon
  history lists and, 236
  screens, background settings for, 303–305
  screens, *NumLock* settings for, 302–303
  security, 181–182
LogPath value, 156–157

• *M* •

machine directory, 136
Machine value, 189
MAKEBOOT.EXE, 43–44
MAKEBT32.EXE, 43–44
Match Case option, 119
Match Whole String Only option, 105
memory. *See also* caches
  areas, basic description of, 20
  system state and, 47
menu(s). *See also* menu bars; specific
    menus
  animation effects, 221–222
  cascading, 77–81
  customizing, 220–223
  depersonalizing, 220–221
  grayed-out options on, 101
menu bar(s). *See also* menus
  basic description of, 97, 99–101, 113–115
  five menus on, 100–101
  in Registry Editors, 97, 99, 113, 114–115
MenuShowDelay value, 223
metabase, 284
Microsoft Management Console (MMC).
    See MMC (Microsoft Management
    Console)
Microsoft TechNet, 240, 260
Microsoft Web site, 187, 193
Microsoft Windows Backup (NTBACKUP),
    141, 216
  backups to diskettes with, 38
  basic description of, 36–37, 44–51, 58
  error messages, 241–242
  files, location of, 144

help, 37
  restore operations and, 258–262
  shortcomings of, 45
  tricks and traps for using, 46–48
MIME types, 142
MMC (Microsoft Management Console),
    28, 193
  basic description of, 68
  customizing, 68, 227
  desktop icons for, 227
  IIS snap-in for, 284
  security and, 193
MMC.EXE, 68. *See also* MMC (Microsoft
    Management Console)
MMSYS.CPL, 69, 76. *See also* Sounds and
    Multimedia control panel
modems speeds, 245
Modify command, 101
modify permission, 183
MountedDevices key, 167
mouse. *See also* double-clicking; right-
    clicking
  control panel for, 74
  cursor shadow effects, 222
  drag-and-drop with, 22, 42, 44
MSC files, 68
MSI files, 148
Multi-String Editor, 117
My Computer
  editing the Registry with, 82–84
  opening, in Explorer view, 227–228
  viewing hidden files/file extensions with,
    134–135
My Documents folder, 56

• *N* •

Name field, 99
names. *See also* filenames
  computer, 20, 64–65
  key, 53, 95, 100, 110, 155
  organization, changing, 325–326
  registered, changing, 325–326
  value, 101–102, 117, 248

navigation pane, 97

NCPA.CPL, 74

NET SHARE command, 51

NETLOGON folder, 145

Network and Dial-up Connections control panel, 74

Network Identification dialog box, 64

Network Identification tab, 244

networking. *See also* Active Directory (AD) database; user profiles
  backups and, 37, 51, 53–55
  client/server, 22, 140, 276
  components, loading order for, 21
  files, organization/location of, 130, 131
  with LANs (local-area networks), 202–203, 216, 244, 268–269
  learning more about, 6
  management of, overview of, 267–278
  mixed-mode, 138
  reporting configuration data, 22–23
  SAM file and, 138–139
  SECURITY file and, 138–139
  services, overview of, 279–288

Networking For Dummies, 3rd Edition (Lowe), 6

New Active dialog box, 229

Normal option, 50

Norton Registry Editor, 88, 106, 244. *See also* Registry Editors

Notepad, 17, 28, 34, 36
  creating batch files with, 229
  editing INI files with, 89
  launching, when opening specific or unknown file types, 22, 230–231
  writing backup batch files with, 55–56

notify permission, 186

Novell NetWare, 140–141, 146, 276

NTBACKUP (Microsoft Windows Backup), 141, 216
  backups to diskettes with, 38
  basic description of, 36–37, 44–51, 58
  error messages, 241–242
  files, location of, 144
  help, 37
  restore operations and, 258–262
  shortcomings of, 45
  tricks and traps for using, 46–48

NTCONFIG.POL, 145

NTDETECT.COM, 47

NTDS key, 286

NTFS (Windows NT File System), 54–56, 179
  file attributes, 133
  permissions, 183

NTFSCopy, 56

NTFSDOS.EXE, 55, 56

NTLDR, 47, 136

NTUSER.DAT. *See also* user profiles
  backups and, 41, 48, 53, 56, 58
  basic description of, 131–132, 139–142
  building new local user profiles and, 205
  .DEFAULT key and, 213–214
  editing, 87–88
  HKU settings and, 174–175
  location of, 201–202, 209, 211
  versions of, comparison of, 211

NTUSER.DAT.LOG, 143, 205

NTUSER.INI, 135, 146

NTUSER.MAN, 141, 214

null strings, 124, 125

NullFile value, 315

NumLock settings, 302–303

objects
  basic description of, 21
  control panel, 79–80

ODBCCP32.CPL, 77

OEMs (Original Equipment Manufacturers), 273, 274

Office (Microsoft), 19, 77, 251–252

OfflineInformation value, 89

On the Internet command, 225–226

Open dialog box, 44

Open field, 79, 88

Open Registry command, 86

Open With dialog box, 85

Open With option, 84–86

Open/Save MRU list, 235

OpenSaveMRU key, 235, 236

optical drives, 37, 44. *See also* removable
    drives
Options command, 88
Options dialog box, 49–50, 261
Options menu, 115–116
organization names, changing, 325–326
Original Equipment Manufacturers (OEMs).
    See OEMs (Original Equipment
    Manufacturers)
Outlook Express (Microsoft), 56
ownership settings, 120–122

● *P* ●

packages, 293–295
Paint (Microsoft), 30, 83
Paint.Picture key, 171–172
parallel ports, 28–29
partitions, 55, 56
passwords
    control panel for, 74
    cracking, 181
    logon security and, 181–182
    recovering lost, 299
    user profiles and, 204–206
PATH variable, 296–298
percent sign (%), 157
Performance Monitor, 189
period (.), 81
permission(s). *See also* permissions (listed
    by type); security
    basic description of, 120–122, 182–183
    delete permission, 186
    keys, 183, 185–191
    NTFS, 183
    shared, 183
    troubleshooting, 245, 251–252
permissions (listed by type). *See also*
    permissions
    change permissions, 183
    create link permission, 186
    create subkey permission, 186
    enumerate subkeys permission, 186
    full control permission, 183, 186, 188, 251
    list folder contents permission, 183

modify permission, 183
notify permission, 186
query value permission, 186
read permissions, 183, 186
set value permission, 186
shared permissions, 183
special permissions, 186
write permission, 183, 186
Permissions dialog box, 112, 120–121
Personal Web Manager control panel, 77
per-user class registration, 141–142
Phone and Modem Options control
    panel, 74
physical structure, of the Registry,
    130–144, 151
Plug and Play, 24, 29, 167, 169
POLEDIT.EXE, 86–88, 147. *See also* System
    Policy Editor (POLEDIT.EXE)
policies. *See also* policy (POL) files
    basic description of, 192–197
    disabling, 242
    group, 184–185, 244–245
    logging of, enabling, 320
    securing computers with, 192–197
    system, 184–185, 242
    troubleshooting, 242–245
Policies key, 164
policy (POL) files. *See also* policies;
    System Policy Editor (POLEDIT.EXE)
    basic description of, 145–146, 179
    creating, 86
    editing, 86–88
power management, 324–325
Power Options control panel, 75, 324–325
Power User rights, 182, 327
PowerdownAfterShutdown value, 324
Print dialog box, 106–107
Print Subtree command, 119
Printer Setup command, 119
Printers control panel, 75
Printers key, 175
printing
    file listings, 136
    part or all of the Registry, 106–107, 119,
        132–136

private INI files, 15–16, 17, 19, 89. *See also* INI files
Processes tab, 83
processor time, division of, 21
ProfileImagePath value, 211
ProfileList key, 212
Programs folder, 98
Prompt User When Slow Link is Detected policy, 245
property sheets, 171
PropertySheetHandlers key, 171
protocols
  DHCP (Dynamic Host Configuration Protocol), 281–282
  FTP (File Transfer Protocol), 284
  IP (Internet Protocol), 280–281, 283
  TCP/IP (Transmission Control Protocol/Internet Protocol), 279–284
PWS.EXE, 77

• *Q* •

QT32.CPL, 77
qualifiers, 134
query value permission, 186
QuickTime 32 control panel, 77
quotas, 249–250

• *R* •

RAM (random-access memory). *See* memory
RDISK, 26
Read Only Mode option, 115, 116, 119
read permission, 183, 186
read+execute permission, 183
Read-only attribute, 132, 133, 134
real-mode editing, 110
recent documents list, 234
Recovery Console, 29, 110, 257–259, 263–264
Recycle Bin, 242
REG files
  basic description of, 147
  construction rules for, 308–309

which don't work on other PCs, 247–248
double-clicking, 96
exporting/importing, 107–110, 119–120, 246–248, 255–257, 307–309
troubleshooting, 247–248
REG RESTORE command, 53
REG SAVE command, 53
REG utility (REG.EXE), 53–54, 58, 233–234, 257
REG_BINARY value type, 99–100, 106, 114, 156, 158
RegDelete command, 235
REG_DWORD value type, 99–103, 114
  basic description of, 156, 158–159
  searching for data in, 106
REG_DWORD_BIG ENDIAN value type, 159
REGEDIT. *See also* Registry Editors
  adding, to your desktop, 97
  adding keys/values with, 102–104
  backups and, 56–58, 59
  basic description of, 14–15, 93–110
  command-line mode, 109–110, 126
  deleting keys/values with, 104–105
  disabling, 87–88
  executable file for (REGEDIT.EXE), 14, 148
  file type settings made with, 229–231
  Find command, 105–106
  graphics mode, 97–109
  handling Class IDs with, 79–80
  help, 63, 96
  making My Computer run Explorer via the Registry with, 227–228
  memory feature, 96
  Print option, 106–107
  remote Registry editing with, 277
  removing, after installing security settings, 185
  restore operations and, 256–257, 262–263
  shortcuts, 97–98
  versions of, 122–123
  viewing the Windows 3.11 Registration Database with, 19
  when to use, 126
  windows, anatomy of, 97–102
Regedit *key,* 124, 125
REGEDIT.REG, 124

REGEDT32, 111–122. *See also* Registry
   Editors
   adding, to your desktop, 111
   adding/deleting keys with, 117–119
   basic description of, 93–94
   behavior, customizing, 115–116
   changing values with, 116–117
   creating sound schemes with, 321–322
   disabling, 87–88
   executable file for (REGEDT32.EXE), 14,
      111, 148
   exporting/importing data with, 119–120
   help, 63, 112, 115
   printing with, 119
   remote Registry editing with, 277–278
   removing, after installing security
      settings, 185
   restore operations and, 256–257
   search feature, 119, 248
   security settings with, 120–122
   versions of, differences between, 112
   when to use, 126
   windows, anatomy of, 112–115
Regedt32 key, 126
REG_EXPAND_SZ value type, 57, 114,
   156–157
REG_FULL_RESOURCE_DESCRIPTOR value
   type, 159–160
Regional Options control panel, 75
registered
   file types, 83–84
   names, changing, 325–326
Registration Database (Windows 3.*x*),
   18–19
Registry Editors, 34, 56–57, 59. *See also*
   REGEDIT; REGEDT32
   adding files types with, 315
   backup procedures before using, 28, 36
   basic description of, 14, 91–126
   comparison table, 94
   disabling, 31, 87–88
   editing without, 61–90
   help, 63, 96, 112, 115, 148
   policies for, 244
   precautions for using, 3, 34, 62–64, 92–93
   remote editing with, 220, 275–278
   restore operations and, 256–257, 262–263
   rules for using, 61–62, 92–93
   running, with Administrator rights, 327
   security and, 139, 185–186, 190–191, 196
   shortcomings of, 23, 62–64
   viewing SECURITY and SAM files with, 139
Registry menu, 100, 114
   Close command, 112
   Export Registry command, 107
   Import Registry File command, 108
   Load Hive command, 118
   Print Subtree command, 119
   Printer Setup command, 119
   Restore command, 120
   Save Key command, 118, 120
   Save Subtree As command, 120
REGISTRY.BKS, 46
REGISTRY.POL, 145
REG_LINK value type, 159
REGMON, 308
REG_MULTI_SZ value type, 57, 95, 114, 117,
   156, 157
REG_NONE value type, 159
REG_RESOURCE_LIST value type, 160
REG_RESOURCE_REQUIREMENTS_LIST
   value type, 160
REGREST, 53
REG_SZ (string) value type, 99–100, 106
   expandable (RG_EXPAND_SZ), 57, 114,
      156–157
   multi-string (RG_MULTI_SZ), 57, 95, 114,
      117, 156, 157
remote access
   editing Registries through, 220, 275–278
   information, in the *RemoteAccess* key, 175
   INI files and, 18
   making backups via, 37
   security settings for, 189
Remote Installation Service (RIS). *See* RIS
   (Remote Installation Service)
RemoteAccess key, 175
removable (cartridge) drives, 28–29, 58
   backups and, 37, 42, 44, 54
   Iomega drives, 37, 42, 44, 54–55
Rename command, 100, 257
REPAIR files, 144

RESET.BAT, 126
RESET.REG, 125
RESOURCEMAP key, 162
Restore command, 120
restore operations. *See also* backups; ERD
   (Emergency Repair Disk)
  basic description of, 29, 132, 253–264
  with DOS, 259
  full, 259–264
  new, with Windows 2000, 26
  partial, 254–259
  rebuilding as an alternative to, 260
RestrictRun value, 243
right-clicking. *See also* context menus
  changing application settings when, 89
  customizing, 22, 30, 84–86
  in Registry Editors, 95
rights
  Administrator rights, 51, 181–182, 190,
    204–205, 207, 327
  Backup Files and Folder rights, 54
  Backup Operator rights, 51
  basic description of, 182
  granting, 182
  group, 182
  Power User rights, 182, 327
RIS (Remote Installation Service), 269
Root key, 167
RSL (Registry Size Limit), 25, 250
Run command, 44, 48, 56, 296–297
Run dialog box, 296–298
Run key, 164
Run MRU list, 234, 236
Run Once feature, 21, 164, 271–274, 326
RunMRU key, 235, 236
RunOnce key, 164, 326
RunOnceEx key, 164

/S option, 110, 125
safe mode boot. *See also* booting
  basic description of, 43
  backups and, 34, 43, 45, 58

restore operations and, 259, 263
  running Registry Editors from, 110
SAM file
  backups and, 35, 40
  basic description of, 40, 132, 138–139
  restore operations and, 258
  user groups and, 182
SAM key, 162
SAV files, 39–40, 144
Save command, 62
Save In field, 57, 108
Save Key command, 118, 120
Save Selections command, 46
Save Settings on Exit option, 116
Save Subtree As command, 120
Scanners and Cameras control panel, 75
scheduled (recurring) backups, 36–37. *See*
    also backups
Scheduled Tasks control panel, 75
Scheduled Tasks utility, 36, 37
screen(s)
  background settings for, 303–305
  NumLock settings for, 302–303
  welcome, 21
scripting
  implementing, 275
  installation method, 268, 269–270
  setting options for, 271–275
scrolling, smooth, 221–222
SDK (Software Development Kit), 169
Search menu. *See also* searching
  For People command, 225–226
  On the Internet command, 225–226
searching. *See also* Search menu
  for filenames, 246, 249
  with the Find command, 105–106,
    248–249
  with REGEDIT, 119, 248
  for values, 105–106, 248
security. *See also* permissions; rights
  changes, backup procedures before,
    28, 36
  clearance, to delete Registry keys,
    118–119

customizing, 179–198
the desktop and, 234–236
history lists and, 234–236
IDs (SIDs), 174, 175, 211–213
improved, with Windows 2000, 24
IP (Internet Protocol) and, 280
for keys, 120–122, 124–126, 183, 185–191
logs, 190, 191
overview of, 180–191
remote Registry editing and, 276, 278
for stored data, 183–184
templates, 193, 195–196
Security Configuration Tool Set, 192–193
SECURITY file, 40, 132, 138–139, 258
SECURITY key, 162
Security menu, 112, 114
server(s), 20, 21
distribution, 273–274
IIS (Microsoft Internet Information Server), 19, 180, 284–285
improving the performance of, 285–287
member, 138
NTUSER.DAT and, 140–141
SAM files and, 138
Terminal Server, 220, 287
Services control panel, 37
Services key, 166
set value permission, 186
setup directory, changing the default location for, 305–306
Setup key, 166–167
setup program(s). *See also* installation; Setup Manager
basic description of, 81–82
choices, recording of, 20
executable files for, 53
SAV files and, 40
text mode/graphics mode, 40, 144
for Windows 3.*x* applications, 18
Setup Manager, 270–275
SFCDisable value, 317
SFCDllCacheDir value, 317
SFCQuota value, 317
SFCShowProgress value, 317
SFP (System File Protection), 316–318

shared permissions, 183. *See also* permissions
sharing violations, 43
Shell key, 173
Shellex key, 171, 173
ShellNew key, 315
SIDs (Security IDs), 174, 175, 211–213
Single MS-DOS mode, 110
size limits, for the Registry, 25, 250
Small Business Networking For Dummies (Weadock), 6
smart cards, 181
"snapshots," 40, 307
SOFTWARE file, 35, 40, 137–138
Software (HKCU\Software) key, 175, 189–191, 196
SOFTWARE (HKLM\SOFTWARE) key, 163–164, 189–191, 196
SOFTWARE.LOG, 143
sorting, the Start menu, 233–234
sound schemes, customizing, 76, 321–322
Sounds and Multimedia control panel, 76, 321
special permissions, 186
speeding up Windows 2000, 31, 220–224
spell-checking feature, 22
SQL (Structured Query Language), 77
square brackets ([]), 17
Start Backup option, 46, 50, 51
Start menu. *See also* menus
customizing, 220–226, 233–234
depersonalizing, 220–221
expanding, 224–225
Find submenu, 225–226
Run command, 44, 48, 56, 296–297
sorting, 233–234
Start Menu folder, 98
startup. *See also* booting
diskettes, 43–44, 58
information, overview of, 20–21
running programs automatically at, 326
status bars, 97, 99, 113
STICPL, 75. *See also* Scheduled Tasks control panel

string (RG_SZ) value type, 99–100, 106
  expandable (RG_EXPAND_SZ), 57, 114, 156–157
  multi-string (RG_MULTI_SZ), 57, 95, 114, 117, 156, 157
String Editor dialog box, 116–117
Structured Query Language (SQL). *See* SQL (Structured Query Language)
superhidden files, 134, 135
SYDM.CPL, 76. *See also* System control panel
SysPrep, 269
System attribute, 132, 133, 134
System control panel, 167, 207, 208, 215
  basic description of, 76
  Hardware Profiles property sheet, 168
  Network Identification tab, 244
SYSTEM file
  backups and, 35, 40
  basic description of, 40, 136–137
  editing, 87–88
System File Checker, 316–317
System File Protection (SFP). *See* SFP (System File Protection)
SYSTEM hive, 143–144
System Internals, 55, 56
SYSTEM key, 164–167
System Policy Editor (POLEDIT.EXE), 24, 147, 192–193
  backup procedures before using, 28, 36
  basic description of, 86–88
  controlling access to control panels with, 69
  creating policy files with, 145
  installing, 86
system state
  backing up, 46–48, 241–242
  basic description of, 46–47
SYSTEM.ALT, 35, 40, 143–144
SYSTEM.INI, 18
SYSVOL folder, 47

• T •

tape drives, 38, 44
Task Manager, 83
Task Scheduler service, 37
"tatoos," use of the term, 196
TCP/IP (Transmission Control Protocol/Internet Protocol), 279–284
TechNet, 19
technical support, 82
TechTips, 306
TELEPHON.CPL, 74
Telnet, 283
templates, 193, 195
Terminal Server, 220, 287
text mode, 40, 144
time zones, 20
TIMEDATE.CPL, 72. Date/Time control panel
topic pane, 97
transmission
  of data, security for, 184
  packets, 280–281
Transmission Control Protocol/Internet Protocol (TCP/IP). *See* TCP/IP (Transmission Control Protocol/Internet Protocol)
Tree menu, 114
tree structure, of the Registry, 152–165
troubleshooting
  ACLs (Access Control Lists), 245
  changes made with the Local Group Policy Tool, 245
  error messages, 239–242, 249–252
  exporting/importing data, 246–248
  INF files, 247–248
  keys, 246–247
  overview of, 239–264
  permissions, 245, 251–252
  policies, 242–245
  problems searching for data, 248
  REG files, 247–248

reporting configuration data to administrators, 22–23
user profiles, 245
TweakUI control panel, 77, 315
  customizing the desktop with, 219–220
  disabling, 88
  when to use, 219–220
Type field, 99
Typed URLs list, 235
TypedURLs key, 235, 236

• *U* •

underscore (_), 65, 101, 156
Undo feature, 62, 96, 112
Uninstall key, 164
uninstall procedures, 28, 34, 35, 164
Unload Hive command, 120
URLs (Uniform Resource Locators), 312–314
Use Transition Effects for Menus and Tooltips option, 109
user profile(s), 21–22, 41, 139–142. *See also* NTUSER.DAT; USRCLASS.DAT
  basic description of, 21, 130, 199–201
  customizing, 199–218, 320
  diverse uses for, 202
  effect of, on the Registry, 209–213
  enabling logging of, 320
  files for, location of, 130–132, 149, 209–212
  hard drive space taken up by, 217
  LANs and, 202–203
  that load slowly, 245
  local, 202–208, 209–210, 216
  managing, 215
  mandatory, 141, 214
  per-user class registration and, 141–142
  roaming, 130, 203–204, 206–207, 210–211, 216
  setting up, 203–208
  troubleshooting, 245
  types of, changing, 208
  when to use, 201–203
  on a Windows 2000 domain, creating, 207
User Profiles tab, 215

USERDIFF file, 142
USERDIFF.LOG, 142
usernames. *See also* NTUSER.DAT
  logon security and, 181–182
  settings for, 139–142
UserPreferencemask value, 222, 223
Users and Passwords control panel, 69, 76, 204–205, 207, 215
Users and Passwords dialog box, 205
USRCLASS.DAT, 174–175, 205. *See also* user profiles
  backups and, 48, 53, 56, 58
  basic description of, 131–132, 139–142
  location of, 201–202, 209, 211
  versions of, comparison of, 211
USRCLASS.DAT.LOG, 205

• *V* •

value(s). *See also specific values; value types*
  adding, 102–104, 155–160
  basic description of, 99, 113–114, 152
  changing, 101
  deleting, 102, 104–105
  exporting/importing, 119–120
  finding, 105–106, 248
  names, 101–102, 117, 248
  putting multiple text entries into single, 95
value pane, 97, 99, 101, 103, 113
value types, 99–100, 102. *See also specific value types*
  basic description of, 156
  exporting, 57
  notation for, 156
VBScript, 235, 236, 326
vendors, 20
Verify Data After the Backup Completes option, 50
version control, 316–318
View menu, 100, 114, 119
View tab, 135
View value, 125

virtual device drivers (VxDs). *See* VxDs (virtual device drivers)
viruses, 185, 187–188
VxDs (virtual device drivers), 16

• W •

wallpaper, 21, 303–305
warning messages, 63, 96
Web browsers. *See* Internet Explorer browser (Microsoft)
welcome screens, 21
white papers, 187
Wilkins, Mark, 3, 180
WINAT.EXE, 36, 37
window(s)
 in Registry Editors, anatomy of, 97–102, 112–115
 size, transmission packet, 280–281
 sizing, 112
 "zooming," 109, 221–222
Window menu, 115
WindowMetrics key, 65
Windows 3.*x* (Microsoft), 15–16, 32
 16-bit programs, 18–19
 device drivers, 16
 INI files and, 13, 18–19
 making startup diskettes from, 44
 use of the term, 4
Windows 95 Registry For Dummies (Weadock and Wilkins), 3
Windows 98 Registry For Dummies (Weadock and Wilkins), 3
Windows 9*x* (Microsoft), 15, 16, 93
 Active Desktop and, 24–25
 backups and, 42–44, 46, 55
 command-line operator, 110
 making startup diskettes from, 44, 55
 Plug and Play features, 24
 policy files, 145–146
 safe mode, 43
 security and, 179, 192
 use of the term, 4
Windows 2000 CD (Microsoft)

backups and, 43–44, 53
 creating startup diskettes using, 43–44
 Registry Editors on, 93
 Resource Kit Tools on, 36, 239–240, 257
Windows 2000 Professional (Microsoft)
 Administrative Tools, 69–71
 basic description of, 2
 backups and, 48
 control panels and, 66–71
 network management and, 267–268
 Registry, size of, 25
 security and, 179, 204
 server performance and, 285
 user profiles and, 204
Windows 2000 Resource Kit, 36, 136, 239–240, 257
 DNS information in, 244
 security information in, 186
Windows 2000 Server (Microsoft), 179, 190, 196–197. *See also* Active Directory (AD) database
 Administrative Tools, 69–71
 basic description of, 2
 CD for, 70, 86
 control panels and, 69–71
 DNS and, 282
 event logs, 318–319
 help, 244
 NTUSER.DAT and, 140–141
 policies and, 145–146, 244
 processor information for, 21
 remote Registry editing and, 276
 restore operations and, 262
 user profiles and, 204, 215
 write caching and, 286
Windows Backup (Microsoft), 141, 216
 backups to diskettes with, 38
 basic description of, 36–37, 44–51, 58
 error messages, 241–242
 files, location of, 144
 help, 37
 restore operations and, 258–262
 shortcomings of, 45
 tricks and traps for using, 46–48

Windows Installer (Microsoft), 250–251, 292–295, 320–321
Windows Internet Naming Service (WINS). *See* WINS (Windows Internet Naming Service)
Windows NT (Microsoft), 22–26, 32, 39, 138, 145–146
  backups and, 53–54
  limitations of the Registry and, 15
  making startup diskettes from, 44
  Registry Editors and, 95–96, 112, 122–123
  right mouse button and, 22
  security and, 179, 181, 184, 192–193, 197
  superhidden files and, 134
  version 4, compatibility of, with material in this book, 3
Windows Scripting Host, 235, 236
WIN.INI, 16, 17, 18
WinLogon key, 164
WINNT folder
  backups and, 38, 47, 48, 50–51
  SYSTEM files and, 136
WINNT32.EXE, 81–82. *See also* setup programs
WINNT.EXE, 81–82. *See also* setup programs
winreg key, 189, 278
WINS (Windows Internet Naming Service), 283
wizards
  Add/Remove Hardware wizard, 28, 55
  Disk Cleanup wizard, 242
  ERD wizard, 27, 29
  Internet Connection Wizard, 89
workstation listings, in the SAM file, 138
write permission, 183, 186

XCOPY command, 34, 44, 55–56

• Z •

ZIP drives, 42, 44, 54–55
"zooming windows" concept, 109, 221–222

Notes

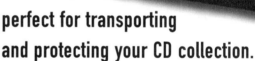

IDG Books Worldwide, Inc., End-User License Agreement

5. **Limited Warranty.**

   (a) IDGB warrants that the Software and Software Media are free from defects in materials and workmanship under normal use for a period of sixty (60) days from the date of purchase of this Book. If IDGB receives notification within the warranty period of defects in materials or workmanship, IDGB will replace the defective Software Media.

   (b) IDGB AND THE AUTHOR OF THE BOOK DISCLAIM ALL OTHER WARRANTIES, EXPRESS OR IMPLIED, INCLUDING WITHOUT LIMITATION IMPLIED WARRANTIES OF MERCHANTABILITY AND FITNESS FOR A PARTICULAR PURPOSE, WITH RESPECT TO THE SOFTWARE, THE PROGRAMS, THE SOURCE CODE CONTAINED THEREIN, AND/OR THE TECHNIQUES DESCRIBED IN THIS BOOK. IDGB DOES NOT WARRANT THAT THE FUNCTIONS CONTAINED IN THE SOFTWARE WILL MEET YOUR REQUIREMENTS OR THAT THE OPERATION OF THE SOFTWARE WILL BE ERROR FREE.

   (c) This limited warranty gives you specific legal rights, and you may have other rights that vary from jurisdiction to jurisdiction.

6. **Remedies.**

   (a) IDGB's entire liability and your exclusive remedy for defects in materials and workmanship shall be limited to replacement of the Software Media, which may be returned to IDGB with a copy of your receipt at the following address: Software Media Fulfillment Department, Attn.: *Windows 2000 Registry For Dummies,* IDG Books Worldwide, Inc., 10475 Crosspoint Blvd., Indianapolis, IN 46256, or call 800-762-2974. Please allow three to four weeks for delivery. This Limited Warranty is void if failure of the Software Media has resulted from accident, abuse, or misapplication. Any replacement Software Media will be warranted for the remainder of the original warranty period or thirty (30) days, whichever is longer.

   (b) In no event shall IDGB or the author be liable for any damages whatsoever (including without limitation damages for loss of business profits, business interruption, loss of business information, or any other pecuniary loss) arising from the use of or inability to use the Book or the Software, even if IDGB has been advised of the possibility of such damages.

   (c) Because some jurisdictions do not allow the exclusion or limitation of liability for consequential or incidental damages, the above limitation or exclusion may not apply to you.

7. **U.S. Government Restricted Rights.** Use, duplication, or disclosure of the Software by the U.S. Government is subject to restrictions stated in paragraph (c)(1)(ii) of the Rights in Technical Data and Computer Software clause of DFARS 252.227-7013, and in subparagraphs (a) through (d) of the Commercial Computer–Restricted Rights clause at FAR 52.227-19, and in similar clauses in the NASA FAR supplement, when applicable.

8. **General.** This Agreement constitutes the entire understanding of the parties and revokes and supersedes all prior agreements, oral or written, between them and may not be modified or amended except in a writing signed by both parties hereto that specifically refers to this Agreement. This Agreement shall take precedence over any other documents that may be in conflict herewith. If any one or more provisions contained in this Agreement are held by any court or tribunal to be invalid, illegal, or otherwise unenforceable, each and every other provision shall remain in full force and effect.

CD Installation Instructions

The *Windows 2000 Registry For Dummies* CD offers valuable information that you won't want to miss. To install the items from the CD to your hard drive, follow these steps.

To install the items from the CD to your hard drive, follow these steps.

1. **Insert the CD into your computer's CD-ROM drive and choose Start⇨Run.**

2. **In the dialog box that appears, type** D:\SETUP.EXE.

   Replace *D* with the proper drive letter if your CD-ROM drive uses a different letter. (If you don't know the letter, see how your CD-ROM drive is listed in My Computer.)

3. **Click OK.**

   A license agreement window appears.

4. **Read through the license agreement, nod your head, and then click the Accept button if you want to use the CD — after you click Accept, you'll never be bothered by the License Agreement window again.**

   The CD interface Welcome screen appears. The interface is a little program that shows you what's on the CD and coordinates installing the programs and running the demos. The interface basically enables you to click a button or two to make things happen.

5. **Click anywhere on the Welcome screen to enter the interface.**

6. **To view the items within a category, just click the category's name.**

   A list of programs in the category appears.

7. **For more information about a program, click the program's name.**

8. **If you don't want to install the program, click the Go Back button to return to the previous screen.**

9. **To install a program, click the appropriate Install button.**

10. **To install other items, repeat Steps 7–10.**

For more information, see the "About the CD" appendix.

IDG BOOKS WORLDWIDE
BOOK REGISTRATION

Register This Book and Win!

We want to hear from you!

Visit **http://my2cents.dummies.com** to register this book and tell us how you liked it!

- ✔ Get entered in our monthly prize giveaway.

- ✔ Give us feedback about this book — tell us what you like best, what you like least, or maybe what you'd like to ask the author and us to change!

- ✔ Let us know any other *...For Dummies*® topics that interest you.

Your feedback helps us determine what books to publish, tells us what coverage to add as we revise our books, and lets us know whether we're meeting your needs as a *...For Dummies* reader. You're our most valuable resource, and what you have to say is important to us!

Not on the Web yet? It's easy to get started with *Dummies 101*®*: The Internet For Windows*® *98* or *The Internet For Dummies*,® 6th Edition, at local retailers everywhere.

Or let us know what you think by sending us a letter at the following address:

...For Dummies Book Registration
Dummies Press
10475 Crosspoint Blvd.
Indianapolis, IN 46256

BESTSELLING BOOK SERIES